Praise for *Women and the Christian Story*

"Dr. Wojciechowski's book, *Women and the Christian Story*, is a wonderfully compact and easily readable history of women in Christianity. It describes in lively and fascinating detail how women throughout the ages have interacted with the male leaders and theologians around them. More importantly, it centers the telling of Christian history around the women themselves. With this book, women are no longer the sidekicks or the backdrop to men's ideas, but they are the idea-makers and history-makers themselves. This well-researched book will enliven any church history course and will show students and readers just how central women's contributions have been to the Christian faith."

—Amy Marga, professor of systematic theology, Luther Seminary

"True to the vocation of a Christian historian, Dr. Wojciechowski takes a therapeutic approach to highlight women's accomplishments rather than focusing on the oppression women have faced, and yet without undermining the riches and depth of experiences that spurred a transformation in women, making them agents of global faith even in its darkest hours. A long-awaited book, more global than some other books available, accessible to non-scholars and students alike, inclusive of the stories of non-Western women as keepers of the faith."

—Sashinungla Pongen, associate professor of church history,
Oriental Theological Seminary, Nagaland, India

"This book tells the real and messy story of Christian women through time and across the globe. Jennifer Hornyak Wojciechowski brings a rich complexity to this history and achieves this without falling into the usual traps of putting Christian women on a pedestal or overlooking their problems or social locations. While some of these stories may be familiar to readers interested in women's history, others are certain to be new and surprising to students of Christian history."

—Nancy Ross, associate professor, Utah Tech University

"The Christian story opens up in beautiful, diverse faces, phases, and spaces when following the webs involving women. Tracking Christian women's involvement from the time of Jesus's first followers through the modern era, Dr. Jennifer Hornyak Wojciechowski has laid out an inviting road map to engage and teach the Christian tradition(s) from an intentionally gender-inclusive perspective. The reader of this book will be energized and delighted."

—Kirsi Stjerna, First Lutheran, Los Angeles/Southwest California
Synod Professor of Lutheran History and Theology, Pacific Lutheran
Theological Seminary of California Lutheran University

"*Women and the Christian Story* provides an engaging and insightful overview of the many ways women from around the world have shaped Christianity through their actions, words, and writings. It combines breadth and depth, stretching from biblical times to the present, while including fascinating details on individual women and their communities. Wojciechowski effectively translates decades of scholarship in both women's and Christian history into a balanced, well-contextualized, and inspirational story for students and general readers."

—Merry Wiesner-Hanks, Distinguished Professor of History Emerita, University of Wisconsin–Milwaukee

Women and the Christian Story

WOMEN AND THE CHRISTIAN STORY

A Global History

Jennifer Hornyak Wojciechowski

Fortress Press
Minneapolis

WOMEN AND THE CHRISTIAN STORY
A Global History

Cover designer: Kristin Miller
Cover image: copyright aeduard | Getty Images (icon from St. Luke's church, in
Kotor, Montenegro, painted by Daškal Dimitrij in the 17th century)

Print ISBN: 978-1-5064-7375-8
eBook ISBN: 978-1-5064-7376-5

Contents

Introduction

This is a story about Christian women; it is also about martyrs, mystics, missionaries, leaders, preachers, theologians, saints, and prophets. It begins two thousand years ago in Israel and continues today with the diverse and rich global faith of an estimated two billion people. It is the story of how women have lived out their faith in different times and places—sometimes subjugated, sometimes in positions of power. The story of women in Christianity is complex and nuanced, and one must resist the urge to present it as a story from oppression to triumph. The actors were imperfect human beings who influenced and were influenced by their cultures and societies—sometimes for better, sometimes for worse. Yes, there were women who triumphed over adversity, but there were also women who oppressed others, and sometimes they were one and the same. At the very root of the story, though, is faith. The women presented in this story were believers, and they dedicated their lives to God, and that faith influenced their actions.

As Joan Didion once astutely pointed out, we tell ourselves stories in order to live.[1] The field of history is many things, but I would argue that it is first and foremost our *stories*. Stories for a people looking for meaning, trying to understand that from which we came so that we can move forward. The major story in this book is that of expansion and development—how a small religious sect grew to a global faith and how women participated in that process. But that does not encapsulate the true beauty and complexity of the story. There are countless smaller stories, countless voices that make up this unwieldy field that spans two millennia on six different continents. Unfortunately, these stories have not all been treated equally. Throughout time, historians have favored a history that elevates men and their accomplishments over women and theirs. Women too often show up as a footnote to the stories of the great men who have supposedly shaped our world alone. Women's stories have been relegated to the sidelines or, worse, lost, but it does not have to be that way.

I remember the first time I realized that there was an entire, albeit small, field of women's history. I had enrolled in a women's history course at my university as an undergraduate student. I loved history; for better or worse, I had already launched myself on the inevitable path to becoming a historian. But I distinctly remember listening, riveted, to the lecturer who told me stories about myself. A history that featured women. We had all been duped by our public school history classes; women had been important figures in the ages that came before us. Of course women shaped our world—they make up roughly half the world's population. How had I not known this?

The history of Christianity does not do much better at recalling the stories of women than secular history does. It may even be worse. Certain traditions have elevated the stories

---

1   Joan Didion, *The White Album* (New York: Simon & Schuster, 1979), 1.

1

of women saints, but for most of history, there was little effort to holistically look at women's role in the development, spread, and practice of the faith. In fact, there were very few attempts to craft any type of systematic women's Christian history before the rise of second-wave feminism. Even then, the field has stayed rather niche, and attempts to bring more women into the historical record have been uneven. Women's history has been plagued by similar problems that have plagued the larger field of history—a favoring of white and affluent figures to the detriment of others.

The idea for this book grew out of my teaching. As I attempted to bring marginalized voices into the classroom, I continually ran into problems finding books for students. I attempted to fill in the gaps through lectures and primary source documents. We are storied people, though, and a modern narrative history of women in Christianity was needed. It is that attention to story that has been particularly prevalent in the creation of this book.

All that said, this book is not long enough. Even if it were a multivolume set, it still would not be long enough. There is simply no way a single book, or even book series, can tell the story of all Christian women, their lives, their experiences, and their contributions to the faith. What this book does do, however, is introduce the topic and provide a general overview. This book interprets and synthesizes a vast body of scholarship into a single accessible volume. It highlights movements, individual women, and events that are critical for understanding the field as a whole. If your investigation is limited to this volume, you will get a solid overview. If you think of this book as your starting place for further study, you will have a framework, a general picture of women's role in the history of Christianity, and the tools to go out and learn more about the topics that you find particularly interesting.

ISSUES IN WOMEN'S HISTORY

Sources

Without question, sources are the biggest challenge when it comes to writing a women's history. Hearing from women in their own words is frustratingly difficult. All historians work with fragments from the past, unable to truly access the full picture, but this is especially so in women's history. Historians use evidence to study and analyze the past. Evidence can take many forms: news reports, diaries, pictures, works of art, legal documents, physical evidence, and so on. There are genuine benefits to this. We know that there is a factual basis for historical claims, but there are also limitations to this evidence-based method. Doing history this way tends to favor cultures with written language over oral cultures, and this method also tends to overrepresent the wealthy, the powerful, and the highly educated. Kings and queens leave a lot more paperwork than peasants! It has also proved true that men left more sources, either accidently or intentionally, than women. The reasons for this are complex and expected, but also unfortunate.

Throughout history, women had less access to formal education (although there are always exceptions). When women did write, their work was less likely to be preserved.

An example from the early church drives home this point. We have so many writings from the church fathers—their texts have truly shaped the faith. We know that there were highly educated women who were their contemporaries and friends and that these women participated in theological and biblical conversations, yet we do not have access to any of their writings. Our knowledge of these church mothers comes to us solely from the writings of men. As time moves forward, there are more sources left by women, but the number of sources pale in comparison to what we have written by men. Therefore, we are constrained by the sources, or lack thereof. Sometimes we are left with conjecture and guesswork, sometimes we are dependent on a few sources to tell us a big story, and far too often stories are just lost.

One of the most consistent sources of women's participation in the church is found in hagiographies, which are writings about the saints. Because they were written to promote the cause of sainthood, they offer up an idealized version of the subject, and again, they are usually penned by men. However, they are often the only source of information on women in the church, particularly women who have been canonized. They are a welcome source of information; however, there are always questions about veracity, and they can be tricky to use to construct a historical narrative. Most hagiographies undeniably contain exaggerations, prominent miracle stories, and versions of their subject that may not be entirely truthful. I have utilized numerous hagiographic accounts in this book, and it is important to note both the benefits and the limitations of these prevalent sources.

Imperfect our sources may be, but they are what we have. I have sometimes likened the task of writing women's history to trying to describe the picture on a puzzle when you only have a few pieces. I am indebted to the many scholars who have come before me, both ancient and modern, who have done amazing work reclaiming the stories of women throughout history. By and large, this book is a big-picture look at the faith. The very nature of the project necessitates making some generalizations and highlighting some figures over others. Hard choices were made over what and who would be included. It is essential to understand that for each person and event included in this book, there are many more that could not be included.

Miracles

Closely related to the issue of hagiography is the issue of miracles, which permeate much of the historical material, especially in regard to the saints. In our post-Enlightenment Western world, there is little belief in the miraculous. Many consider the spiritual realm the stuff of fantasies, and even biblical passages that refer to miracles or demonic possession are often thought to be either allegorical or an explanation of things that people could not understand due to a lack of science or technology. That said, throughout most of history, and in many places around the globe today, miracles, heavenly beings, demons, and magic are a real and accepted part of life. One may even see the rise and proliferation of charismatic forms of Christianity, with their emphasis on miracles and spiritual warfare, as a reaction to this rationalist view of faith. When considering those facts, it is the rational West that is the outlier on this issue.

Stories of miracles, divine intercession, the intercession of saints, and mystical relationships with God are ever present in hagiographies, biographies, and even some scholarly histories. A significant portion of the women examined in this book reportedly experienced or performed miracles. I do not believe it is my place to assess whether each account of the miraculous is genuine or not; therefore, the miracles are presented as part of the story. It is up to each individual reader to decide whether to take these accounts as fact or fiction.

Extreme Asceticism

A much less pleasant topic that needs to be addressed is the issue of extreme asceticism and self-mortification. There are numerous examples of women throughout the book who practiced forms of penance that would be considered self-harm today. Consistently throughout Christian history, women have starved and tortured themselves in the name of God. While I purposefully do not glorify those aspects of their lives, I believe it is important to situate these behaviors within their context. In many times and places throughout Christian history, believers, both men and women, have practiced such behaviors.

Often this mortification of the flesh was seen as a mark of holiness—though it must also be noted that frequently there was pushback from ecclesial authorities against its most extreme forms. Yet on a popular level, the women who were particularly brutal with their penance, such as Catherine of Siena or Rosa de Lima, were considered living saints, and their behavior had immense influence on why others saw them as exemplars of holiness.

Truth be told, people still practice varying forms of starvation and body alteration today, though more frequently now it is for ideals of cultural beauty rather than perceived holiness. Remember definitions of holiness and insanity are cultural. While today we would consider many of these practices a sign of mental instability, this was not the case in previous times and cultures, in which they were instead seen as signs of holiness. Hair shirts, metal crowns of nails, and the plethora of other methods people have used to torture themselves in the name of God have thankfully fallen out of favor, but other forms of religious fervor have, of course, continued.

A Positive Look at Women's History

Many of the previous histories of women have focused on power structures and the wrongs committed by churches, and there are valid reasons for this. Women have consistently been marginalized by power structures for thousands of years, and understanding those power structures is essential when looking to dismantle them. While this book recognizes the importance of that work, it is not the primary emphasis here. This is a narrative account that focuses on women, not the men and institutions that have oppressed them. Therefore, I put women, their experiences, and their accomplishments at the center of this book. I highlight their resilience, not their oppression.

On a similar note, I do not present the universal church to be the enemy of women. The relationship between structures of power and women is far more complicated than that simplistic dichotomy. The good versus bad mentality is not the way forward. The universal church is made up of a plethora of denominations and movements and billions of different people. One cannot sum up "the church" with simple statements of right and wrong. Were there times when official church hierarchies implemented oppressive policies against women? Yes. Were there times when official church bodies lifted women up and provided them a place to flourish and grow? Also yes. To ignore either side of that coin would be a detriment to our story.

OUTLINE OF THE BOOK

The argument that women have been integral members of the Christian faith and that they have been involved in all aspects of Christian life including defining the faith, missions, leadership, and theological development is the foundation of this book. Women are not footnotes to the story; from the women standing near the cross to the women who are teachers and preachers today—women *are* the story. And if we want to truly understand a story, we need to go back to the beginning, which is the time of the earliest apostles in the first century. The book moves along chronologically with each chapter highlighting a theme or themes that come to the forefront in that particular era. This thematic element becomes especially prominent from chapter 8 onward. It is important to recognize that while I use chapter themes throughout the book, these themes are both timely and timeless. For example, the dominant theme of the first chapter is women following an illegal faith. We examine how Christian women operated as an oppressed group within a hostile empire, but Christianity has been illegal in various places and times, so that thematic element also shows up in other chapters. Similarly, evangelism is the primary theme of chapter 9; however, this, too, is a recurring theme throughout Christianity. Just because a theme is highlighted in one era, it does not mean it is not present elsewhere.

One does not need to be an expert in Christianity history to approach this book. For ease of comprehension, most chapters begin with a short overview of pertinent general history that serves as background information. For theological concepts or references to certain people or events that are either more obscure or tangential to the story, there are explanations in the footnotes.

The first chapter looks at the earliest Christians and at a variety of ways in which women, situated within their own context, lived out their faith in an empire that was hostile to their beliefs. We begin with a brief examination of the ancient world; life for women in Greco-Roman society; the role women played in the Gospels, the Epistles, and early Christian literature; the offices of prophet, deacon, and widow; and finally an in-depth look at martyrdom.

The conversion of the Roman Empire and the rise of monasticism are the focus of the second chapter. During these years, there were women who opted to forgo the traditional roles of wife and mother and lived in community with other women. This chapter looks at women leaders in the blossoming monastic movement, women as mothers, and royal women. The chapter addresses larger issues of gender, holiness, and women's leadership and scholarship in the ancient world as well.

The third chapter deals with the decline of the Roman Empire, the expansion of Christianity, and the shift of Christianity to the north after the rise of Islam. In the West, a complex landscape of small kingdoms and languages emerged from the crumbling Roman Empire. Political marriages were used to forge alliances, and Christian wives were influential throughout Europe in converting various kingdoms. This chapter also examines Eastern figures such as Empresses Theodora and Irene in Byzantium, and Olga and Anna Porphyrogenita's influence on the conversion of Kyivan Rus.

Monasticism in the high to late Middle Ages is the focus of the fourth chapter. Barriers to the monastic life created the atmosphere for the establishment of a lay monastic movement known as the beguines, which was later suppressed. Meanwhile, monastic women had access to education and experiences that many others did not have. Women wrote, preached, worked as scholars, participated in church renewal movements, and advanced theological developments. Special attention will be paid to Hildegard of Bingen, Clare of Assisi, Birgitta of Sweden, Catherine of Siena, Julian of Norwich, and Joan of Arc.

Chapter 5 deals with the tumultuous time of the Protestant Reformation in Europe. We consider society's views of women as either wife and mother or religious sister. There is an examination of women who participated in the Protestant reformation, such as pastors' wives, pamphleteers, and theologians. Highly influential women, such as Katharina von Bora, Teresa of Ávila, and the queens Mary I and Elizabeth I, are examined in more detail.

The "discovery" of the Americas in the late fifteenth century is one of the most significant moments in Christian history. The contact between peoples and the transference of culture, religion, goods, and diseases forever changed the trajectory of both the Christian faith and society at large. Chapter 6 focuses on women in the Americas in the time of exploration and colonization. In Catholic Latin America, we examine the Virgin of Guadalupe, the influence of convents, and the role of laywomen called *beatas*. In religiously diverse North America, the focus is primarily on the disparate experiences of American Indian, Puritan, and Quaker women.

Chapter 7 focuses on the eighteenth century—a time in which ideas of equality and self-governance began to permeate society, even if those ideals were rarely extended to women. Religiously, the rise of more emotional expressions of faith acted as a counter to the rationalism of the Enlightenment. In the West, women became increasingly involved in religious movements like Methodism and Pietism; female leadership and influence in these movements are explored. This chapter will also examine the beginnings of Protestant missions, particularly among the Moravians. Mother Ann Lee and the Public Universal Friend, two American Revolution–era prophets, are examined as well.

Chapter 8 is devoted to global missions, though it is not a systematic summary of the movement, which would be impossible in one short chapter. Instead, the chapter gives glimpses and stories from the perspectives of both women missionaries (and missionary societies) and the women receiving (or rejecting) the message. These stories are fragments, parts of a complicated and unruly whole. But through these glimpses, you can see determined women, for better or worse, shaping their own destinies and shaping the world around them.

While women who preached can be traced to the very earliest days of the church, the nineteenth and twentieth centuries saw an explosion of women evangelists and church founders. Chapter 9 focuses on famed evangelists such as Jarena Lee, Amanda Berry Smith, Phoebe Palmer, Catherine Booth, and Aimee Semple McPherson and how their public ministries both brought people to faith and pushed boundaries. Following this will be a brief examination of women's ordination in the nineteenth century. Mary Baker Eddy, Ellen G. White, and Teresa Urrea, who are all religious leaders that fall outside of traditional nineteenth-century Christian norms and expectations, are also examined.

Christian women have been engaging in acts of charity since the earliest days of Christianity. It wasn't until the modern era, however, that Christian women became active in *organized* reform movements. Chapter 10 focuses on both how women organized and three large-scale reform movements that have been particularly prevalent: abolition / civil rights / anti-colonialism, women's rights, and temperance.

The eleventh and final chapter is focused on the twentieth century. It is broken down into four general categories: shifting trends in global Christianity, a century of suffering, a century of hope, and a century of advancement. Trends in global Christianity highlight the shift from European/American Christian dominance to the growth and vibrancy of African and Asian Christianity; a century of suffering examines the persecutions and death that featured too prominently in the twentieth century; a century of hope looks at important social reform movements; and a century of advancement focuses on women's ministries, leadership, ordination, and entrance into the academy and theological studies.

CHAPTER 1

Following an Illegal Faith (30–300)

Jesus said to her, "Mary!" She turned and said to him in Hebrew, "Rabbouni!" (which means Teacher). Jesus said to her, "Do not hold on to me, because I have not yet ascended to the Father. But go to my brothers and say to them, 'I am ascending to my Father and your Father, to my God and your God.'" Mary Magdalene went and announced to the disciples, "I have seen the Lord"; and she told them that he had said these things to her. (John 20:16–18)

Mary Magdalene, who is mentioned in all four Gospel accounts, has long been remembered as the "apostle to the apostles" in many Christian traditions. Therefore, it was a woman that Jesus first sent to proclaim the resurrection, and women continued to be capable evangelists, leaders, organizers, writers, and martyrs throughout the period of the early church. This prevalence of women is often forgotten when people look back at the earliest years of Christianity; however, it is not an exaggeration to say the church could not have grown as rapidly or as fruitfully without the dedicated support of these earliest believers.

If women consistently participated in the faith from the beginning, how did that look in practice? How did women engage with a new religion that ran counter to many societal expectations and accepted religious traditions of the day? This chapter begins with a survey of women's roles and experiences in the ancient world. By understanding the norms of the Greco-Roman world in particular, we can better interpret how Christian women adhered to or subverted those norms. Attention will be paid to how class and status of either free or enslaved influenced women's opportunities and challenges.

A detailed look at women in the Gospels, Epistles, and early Christian texts follows. These texts provide examples of which official and unofficial positions women held in the early church, such as the roles of deaconess, widow, and prophet. Even though there is some uncertainty as to how these roles were defined and performed, better understanding these positions not only helps us interpret ancient Christianity but also has implications for the faith today. Through early Christian non-biblical texts, we can better understand how the Christian feminine ideal was understood and portrayed.

The most influential public witnesses in the early church were martyrs; therefore, martyrdom tales from both the Roman and the Persian Empires will be examined. Gender and class had little bearing on whether or not an individual would be arrested—a Christian was a Christian, and that was illegal. Both men and women, rich and poor, free and slave died in the arena, side by side as equals, but that does not mean that their experiences were the same. Issues of sexual violence and motherhood added layers of complexity for women of all classes.

At its very core, within all these different aspects of the faith in the early church, this chapter looks at how women, situated within their own context, lived out their faith. How women found ways to be faithful when facing challenges and hardships associated with devotion to a religion that had been deemed illegal, and how they found meaning in the worship of a God killed and rejected by secular society but who gave them profound purpose and courage in the face of seemingly unbeatably odds.

HISTORICAL BACKGROUND

The story of Christianity is imbedded in history. Jesus of Nazareth was born into a particular time and place, and he and his first followers operated within that cultural milieu. Jesus preached a powerful and transformational message that was largely directed to those on the margins of society, including women. Little is known of Jesus's early life, though around the time he was thirty years old he began a public ministry that included preaching, healing, exorcisms, and calls for religious reforms. From scriptural accounts, we know that Jesus had many women followers, and those women learned from him, participated in evangelism for the blossoming movement, and supported him and the movement financially.

Jesus was executed around the year 30 CE by Roman officials. He died brutally by crucifixion—a common Roman execution technique for dissidents that was designed to instill fear and submission. A first-century bystander would have surely believed this was the end of the Jesus movement. The founder had died, and most of the leaders were scattered and disheartened. Then something truly remarkable happened. Jesus's followers began to claim that he had risen from the dead. Each of the Gospel accounts reports that a small group of women were the first witnesses to the resurrection. Scholars have even used this detail of women as the first witnesses to argue for the veracity of the resurrection accounts. Women were not considered reliable witnesses, and no one that was looking for credibility would have fabricated a resurrection story featuring women so prominently. If these stories described women proclaiming the resurrection first, the argument goes, then they must truly have been the first witnesses.[1]

The stories of the resurrection spread like wildfire. Participants in the Jesus movement, both men and women, were transformed from defeated and downtrodden followers of an executed charismatic figure to empowered missionaries bringing the good news of a resurrected messiah to the nations. They believed and acted on the commandment *to make believers of all nations*. Within three hundred and fifty years, this tiny splinter sect of Judaism had grown immensely and become the official religion of the Roman Empire, with other Christian communities scattered across the known world.

---

1 N. T. Wright, *The Resurrection of the Son of God* (Minneapolis: Fortress, 2003), 607.

THE GREAT CIVILIZATIONS OF THE FIRST CENTURY

As far as we know, Jesus spent his entire life in Judea, but his followers traveled to the ends of the earth spreading their gospel message. To understand the lives of early Christian women, it is necessary to survey the world in which they lived. The modern reader may find the interconnectedness of the ancient world surprising. Travel, economic trade, and cultural transference were realities of the time. Merchants traveled trade routes, such as the well-known Silk Road, and soldiers traveled great distances during military campaigns. Ships transported goods all over the known world; Roman coins and goods have been found as far north as Scandinavia and as far south as modern-day Uganda.[2] Along with the transfer of goods, travelers brought culture and religion with them.

There were four major civilizations during the time of Christ. The Greco-Roman civilization was the center of the most significant Christian spread. This was by no means a monolithic culture; it incorporated numerous diverse languages and peoples, all living under Roman imperial rule. While linguistic and cultural differences remained, they were bound by a common Greek language and culture that had spread as a result of the Greek conquests centuries before. The Roman Empire was religiously diverse, and the Romans allowed their subjects to maintain their own deities as long as they also sacrificed to the imperial cult, a point that would cause considerable hardships for early Christians.

East of the Roman Empire was the Persian Empire under the rule of the Parthians. The Persian Empire, like the Roman one, included a variety of languages, cultures, and traditions. Their major religion was Zoroastrianism, a dualistic religion founded in the sixth century BCE by the Iranian prophet Zoroaster, though other religions were largely tolerated. In the Indian subcontinent and other areas of South Asia, the Indian civilization was dominant, with Hinduism, Jainism, and Buddhism as popular religions. In East Asia, China emerged as a unified civilization. Confucianism was growing among the members of the upper class during Jesus's lifetime. Culturally, all four of these ancient civilizations had robust urban centers, rich literary traditions, and deep religious roots. Outside these four dominant civilizations, there were many other cultures, kingdoms, tribes, and faiths making up a diverse world.

WOMEN'S LIVES IN THE FIRST CENTURY

Within this complex web of ancient cultures, religions, and politics, women lived their lives. Their voices were too often left out of official writings and history books, but they profoundly influenced their world. There was no single experience for women in the ancient world but countless experiences that were influenced by culture, religious affiliation, family, class, and status of free or slave.

2　Dale T. Irving and Scott Sunquist, *History of the World Christian Movement, Volume 1: Earliest Christianity to 1453* (Maryknoll: Orbis, 2001), 5.

Christianity was born in Israel among its Jewish population. While the Christian faith quickly expanded to the gentile world, a brief examination of the lives of Jewish women is needed before we move to a more detailed examination of the Greco-Roman culture at large. Israel had endured a series of different military conquests throughout the centuries, and by the time of Jesus's birth, it had been under Roman control for about sixty years. Modern scholars have argued that the women living in Jesus's homeland of Galilee were some of the poorest people in the world in the first century.[3] Roman economic policies had evicted Jews, especially Galileans, from their lands, and the people of Israel were being crushed under the Roman tax system—Israelites were forced to pay taxes to the local Herodian rulers, a tax to Rome, and a third tithe to the temple. This triple taxation was especially devastating to poor and rural communities, which were barely surviving. The political and economic oppression faced by the Jewish people led to political instability and the occasional outburst of violence and subsequent Roman suppression. This came to a breaking point during the First Jewish–Roman War, which ran from 66 to 73 CE and resulted in the destruction of Jerusalem and the Jewish Temple, thus ending the temple system and pushing many more Jews into exile.

Despite rural Israel's poverty and trials, women of the lower agrarian class likely had more freedom in certain ways than wealthier women. Because agrarian families needed all family members' labor, women were not secluded in the home like wealthy women often were. They would have participated in the daily running of their homes, lands, and families. They likely interacted with men in various settings, though it was uncommon for unrelated men and women to converse in public.

Typical for the time, Jewish girls were married young. Women did not have access to divorce, though men did. Divorce was particularly disastrous for a woman living in the first century since there were few options besides dependence on a husband or father. In light of this fact, one should take Jesus's condemnation of divorce as being supportive of women and women's well-being, not restrictive. First-century Jewish women did have inheritance rights, but precedence was given to male inheritors.

There is debate as to whether women were educated in matters of the Torah during this time, but it would have been uncommon if it happened at all. Women had few public religious duties, though there were exceptions, especially among Jews living in the diaspora, where there is some evidence that women may have headed synagogues. Women were not allowed to serve as temple priests in Jerusalem though. In this regard, Judaism differed from the larger Greco-Roman world, where women were able to serve as temple priestesses for various deities.[4]

While Christianity was born in the heart of Israel, it very quickly expanded to the larger world. According to tradition, the apostles traveled around the world following Jesus's commandment to make believers of all nations. We do not know what happened to Jesus's close female followers since scripture and tradition are silent on the issue; however, it is reasonable to assume these women engaged in evangelism, and early missionaries

---

3 Christine Schenk, *Crispina and Her Sisters: Women and Authority in Early Christianity* (Minneapolis: Fortress, 2017), 6.

4 Schenk, *Crispina and Her Sisters*, 7–14.

found many gentiles who embraced their message. The new Christians existed within a complex culture with norms and expectations that influenced the lives of believers. At numerous places within Paul's letters especially, we see allusions to the larger culture, familial relationships, and assumptions and exceptions regarding gender relationships. While it is important to remember the variety of different cultures within the Roman Empire, what follows is a brief examination of common norms.

The concept of an ancient family is different from the modern Western view of family. However, maintaining familial bonds, raising children, and supporting one another are experiences shared by families throughout time. Within the Roman family, the *paterfamilias* was the head of the household, with all women, children (both male and female), and slaves subject to his leadership. Much has been said about the *paterfamilias*'s control over this family and the powers awarded to him, such as the right to kill his own family members. While there were tyrannical family heads, one must not assume this was always the case. There are examples of writings from the time that show the love and devotion fathers felt toward their children, both sons and daughters.[5]

It was an expectation that all freeborn women would marry and have children, with the exception of vestal virgins or other priestesses. Women generally married young, within their teenage years, to an older man through an arranged marriage. Women were discouraged from marrying below their own social class, though this ideal was not always followed, and men were not bound by these social expectations. There were two types of marriage contracts in the Roman world: *cum manu*, in which wives were legally under their husband's control and everything the wife acquired prior to her marriage would become property of her husband, and *sine manu*, where the wife remained legally under the control of her father or another male guardian. By the first century, *sine manu* marriages were the norm, and through this type of marriage, a woman would inherit from her father's estate when he died, giving her increased control of her own assets and affairs. Conflicts between husbands and fathers were not unheard of, and it was possible for a father to dissolve his daughter's marriage. While the *paterfamilias* ultimately had control of his family, his wife, the family's matron, exercised significant influence on the family, and this influence would have increased if she were widowed.[6]

There was a sexual double standard between upper-class men and women. It was commonplace for men to have concubines, pay for prostitutes, and engage in sexual activity with their slaves. Men faced no legal repercussions for any of these sexual exploits. Conversely, female infidelity was a criminal act that could result in the loss of half a woman's dowry and a third of any property, and her husband had to divorce her or face legal penalties himself. These laws were designed to control female reproduction and ensure paternity in the elite Roman families.

---

5 For example, writing from exile in the first century, Cicero expressed how much he missed his daughter Tullia: "What of the fact that at the same time I miss my daughter? Such faithfulness, such unassuming conduct, such intelligence! The very likeness of me in her face, in her speech, in her mind!" (Cicero, *Letters to His Brother Quintus* 1.3.3) as quoted in Bonnie MacLachland, *Women in Ancient Rome: A Sourcebook* (London: Bloomsbury, 2013), 96. These are the words of a man who clearly loved and respected his daughter—feelings many Roman fathers would have shared.

6 Schenk, *Crispina and Her Sisters*, 16–20.

Once married, it was expected that women would have children, and giving birth and caring for children were major endeavors for women of all social classes. The process of birth was dangerous, and infant mortality rates were high, with an estimated third of children dying within their first year of life. Despite the expectation to have children, there is historical evidence that rudimentary forms of contraceptives were used, and abortions were performed.[7] It is of note that both Jews and Christians wrote strongly against abortion—Jews attributed it to something that is associated with the nations, and Christians, according to the *Didache*, associated it with the "Way of Death."[8] Regardless, there was a glut of unwanted children, and the ancient Greco-Roman world engaged in the practice of exposure, which is technically different from infanticide, though only marginally so. Evidence points to this being a relatively accepted practice, with people abandoning babies at common places such as temples, crossroads, and garbage heaps. These abandoned children provided a ready supply of slaves for society if they were picked up before they died. It is well known that early Christians picked up exposed children and raised them.

Upper-class families valued education for all of their children regardless of gender, though education likely was different for boys and girls. Upper-class girls were educated to run a large household, which took significant skill. Mothers were the primary educators when children were young, though fathers tended to take over the role from the age of seven to sixteen. Nurses, often employed by upper-class families, also played important roles in educating children. By their mid-teenage years, boys would either be tutored or sent to school to be formally educated in rhetoric, philosophy, geometry, music, and astronomy. The standard education for girls is less clear, though they were more likely to be tutored at home. There is evidence that there were women who participated in philosophical circles, and there are accounts of specific women who were well versed in a variety of fields. It is not unreasonable to assume that many, if not the majority, were educated. There is evidence that philosophical education became increasingly valued for men and women regardless of social class and that many people had access to public philosophers. There was also an increase in public libraries where anyone could gain information, though these were more prevalent and accessible in urban centers.[9]

Whereas education for the upper classes in the Roman Empire was expected regardless of gender, education for the working classes, agrarian families, and slaves was far less assured. There are scholars who argue that most people received at least a basic education in reading, writing, and counting, though most of the population remained functionally illiterate. Most children living in an agrarian setting would have started helping out around the house and land as soon as they were physically able, which left little time for study. Slaves held a variety of positions in society, and their levels of education varied. Some slave children were educated in trades, and occasionally, slaves received excellent

---

7 Soranus of Ephesus, *Gynecology*, trans. Oswei Temkin (Baltimore: Johns Hopkins University Press, 1991).

8 "The Didache, or Teaching of the Twelve Apostles," in *The Apostolic Fathers*, vol. 1, trans. Kirsopp Lake (London: William Heinemann, 1919), 309–333.

9 Schenk, *Crispina and Her Sisters*, 41–42.

educations. There were slaves that went on to have careers as librarians, tutors, and teachers, but most lived hard lives marginalized in a society that denied them even personhood.

In the first century BCE, Rome was facing a population decline. Men were postponing marriage, and divorce was common, especially among the upper classes. These marriage habits, compounded with the abysmal life expectancy of a meager twenty-five years, were causing a crisis. In 17 BCE, to combat the decline and what was considered immoral behavior, Augustus Caesar passed legislation to encourage larger families. Up until this point, freeborn women, while able to inherit property, did not have the right to administer it without a legal male guardian called a *tutela*. To encourage women to have more children, any freeborn woman who had at least three children and any freed woman who had at least four children would be able to manage her own affairs without a male guardian. Emperor Claudius later abolished the *tutela* altogether, so any female Roman citizen could manage her own property after the death of her father. This legislation was particularly freeing for women of the lower classes. Women owned their own businesses and participated in public affairs even if they were officially barred from voting or holding public office. Business was an area where they could have held influence within the society.[10]

In sharp contrast to the relative freedom elite women enjoyed, or even the more modest opportunities that freeborn women had, enslaved women faced numerous hardships. Christianity spread quickly among slaves, and an examination of ancient slavery sheds light on their experience and why the faith may have appealed to this group. Slaves were considered private property and had no rights or control over their own bodies, and both female and male slaves were expected to be sexually available to their owners—it was not considered scandalous because they were property. An owner was able to physically harm or even kill a slave without consequence. Under a system of such blatant sexual exploitation, female slaves were exposed to the risk of pregnancy. A slave's child was considered property of the owner, and the slave owner could abandon the child, sell the child, or decide to raise the child as a slave. Girls born to slaves, or abandoned and claimed, were often forced into a life of prostitution and further sexually exploited to produce children.

It must be noted that some early Christians did own slaves, as is made clear in Paul's letter to Philemon. We do not know how much, if at all, adherence to early Christianity influenced slave owners' treatment of their slaves. While Paul recommends that masters treat their slaves right and fair, he also tells slaves to obey their masters in everything. Considering the frequency with which slaves were sexually exploited by their owners and the fact that the exploitation was considered the cultural norm, one does come to the uncomfortable question of what Paul includes in his recommendation. On the other hand, a slave literally had no choice, so Paul's recommendation to obey could also be seen as acceptance of a cultural reality that if slaves tried to resist, they would face punishment or death, rather than as support for a sexually exploitive system.[11]

---

10 Schenk, *Crispina and Her Sisters*, 18–19.

11 Carolyn Osiek and Margaret Y. MacDonald, *A Women's Place: House Churches in the Earliest Christianity* (Minneapolis: Augsburg Fortress Press, 2006), 95–117.

WOMEN IN THE NEW TESTAMENT AND EARLY CHRISTIAN LITERATURE

In that gray area that spans biblical studies and the earliest history of Christianity, numerous women have been associated with Jesus and Paul. This area of study has been of particular interest to feminist historians and scholars due to the clear participation of women in a variety of roles in the early church. Paul's writings against women speaking and teaching have been used for millennia to keep women silent, yet the scriptures often paint a remarkably different picture of women as faithful followers of Jesus and hardworking messengers of the good news.

With the background information of the lives and roles of women in the first century, we can turn to these stories once again with fresh eyes and a new appreciation for the roles these women played. Everything in the scriptures indicates that Jesus broke with first-century gender assumptions. His relationships with women are consistently respectful and affirming. On numerous occasions, he is rebuked by his male apostles for consorting with the wrong type of women, or women in general, only for him to defend his actions and support the women.

Sadly, we only know of a small number of the women who were active in Jesus's ministry, though through their examples, we can make assumptions about women in the biblical era. One such person is the Samaritan woman who only appears in John's Gospel (John 4:1–42). When Jesus is returning to Galilee from Judea, he passes through Samaria. Tired from his journey, he sits near Jacob's well and asks a woman for a drink while his disciples go into town to buy supplies. Their conversation defies societal expectations. There were long-standing hostilities between Jews and Samaritans, and generally, unrelated men and women would not converse in public. Throughout their conversation, the woman comes to the realization of who Jesus is, and he confirms to her that he is indeed the Messiah. She returns to the city, where she begins to proclaim that Jesus is the Messiah. One could make the case that the Samarian woman was one of Jesus's first missionaries—the fact that she took her message outside of Israel is of particular interest as well.

Mary and Martha are two other examples of women who were influential in the early Jesus movement. The two sisters, who appear in both Luke's and John's Gospel accounts along with their brother Lazarus, know Jesus well. In Luke's Gospel, the disciples come to Martha's home, and she prepares a meal for her guests while Mary sits by Jesus and listens to what he is saying. Mary's choice leads to domestic strife when Martha openly complains to Jesus about Mary's unwillingness to help with the housework. Jesus sides with Mary, saying she has chosen the better part. Since we know Jesus taught Mary and defended this activity, it is likely he taught other women as well.

We see these sisters again in John 11:1–44. The sisters send word to Jesus that their brother Lazarus is ill. Jesus is delayed in coming to their house even though the text states that he loves all three of the siblings. By the time Jesus arrives, Lazarus has been dead for days, and Martha scolds Jesus with the words "Lord, if you had been here, my brother would not have died" (John 11:21). Martha once again confronts Jesus to express her unhappiness, but she also shows her faith and devotion to Jesus by stating that she knows he is the Messiah and that she believes he can raise her brother from the dead.

While the aforementioned women make brief appearances in the Gospels, Mary, the mother of Jesus, and Mary Magdalene both take on more significant roles. The most celebrated woman in the Bible is Jesus's mother, Mary. She has many titles (Mother of God, the Blessed Virgin, *theotokos*, Queen of the Heavens, etc.), highlighting the love and respect believers have shown her. Mary has long been seen as the epitome of faithfulness. There have been countless works of art, awe-inspiring cathedrals, poems, hymns, and prayers devoted to her; there are liturgical feast days, devotional practices, meditations, pilgrimages, and festivals in her honor. Mary's influence on the church cannot be overstated.

We first meet Mary when she is a young virgin, engaged but not yet married, living in Nazareth in Galilee. Considering the social conventions of the time, she was likely in her mid-teenage years. Luke's Gospel gives a full account of her interaction with the angel Gabriel in which he greets her with this famous line: *Hail Mary, full of grace, the Lord is with you.* As opposed to Zachariah's faithlessness, recorded in the previous chapter, this young woman believes, willingly agrees to bear the Messiah, and recites some of the most beautiful lines in scripture, the Magnificat (Luke 1:46–55). When her son is an adult, she continues to play a role in Jesus's life and ministry. She is present at his first miracle, and she stands with her son at the crucifixion.

Additional information about Mary comes from the second-century noncanonical document called the *Gospel of James*.[12] Throughout this account, supposedly written by Jesus's brother James, the reader is given a background on Jesus's earthly family, including Mary's parents and the miraculous circumstances surrounding her birth. She is given over to the temple at the age of three, and at twelve, the temple priests task Joseph, an older widower, with keeping Mary at his home. There is great confusion and accusation surrounding Mary's pregnancy, but both Joseph and Mary are found innocent by the temple priests. One of the more pertinent stories included in this gospel is the account of Mary's delivery of Jesus in a cave. When Mary goes into labor, Joseph runs to get a Hebrew midwife, who delivers the child. After the midwife leaves, she meets a women named Salome and tells her of the miracle she just witnessed. Refusing to believe, Salome, in what sounds similar to Thomas's statements of disbelief in the resurrected Christ, says that she will not believe that a virgin gave birth until she has "inserted her finger and investigated her." Salome goes to the cave and does just that, but as punishment her hand is "consumed by fire." An angel appears, and Salome worships the infant Jesus and is healed.[13]

---

12 The Bible contains four recognized Gospels: Matthew, Mark, Luke, and John. However, there were as many as thirty early texts that could fall into this genre—most are only known to us as fragments or in quotations in other works. Some of these gospel texts, such as the *Gospel of James*, were widely read and continue to be used by various Christian communities today though they never had the authority of the canonical Gospels. Others, such as the *Gospel of Thomas*, were lost and only recently recovered.

13 *Protoevangelium of James* in *From Ante-Nicene Fathers*, vol. 8, edited by Alexander Roberts, James Donaldson, and A. Cleveland Coxe, trans. Alexander Walker (Buffalo, NY: Christian Literature Publishing Co., 1886). Revised and edited for New Advent by Kevin Knight, http://www.newadvent.org/fathers/0847.htm, chaps. 19–20.

Throughout this account, there is a preoccupation with Mary's virginity that is not present in the four canonical Gospels, even providing "proof" through Salome's folly. There is also a goal of elevating Mary's own conception and upbringing to show God's favor from before she was even born. Her conception story reminds the reader of Abraham and Sarah—the childless couple blessed with a child in their old age. Once Mary is born and brought to the temple, the *Gospel of James* tells the reader that "she was fed like a dove and received food from the hand of an angel." The Gospel of James establishes that Mary is not just any woman but one that has been chosen and blessed.

While it has sometimes been the pattern to paint Mary into the picture of perfect female submission, this is an incomplete analysis. While she submitted to and loved God, she also threw off societal expectations and pressures to follow her faith. She was a member of a highly marginalized group, she came from a poor region in an occupied country, and the prospects for a young, unmarried pregnant woman at the time were abysmal. Her trials and suffering have served to comfort and uplift women throughout Christian history.

Another Mary—Mary Magdalene—appears as an important witness to Jesus's death and resurrection. Despite Christian tradition teaching she was a prostitute, there is nothing in scripture to indicate she was. Her name implies she was from the city of Magdala, a town on the Sea of Galilee, and she was likely a woman of some means since it is indicated that she supported Jesus and his ministry financially.

Jesus's apostles scattered after his arrest, but at least a small group of women stayed, and Mark identifies three of them: Mary Magdalene, Mary, the mother of James, and Salome (Mark 16:1). The group of women witnessed the crucifixion and saw where Jesus was buried, and some of them returned on the first day of the week to anoint the body. Just like Jesus's mother, Mary, Mary Magdalene and the other women did not abandon Jesus. Although the accounts vary between the different Gospels, Mary Magdalene is identified in each one as being the first to witness the resurrection. In Matthew's Gospel, the women meet and embrace Jesus, and Jesus himself tells Mary Magdalene and the others not to be afraid and to go and tell his brothers of his rising (Matt 28:8).

It is significant that this group of women is the first to witness the resurrection. They are the first to see and speak with the risen Jesus, and they are the first to receive the commandment to proclaim his resurrection. While this is the last time Mary Magdalene appears in the scriptures, it seems likely she would have continued to proclaim the good news and participate in the growing Jesus movement.

PAUL AND WOMEN

Paul's relationship with women is complex. He has been lifted up as a liberator of women and condemned for oppressing them. His statements in the Epistles seem to contradict each other in various places, leaving a legacy of confusion regarding his actual stance on women in the early church. Some scholars have pointed out that his harshest words against women come from his disputed letters and have questioned whether he penned them at all (these include Colossians, Ephesians, Titus, 2 Thessalonians, and 1 and

2 Timothy). Regardless of the authenticity of these particular letters, Paul can be seen as a man who waffles between the revolutionary message of the gospel and traditional views of gender in the ancient world. Indisputably, gender and class barriers broke down in the new Christian communities, but these communities were functioning in a world with firm ideas on what the role of women should be. Paul's letters are just that: letters. We do not necessarily have the full picture, or even the full conversation in some instances. For example, in 1 Corinthians 14:33–36, Paul commands women to be silent in church. This contradicts his many other references to women being active in churches and ministries. While there have been many hypotheses on this contradiction, it is one of the more confusing and, unfortunately, misused statements in Paul's letters.

Despite some of Paul's statements on women, he counted many as co-laborers in evangelism. In his letter to the Romans, Paul commends four different women as having labored for the Lord: Mary, Tryphaena, Tryphosa, and Persis (Rom 16:6, 12). He also commends Priscilla and her husband, Aquila (Rom 16:3), for their missionary work. Similarly, Andronicus and Junia (Rom 6:7) are listed as apostles in the same chapter. Paul notes that they were in prison together and that the couple had been in Christ before he was. A note must be made about Junia. Virtually all early Christian writers assumed Junia was a woman, but beginning in the medieval period, Junia began to be translated as Junias, the masculine version of the name. The belief at the time was that women could not hold the title of apostle. However, while Junia was a common name in the ancient world, there is no other example of the name Junias existing in ancient literature.[14]

Another leader who is referenced in Romans 16 is Phoebe, who acts as Paul's envoy in Rome. He commends his sister Phoebe, a deacon of the church of Cenchreae (Rom 16:1–2) to the Christian community in Rome. He explains that she has been a benefactor to many, including Paul. It is of note that Paul uses the term *diakonos* or deacon in the masculine form. We do not know exactly what that title entailed this early in the church, but she was a woman of importance in her church. Her title of benefactor implies she was a woman of considerable means who had independence. Another independent woman of means is Lydia, who appears in Acts 16. The text states that she was from the city of Thyatira and that she was a dealer of purple cloth. After hearing Paul speak in Philippi, she and her household are baptized, and she then invites Paul to stay at her home. There are certain things that can be inferred from the short passage about Lydia. She was an independent woman of means, but she was probably not part of the elite upper classes since she was a merchant. She had other people living within her household; whether they were relatives, slaves, or both, we simply do not know. Finally, there is Nympha, who only gets one line in Paul's letter to the Colossians: "Give my greetings to the brothers and sisters at Laodicea, and to Nympha and the church in her house" (Col 4:15). While it is a short reference, we can once again infer that she was a woman of means and importance who hosted a church in her home, though what her exact role entailed is again unknown.

---

14 For an extensive overview of Junia, see Eldon Jay Epp, *Junia: The First Woman Apostle* (Minneapolis: Augsburg Fortress, 2005).

WOMEN IN EARLY CHRISTIAN LITERATURE

While the Gospels and the Epistles rightfully provide a strong foundation for our knowledge of women's activities in the earliest church, there are numerous other writings such as the noncanonical gospels, writings of the church fathers, and popular literature that can inform our understanding. The *Acts of John* and the *Acts of Paul* provide us with examples of two early Christian women whose stories more closely resemble fantasy literature than real life. Regardless of the veracity of these stories, they provide fascinating examples of the cultural feminine ideal, and they also demonstrate examples of Christian women rejecting cultural norms to follow Jesus.

In the *Acts of Paul and Thecla*, which is part of the longer *Acts of Paul*, we meet Thecla, who proves to be the heroine of this story, while Paul largely takes a secondary role. The sheer fantastic nature of the account suggests plenty of literary embellishment, and there is some scholarly debate as to whether Thecla was even a real person. In the ancient world, it was assumed she was real, and she continues to be venerated as a saint in various Christian traditions today. In the city of Seleucia, where she supposedly lived out the remainder of her life, there was a popular shrine and pilgrimage site at the location of her tomb. Both Egeria and Gregory of Nazianzus famously visited the site in the fourth century.

The story of Thecla opens with Paul preaching while Thecla sits by the window of a nearby house listening "day and night" to his message of chastity. When Paul is arrested and brought before the governor, Thecla stands beside him. When Thecla refuses to marry her fiancé, Thamyris, her mother demands Thecla be burned to death publicly as a sort of lesson in terror to deter other women from acting like this. Her mother's response is shocking, but it also demonstrates how radical Thecla's actions were. She not only rejected her family and fiancé but also disrupted the social order. Her mother's fear that other women will act in this manner is palpable.

The first of many miracles occurs when God sends a horrific rain and hailstorm to the site of Thecla's burning pyre. The story notes that many in the audience die, while Thecla is saved, goes to find Paul, and then begins an exciting adventure. One of the more entertaining episodes, in an all-around lively and enjoyable story, is Thecla's escapades in Antioch. There, she spurns the advances of a powerful man, who drags her before a governor who once again sentences Thecla to death—this time in the arena. What follows is another fantastic episode. First, she faces wild beasts, but a lioness protects her. Then, spotting a pit of water filled with vicious seals, she jumps in and baptizes herself while the onlooking crowd weeps. Next, she miraculously escapes being torn apart by bulls. In the end, Thecla preaches to the governor from the arena and is released. The story concludes with a note that Thecla later reconciles with her mother, thus demonstrating her powerful ability to forgive, and then sets off for Seleucia, where "she enlightened many people with the word of God."[15]

While the miracles are both amazing and entertaining, there are critical items in this story that need to be examined. First, Thecla acts as an independent agent despite being

---

15 "Acts of Paul and Thecla," in *Women in the Early Church*, ed. Elizabeth Clark (Wilmington, DE: Michael Glazier, 1983), 79–88.

a single young woman—something that was exceedingly rare in the Greco-Roman culture of the day, even within Christian communities. She rejects multiple marriage proposals, instead choosing to travel and evangelize. Not only is this tolerated, but it is also endorsed; Paul commissions her to spread the gospel after proving herself. Second, she baptizes herself. Generally speaking, people do not baptize themselves, especially in pits of water filled with predators, so this in itself is a rather surprising event. Prior to this, Paul had refused to baptize her when she asked him, but he does recognize this highly unusual event as a valid baptism. While there is some debate as to whether women were ever ordained priests in the early church, which will be discussed further below, it is significant that Thecla was performing sacraments without any discussion of her gender at all. Third, she goes on to have a career as an evangelist, and apparently, she was a very successful one since the story reports that many were enlightened. Continuing with the adventurous quality of the story, she travels all the way to Seleucia, which was in the Persian Empire, to spread the message.

Thecla's story was wildly popular with early Christians. There is evidence that devotion to her spread all around the Mediterranean Basin, including different churches and shrines dedicated to her. While one might assume her popularity waned as the church became more patriarchal in nature, this appears to be untrue. In the mid-fifth century, a priest in or near Seleucia wrote *The Life and Miracles of Saint Thecla*, which added more to her story. The first part of the text is a retelling of the *Acts of Paul and Thecla*, and the second part chronicles the miracles performed at Thecla's shrine in Seleucia. In *Life and Miracles*, Thecla is referred to not only as a virgin but also as a martyr and an apostle. Also of note, Thecla's teaching and baptizing are expanded. Significantly, she teaches an Arian bishop to accept the Trinitarian confession, thus inserting her into the much later Arian controversy on the side of Nicene Orthodoxy.[16] She only baptizes herself in the *Acts of Paul and Thecla*, but in *Life and Miracles*, she baptizes others, both women and men.[17] Thecla defies not only Greco-Roman societal expectations but also Christian conventions regarding women's roles. She is a public figure who travels and teaches while also administering at least the sacrament of baptism. *Life and Miracles* places her as one of the defenders of the Orthodox faith even though her life predated the Arian controversy.

An interesting comparison to Thecla is the figure of Drusiana, who appears in the *Acts of John*. Like Thecla, Drusiana is an example of a pious woman who fought to be chaste, and she performed miracles. According to the *Acts of John*, Drusiana and her husband, Andronicus, were early Christians who decided to live a celibate marriage despite early resistance from Andronicus, who locked her in a tomb for refusing his sexual advances.

While the apostle John is staying at their house in Ephesus, a man named Callimachus, who is referred to as a messenger of Satan, falls in love with Drusiana. Drusiana becomes distraught that she would become a "stumbling block for a man uninitiated in Godliness!" She dies while grieving for Callimachus and is buried in a tomb. This is not the end of

---

16 The Arian controversy was a series of disputes about the very nature of Christ in the early church. Arius, a priest, argued that Jesus was *created* and not of the same substance as the Father. Arianism was deemed a heresy at the Council of Nicaea in 325, though conflicts between Arians and Trinitarian Christians continued long after the council.

17 For a more detailed examination of this text, see Scott F. Johnson, *The Life and Miracles of Thekla: A Literary Study* (Washington, DC: Center for Hellenic Studies, 2006).

the story, however, and Callimachus bribes Andronicus's steward to open the tomb so that he can rape Drusiana's corpse. Before he can act on his abhorrent plan, a snake appears and kills both the steward and Callimachus.

The next day John, Andronicus, and some other men go to her tomb and find a "beautiful man" there. This beautiful man tells John that he found Drusiana nearly defiled and that John is to raise her from the dead. The man departs, and John and the others are left with the dead steward and Callimachus, who still has the sleeping snake on his chest. John first raises Callimachus, who, through this ordeal, comes to faith. Andronicus then begs John to bring Drusiana back from the dead. After Drusiana's resurrection, she decides to raise the immoral steward from the dead. The steward, however, remains unchanged and dies shortly thereafter.[18]

Whereas Thecla was the unquestioned hero in her tale, Drusiana plays a more ambiguous role in the *Acts of John*. Her commitment to chastity is her most celebrated quality—she even chooses death lest she cause a man to stumble in faith. As a major figure in the story, she spends a surprising amount of time dead. God's favor toward her is proven by the protection of her body from violation, though her death acts as a vehicle for Callimachus's radical transformation. This emphasis on Callimachus's conversation is further emphasized when Andronicus asks John to bring his wife back from the dead as John is celebrating Callimachus's salvation. While John does not hesitate to do so, Callimachus is his primary concern. As he is praying for Drusiana to be restored, he says, "Let your name be glorified by us, and raise Drusiana, that Callimachus may be further established in the One."[19] Even her resurrection is for the benefit and the salvation of Callimachus.

Thecla and Drusiana demonstrate two sides of the womanly ideal in the early Christian church. Both women embrace a life of chastity despite the dire consequences: one was almost burned to death, while the other was entombed. Their commitment to chastity is lifted up as the ideal for women through both of these stories. It is only after each woman dedicates her life to virginity and suffers for it that she starts to exhibit miraculous behaviors. God favors them because of their holiness, and their holiness is overwhelmingly defined by their chastity in these texts. Of course, each woman does exhibit other important and venerable qualities. They hold to their faith throughout various trials, and they are rewarded by divine intervention. Although Drusiana's participation in evangelism is a bit tangential, both women do act as evangelists. In fact, after the adventures of her youth, Thecla becomes best defined by her ability to teach and evangelize. Finally, one cannot discount both women's almost divine ability to forgive. Drusiana forgives both her husband for locking her in a tomb and Callimachus for his unwanted advances and his dastardly plan to violate her corpse, while Thecla forgives her mother for insisting that she be burned at the stake. Through these two stories, we can start to put together a picture of ideal faithfulness in a woman in the era: devotion to God, commitment to chastity, a

---

18 Paola Francesca Moretti, "The Two Ephesian Matrons: Drusiana's Story in the Acts of John as a Possible Christian Response to Milesian Narrative," in *The Ancient Novel and Early Christian and Jewish Narrative: Fictional Intersections*, eds. Marília P. Futre Pinheiro, Judith Perkins, and Richard Pervo (Groningen: Barkhuis, 2012), 35–48.

19 "The Acts of John" in *The Apocryphal Acts of the New Testament*, trans. M. R. James (Oxford: Clarendon Press, 1924), sec. 79.

willingness to put faith before social convention, and a powerful ability to forgive those who have wronged them. While their stories incorporate elements of exaggeration and fantasy, the qualities these women exhibit were undoubtedly real ideals.

OFFICIAL ROLES IN THE CHURCH: PRIESTS, PROPHETS, DEACONS, AND WIDOWS

The formal structure of the Christian church emerged early but lacked a strong hierarchy as there was not uniformity among all Christian communities. Generally, there were deacons, presbyters, and bishops who united the one church in an area. Presbyters and deacons were accountable to the bishop, and the bishops were accountable to each other and to the people. Guidelines for the ordination of deacons, priests, and bishops and instructions for conducting worship were recorded in a mid-third century document called *Apostolic Tradition* by Hippolytus of Rome, though he asserts that these practices were handed down from the earliest days of the church.[20]

There has been significant debate in recent decades as to whether women in the early church acted as priests. The most obvious reason for this debate is the question of women's ordination today. Unfortunately, we cannot definitively answer the question based on available evidence. From biblical accounts alone, we know women carried a variety of titles including deacon, teacher, and apostle, though we cannot be entirely sure how those roles functioned in the very early church. There is archeological evidence that women may have held roles as presbyters or even bishops in the early church as well, though there is no definitive proof. There is recorded evidence that enslaved women did hold levels of leadership, a prospect that must have been utterly shocking to the larger community.[21]

Despite the ambiguity of how exactly women leaders functioned in the early church, it is well established that women gradually became less influential as the church became more structured and regulated. There are various reasons why women lost power and influence as time went on; significant was the attempt to make Christianity look more respectable in the eyes of the larger society. The early church was plagued with unsubstantiated rumors that were causing problems for the early Christian communities, and it is undeniable that the earliest Christians embraced a lifestyle that was countercultural. While women were gaining more rights in society, this was controversial, and there could have been a push within Christianity to embrace a more traditional view of family and gender to appear more respectable, especially in light of their other public relation problems.

Even with the restriction of women's activities as time passed, there were consistent roles women could and did assume in the early church, such as widow and deaconess. The role of a widow was originally for women who were worthy of receiving help from the community due to their righteous life and lack of family and resources.

---

20 *The Apostolic Tradition of Hippolytus*, trans. Burton Scott Easton (Cambridge: Cambridge University Press, 1934), 1:1–15.

21 "Correspondence of Pliny and Trajan," in *Readings in World Christian History, Volume 1: Earliest Christianity to 1453*, eds. John W. Coakley and Andrea Sterk (Maryknoll: Orbis Books, 2018), 23–24.

Widows would be registered, along with orphans, to receive assistance. First Timothy offers a revealing passage on widows. The epistle states:

> Let a widow be put on the list if she is not less than sixty years old and has been married only once; she must be well attested for her good works, as one who has brought up children, shown hospitality, washed the saints' feet, helped the afflicted, and devoted herself to doing good in every way. But refuse to put younger widows on the list; for when their sensual desires alienate them from Christ, they want to marry, and so they incur condemnation for having violated their first pledge. Besides that, they learn to be idle, gadding about from house to house; and they are not merely idle, but also gossips and busybodies, saying what they should not say. So I would have younger widows marry, bear children, and manage their households, so as to give the adversary no occasion to revile us. For some have already turned away to follow Satan. If any believing woman has relatives who are really widows, let her assist them; let the church not be burdened, so that it can assist those who are real widows. (1 Tim 5:9–16)

There are numerous points worthy of discussion in the above quote. Only widows without any other resources could qualify for community support. Considering the probable financial constraints of the early church, this makes sense. There is also a level of behavioral expectation expressed here that may be surprising to the modern reader. Widows brought life experience and wisdom to impart to younger members of the community, but they also had a level of independence in the ancient world that was unique. The restrictions on a widow's behavior were, at least in part, attempts to limit their freedom and independence.

By the beginning of the second century, widows took on a new role, almost as a special order to which they were appointed, called "office of the widow." A widow was not ordained, but she was obliged to live a life of chastity. Hippolytus of Rome recommended that widows and virgins fast and pray frequently.[22] Widows provided education to younger women and children, were agents of evangelism, and provided support to needy members of the community (both the Christian community and the community at large).

Another role open to women was that of deacon or deaconess. As we saw in Paul's letter to the Romans, Phoebe was introduced as a deacon, though there is much we do not know about this title. It is unknown whether female deacons were common and what their duties entailed. By the end of the first century, male deacons were a recognized part of the church, but whether women held the role in the same way is simply unknown. By the end of the third century, however, the role of the *deaconess* had emerged, and the role was particularly common in the Eastern churches. The major source of information about deaconesses comes from a text called *Didascalia Apostolorum*, and it includes an entire section on the ordination of deaconesses, though the text also states that women cannot baptize. A deaconess's main tasks were visiting the sick and *receiving* baptized women when

---

22 *The Apostolic Tradition of Hippolytus*, 3:25.

they emerged from the water; this likely was seen as necessary for preserving modesty since early Christians were typically baptized in the nude. Deaconesses had additional duties such as distributing resources to the poor, finding seats for women at church, acting as intermediaries between women and male clergy, and teaching new Christian converts about Christian life.[23]

The institutionalization of these two roles for women in the church was a double-edged sword. On the one hand, women had a recognized role and function in the church, where they did perform important duties. On the other hand, those official roles were increasingly being held by single women, while married women were losing influence. The establishment of an official office for deaconesses and widows also inevitably gave bishops more control over these women.

Prophet was the most ambiguous role that women could hold in the ancient church; it was open to both men and women, and it was an important part of the faith. The *Didache* even gives advice for determining whether a person is a genuine prophet or not.[24] Although prophecy played a role in the early church, there were also tensions between the established church and prophets. Prophecy provided an alternative route to church authority, bypassing official ordination and sacraments since prophets claimed their authority directly from God. This tension between prophets and established leadership plays out repeatedly throughout Christian history.

New Prophecy, also called Montanism, was a particularly influential stream of prophetic Christianity that arose in the late second century but was condemned as heretical by the established church. Unfortunately, we know little more than the basic facts surrounding the founding of the movement. The name most associated with the movement was a prophet named Montanus who was from Phrygia. He experienced ecstatic possession and was apparently a talented church organizer. Equally important were two women, Priscilla and Maximilla; both were prophets and held official and ordained leadership roles within the movement. While there is speculation that women may have held positions as priests in the early church, New Prophecy is the only movement for which we have firm evidence that women were ordained priests. In fact, Priscilla, Maximilla, and another woman named Quintilla all functioned as bishops.

TALES OF MARTYRDOM OR FOLLOWING AN ILLEGAL FAITH

Of all the roles women held in the early church, that of martyr was likely the most profound and influential. It was a powerful expression of Christian faith, and all attempts to crush Christianity through violent oppression only resulted in spreading the faith further. In martyrdom, women and men died side by side as equals, and it was a way in which the most marginalized people were able to resist both the culture and the state.

---

23 *Didascalia Apostolorum*, trans. Margaret Dunlop Gibson (London: C. J. Clay and Sons, 1903), chap. XVI.
24 *Didache*, 11:3–12.

Generally speaking, people in the ancient world received their religion and their culture from their homeland. The Roman Empire was relatively tolerant of religious pluralism; practically, a level of religious tolerance was necessary in a large empire that consisted of many different ethnic and religious groups. Regardless of religious affiliation, people living under Roman rule were expected to venerate the emperor and offer up prayers to the Roman gods for the empire's well-being. This was a requirement for being a good citizen, and with the exception of the Jews, few people took issue with it; most faiths in the ancient world were polytheist. It was assumed that other gods were indeed real, and it was quite possible to offer sacrifice to another god while staying loyal to your own. Judaism was of course the exception; however, Roman authorities recognized Judaism as an old and venerable religion, and Jews were exempt from the requirement of sacrificing to Roman gods, for the most part.

For the first few decades after Jesus's death, Romans did not distinguish between Judaism and this new Christian faith, and Christians reaped the benefit of not being expected to sacrifice either. However, as Christians developed new communities, comprised of both Jews and gentiles, and distinguished themselves further from their Jewish roots, Rome and its people came to realize that Christianity was something different and new—and something suspicious. There were rumors that Christians were cannibals and incestuous, and they were often accused of being atheists, which seems odd now, but Christians denied the existence of all gods besides their own (or accused the other gods of being demons, which did little to endear them to their polytheistic neighbors).

The first known large-scale killing of Christians occurred in 64 CE after the Great Fire of Rome destroyed much of the city. Nero, who was an unpopular emperor, found it advantageous to blame the unpopular Christians for starting the fire, thus diverting negative public opinion from himself. It is estimated that hundreds of Christians were killed, and according to Clement of Rome, both Peter and Paul were executed in this purge.[25] While terrible, the event was more of an isolated slaughter than any sort of systematic persecution.

Persecution remained sporadic and localized, though surely always in the back of all believers' minds. A fascinating exchange between the emperor Trajan and the administrator Pliny the Younger, the governor of Bithynia, between the years 111 and 113 speaks to the difficult position Christians could find themselves in. In the exchange, Pliny seeks guidance as to how to deal with the Christians in his province. He has found that Christians are being persecuted, but he seems confused as to why. He casually mentions how he tortured two enslaved female deacons to confirm what he had learned about this group. He reports that Christian activities consist of assembling before daylight to sing a hymn to Christ as a god; then they bind themselves with an oath not to commit any wrongdoings, and when they are done, they meet again to eat, but it is only ordinary food. Also of note, Pliny reports that the contagion of this superstition had spread not only in the cities but also to the villages and countryside and to men and women of every rank. Pliny reports that he executed some Christians and sent the Roman citizens off to Rome. He released

---

25 Clement of Rome, *First Epistle*, 5:4–6.

any who were able to recite a prayer to the gods and offer incense and wine to a statue of the emperor. In response, the emperor confirms that Pliny has done well. Christians are not to be sought out, but they must be punished if accused and convicted.[26]

Things changed when Marcus Aurelius became emperor in 161. He was well educated and a philosopher, but his tenure as emperor was plagued by various disasters, and he blamed Christians for bringing the wrath of the gods upon the empire. He supported the persecution of Christians, and it was under his reign that Justin Martyr was killed and a woman named Felicitas watched her seven sons martyred before being martyred herself. This round of persecutions ended with Marcus Aurelius's death in 180.

By the beginning of the third century, the political situation for Christians grew worse again. Roman rule started showing signs of decline, while Christianity continued to spread among the ranks in Roman society. Emperors wanting to instill greater loyalty in their subjects became increasingly suspicious of Christians. There were four major waves of persecution in the Roman Empire, beginning under the rule of Septimius Severus—this was the wave that took the lives of Perpetua and Felicity, to whom we will turn shortly. Under the reign of Decius, another wave of persecution began in the year 250; eight years later, Valerian renewed the efforts. The final wave of severe persecution began under Galerius in the eastern part of the empire and Diocletian in the western part.

While the fourth century brought an end to persecution for Christians living under the Roman Empire, leading to a flourishing of monasticism and an establishment of doctrine, the opposite was true for Christians living under Persian rule. In fact, in the Persian Empire, what is remembered as the Great Persecution began around the year 340. It is somewhat ironic, but the favored position of Christianity in Rome led to a deep distrust of it in Persia.

In both Roman and Persian Christianity, martyrdom became a major expression of faith, and there are many martyrdom accounts about women. A consistent theme that runs through them is the graphic nature of the violence inflicted on them. The gruesome violence is quite distasteful to the modern reader, and there are numerous instances when it seems the violence has been elaborated upon. However, these tales were written to demonstrate believers' ability to suffer greatly for the faith, and they also show the dangers particular to women. Women faced not only physical violence and torture but also the threat of sexual violence.

The *Acts of the Martyrs* is written in a variety of forms and styles, including moving narrative accounts and formal trial accounts. One of the earliest accounts is of a woman named Blandina who was martyred in Lyons in 177. The Christian community in Lyons was largely comprised of immigrants from Asia Minor and faced significant persecution. According to the text,

> in the first place, they heroically endured all that the people *en masse* heaped on
> them: abuse, dragging, stoning, imprisonment, and all that an enraged mob
> is likely to inflict on their most hated enemies. They were dragged into the

---

26 "Correspondence of Pliny and Trajan," 23–24.

> forum and interrogated before the entire populace by the tribune and the city authorities. . . . From then on the blessed martyrs underwent torments beyond all description.[27]

From there, the account goes on to describe the tortures Blandina endured. She shows such bravery and strength that even those torturing her throughout the night are exhausted and state that there is nothing else they can do to the woman and that they are surprised she is still alive. The next day, she and three men are brought to the arena to be publicly tortured and killed. At one point, she is hung from a post, and "she seemed to hang there from a cross. . . . They saw in the person of their sister him who was crucified for them, that he might convince all who believe in him that all who suffer for Christ's glory will have eternal fellowship in the living God."[28] Blandina miraculously survives this ordeal as well. After more accounts of torture and her bravery, Blandina finally dies. Her account is shocking in both its brutality and the respect given to her. Her comparison to a Christ figure is especially remarkable.

Another tale from the *Acts of the Martyrs* is the "Martyrdom of Agapê, Irenê, and Chionê," which occurred during the final persecution in the Roman Empire under Diocletian in the year 304. While there is elaborate mythology surrounding these women, who are considered saints in the Christian tradition, there is little evidence of their lives outside the records of their trials. More than likely, the three women left their families and fled to a mountain after Diocletian's edict that anyone in possession of Christian scriptures needed to surrender them or face death. There they formed a community of women so that they could live as Christians away from the emperor's persecutions; however, they were found and arrested. They along with their other female companions Agatho, Cassia, Philippa, and Eutychia were charged with refusing to eat sacrificial food and brought before the prefect. All seven women remained strong under questioning and refused to eat the sacrificial food or repent of their behavior. As a result, Agapê and Chionê were sentenced to death by burning, while the other five were imprisoned. Eutychia was imprisoned because she was pregnant (supposedly by God and not a man), and the rest were at least temporarily spared because of their youth. Throughout the trial, the prefect seemed as frustrated by the women's refusal to listen to decrees as he did by their commitment to Christianity. Indeed, it must have been infuriating to him that a group of young women, so lacking in any formal power or authority, stood firm in their convictions, choosing death over sacrificing to other gods.[29]

Crispina, too, was martyred during the reign of Diocletian in the year 304, and her story stands out because of her strong personality. Her trial account reveals a witty and determined woman who verbally spars with the proconsul. When the proconsul points out that the entire province of Africa has sacrificed, she replies, "May they never find it easy to make me offer sacrifice to demons: but I sacrifice to the Lord who has made heaven

---

27 "Acts of the Martyrs," in *In Her Words*, ed. Amy Oden (Nashville: Abingdon Press, 1994), 39.

28 "Acts of the Martyrs," 40.

29 "Acts of the Martyrs," 41–44.

and earth, the sea, and all things that are in them." And when he threatens to behead her for refusing to sacrifice, she retorts, "I should thank my God if I obtain this. I should be very happy to lose my head for the sake of my God. For I refuse to sacrifice to these ridiculous deaf and dumb statues." Between her refusal to sacrifice and the fact that she called the Roman gods both demons and ridiculous, it is little surprise that she was indeed sentenced to death.[30]

THE PASSION OF PERPETUA AND FELICITY

One of the most famous tales of martyrdom, regardless of gender, is that of Perpetua and Felicity. It is believed that Perpetua wrote most of the account herself, and it remains one of the only accounts of the early church written by a woman. In addition to Perpetua's first-person narrative of her imprisonment, there is an introduction written by an editor, possibly Tertullian, an account of the dream of her companion in prison, the presbyter Saturus, and some final additional material about the death of Perpetua and Felicity and the other martyrs. In addition to the martyrdom itself, the account gives us invaluable information on Roman family relations and motherhood, and it demonstrates how gender roles and gender inequality melted away in the arena.

The martyrdom account takes place in the North African city of Carthage under the persecution of Emperor Septimius Severus in the years 202–203. While it is possible embellishments were added to the tale, the story is believed to be true. The account describes Perpetua as twenty-two years old, respectfully born, liberally educated, and married with an infant son. Perpetua was a catechumen, or in the process of conversion, at the time of her arrest. The emperor had outlawed, by punishment of death, conversion to Christianity, so the situation is logical considering the nature of this particular persecution.

Her husband is curiously absent from the account. Legally speaking, Perpetua most likely stayed under the authority of her own father, as was the custom at the time. However, Perpetua's son legally would have belonged to her husband, though it is her father, the maternal grandfather, who takes the child from her. It is possible her husband was already dead, though this, too, seems unlikely since Perpetua was called a matron and not a widow. Regardless of the identity of Perpetua's husband, it was her father who consistently acted as the male authority in her life, begging her to recant to save her life. In their first encounter in response to his pleas to recant, she tells him:

> Father, do you see, let us say, this vessel lying here to be a little pitcher, or something else? And he said, "I see it to be so." And I replied to him, "Can it be called by any other name than what it is?" And he said, "No." "Neither can I call myself anything else than what I am, a Christian."[31]

---

30 "Acts of the Martyrs," 44–46.

31 "The Martyrdom of Perpetua and Felicity," in *Readings in World Christian History, Volume 1: Earliest Christianity to 1453*, eds. John Coakley and Andrea Sterk (Maryknoll: Orbis, 2004), 1:2.

Her father then physically attacks her. Perpetua describes fearing he would tear her eyes out, but then he leaves. During other confrontations between the two, her father admits she is his favorite child, and he cannot bear to see her killed. During her trial, he once again begs her to recant. He is beaten in front of her, which causes her significant suffering, but she stays firm. Perpetua remains strong in her faith throughout all of their interactions, consistently rejecting her father's pleas and subverting the social order of the day to follow Christ. She has a new authority in her life, and it is not her earthly family. At the time of her arrest, she is unsure what her future holds. Her brother, who is also a believer but not imprisoned, encourages her to pray for a vision. Throughout her imprisonment, she receives four visions, which she describes as gradually preparing her and the other imprisoned Christians for their martyrdom.

While Perpetua is the main focus of the tale since she penned most of the account, there was another woman suffering along with her, Felicity, who was a slave. Often Felicity is identified as Perpetua's slave, but there is nothing in the text to indicate that is the case. Felicity is pregnant at the time of her arrest, and the account states that she is concerned that her companions will be executed before her because pregnant women cannot be publicly punished. After fervent prayers, Felicity goes into labor a month early. As she suffers from labor pains, she is taunted by the jailers: "You who are in such suffering now, what will you do when you are thrown to the beasts, which you despised when you refused to sacrifice?" Felicity replies, "Now it is I that suffer what I suffer; but then there will be another in me, who will suffer for me, because I also am about to suffer for him."[32] After the birth, Felicity rejoices that she survived the birth so that she can fight the wild beasts, going from the "midwife to the gladiator." Felicity's family situation is worth noting. As a slave, Felicity could not have been legally married, and neither her owner nor the father of her child (they could have been the same person) make any attempt to claim the child. The text says a Christian woman brought up Felicity's girl as her own daughter, which would have greatly comforted Felicity. Not only would her daughter be raised as a family member and not as a slave, which would have been typical, but she would also be raised as a Christian.

When it comes time for their executions, the two women are stripped, clothed in nets, and brought into the arena together to fight a fierce cow. The account states that the crowd shudders as they see them: one woman delicate in frame and the other with breasts dripping from her recent birth. It is certainly of note that the crowd is upset by the condition of the women. The brutality of throwing two young women, one with breast milk dripping down her body, is too much for even this crowd. Consequently, both women are then recalled and dressed in loose-fitting clothing, which apparently solves the crowd's reluctance to enjoy their violent deaths. The women perform courageously in the arena. At one point, Perpetua even stops to fix her clothing to preserve her modesty and puts up her hair, not wanting to die looking like she is in mourning. In the end, both women, after being gored by the mad cow, die by the sword. Perpetua guides the wavering blade

---

32 "The Martyrdom of Perpetua and Felicity," 5:2.

of the gladiator, the editor noting that a woman such as her probably cannot be killed unless she wills it.[33]

Unlike so many other accounts of early Christianity that celebrate virginity, motherhood is a running theme. At the beginning of the account, Perpetua is anxious for the welfare of her child; she is later allowed to have her son in prison with her, which gives her great comfort. We get an account of Felicity's labor and a discussion of engorged breasts and breast milk. Motherhood and the physical experiences that go along with it play a role in the story. These are experiences unique to women facing martyrdom. The fact that they are facing death in the arena while contending with concern over their infant children, the physical pains of labor, and the discomforts of breastfeeding adds to their bravery. These bodily occurrences are not viewed as inferior or sinful but as simply a fact of life for young women of childbearing years.

An interesting comparison to the Roman martyrdom accounts is that of Anahid, a fifth-century Persian martyr. In many ways, the Persian martyrdom accounts are similar to the Roman accounts—women die brutally while demonstrating significant courage and inspiring others through their unrelenting faith. In other ways, the cultural context is different, and in the following story, the violence is particularly gruesome and features prominently.

The story of Anahid takes place after the great Persian persecutions, in the mid-400s when Christianity had become a recognized minority religion, and it was mainly aristocratic Zoroastrian families who were banned from converting. Had Anahid not been the daughter of a Zoroastrian Mobed (cleric), she might have been able to live out her life in peace, but due to her connection with Zoroastrianism, she suffered terribly for her faith. At the beginning of the martyrdom account, Anahid is possessed by a demon, and her desperate father, the Mobed Adurhormizd, is looking for a solution. After Magian sorcerers, Manicheans, and Jews all fail to help her, he seeks the help of a Christian holy man named Pethion. Pethion heals her, first from the demon and later from leprosy, and eventually both Anahid and her father are converted to Christianity. As a Zoroastrian cleric, Adurhormizd is martyred first. After his death, prominent Zoroastrian men of the region seek out Anahid, who willingly comes to face trial.

Once Anahid stands in front of the men, they are shocked by her incredible beauty. The head Magian offers to marry her, or if she would prefer, he offers his son as a husband. He begs her to marry and save her life. When she rejects the Magian and his son, the Magian becomes furious and has her beaten. What follows is a lengthy account of tortures and miraculous healings. In the end, they bring Anahid to a hillside, attach her to four iron stakes, smear her with honey, and leave her for the animals. Instead of eating her, the animals and insects surround her body and protect her. After seven days, the local Christian community comes to the spot, and the animals let the Christians enter. Anahid prays and then dies, though when the clergy reaches her, it appears as though she has

---

33 "The Martyrdom of Perpetua and Felicity," 6:4.

already been dead for days. The end of the account says that Anahid died on June 18 in the ninth year of Yazdgard, King of Kings, which places her death around the year 445.[34]

Anahid is not the only Persian martyrdom tale that features powerful men proposing marriage to Christian women who then reject them. There are additional martyrdom tales of women refusing the advances of powerful men and only then being tortured and killed. In the story of the martyr Tarbo, she, her sister, and their servant are tortured and killed after Tarbo refuses the advances of a Mobed.[35] Similarly, in the tale of Martha, daughter of Posi, it is only after she rejects the idea of marriage and children that the Mobed sentences her to death.[36] There is a recurring theme of men being driven to violence and murder not by a woman's faith but by her rejection of either their sexual advances or sexual relationships in general. It is a disturbing feature, but it speaks to the additional danger women faced when they defied cultural norms in the name of their faith.

---

34 "Anahid," in *Holy Women of the Syrian Orient*, eds. and trans. Sebastian P. Brock and Susan Ashbrook Harvey (Berkeley: University of California Press, 2008), 82–99.

35 "The Martyrdom of Tarbo, her Sister, and Her Servant," in *Holy Women of the Syrian Orient*, 73–76.

36 "The Martyrdom of Martha, Daughter of Posi Who Was a Daughter of the Covenant," in *Holy Women of the Syrian Orient*, 71–72.

CHAPTER 2

Women under Empire (300–500)

The persecutions in the period of the early church did not suppress the spread of Christianity. Instead each wave only succeeded in bringing more people to the faith. By the opening of the fourth century, a significant portion of the Roman upper class, women in particular, had embraced Christianity. While Christianity continued to spread, changes that would forever influence the nature and trajectory of the faith were occurring within the Roman Empire. Within a few short years, Christianity went from an illegal religion to the religion of the empire. The conversion of Emperor Constantine remains one of the most significant events in Christian history. There has been great historical debate as to what was gained or lost with this conversion, but regardless of moral judgments, the event was pivotal religiously, politically, and societally, and the legalization ushered in a new era for Christianity.

When Christianity became legal, believers had to adjust to living under a government that not only tolerated Christianity but eventually actively promoted it. This was a profound change in their circumstances; this shift could be difficult for Christian communities, even if legalization of the faith was generally beneficial for them. Inevitably the faith transformed due to the dynamic change in political and cultural circumstances. Two benefits that emerged from the legalization were the standardization of doctrine through church councils and the proliferation of the monastic life.

During these early years of legalization, Christian women increasingly opted to forgo the traditional roles of wife and mother to live in communities with other women. While there was an increase in societal acceptance of this lifestyle, it often proved difficult for women, especially if their families were unsupportive. Some women escaped to the deserts, while others built monastic communities within urban centers. Regardless of their location, the process represented a shift in attitudes toward women during the era. Virginity and monasticism became the preferable states for Christian women. The women we know the most about were respected for their willingness to reject marriage and motherhood. Sometimes this rejection occurred even after marrying and having children—there are stories celebrating women for leaving their children behind to embrace the monastic life. Gender remained an important factor in this era. Women, largely viewed as the weaker sex, were revered when they were able to "transcend" their gender and become more like men. This is highlighted in various stories about the saints, which include a genre of writings about holy women who became "like men."

While monasticism may have been considered the preferable path, most women still married and had children. From the writings of various church fathers, we can glean the role and influence Christian mothers exerted over their husbands and children. While these writings about mothers represent a relatively small number of women, they can give us a glimpse of what it was like to raise devout children in the late Roman Empire.

One particularly fascinating area in which gender, power, and religious authority come to a head is that of high-born royal women, especially those from the Byzantine East, who established themselves as influential religious figures. Public shows of religiosity, feuds with religious leaders, and influence on the establishment of religious policies further complicate the picture of how women functioned within this particular cultural context.

HISTORICAL BACKGROUND

By the turn of the fourth century, the Roman Empire was in disrepair. Warfare with the Persians to the east and the Germanic tribes to the north overextended the Roman military. High taxes were draining the people, and waves of new religions were making their way through the empire, proving the people had little faith in the old Roman gods. Responding to the increasing number of challenges, Emperor Diocletian divided the empire into a tetrarchy, or in other words, he divided it into fourths. Unsurprisingly this proved to be an unstable ruling arrangement. Power plays and intrigue became common occurrences among the four rulers.

In 306, Constantinius, who was ruler over Spain, Britain, and Gaul, died, and the army proclaimed his ambitious son, Constantine, his replacement. In 312, Constantine marched against his co-emperor Maxentius, who ruled Italy and North Africa. On the eve of a decisive battle, Constantine received a vision: he saw the first two letters of Christ (chi-rho) and heard the words "In this, conquer." He commanded the symbol be put on his soldiers' shields before they went into battle. He took Rome and became the sole ruler of the western portion of the empire; later he gained control over the entire empire.

Like emperors before him, he wanted to recapture the old glory of Rome, though he believed he could better accomplish this through worship of the Christian God rather than the old Roman deities. The legalization of Christianity must have felt like an answer to Christians' prayers after the many persecutions and hardships they had faced in the centuries prior, but legalization was not an entirely smooth transition. Christian faith and opposition to Roman authorities had long been virtually indistinguishable. Each martyrdom was a resistance to earthly authority. Secret church services undermined the state. The refusal to marry and participate in typical Roman family patterns disrupted social norms. Suddenly martyrdom was off the table, at least within the Roman Empire. Church services were not only legal, but in many cases, Christians received funds to build churches. Celibate Christian life was celebrated instead of reviled. Christians gained political import and began working with the very Roman officials who had once tortured and executed members of their faith communities. Christians who had once been in the arenas fighting for their lives were now more likely to be spectators than victims. What began as a countercultural movement gradually became more accommodating of typical Roman life—accepting norms and practices of the larger society. Against this there would always be pushback from certain Christians, but the culture creep continued. Access to power changes institutions after all.

There were significant advantages to the legalization of the faith. Due to the increased freedom, the period after legalization became the era of the great church fathers—men such as Augustine, Jerome, the Cappadocians, and John Chrysostom wrote influential Christian texts that shaped the faith. The Councils of Nicaea, Constantinople, Ephesus, and Chalcedon established the nature of Christ, asserted the Virgin Mary as the *theotokos* or God-bearer, and defined the Trinity among other important issues. Women were largely left out of these conversations; the church fathers were all men, and the councils were for male clergy. That does not mean women did not speak or write on these topics during the fourth and fifth centuries. It seems likely they did; however, virtually nothing has been saved. There are only three undisputed extant writings by women from this period: *Cento* by Faltonia Betitia Proba, *The Martyrdom of St. Cyprian* by the Empress Eudocia, and *The Pilgrimage of Egeria*. Of these *The Pilgrimage of Egeria*, which will be examined later in this chapter, is the only factual and personalized account.[1] While it offers interesting information and a rare glimpse of a woman's perspective from this era, it is rather limited by the fact that it is a travel narrative. There were plenty of women who had the education and skillset to write great Christian works, but if they were written, the works were either not saved or left unattributed. From the writings of men, we know of the brilliance, piety, and influence of many women of the time, such as Melania the Elder, Melania the Younger, Marcella, Paula, Eustochium, Macrina, and Olympias. Yet sadly, we have no writings from any of these women's own pens. Because there are so few extant writings dating from this era by women, we must largely rely on male writers to access information on women. These male writers had personal relationships with women, but they also had their own lenses and views regarding them, all of which were not necessarily flattering.

One additional challenge when studying women of this era has to do with wealth and social class. The women we know the most about were overwhelmingly members of the aristocracy, specifically wealthy widows and upper-class committed virgins. Often it is their proximity to the church fathers that has preserved the memories of these women. While the information on well-known aristocratic women is valuable, it is admittedly not representative of most women of the time.

Many Christian women of the era, from a variety of social classes, were committed to asceticism. Celibacy and simple living had long been part of Christian life, but the fourth century saw a true proliferation of an ascetic framework. When Christianity had been a persecuted religion, the very association with the faith was a demonstration of one's commitment to Christ. The clear and present danger of martyrdom vanished, and conversion to Christianity became a safe and eventually politically advantageous choice. The rich and powerful gained dominance in the church. Corruption spread throughout the clergy. Now that the church was free to flourish without threat of persecution, it faced a deeper

---

1 Gillian Cloke, *This Female Man of God: Women and Spiritual Power in the Patristic Age, AD 350–450* (London: Routledge, 1995), 13.

existential problem. How can one be a true Christian in a time of laxity and growing corruption? How can one be a true Christian when the church and the world seem to be merging into one entity? The legalization that felt like such a blessing from God to some felt like a snare to others.

For many the solution to this problem was monasticism. A commitment to virginity and asceticism became a new type of sacrifice—a new sort of martyrdom. The pattern of rejecting society to embrace solitude or communal living outside the mainstream became increasingly popular. The monastic Christian tradition began before the fourth century; in fact, the most famous of the desert ascetics, St. Anthony of the Desert, retreated to the Egyptian desert prior to Constantine's conversion, but it was after Constantine that the movement exploded in popularity. The practices of the ascetics ranged from regimented to fanatical.

As Christianity became more worldly, women retreated to the deserts, intent on detaching themselves from society and living a life of solitude. To begin such a spiritual journey, one would generally seek out a spiritual guide, such as an *amma*, or spiritual mother, who lived the ascetic life and had obtained a level of wisdom and maturity. It is through this process of ascetic apprenticeship that desert *ammas* and *abbas* (*spiritual fathers*) would find themselves surrounded by eager Christians despite their retreat from society.

The life of a desert ascetic was harsh. Often they would only eat one vegetarian meal a day, though ancient sources also describe ascetics who ate only bread, water, and salt. Ascetics would sleep little and spent much of their time in prayer, they rarely bathed, and most were committed to supporting themselves and working hard. Suppressing passions and exerting control over the body were critical, as was solitude, whether alone in the desert or in a cell in a monastic community. Pilgrims would seek out these holy figures, looking for wisdom and guidance. From this, we have recorded sayings from the desert mothers. Common themes emerge from these sayings, such as the importance of seeking God, prayer, repentance, penance, obedience, silence, and manual labor.[2]

Increasingly, the solitary retreat from society that first dominated this early period gave way to cenobitic (meaning communal life) monasticism. While not the founder, Pachomius deserves credit as an early and important organizer of this type of lifestyle. His monastic rule demanded that any who joined the community relinquish their wealth and promise obedience to their superiors. All monks were required to perform labor willingly, seeing nothing as below them. Pachomius's sister, Mary, founded communities for women as he was founding them for men, and these were typically less fanatical than the lone monastics. This theme of brother and sister (whether related by blood or perhaps in spirit) establishing monasteries together is a recurring theme throughout Christian history.

---

2 Laura Swan, *The Forgotten Desert Mothers: Sayings, Lives, and Stories of Early Christian Women* (New York: Paulist Press, 2001), 32–70.

MONASTIC LEADERS IN THE WESTERN EMPIRE

Despite the popularity of desert monasticism, one did not necessarily need to escape to the deserts of Egypt to live a holy life. Some women who were unwilling or unable to move to the desert built for themselves monastic havens within urban centers. A pioneer of urban monasticism was a woman by the name of Marcella (c. 312–410). Much of what we know about Marcella comes to us from Jerome, who was one of her friends. Many of the other high-profile Christian women of the time were associated with her in some regard. She was a brilliant scholar, a strong leader, and widely influential.[3]

Marcella was born into a wealthy aristocratic family; she married young, as was expected of upper-class women, but was widowed after a mere seven months. When her mother tried to arrange a second marriage to a much older man, Marcella refused. Jerome reports that Marcella learned of aspects of the monastic life, including Anthony of the Desert, Pachomius, and the monasteries in Thebaid, from some Alexandrian priests who were seeking refuge in Rome. Inspired by these desert monastics, Marcella created a spiritual haven right in the city of Rome. She took a vow of celibacy and opened her home to women pursuing a spiritual life. Jerome reports that Marcella lived as an ascetic for many years; she fasted moderately, abstained from meat, and would only drink wine for medicinal purposes. While she kept a disciplined life, she was not fanatical. Conversely, her younger sister, Asella, was far more extreme and chose to live in solitude.

Marcella became a respected scholar, particularly regarding biblical interpretation and translation. She studied the Bible in private with Jerome, whose expertise was well known, and encouraged an intellectual atmosphere in her home. She was so well versed in scripture that priests would come to her with difficult questions, especially after Jerome left Rome. Jerome notes:

> When she was thus questioned, she would reply as if her answer was not her own but from me or some other man, in order to confess that what she taught she herself had learned from others. For she knew that the apostle had said, "I do not permit a woman to teach" and she would not seem to inflict an injury on the male sex and on those priests who were enquiring about obscure and doubtful positions.[4]

Despite Jerome's description, it seems likely that the men who came to Marcella were very aware of her intellectual prowess, though she employed great modesty in her abilities either due to her nature or perhaps out of necessity as a woman.

Marcella continued her urban monastery until the Goths sacked Rome in 410. Enemy soldiers broke into her home looking for gold, and when Marcella told them she had

---

3 Jerome, "To Principia, Letter 127," in *From Nicene and Post-Nicene Fathers, Second Series*, vol. 6., eds. Philip Schaff and Henry Wace, trans. W. H. Fremantle, G. Lewis, and W. G. Martley (Buffalo, NY: Christian Literature Publishing Co., 1893). Revised and edited for New Advent by Kevin Knight. https://www.newadvent.org/fathers/3001127.htm.

4 .Jerome, "To Principia, Letter 127:7."

none, they beat her severely. Apparently moved by some compassion, or perhaps driven by guilt for beating an elderly woman, the men then dropped her and her young associate, Principia, at the basilica for refuge, where the women remained until it was safe to return to their home. Sadly, Marcella died soon after from her injuries.

Two of the women closely associated with Marcella's monastic community were Paula (347–404) and Paula's youngest daughter, Eustochium (c. 368–419). Like Marcella, much of what we know about Paula comes from Jerome, with whom she was close friends for many years. Paula, too, came from aristocratic Roman stock, her family wealthy and ancient. In a letter addressed to Eustochium after the death of Paula, Jerome states that Paula's father was "said to have in his veins the blood of Agamemnon who destroyed Troy after a ten years siege," though, of course, it is Paula's faithfulness that is worthy of praise and not her ancient family.[5] Paula married a man from another elite Roman family, and they had five children: four girls and finally a boy, after whom she stopped having children. Jerome states that it was obligation to produce a male heir, not desire, that fueled her reproduction. After the death of her husband in 380, she was free to pursue a life of holiness in Marcella's home. She quickly became one of the better-known Christian women in the city.

Again like Marcella, Paula was an ardent student of scripture. She studied with Jerome, who said that her skill in Hebrew surpassed even his own. Her close relationship with Jerome led to rumors of sexual impropriety; however, there is no evidence that either broke their commitment to celibacy. Rumors aside, they were close friends who cared deeply for each other.

When Pope Damasus, for whom Jerome had been secretary, died, Jerome left Rome for Palestine. Soon after, Paula and Eustochium left the city as well, but leaving Rome was no small feat for Paula. An account of her children, including her still-young son Toxotius, pleading with her to stay with them is heart-wrenching all these years later. According to Jerome:

> But still Paula's eyes were dry as she turned them heavenwards; and she over-came her love for her children by her love for God. She knew herself no more as a mother, that she might approve herself a handmaid of Christ. Yet her heart was rent within her, and she wrestled with her grief, as though she were being forcibly separated from parts of herself.[6]

She was able to detach herself from her children and pursue the life of holiness to which she felt called. It is worth noting that Paula is being praised for her ability to separate herself from her family. It is virginity and celibacy—not motherhood—that Jerome is promoting as the ideal state for a religious woman.

---

5   Jerome, "To Eustochium, *Letter* 108.3," in *From Nicene and Post-Nicene Fathers, Second Series*, vol. 6., eds. Philip Schaff and Henry Wace, trans. W. H. Fremantle, G. Lewis, and W. G. Martley (Buffalo, NY: Christian Literature Publishing Co., 1893). Revised and edited for New Advent by Kevin Knight. http://www.newadvent.org/fathers/3001108.htm.

6   Jerome, "To Eustochium, Letter 108.6."

After their departure, Paula and Eustochium met Jerome in Antioch in the year 385. They spent the next year traveling all over the Holy Land and Egypt, finally ending up in Bethlehem, where they set up a joint monastic community. Jerome led the community for men, while Paula, and later Eustochium, led the community for women.

It was in Bethlehem that Jerome produced the Latin Vulgate, which would become the standard Bible translation in the West for over a thousand years. The role of Paul and Eustochium in the production of the Vulgate brings up serious questions concerning the role of women in early church scholarship. While Jerome is credited as the sole translator, he admits in his own letters that he was often prompted by Paula to consider particular ideas or insights. Jerome says that he taught the women Hebrew and that Paula's abilities with the language surpassed his own. Considering their close relationship and Paula's skills, it is not unreasonable to assume Paula (and perhaps Eustochium) played a role in this incredibly important project. Unfortunately, with the sources available, it is impossible to know exactly what role, if any, the two women played. This episode highlights what possible theological contributions women made to Christianity that have been unattributed.

Concerning Paula's lifestyle, once in Bethlehem, she was extreme in her asceticism and lavish in her generosity. She did not bathe unless she was very ill, her fasts were severe, and she slept little, spending most of the night in prayer. While she kept extremely strict practices, she did not expect the women living in her monastery to hold such a strict regimen. She took it upon herself to give away her fortune, and when she ran out of money, she took out loans to keep giving—sometimes taking out loans to pay off previous loans. When she died, she left Eustochium with such debt, Jerome states somewhat disapprovingly, that outside of a miracle from God she had little hope of repaying it.

History has remembered Jerome as one of the great church fathers, and Paula and Eustochium have long been considered little more than footnotes to his story. However, a brief but fascinating section in Palladius of Aspuna's *Lausiac History* may point to a rather different reality during their lifetimes.[7] In Palladius's section on holy women, he describes Paula as follows:

> The mother of Toxotius, a woman greatly advanced in her spiritual way of life. A certain Jerome from Dalmatia became a stumbling block for her. She was capable of flying higher than everybody, for she was very talented, but in his jealousy he stood in her way, having won her over to his own point of view.[8]

Of Eustochium, whom he had not met, he wrote that she was known as a woman of extreme discretion, running a community of fifty women.

After Paula's death in 404, she left Eustochium in charge of the community. Eustochium was the fourth daughter of Paula, and unlike her other siblings, who married, she committed herself to the life of a Christian virgin at a young age, traveling with and assisting

---

7 Palladius was a friend to Melania the Elder and Rufinus, who had a significant dispute with Jerome over the theology of Origen that likely influenced Palladius's scathing comments on Jerome.

8 Palladius of Aspuna, *The Lausiac History*, trans. John Wortley (Collegeville: Liturgical Press, 2015), sec. 41.

her mother. She, too, had a close relationship with Jerome, who seemed to view her as a sort of spiritual daughter. She raised her niece Paula the Younger at their monastery in Bethlehem. In an interesting and telling event, when Eustochium died, Paula the Younger took over the community despite being a mere eighteen years old. It was her lineage, not her experience, that qualified her for the position. This passing along of leadership on familial lines was not uncommon at the time.

MELANIA THE ELDER AND YOUNGER

Melania the Elder (c. 350–410) was a contemporary of Paula's and similarly a member of the Roman aristocracy. She was born sometime in the middle of the fourth century, though the exact date of her birth is unknown. Palladius writes that she was a Spaniard by birth but later moved to Rome; her grandfather was consul, and she was the wife of a high-ranking man.[9] She was married at the age of fourteen, and she was widowed and lost two of her three children within a short period of time when she was about twenty-two years old. Following this she decided she wanted to retreat from Rome, leaving behind her one surviving child, a son named Publicola. She sold her possessions and fled the city in secret, fearing she would be stopped by family and state authorities. After traveling and visiting the desert fathers in Egypt, she settled with her friend and religious companion Rufinus of Aquileia in Jerusalem, where she built a monastery for women.

Melania the Elder was an intelligent and highly educated woman, and she was incredibly well read, keeping an impressive personal library even after rejecting most worldly possessions. She was involved in a controversy surrounding the theologian Origen, whom she profoundly admired.[10] In fact, it was her defense of Origen that hurt her reputation in later years when the established church rejected much of Origen's writings. Jerome, who once had many words of praise for Melania, eventually wrote of her treachery, and when an account was later written about her granddaughter Melania the Younger, she was not even mentioned due to her commitment to Origenism.

Although Melania the Elder retired to the desert, she did not stop interacting with the world around her. In a telling episode, she was mistaken for a slave and arrested by the consul of Palestine. There would be no quiet suffering for Melania; she quickly pulled her rank:

> I am the daughter of N——, the widow of N——, and the servant of Christ; do not despise the meanness of my appearance. I am capable of raising myself up if I want to; you cannot terrify me in this matter or take what is mine. This I

---

9 Palladius, *Lausiac History*, sec. 46.

10 Origen of Alexandria (c. 184–253) was an early Christian theologian. His literary output was enormous, and he was tremendously influential on Christian thought. While much of his theology is considered orthodox, there were aspects, such as the preexistence of souls and universal salvation, that were later rejected as heresies. These teachings have at various points in history caused great suspicion toward his work in general.

> revealed to you so you do not unwittingly incur charges. Like a falcon, one has
> to make use of pride against the insensitive.[11]

She was released with an apology.

She continued to exercise authority in Egypt, financially supporting churches, monasteries, and people. She became involved in church politics, and she mediated a schism within the Antiochian church and reportedly brought a number of monks back to an orthodox position concerning the Holy Spirit. She was also known to berate male clergy who seemed to have faltered in their holiness. It seems she always maintained an attitude of authority that was likely rooted in her highborn status.

At the age of sixty Melania decided to return to Rome to check in on her family, and Palladius reports that she led them out of Rome to pursue a holy life shortly before the city was sacked in 410.[12] Her visit was likely due in part to concern for her granddaughter and namesake Melania the Younger (383–439). Melania the Younger was the daughter of Publicola and his wife, Albina, and at the age of fourteen she married a man named Pinianus. Combined, the couple had one of the largest fortunes of the day. It appears the younger Melania had always preferred a religious life, but she married out of duty and agreed to produce two heirs. While sources vary, it seems the couple had either two children who died young or one child who died and a failed pregnancy. Regardless, after the death of their young children, Melania convinced Pinianus to forgo traditional marriage, devote their lives to God, and live a celibate life together. Their two prominent families tried to stop them; Publicola even threatened disinheritance, an empty threat since Melania was his only heir. In the end, the couple managed to liquidate most of their assets in Italy and Spain shortly before the Gothic invasion and left Rome. Their travels first took them to North Africa, where they were able to liquidate their African estates. There, to Augustine's embarrassment, the residents of Hippo tried to detain them, but they settled in Thagaste. After seven years, the couple moved to Jerusalem. They arrived at the Mount of Olives in 417 and established a double monastic community where Albina served as *amma* for the women and Pinianus served as *abba* for the men. However, it appears Melania was the informal leader, and she established the rule for the community.

As with her grandmother before her, an ascetic life devoted to God did not erase her aristocratic leanings. She remained a high-profile person known for building churches and having a successful healing ministry. She traveled freely within aristocratic circles even after her retreat from society. Toward the end of her life, her uncle Volusianus invited her to Constantinople for the wedding of the Western emperor, Valentinian III, to Eudoxia, the daughter of the Eastern emperor, Theodosius III, in 436. Melania accepted immediately with the plan of converting her unbelieving uncle. Despite his pleas to let him make his own choice in the matter, she brought in the patriarch of Constantinople, who promptly baptized him. In addition to pressuring family members into baptism during

---

11 Palladius, *Lausiac History*, sec. 46.

12 Palladius, *Lausiac History*, 54.

her time in Constantinople, Melania managed to convince the empress to take a pilgrimage to the Holy Land, a trip in which Melania played a heavy role.[13]

The two Melanias make for an interesting comparison. They both complied with societal pressure to marry and produce heirs, and it is worth dwelling on the fact that Melania the Younger, who was named for her illustrious ascetic grandmother, was still pushed into marriage despite the clear respect the family held for Melania the Elder. As the sole heir to her family's fortune, the pressure to have children was surely strong for the younger Melania. It was only after the traumatic loss of two children that she forged a new path as an ascetic along with her husband.

MONASTIC LEADERS IN THE EASTERN EMPIRE

There were numerous prominent monastic Christian women who emerged in the Eastern Empire, one of the most notable being Macrina (c. 330–379). What we know of her comes from a biography by her brother Gregory of Nyssa, probably written shortly after her death. Gregory and Basil of Caesarea (another of Macrina's brothers), along with their friend Gregory of Nazianzus, were critical in establishing the doctrine of the Trinity, but throughout the biography of Macrina, it becomes clear that she, too, was a pioneer in Christian holiness and thought. The affection and respect that Gregory felt toward his sister take center stage as he writes about her life and influence among her illustrious family.

The letter opens with the following:

> My apology must be that the subject on which you bade me write is greater
> than can be compressed within the limits of a letter. . . . In this case it was
> a woman, who provided us with our subject; if indeed she should be styled a
> woman, for I do not know whether it is fitting to designate her by her sex, who
> so surpassed her sex.[14]

Praising women for being unlike other women or being like men is a common theme throughout this era. In this case, Macrina surpassing her womanhood has to do with her faith, her leadership, and her intelligence. A few lines later Gregory of Nyssa argues that Macrina raised herself by philosophy to the height of human virtue.

The story begins before Macrina was born. Macrina's mother, Emmelia, wanted to pursue a monastic life, but since both of her parents were dead and she was reportedly very beautiful, she decided to marry a pious and scrupulous man to be her protector lest she be abducted by lustful men. This once again highlights the reality for women in the ancient world. Even if a girl or woman desired a life of virginity, oftentimes it was simply

---

13 Gillian Cloke, *This Female Man of God: Women and Spiritual Power in the Patristic Age, AD 350–450* (London: Routledge, 1995), 183–184.

14 Gregory of Nyssa, "Life of Macrina," in *Readings in World Christian History, Volume 1: Earliest Christianity to 1453*, eds. John W. Coakly and Andrea Sterk (Maryknoll, NY: Orbis Books, 2018), 147.

not an option. Macrina was their firstborn child, and Gregory records the miraculous nature of the birth. Emmelia had a dream during her delivery in which an angelic figure addressed the child as Thecla, which became Macrina's secret name. This is an obvious reference to the famed Thecla of the *Acts of Paul and Thecla*, who chose the virgin life, performed numerous miracles, and became a teacher and missionary for the faith. Despite the importance of Christian devotion in Macrina's family, Macrina was not destined for the virginal life either. Gregory states that by the age of twelve her beauty was such that suiters flocked to her parents, and her father picked a young man for her to marry. Marital plans were cut short when the young man died shortly after their betrothal. Normally the family would have sought out another match, but at this point, Macrina argued that her betrothal was the equivalent of marriage and that she must remain loyal to her betrothed, who was not dead but, thanks to the hope of the resurrection, only absent.

It is not entirely clear whether Macrina felt deep loyalty to her betrothed or saw an opportunity to forgo married life and grasped on to it—or perhaps a combination of both. Her personal feelings aside, she made a convincing case to her parents and was allowed to stay single and at home with her mother. Thus Macrina took on the roles of both widow and virgin.

Unlike the relationship described between Paula and Eustochium, where Paula is the leader and Eustochium her faithful daughter, Macrina was obviously the leader in her family. While the biography is unquestionably written to glorify her life, Macrina did hold an important and influential role in a family full of important and influential people. Macrina is described as encouraging her mother to reject the worldly life—to wean Emmelia from luxury, as Gregory puts it. It was Macrina who convinced her mother to regard their servants as equals. When Basil came home from the university "puffed up with pride," it was Macrina who set him down the path of rejecting the glories of fame and encouraged him to embrace the religious life. Macrina was the one who raised her youngest brother, Peter, who went into the priesthood. When Gregory of Nyssa came to see her at the end of her life, she admonished him as well. As he told her of his troubles, such as his exile at the hands of the emperor, she said to him:

> But you are renowned in cities and peoples and nations. Churches summon
> you as an ally and director, and do you not see the grace of God in it all?
> Do you fail to recognize the cause of such great blessings, that it is your par-
> ents' prayers that are lifting you up on high, you that have little or no equipment
> within yourself for such success?[15]

Gregory of Nyssa cherished her words. One wonders if Macrina desired the illustrious careers of her successful brothers. Her intelligence and dedication could have given her a life of renown had she not been a woman.

Gregory's narrative concludes with a tantalizing section alluding to all the things he did not include. He states that he has omitted an extraordinary agricultural operation

---

15 Gregory of Nyssa, "Life of Macrina," 153.

during a famine, miraculous healings, exorcisms of demons, and true predictions of the future. He says he has left out these miraculous details because he fears people, especially nonbelievers, will reject the biography. A practical tactic on his part, but these lines hint at a much larger life than what is recorded in his short biography.

An influential contemporary of Macrina was Olympias, born sometime in the 360s. She was a wealthy, highly educated, and well-connected woman. Among her Christian friends and supporters were John Chrysostom, with whom she was quite close, Macrina, Basil of Caesarea, Gregory of Nyssa, and Gregory of Nazianzus. She was the daughter of an imperial officer and member of the imperial court in Constantinople. Her parents died when she was young, leaving her a large fortune and extensive landholdings in the Eastern Empire.

She was married briefly as a young woman to the prefect of Constantinople, but the man died a few days after their wedding. They never consummated their marriage, and Olympias claimed to be both widow and virgin. Emperor Theodosius tried to force Olympias into a second marriage, but she refused. She explained her reasoning to the emperor as such:

> If my king, the Lord Jesus Christ, wanted me to be joined with a man, he would not have taken away my first husband immediately. Since he knew that I was unsuited for the conjugal life and was not able to please a man, he freed him, Nebridius, from the bond and delivered me of this very burdensome yoke and servitude to a husband, having placed upon my mind the happy yoke of continence.[16]

For defying him, Theodosius put her and her property under the control of the city prefect, Clementinus, until her thirtieth birthday, hoping she would relent and accept the marriage. Clementinus went as far as denying Olympias access to churches or the city's bishops. Yet Olympias would not relent and thanked the emperor for relieving her of her wealth. In 391, when Olympias was not yet thirty, her property was returned, allegedly because of her reputation for holiness. Once in control of her own finances again, she was able to distribute significant amounts to the poor and support numerous bishops, virgins, and ascetics.[17]

The bishop of Constantinople at the time, Nectarius, ordained Olympias as a deaconess. Using some of her remaining property in Constantinople, Olympias built a monastery for herself and some other women at the south edge of the cathedral. Eventually her monastery would grow to 250 women, including three other deaconesses: Martyria and Palladia, who were Olympias's sisters, and another relative named Elisanthia. At the monastery, the women engaged in learning, prayer, and service to the poor. Olympias lived a

16 *Life of Olympias, Deaconess*, 3, quoted in Elizabeth Clark, *Women in the Early Church* (Wilmington, DL: Glazier, 1983), 225.

17 Gillian Cloke, *This Female Man of God: Women and Spiritual Power in the Patristic Age, AD 350–450* (London: Routledge, 1995), 94–95.

typical ascetic life, abstaining from meat, sleeping little, bathing rarely, and wearing simple clothing. She also catechized women of the city who were not Christians.

Olympias is well known for her friendship with John Chrysostom, who was both the patriarch of Constantinople and an avid proponent of the ascetic life. *Life of Olympias, Deaconess* states that Chrysostom visited Olympias's monastery continuously and sustained the women with his wise teachings. When Chrysostom was exiled in 404, Olympias continued to support him and all those who were with him financially. During his exile he suffered from loneliness and depression, and Olympias was his confidant and the recipient of many letters; his absence reportedly pushed her to depression. In the end, her association with Chrysostom also led to her exile from Constantinople. She died in Nicomedia in the year 408.

Olympias, like so many of the other wealthy widows and virgins examined in this chapter, was able to live a religious life partially due to her great wealth and privilege within society. While she initially submitted to a marriage, she defied an emperor when pushed toward another. Her wealth and extensive landholdings enabled her to support people and causes she cared about and to build a monastery she could run herself.

The aforementioned stories demonstrate that women of the era exercised considerable influence in certain areas of Christianity, particularly the development of monasticism. These stories also reveal how difficult it was for women to forge their own paths and devote their lives to God. Even these women, who were wealthy and privileged in so many ways, still had limited control over their own lives. One suspects a number of them would have been great scholars and theologians had the opportunity arisen. And what of the women who did not have the financial means to liquidate their ample assets and escape to the desert? While women lower on the economic scale were likely less secluded, they had fewer resources. We do know the majority of women monastics were not affluent, so women of all classes fled to the desert or various monasteries.

THE WOMEN WHO BECAME MEN

While there are examples of pious and influential women, by and large, men had more power and more influence, and following commonly held cultural beliefs, men were considered fundamentally superior to women. This underlying cultural misogyny plays out in a surprising number of stories about women who became like men. There are as many as twelve known monastic tales about women who disguised themselves as men to escape marriage, join monastic communities, or gain independence. Among the women recorded in this genre are Mary/Marinos, Matrona of Perge, Euphrosyne of Alexandria, Apollinaria/Dorotheos, Eugenia/Eugenios, Susannah/John, and Theodora/Theodore. It is worth noting that all the aforementioned individuals are considered saints; there is, however, questionable historical veracity to these stories. There are highly sensationalized common features among them, including false accusations of rape and seduction against these figures. The stories reflect a genre of ancient Christian literature that seems to imply that women literally have to turn into men to be completely holy. What follows is a short

summary of two of the stories that are representative of the genre. Before their trans-
formations, the subjects were both beautiful women who tempted men.

The first tale is that of Pelagia, who converts to Christianity with the help of a bishop
named Nonnos in the city of Antioch (though Antioch is not his see). The story is nar-
rated by "Jacob," who is Nonnos's deacon. There is scholarly speculation that this account
is a literary elaboration of the prostitute mentioned in John Chrysostom's Homily 67 on
Matthew. If that is the case, then Pelagia, or at least the real woman on whom Pelagia is
based, lived in the fourth century. This story was popular, and it is likely that a number of
later, completely fictitious accounts were based on it.

According to the tale, Pelagia was a wealthy and exceedingly beautiful prostitute who
lived in Antioch. She was so alluring that the narrator states, "Her appearance invited
everyone who set eyes on her to fall in love with her."[18] She was wealthy enough to own
numerous slaves who tended to her, and the account describes her as wearing gold and
jewels as she rode a donkey through the streets. She supposedly brought on the ruin of
many men. Yet despite her past, Pelagia becomes a Christian, receives the sacraments, and
rejects her wealth. There are elements of the fantastic included in the story, such as when
Satan arrives and essentially throws a temper tantrum over Pelagia's conversion. The tale
in Antioch concludes with the disappearance of Pelagia, and Nonnos and Jacob leave
the city.

The tale picks up three years later when Jacob visits Jerusalem. Nonnos tells him to
visit a monk named Pelagios, who is a eunuch. This eunuch is indeed Pelagia, though
Jacob does not recognize her because her beauty has vanished. Her face has become ugly,
her eyes hollow, and her body emaciated from ascetic living. Even her voice has turned
into a man's voice. While Jacob is still in Jerusalem, Pelagios dies. It is after her death that
it is discovered that Pelagios was indeed the woman Pelagia, and the people rejoice, saying,
"Praise to you, Lord; how many hidden saints you have on earth—and not just men, but
women as well!"[19]

The second tale of a woman becoming a holy man is that of Anastasia. The story is
part of a late sixth-century cycle of stories about Abba Daniel of Sketis. The story opens
with Daniel and a disciple going out into the desert to visit a dying eunuch living in a cave
eighteen miles from Skete. As Daniel's disciple is preparing the body for burial, he notices
the old eunuch has breasts but does not mention this fact until the two men are on the
journey home. Daniel replies that he did know the eunuch was a woman and proceeds
to tell the disciple her story. The eunuch was a patrician lady of high rank named Anastasia who had been pursued romantically by Emperor Justinian, but Empress Theodora
jealously forced her to flee to Egypt, where she built a monastery. Once Theodora died,
Justinian wanted to bring Anastasia back to Constantinople, so she fled into the desert.

---

18 Sebastian P. Brock and Susan Ashbrook Harvey, *Holy Women of the Syrian Orient* (Berkeley, CA: University of California Press,
    1998), 43.

19 Brock and Harvey, 61.

She asked Daniel for help as the emperor's soldiers were searching for her. Daniel gave her a cave in the desert and men's attire, and she stayed there for twenty-eight years.[20]

While the two tales were written centuries apart and occur in different places, they share commonalities. Both Pelagia and Anastasia were women of exceptional beauty who became like men in their desire to be holy. Both became unrecognizable and were discovered as women only after death when their withered breasts were noticed in the burial process. Their extreme fasting—or in reality, starvation—would have stopped menstruation, shrunk their breasts, and eliminated their bodies' natural shapes. It is as if their sexuality and femininity needed to be destroyed before they could truly become holy.

The conclusion of Pelagia's tale is telling. The people celebrated after her death because saints could indeed be women. The implication is that the people believed only men were capable of being holy and that this revelation caused them to see that women were capable of holiness too—but, of course, only after taking on the role of a man. Like Gregory of Nyssa commenting that Macrina so surpassed her sex that he did not know whether to style her a woman at all, it was the ultimate accomplishment for a woman to shed the inferior quality of her womanhood and become like a man.

CHRISTIAN MOTHERS

Despite the draw to live a life of asceticism in the desert, most Christian women married and had children. Due to their proximity to the church fathers, we know of a number of mothers who influenced their well-known children, such as Nonna, the mother of Gregory of Nazianzus; Emmelia, the mother of Macrina, Basil the Great, and Gregory of Nyssa; Anthusa, the mother of John Chrysostom; and likely the best known of all, Monica, the mother of Augustine of Hippo. Interestingly, due to the marriage arrangements of the late Roman era, a woman may have controlled wealth that she inherited from her family of origin, but she had no claim to any of her husband's property or technically even her own children. Yet even if she had no legal control over her children, she gave birth to them and raised them, and her influence on them was often significant. There are common themes throughout these stories that indicate how influential mothers were on their children in a variety of capacities, whether that was through educating their children, devoting them to God, praying ceaselessly for them, or even pushing them into a particular religious vocation.

The examples of Monica and Nonna show the influence that a wife and mother could have on the faith of her family. Both women were Christian but married to individuals who were seen as socially acceptable choices but were not Christians. Each took a different tactic with her husband's unbelief. Monica, whose husband apparently had a bad temper, was a silent and enduring witness who eventually won her husband over to her cause. Her son Augustine was another story. Her commanding presence fills his *Confessions*. With her relentless prayers and persuasion, there is no doubt that she was the most influential

---

20 Brock and Harvey, *Holy Women of the Syrian Orient*, 142–149.

figure in his conversion.[21] Nonna, unlike Monica, took a much more direct approach with her husband. According to her son, Gregory of Nazianzus, she prayed relentlessly for the conversion of her husband, but she did not leave her efforts with God alone. She employed various means to influence her husband, including rapprochements, warnings, and even estrangements, and her efforts paid off. Her husband was baptized and three years later became the bishop of Nazianzus, and in addition she raised children who were strong in the faith, including her son Gregory, who is one of the most respected and influential church theologians in history.

Emmelia was born into a Christian family, and her father had even been martyred during the Diocletian persecution. Unlike Nonna and Monica, she married a Christian, though she had desired a monastic life when she was young. When her daughter Macrina made the case for her own monastic life after the death of her betrothed, Emmelia agreed and eventually joined her. While Macrina's biography describes Macrina and not Emmelia as the leader within their monastic community, Emmelia's influence on her family was significant. Three of her ten children became bishops, and five became saints.

Finally, Anthusa was a major influence in the life of her son, John Chrysostom. Widowed at a young age, she decided to stay single and raise her talented son on her own. She was well educated and decided to teach him at home during his youth and later sent him to be educated in speech and theology with prestigious teachers. When her son decided to become a monk, she begged and pleaded with him not to leave her. She was apparently convincing, because he stayed with her until her death.

Of course, these four mothers represent just a small sampling, but their dedication to and influence on their families open a window into the ways in which women, while limited in formal power, commanded great influence over their spouses and children.

WOMEN PILGRIMS

Pilgrimage was an important expression of faith in the ancient church. It was a way for believers to connect with their Christian faith through physical proximity to the various holy sites, holy objects, and saints found throughout the empire. The Holy Land, including Jerusalem and the surrounding regions, was the center of the pilgrimage movement. The site of the crucifixion was the most popular in the Holy Land, but pilgrims also sought out other places mentioned in the New Testament, such as the Garden of Gethsemane, the pool of Siloam, the Tower of David, the site of the nativity in Bethlehem, and the site of Christ's baptism in the Jordan. People also trekked to various Old Testament locations, such as Mount Sinai. There were sites that appealed specifically to women, such as the spring on Mount Sinai where bathing in the waters was supposed to aid with conception; the well at Sychar where Christ talked with the Samaritan woman; and the

---

21 Augustine of Hippo, *Confessions* (Oxford: Oxford University Press, 2009).

tomb of Rachel near Bethlehem. While the Holy Land was the most popular destination, Christians took pilgrimages to Syria, regions of Asia Minor, Egypt, Rome, and Constantinople as well.[22]

The most well-known woman to go on pilgrimage to the Holy Land—Helena, the mother of Emperor Constantine—set a precedent for later women. Named augusta in 324, Helena traveled to Jerusalem in 326 and 327. According to sources, while in the Holy Land, she identified the sites associated with the crucifixion and resurrection and is believed to have discovered a piece of the true cross and the tomb from which Jesus rose from the dead. After Helena's famous and productive pilgrimage, pilgrimages to the Holy Land increased for both women and men. Constantine and his successors continued to sponsor churches both in the Holy Land and at the sites of famous saints around the empire, which only increased the practice of pilgrimage.

Diary of a Pilgrim by Egeria is a remarkable first-person account of travel to the Holy Land. It gives us a glimpse into the experience of an extended pilgrimage for a woman in the late fourth century. The manuscript itself is fragmentary, with only about one third of Egeria's journey available. The only surviving copy was created in the eleventh century and then lost until it was discovered in 1884 in a monastic library in Arezzo, Italy. Outside of the document itself we know nothing of Egeria. There has been scholarly debate as to where she was from and who exactly she was, but there are no definitive answers. Scholars have suggested Spain or Gaul as her homeland. At one point in her narrative, she compares the Euphrates with the Rhone, which implies familiarity but does not prove point of origin either. She has often been referred to as a nun or an abbess because she addresses her writings to the "venerable ladies my sisters." However, that does not necessarily prove monastic association. In fact, the length of her pilgrimage, which was over three years, may point to the fact that she was not a nun or abbess. She undoubtedly was educated since she was able to pen this account—though it seems she did not receive the very high-level education that someone like Paula or Melania the Elder received—and she had access to significant funds to finance the trip. In the final analysis, while there are certain aspects of her origin and lifestyle that can be inferred from the letter, there is still much uncertainty surrounding the person of Egeria, but this mystery does not take away from the importance of her narrative.

Egeria's pilgrimage took place from 381 to 384. She first sailed to Constantinople from wherever her origination point was and then traveled through Asia Minor, Mesopotamia, Syria, Palestine, and Egypt using the Bible as her guide. The narrative is broken into two distinct halves, the first being the travel narrative and the second a detailed description of the daily services and liturgical year in Jerusalem. Pertaining to her travels, she often rode a donkey, though she would walk when the terrain made it too difficult for the donkey to carry her. This was not a solitary endeavor. She traveled with a group of religious pilgrims, and the trip was one of much socialization, though we do not know exactly who her companions were. The pilgrimage itself was physically taxing, with activities that included climbing Mount Sinai. She and her traveling companions received

---

22 Carolyn L. Connor, *Women of Byzantium* (New Haven: Yale, 2004), 29–30.

hospitality and guidance from monks throughout their journey. In the second half of her book, she provides valuable information on the history of the liturgy, details about church architecture she comes across, and details of the monastic life.[23]

ROYAL WOMEN OF BYZANTIUM

Not all influential women were monastics or mothers of church leaders. A small but powerful group of women, namely women who were members of royal households, held an unusual amount of influence over the role of the church in society, different theological developments, and church politics. Often royal women were explicitly religious publicly, and many were indeed pious; however, it was also common for women of a royal household to have differing opinions to the church leadership. Feuds between patriarchs and empresses occurred on more than one occasion.

The elevation of Theodosius, remembered as Theodosius the Great, to the position of emperor of the East in 379, heralded a new era of Christian leadership. Theodosius's first wife, Aelia Flavia Flaccilla, a woman respected for her character and devotion to the Christian faith, set the tone for future Eastern empresses. The exact date of their marriage is unknown, but by the time Theodosius arrived in the East, Flaccilla had already given birth to two children—a girl named Pulcheria, who died young, and a boy named Arcadius. She gave birth to a second son, named Honorius, in 384. Eventually both of her sons would become emperors. Arcadius was elevated to the rank of augustus in 383 by his father. While the designation meant little since he was still a child and his father was truly the ruling monarch, it did signify the continuation of Theodosius's imperial line. Either at the same time or shortly after, Flaccilla was made augusta. Her elevated rank, which did not give her the same official power as her husband, was tied to her childbearing. Gregory of Nyssa gave the funeral oration after her death, from which we can learn of her life and character. According to Gregory, she was the rudder of the empire, the image of philanthropy, a monument of chastity, both humble and exalted, both modest and bold, zealous in her faith, and a pillar of the church.[24] One can assume there is a certain level of exaggeration in Gregory's words. She was the emperor's wife, and anything but the highest praise at her funeral would have been unsatisfactory. However, her public career does show that she was a defender of the faith, and she rejected the perennial heresy of the day: Arianism. She was committed to philanthropy within her city, and perhaps most important of all for the wife of an emperor, she successfully brought forth heirs.

Flaccilla's son reigned after his father died, and he was a weak emperor, but his wife, Eudoxia, proved a worthy augusta. She was the daughter of a Roman mother and a Frankish general. She married the new emperor, Arcadius, in the year 395. She gave birth to five children during her nine years of marriage: Flaccilla, born in 397, Pulcheria, born in 399,

---

23 Anne McGowan and Paul F. Bradshaw, *The Pilgrimage of Egeria* (Collegeville, MN: Liturgical Press, 2018), 1–26.

24 Kenneth G. Holum, *Theodosian Empresses: Women and Imperial Dominion in Late Antiquity* (Berkeley: University of California Press, 1989), 23.

and Arcadia, born in 400, were all girls. In 401 she gave birth to the long-awaited male heir, Theodosius, who would later be known as Theodosius II. She had another daughter, named Marina, in 403. Eudoxia died in 404 from complications during her sixth pregnancy. Interestingly she was given the rank of augusta in 400, before her son and imperial heir was born.[25]

Although Eudoxia was an ardent Christian, devoted to relics of the saints, and fond of building churches, she is well known for her disastrous feud with John Chrysostom, the patriarch of Constantinople. Eudoxia undoubtedly had a strong personality and was an astute politician. Her "imperious attitude" is well documented, and none of these qualities endeared her to the bishop. Chrysostom, who reportedly was appointed patriarch against his will, was a champion of asceticism, had a strong belief in justice, preached that the earth was common property, and was an outspoken critic of wealth and extravagance. In truth, he managed to offend a great number of people in Byzantium—not just the empress. Chrysostom did have relationships with some women; his close friendship with Olympias is discussed above. However, he fundamentally saw women as carrying the taint of Eve. He especially disapproved of women exercising political control, as Eudoxia did, and he even referred to her as a "Jezebel." It was only a matter of time before the patriarch's enemies managed to get him banished, a task Eudoxia initiated with the emperor.

Unfortunately for Eudoxia, while many members of the elite society disliked Chrysostom, the general population of Constantinople loved him, and the people protested his exile en masse; mobs even burned the Church of Hagia Sophia in protest. Around the same time, Eudoxia's eldest daughter died. Eudoxia's personal tragedy, combined with the civil unrest, convinced her that God was punishing her for her mistreatment of Chrysostom, so she begged him to return, which he did. The peace between the two lasted for a few months. Following an unveiling of a silver statue of Eudoxia that prompted much celebration and noise, Chrysostom, not disposed to keeping criticism of the empress to himself, once again spoke out publicly against Eudoxia. This time he was banished permanently. Six months later, in October of 404, Eudoxia died from pregnancy complications. Historians have often commented that the stress from the Chrysostom affair led to Eudoxia's death. While it is certainly true that the feud with the patriarch would have been stressful, it is unlikely that it was the sole cause of her death. The death of her eldest child would have had a profound impact on Eudoxia's mental health, perhaps more so than her fight with the patriarch. That said, pregnancy and childbirth were a dangerous business in the fifth century and the leading causes of death among women of childbearing age; many women died in childbirth without a feud to blame the death on.[26]

The most influential of all the royal women was Eudoxia's oldest surviving daughter, Pulcheria. In the year 412, Pulcheria, at the age of fifteen, officially took control of the imperial family and became the guardian of her younger brother, Theodosius II, who was elevated to emperor when their father died. She assumed a role of extreme piety and humility and enforced it on the rest of her family. The imperial palace resembled a

---

25   Carolyn L. Connor, *Women of Byzantium* (New Haven: Yale University Press, 2004), 53–54.

26   Connor, *Women of Byzantium*, 54.

monastery under Pulcheria's influence. She, Theodosius II, and their two surviving sisters would chant antiphons and recite scripture daily, they fasted on Wednesdays and Fridays, and the sisters gave up luxurious clothing and cosmetics and rejected the idle behavior common to the aristocracy. Pulcheria made a vow of virginity to God in a public ceremony in the Hagia Sophia, and her sisters followed suit. In 414 Theodosius named her augusta, and it is reported that she took over the government for her brother, who had little interest in ruling his empire.

A moment must be spent on the three sisters' decision to publicly embrace virginity. While Pulcheria was undeniably a dedicated Christian, there are other reasons a vow of virginity would have been advantageous. Three virgin sisters brought stability to a potentially dangerous period for the young and inexperienced emperor. By forgoing marriage, they were rejecting possible suitors, who would inevitably bring complicated family situations and perhaps even aspirations for the throne themselves. Theodosius and his sisters could act as a united family unit, keeping power to themselves. The sisters kept usurpers from the throne, and Pulcheria in particular maintained power and influence with the emperor. This arrangement would continue until the emperor decided to marry.

The story of Theodosius's marriage is rather romantic but likely not entirely accurate. The story goes like this: At twenty, the emperor decided he would like to marry. He told Pulcheria of his desire, and she started to look for women of aristocratic rank, though Theodosius assured her that he would marry a woman of lower rank if she were beautiful. Meanwhile, a young woman named Athenïas came to Constantinople seeking an audience with the empress to discuss a grievance. Her father, an Athenian sophist, had died, leaving his estate to her two brothers—thus rendering her destitute. Pulcheria was struck by Athenïas's beauty and intelligence. After being assured by Athenïas's two aunts that she was a virgin and well educated, Pulcheria told her brother of the young woman. Theodosius called for the girl to come to his apartments so that he could observe her from behind a curtain, and the young emperor fell in love with the beautiful Athenian woman. Athenïas converted to Christianity, took the Christian name Eudocia, and married the emperor.

It is undisputed that Athenïas married Theodosius in the year 421. She was baptized shortly before taking the name Eudocia. Pulcheria's role in the story, however, is debated. While it does seem likely she would have had some influence over who Theodosius married, it is unlikely she orchestrated the entire thing. Some scholars have suggested Pulcheria would have rejected a woman who was not of aristocratic stock. However, upon further reflection, she may have considered a woman of lower rank preferable. After all, the three sisters of the emperor rejected marriage at least in part to keep powerful men out of the palace. Having the emperor marry someone with no familial or political connections likely seemed advantageous. It also seems unlikely that the story of the lost inheritance is true since both of Eudocia's brothers came to occupy positions of power within Theodosius's government. Doubtless there is some truth to this story, though to what degree has been lost to history. Eudocia was elevated to the rank of augusta in 423 after the birth of her first child, a girl, in 422—thus carrying the same rank as Pulcheria. Eudocia, a professor's daughter, was concerned with education. She was likely instrumental in the refounding of the University of Constantinople and in Theodosius's edict that led to the advancement and privileging of professors in society. Eudocia was a well-known literary figure at the time, and she wrote a number of hagiographic works, including *The Martyrdom of St. Cyprian*, which is one of the few extant examples of writing by women in this era. Despite her pagan beginnings, she was a committed Christian, and she even attended the Council of Ephesus in 431. In 437–438, Eudocia made a pilgrimage to the Holy Land, traveling with Melania the Younger after being persuaded to do so at the marriage ceremony of her daughter.

Unfortunately for Eudocia, her marriage would not last. It was rumored she had an affair with a man named Paulinus, who had been a close friend of the imperial family. Theodosius executed Paulinus, and soon after, Eudocia left Constantinople for Jerusalem, where she spent the remainder of her life, estranged from her husband. Interestingly Theodosius let her retain her title of augusta, and she was able to control considerable wealth and land ownings, which enabled her to take on various building projects. When she died in 460, she was buried in the Church of St. Stephens, which is one of the churches she had built.[27]

Interestingly Pulcheria also lost influence with the emperor around the same time Eudocia into self-exile. Pulcheria moved out of the palace and lived with her circle of ascetic women. She was able to reconcile with Theodosius shortly before his death in 450, which proved opportune for her. Theodosius II had only one surviving child, a daughter named Licinia Eudoxia, who had married the Western emperor Valentinian III in 437; therefore, Theodosius had no male heir. Pulcheria ruled briefly as sole empress following his death, but then she decided to marry a soldier named Marcian, though the two reportedly had a celibate marriage. In this unusual circumstance, it was Pulcheria who elevated Marcian to the rank of emperor, and it was the two of them that convened the Council of Chalcedon in the year 451. Pulcheria died in the year 455, leaving Marcian to rule for another two years before his own death in 457. Pulcheria was the last person to rule in the Theodosian line.

The Theodosian women, especially Pulcheria, wielded power and influence in both the temporal and ecclesiastical realms. Pulcheria was involved in the Council of Ephesus in 431, and twenty years later, Pulcheria and her husband, Marcian, called the Council of Chalcedon in 451; these two councils are considered the third and fourth of the great church councils of the early church. Pulcheria presided as imperial officer over the council in place of her new husband, at which she was hailed as the new Helena (a reference to Constantine's pious mother). She is arguably one of the most influential women in the early church, and she is in fact honored as a saint in both the Eastern and Western churches for her contributions to the faith. Pulcheria and the Theodosian women set a precedent for the later Byzantine empresses, who were both powerful rulers and devoted Christians.[28]

---

27 Connor, *Women of Byzantium*, 59–60.

28 Connor, *Women of Byzantium*, 55–60.

CHAPTER 3

Expansion and a Move North (500–1000)

In the tenth century, a woman by the name of Hrotsvith produced a number of writings in Latin. She was a secular canoness at Gandersheim Abbey in modern-day Bad Gandersheim in Lower Saxony, Germany.[1] Gandersheim was a remarkable convent with first aristocratic and then royal and imperial association. We know, for example, that Hrotsvith's abbess and close friend, Gerberga II, was the emperor's niece. In addition to its aristocratic status, the convent was independent. It had its own courts, minted its own coins, had its own representatives at the imperial assembly, and had direct protection from the Papal See. All the women in residence were of noble birth; some took the veil, while others were canonesses. As a canoness, Hrotsvith could retain her own fortune, keep servants, welcome guests, and come and go from the convent without difficulty.[2]

The atmosphere at Gandersheim was intellectual, and the women were encouraged to read major authors both Christian and pagan. The library at Gandersheim, to which Hrotsvith had access, contained classical and theological works including those by Virgil, Horace, Terence, and Ovid. Considering the intellectual atmosphere and Hrotsvith's relative freedom both physically and intellectually, Gandersheim was a place in which she could flourish as an author. Hrotsvith's writings can be broken into three genres: metrical legends, dramas, and contemporary history written in metrical form. It is her dramas that are of particular note; there are no extant dramas besides hers "between the comedies of classic times and the miracle plays."[3]

In a time in history that is often referred to as the "Dark Ages," Hrotsvith demonstrates that scholarly endeavors were not only possible for women but sometimes even encouraged. She also symbolizes the fluidity between monastic and secular life that is a dominant theme in this particular time in history. While her privileged position in society must be noted and one must not understand her opportunities as universal, she reminds us that women continued to be important religious figures as the era of late antiquity turned over to the Middle Ages.

---

1 Canonesses in medieval Europe were women who withdrew to a monastery to live a pious life, but they did not become nuns and they did not follow a monastic rule. Canonesses were typically aristocratic women, and the position provided them a respectable alternative to marriage without having to make religious vows.

2 Peter Dronke and Ernst Michael Dronke, *Women Writers of the Middle Ages: A Critical Study of Texts from Perpetua to Marguerite Porete* (Cambridge: Cambridge University Press, 1984), 55–56.

3 Lina Eckenstein, *Woman under Monasticism: Chapters on Saint-lore and Convent Life between A.D. 500 and A.D. 1500* (New York: Macmillan, 2013), 161.

After the fall of Rome, Christianity was radically transformed. It went from being the religion of a powerful global empire to operating in a chaotic political landscape with shifting power structures, power vacuums, and a crumbling infrastructure. With the rise of Islam in the Arabian Peninsula in the early seventh century, Christianity was increasingly forced north, most notably into Europe. Therefore, the expansion and shifting centers of Christianity are themes that run through the early Middle Ages.

During this time, distinct religious traditions developed within Christendom. Believers operated in disparate political and cultural milieus, and the Christian faith was influenced by these differences. Because this diversity was based on location, this chapter is divided by geographic region: Western Europe, the Byzantine Empire, and Kyivan Rus. While one could make an argument for dividing the chapter between nuns and women who lived in the world, this divide is surprisingly fluid. By focusing on geographic region, we can examine how these areas, which represent major strongholds of Christendom, produced influential religious practices and theological traditions that remain important in today's world.

In Western Europe, a complex landscape of small kingdoms and languages emerged from the crumbling Roman Empire. Political marriages were used to forge alliances, and Christian queens and wives were influential throughout Europe in converting various kingdoms. Powerful abbesses affected both church politics and the world around them. Finally, evangelistic nuns were active participants in the conversion of the people. In the Byzantine Empire, empresses and other women of the royal household continued to be authoritative Christian figures. When external warfare and internal crises threatened the faith, women played a role in stabilizing the country and religious practices. In the development of Russian Christianity, women were key players in the conversion of Kyivan Rus.

WESTERN EUROPE

In truth, one cannot speak of anything remotely resembling modern Western Europe in the early Middle Ages. The crumbling of the Roman Empire in the West left a chaotic political and social situation. What remained were numerous separate kingdoms, a wide variety of languages, and little to connect the disparate groups besides an eventual adherence to the Catholic faith. Indeed, it was the church that provided an administrative network, sponsored education, controlled extensive landholdings, and interacted closely with local political leaders. Through this chaos, the bishop of Rome—or the pope—came to be the most influential person in the West. While there were popes who were primarily concerned with power, others were genuinely concerned with the well-being of the people and stepped up to provide the stability that was so needed when secular authorities were simply unable to do so. For example, Gregory the Great, pope from 590 to 604, redefined the office, engaged in activities such as distributing food to those in need, collected taxes, maintained legal records, arranged holy days of prayer to end epidemics, negotiated political settlements with warring enemies, and even reorganized the administration of the papal states. Activities such as these unquestionably changed the role and function of the church for future generations.

Despite the different paths to Catholic domination throughout the European kingdoms, women played a pivotal role in the spread of Catholic Christianity in Western Europe during the early Middle Ages. Often it is queens who are best remembered for their Christian influence on their unbelieving husbands, but it was nuns and abbesses who likely played a much larger role in the actual conversion of the people. Monasteries, which sprung up all over Europe, became centers of evangelism, learning, and hospitality.

Until the seventh century, the story of Christianity was one of explosive growth, with its move into both Eastern and Western Europe being most notable. The tides were changing, though, and what is probably the most influential event in the history of Christianity was in fact not Christian at all. Throughout the course of the seventh century, over half of the world's Christians came to live under another religion, Islam, which was founded in seventh-century Arabia and then quickly expanded to become a world power. Even for Christians living outside of Islamic-controlled areas, the faith would continue to have significant influence on their lives. Islam continued to be a factor—sometimes front and center, sometimes quietly in the background—in many political happenings over centuries in the Christian lands. One of the most significant ramifications of the Islamic conquests is the association of Western Europe and Christianity. As Christian lands in North Africa and the Middle East fell to Islamic forces, Christianity gained traction in Western Europe, and eventually a European expression of Christianity became so dominant that Western Christians often forget that there was a time when Christianity was not European.

What follows is an examination of women's roles in early medieval society in what is now Western Europe, focusing primarily on the British Isles and the Frankish kingdoms on the European continent. There was substantial cultural and religious transference between the societies, and marriages were common between the royal households. Yet each context has unique features regarding both conversion efforts and cultural distinctions.

Previous scholarship tended to separate the lives of married women and monastic women, but this binary could be surprisingly fluid, and separating women on these lines is problematic. Monasteries were far less isolated from the world than one might assume. Queens and other noblewomen were sometimes raised in monasteries, and some entered monasteries either as young women or later in life after being widowed. Close ties between monasteries and aristocratic houses were common, and even monastic separation between genders was not a given during this time.

Ireland

We start our examination in Ireland with its rich Christian past and distinctive form of Catholicism. The person most associated with Irish Catholicism is St. Patrick, and one cannot truly talk about early Irish Catholicism without first discussing him and his expansive missionary efforts. British by birth, Patrick was kidnapped and forced into slavery in Ireland sometime early in the fifth century. After six years of bondage, he escaped to Gaul and joined a monastic community. Amazingly, he felt called back to the land of his captors to missionize the people. He reportedly converted thousands, both kings and slaves, ordained many priests, and established a monastic movement that grew rapidly.

Over the next couple of hundred years, Christianity flourished, and monasteries became centers of the faith. Ireland was largely agrarian with few urban centers, so it was monasteries that emerged as centers of culture and learning throughout the country. Having little contact with the Roman Church, Irish Christians developed distinctive practices. Some of these distinctive qualities would become standard within Roman Catholicism, and some would be eliminated as time passed. One such element that was kept and flourished was the practice of private and frequent confession. Other elements that were later rejected by the Catholic Church, notably in the Synod of Whitby, to which we will shortly return, were an alternative dating of Easter and certain styles of tonsure for male monastics. An especially notable feature was the prominence of large double monasteries led by an abbess.

One of the most fascinating and yet frustratingly elusive women in early Irish Christian history is Brigid of Kildare. There are numerous hagiographic texts written about Brigid, but the earliest dates from a century after her death. These texts give few concrete facts about her life; instead, they are most concerned with advancing her religious cult. To complicate the situation further, she also happens to share the name and certain attributes of an old Irish goddess. The lack of evidence-based historical sources and her commonalities with a local deity have led some historians to question whether Brigid even existed as a historical person. Yet Brigid has long been a wildly popular saint both in Ireland and abroad, and she is one of three patron saints in Ireland along with Patrick and Columba. In Ireland alone, she is currently the patron saint of 127 churches, 116 holy wells, and various convents, monasteries, and other religious houses. She has a significant following in Britain, the European continent, and even some areas of the Americas.[4]

Despite the shaky historical evidence, it seems more likely than not that she did exist and that her legend gradually gained attributes of the goddess Brigid as her cult grew in popularity. While the facts of her life are sparse, we can get a basic picture of this beloved saint. She was probably born sometime around the year 450. Her father was a noble named Dubthach (or Duffy), and her mother was one of his slaves. It is likely Brigid became a Christian when she was young, certainly before the age of marriage, because when her father and brother tried to arrange a marriage for her, she refused, and eventually her father allowed her to become a nun. After taking the veil, Brigid gained a reputation for charity, good works, and the performance of signs and wonders. She is credited with founding the double monastery at Kildare, where she served as the first abbess. She lived a long life for the time, probably about sixty years. After her death, the monastery of Kildare was active in promoting her cause of sainthood, and Kildare became a site of pilgrimage.

The circumstances of her birth and dedication to the faith are typical of hagiographic literature, and the story of her life is plausible. Women leading double monasteries in

---

4 Noel Kissane, *Saint Brigid of Kildare: Life, Legend, and Cult* (Dublin: Open Air, 2017), 17. Kissane's book provides a fascinating study of Brigid, available sources about her life, and the history of her cult.

Ireland was a common enough occurrence, and numerous abbesses in the early Middle Ages were known for their miracles and charity. The apparent fusing of St. Brigid and the popular pre-Christian goddess Brigid, though, make the story of this saint particularly interesting. St. Brigid's feast day is celebrated on February 1, which is the same day as Imbolc, a pagan festival associated with the goddess. St. Brigid also shares some imagery with the goddess, such as cattle and fire. While conjecture, my belief is that as Christianity grew in popularity, these two popular female figures, who shared a name, inevitably became intertwined into one person, St. Brigid. To the modern reader, this fusion of religious figures may seem odd, but it can be a common occurrence when a country or a people is in the process of embracing a new religion. Elements of the old can legitimize the new or make the new seem like a continuation of the old.

Britain

The largely accepted story of Britain's conversion to Christianity centers around a group of Roman Catholic missionaries led by Augustine of Canterbury. The involvement and influence of this group of missionaries are undeniable, but a closer examination of the situation points to heavy involvement of women, both royal and monastic, in the conversion of the English people.

The story of Augustine's mission, as told in the Venerable Bede's *Ecclesiastical History of the English Nation*, is a romantic tale that has endured through the ages. The story begins with Gregory the Great (540–604), before he became pope, in a marketplace in Rome. There he came across two boys with a fair complexion being sold as slaves. Gregory inquired about their origin and was told they were Angles from Britain and were pagan. He famously replied, "Not Angles, but Angels!" Thus, he was inspired to missionize these foreign peoples, but his request was denied by the current pope. After Gregory became pope, he sent the monk Augustine with another forty or so missionaries. When Augustine arrived in Kent at the very end of the sixth century, England was little more than a collection of villages led by local warring kings.[5]

To assume that, prior to Augustine's arrival, England had no knowledge of Christianity would be a mistake, however. It must be remembered that what is now England had been part of the Roman Empire, which had embraced Christianity and in fact even outlawed all other forms of religion. Of course, Britain was on the outskirts of the empire, and the last of the Roman troops were moved out of London in 407, not long after non-Christian religions were outlawed. Most of the populace likely was pagan even under Roman occupation, but Christianity had a presence. Then there was the flourishing of Irish Christianity, which would have been known to the English.

When Augustine and his envoy arrived in Kent, they contacted the local king to state their intentions, a necessary step to avoid being killed, and found the king, named Ethelbert, married to a Christian wife named Bertha. Bertha deserves a prominent place in the history of Christianizing Britain; in fact, it has been speculated that it was Bertha who initially *requested* that Pope Gregory send missionaries to her adopted homeland. While

---

5 Bede, *The Ecclesiastical History of England*, trans. A. M. Sellar (London: George Bell and Sons, 1907), 83.

that theory lacks the romantic quality of Gregory in the marketplace, it also seems to be more likely. Or perhaps the truth lies somewhere between the two stories.

Bertha was born a Frankish princess, the daughter of King Charibert and Ingoberg. She was also the great-granddaughter of Clotilde, who will be examined shortly. In the custom of making political matches with royal daughters, Bertha was sent to marry Ethelbert of Kent sometime in the 570s. The marriage contract stipulated that Bertha would be able to practice her religion freely and bring with her a private chaplain, Bishop Liudhard, and some other clergy. Ethelbert even gave her an ancient church near Canterbury that had been built by the Romans. So, when Augustine arrived in 597, there was already a Catholic queen, Catholic clergy, and a small worshipping community.[6]

It was not unusual to have a royal household practicing different religions. As influential as a Christian queen may have been, the faith of the king set the religious tone in a particular land. The conversion of King Ethelbert happened surprisingly quickly after Augustine's arrival. It was somewhere around Christmas in 597 when he and ten thousand of his subjects were baptized. The swiftness suggests Ethelbert had been influenced by his wife and her faith prior to the missionary envoys' arrival. After the conversion, Pope Gregory wrote to the king and queen congratulating them; he compared Ethelbert to Constantine and Bertha to Helena—thus tying them closer to Rome's past.

A similar conversion pattern played out again with Ethelbert and Bertha's daughter Ethelburga in Northumbria some thirty years after her father's conversion. Ethelburga married the Northumbrian king Edwin in 625. When Edwin proposed marriage to Ethelburga, the reply from Kent was that if he were to marry her, he would need to convert to Christianity first. The truth of the matter was that the marriage was a solid political alliance for both Northumbria and Kent, so when Edwin proposed a compromise of considering conversion and allowing missionaries into Northumbria, Kent agreed to the terms. Ethelburga arrived in Northumbria with Paulinus, who acted as her mentor and a missionary and bishop to the region. Edwin waffled regarding whether or not to embrace Christianity. Bede reports that Edwin would sit for hours and deliberate what religion he should follow. Two years after his marriage to Ethelburga, Edwin decided to accept baptism on April 12, 627, in a hastily built church in the city of York.[7]

It was a violent time in history, and Edwin lived only five or six years after his conversion. He and his eldest son were murdered by a rival king named Penda of Mercia, and his household fled Northumbria. Ethelburga, her children, and Paulinus returned to Kent. Edwin's great-niece Hilda, who was baptized with him in 627, also survived the attack and became one of the most influential Christian women in English history.[8]

Hilda of Whitby, known as Hild of Streanaeshalch during her lifetime, was probably born in 614. She was trained in the faith by Bishop Paulinus and was baptized when she was thirteen years old. It should be remembered that in this time and place, at thirteen

---

6 Anne E. Inman, *Hild of Whitby and the Ministry of Women in the Anglo-Saxon World* (Lanham: Lexington Books/Fortress Academic, 2019), 40–46.

7 Bede, *Ecclesiastical History of the English Nation*, trans. Lewis Gidley (Oxford: Oxford University Press, 1870), 152. This text was originally written in 731 CE.

8 Inman, *Hild of Whitby*, 11–12.

one was considered an adult, and she more than likely had agency in this decision. According to Bede, she spent thirty-three years in the world and thirty-three years devoted to God, though there is little other information on her life before she entered a monastery. Considering the customs of the time, it seems likely she married, though this is merely conjecture since there is no record of a marriage. It is also unknown where she went or what she did after Edwin was killed. Scholars have suggested that she went to various places, including Kent, Gaul, and Bamburgh, which was a stronghold in Northumbria that held out against Penda. Considering her later ecclesial career and association with the Irish Church, Bamburgh seems the most likely scenario.

Hilda's association with Irish Christianity may seem surprising considering she was baptized into the Roman rite. The explanation for this change in association has much to do with two brothers and their rise to the Northumbrian throne. Edwin became king of Northumbria by killing the previous king, a man by the name of Ethelfrith, in 616. Ethelfrith's two sons, Oswald and Oswy, escaped and were raised in exile in Dalriada in what is now Scotland. They had been converted to Christianity by the monks on the island of Iona, which had been founded by the great Irish missionary Columba in the 560s; therefore, their faith was that of the Irish variety. Both brothers would be king, Oswald first and Oswy second, though the story of their lives is beyond the scope of our investigation here. It was Oswald who, concerned with continuing the conversion of his lands, requested Aidan, a monk at Iona, to establish a monastery in Lindisfarne to continue with the Christianization, and Aidan had significant influence on Hilda.

Hilda's story picks up in 647 with her living in East Anglia and preparing to join her sister at a monastery in Chelles in the Frankish lands. However, prior to her move to the Continent, Aidan persuaded her to return to Northumbria, become part of the Ionian mission, and establish a new community. Joining her sister at Chelles would have been a logical choice, if she had become a widow. Her decision to instead join Aidan is on the face of it surprising and likely speaks to a previous relationship of some kind between the two. The name and location of Hilda's first monastery have been lost, though in 649 Aidan appointed her abbess of the abbey at Hartlepool. After a number of years of running Hartlepool, Hilda was moved to the much larger monastery at Streanaeshalch, which later became known at Whitby.

Whitby was a large double monastery. As abbess, Hilda ran the complex with both monks and nuns under her authority. The monastery housed a church, a scriptorium, an infirmary, and various functional buildings devoted to trades such as textile production. It was a respected center of learning at the time, and it produced a number of priests, bishops, and theologians. Whitby had a close association with the royal house of Northumbria. When Hilda was still at Hartlepool, she was given King Oswy's infant daughter, Aelffled, to raise. It should also be assumed that Whitby then had the capability of receiving the nobility and hosting banquets. Aelffled would later become abbess of Whitby.

While Aidan and Oswy were influenced by Irish Christianity, the Roman form was gaining popularity, especially in Kent. The problem of having two competing forms of Catholicism came to a head in Northumbria. The differences should not be overemphasized. They were both legitimate forms of the Catholic faith in doctrine, and most practices were the same between the two forms. However, issues such as the date of Easter caused problems. As Bede recounts, this issue was a particular problem for the royal household since Oswy was Celtic but his queen, Eanfled, was Roman. Sometimes the king would be feasting for Easter while his wife was still observing the Lenten fast. Oswy's own sons had taken to the Roman way, though his daughter Aelffled, being raised by Hilda, likely practiced the Irish dating.

The king called the Synod of Whitby in 664 to contend with the issues of both Easter and tonsure.[9] Bishops, abbots, kings, and queens attended the synod at Hilda's monastery, and it seems obvious that Hilda played some part in it. It was inevitable that the Roman side would win. The Irish supporters gracefully accepted the ruling, and Hilda exerted her own influence to keep the peace around the ruling. Hilda continued to serve as abbess until her death in 680 at the age of sixty-six. It is reported that she continued to teach even on her deathbed. The Venerable Bede wrote:

> Her prudence was so great, that not only meaner men in their need, but sometimes even kings and princes, sought and received her counsel; she obliged those who were under her direction to give so much time to reading of the Holy Scriptures, and to exercise themselves so much in works of justice, that many might readily be found there fit for the priesthood and the service of the altar.[10]

She was indeed a great leader in a time of change. After her death, Aelffled, whom Hilda had raised, and Aelffled's mother and former queen, Eanfled, took over as joint leaders of Whitby. Hilda's role of leading a double monastery was not an anomaly. She represents the intertwining of monastic houses with royal households and shows how women born of aristocratic rank could exercise considerable authority within the church and therefore society.[11]

The Frankish Lands

When the Roman Empire finally fell and the last emperor was overthrown in 476, Gaul had been ruled by various Germanic tribes for quite some time. The Visigoths had been in Aquitaine since 418, and the Burgundians had been in the Rhone Valley since around 440. The Franks came into Gaul from the north and the east, and in 481 Clovis became king of a small region in northern Gaul and began his wars of conquest—first uniting the Frankish kingdoms and then conquering lands from other tribes. He pushed the Visigoths out of Aquitaine and into what is now Spain and eventually came to rule much of what is now modern France. He established the Merovingian era, which was a time of rapid social change and would last until the rise of the Carolingian dynasty in 751. The culture that

---

9   Tonsure is the practice of cutting or shaving some or all of the hair on a monk or priest's head. The Irish and Romans both had forms of tonsure, but the Roman Church left a fringe of hair around the head while the Irish Church shaved in front of a line running from ear to ear.

10 Bede, *The Ecclesiastical History of England*, trans. A. M. Sellar (London: George Bell and Sons, 1907), chap. XXIII.

11 Linda Kulzer and Miriam Schmitt, *Medieval Women Monastics: Wisdom's Wellsprings* (Collegeville: Liturgical Press, 1996), 13–32.

emerged was neither Roman nor of the old Germanic tribes but something new. Women were primary drivers of the establishment of this new society and the subsequent spread of Catholic Christianity. Intermarriage between Gallo-Romans and the Franks, especially Gallo-Roman women and Frankish men, was common. Thus, women would leave their families of origin and transplant their beliefs and customs to their new families and transfer these beliefs to their children.

Few women exemplify this pattern of cultural and religious transference better than Clotilde. She was born a princess in the kingdom of Burgundy sometime in the 470s. Her mother was a Gallo-Roman and her father the Burgundian king Chilperic. Her mother had been Catholic and had perhaps converted her husband. Clotilde, influenced by her mother, was also Catholic. In surprisingly normal familial circumstances for the time, her uncle Gundobad murdered both of her parents and exiled her older sister, though he kept Clotilde and raised her in his home. Gregory of Tours wrote that Clotilde was saved due to God's intervention, which may be true, but there was likely a political reason as well. Her beauty and manners are noted in sources, so it is probable that her uncle, now king of Burgundy, believed he could make an advantageous political marriage through her, and he did just that by marrying her off to Clovis.

At the time of their marriage, Clovis was a pagan. According to sources, Clotilde pleaded with him to accept Catholicism, which he initially refused. Despite his insistence on remaining loyal to his gods, she had their first child baptized. Sadly, the boy died shortly thereafter, which caused Clovis to blame the baptism for his son's death, leading to strife between the couple. Clotilde baptized their second child despite his protests, and that child survived. While Clotilde continued to persuade and pray for her husband to convert to Catholicism, his actual conversion moment happened while he was at war. In a story that recalls Constantine's conversion event roughly two hundred years earlier, Clovis prayed to Jesus to free him from danger while he and his men were losing a military battle. Shortly thereafter the tide changed, and Clovis was victorious. He returned home and told his wife of his miraculous win. She called a bishop, and Clovis accepted baptism. Following his baptism, Clovis built churches on his lands and practiced almsgiving. This conversion apparently also inspired Clovis to continue to expand his own kingdom. He reasoned that the heretical Arian Christians and pagans should not hold the majority of Gaul; thus he set out to claim Gaul for Catholic Christianity.

Clovis's conversion is considered a critical moment in European history, and the influence of his wife is certain in both his conversion and his impact on the religion of his subjects. The story of Clovis and Clotilde is also a helpful example of the religious complexities of this time and place. Arianism, Catholicism, and indigenous European beliefs were all present and interacting within the society and even within the same families. Clovis was originally pagan, he had sisters who were Arian, and he took a Catholic wife. Especially among the nobility, situations like this were not uncommon.

Clovis died in 511, and his kingdom was divided between his sons. Clotilde retired to the Abbey of St. Martin of Tours. It should not be assumed, however, that Clotilde isolated herself from the world once she entered into a monastery. She continued to be involved in politics and the lives of her children until 531. Scholars have speculated that when her sons went to war against their cousin Sigismund, the son of the man who had murdered Clotilde's parents, she was behind the attack, though there is no actual proof of her involvement.

Devoting herself to the religious life did not prevent personal tragedy either. Her daughter, who shared her name, was married to the Arian king of the Goths Amalaric. He physically abused her to the point that her brothers raised an army against him and his followers. Although Clotilde's sons were victorious and killed Amalaric, her daughter died on the way back home. One of the most tragic moments of her life, though, was the murder of two of her grandsons at the hands of one of her sons. Her eldest son had died, leaving his three sons in her care. Concerned by Clotilde's affection for the boys, her son Clothar tricked Clotilde into sending the boys to him, and then he murdered two of them. The third boy escaped and eventually chose a religious life. Clotilde was devastated by the deaths of the boys.[12] Unfortunately, this violence and intrigue were far too common in the era, and women were often caught up in the fallout.

Another woman who suffered from the violence of the era was Clotilde's daughter-in-law Radegund. It is not known whether Clotilde ever knew Radegund, though it is certainly possible. The women had much in common, including tragic childhoods, marriages to kings, and lives within a violent society where they witnessed the murders of people they loved. Perhaps the most significant similarity, though, is that both women are recognized as canonized saints.

Radegund was born a Thuringian princess and took on the role of a pious Frankish queen. She is also one of the most documented people, not just women, of her era. The events of her life were recorded by Radegund's friend and confessor Venantius Fortunatus and Gregory of Tours in two separate works. A fellow nun named Baudonivia also wrote a supplemental document on her life. While the works are hagiographic, they do contain valuable information on her life and temperament.

The exact date of Radegund's birth is unknown, though it was likely around the year 520. Like Clotilde, Radegund's family was murdered by an uncle who took her to be raised in his own home. Her uncle and his house were later slaughtered by Clovis's sons in an act of retaliation for breaking a treaty with the Franks and murdering a number of women and children. Instead of killing Radegund, Clovis's sons gambled for her, and Clothar won. She was still a child at the time, so she was taken to a monastery to be raised as his future wife. By the time they were married, Clothar had had numerous wives, though the sequence and overlap are not entirely understood. It is highly likely, though, that at least some of the marriages were polygamous.

Radegund's biographers emphasize her almsgiving and humble works while she was queen. Even while married to Clothar, she engaged in acts of extreme asceticism such as prostrating herself on a hair cloak near the privies in the cold. This self-torment would only increase over time. She cared for the poor and prisoners and begged her husband not to execute criminals. Apparently, her husband complained that she was more like a nun than a wife. After Clothar murdered her only surviving brother around the year 550, she

---

12 Jo Ann McNamara, *Sainted Women of the Dark Ages* (Durham: Duke University Press, 1992), 38–50.

dressed as a nun and went to Médard, the bishop of Noyon, and insisted he consecrate her to the church. Médard was in a tricky political situation, but he consecrated her as a deaconess. Deaconesses were not common in Western Europe at the time, but it proved a perfect solution for the married queen who desperately wanted to live her life as a nun. Despite her desire to live away from her husband, Clothar financially supported Radegund's religious life, and he may have been the one to negotiate the endowment for the monastery she founded at Poitiers, where she settled after his death.

In addition to almsgiving, manual labor, and prayer, Radegund practiced self-mutilation, which was not typical behavior at the time. She bound herself in chains until she bled and burned herself. She was also known for performing miracles, such as healing the blind and even raising the dead. The religious cult surrounding Radegund is quite fascinating. The written works about her life were clearly penned to appeal to wide audiences and elevate her position as a religious leader. These actions highlight both her extreme religious devotion and her fanaticism, but they also reveal her strong-willed personality. Despite incredible odds she was able to leave her husband, who was a king, and force a bishop into consecrating her in spite of the act being a very dangerous political move for the cleric. As the head of a monastery that was royally founded and privately endowed, she had a certain level of freedom from church leadership as well. Radegund was an independent woman and a force to be reckoned with.[13]

Conversion of the People

Just because the aristocracy embraced the Catholic faith, it does not mean that everyone else was suddenly willing to throw out their gods and traditions and embrace those of their overlords. It will come as no surprise that forced baptism and the outlawing of native religious practices proved to be inadequate evangelism, and many people remained committed to their old gods. The process of bringing Christianity to the people was largely spearheaded by nuns and monks who devoted their lives to evangelism. Whereas priests and bishops were tied to their geographic area, monks and nuns had freedom to go out and convert. By the seventh century a pattern of itinerant preaching had emerged in Western Europe. Both monks and nuns, often originating from the British Isles, traveled through the Frankish lands, establishing monasteries that would serve as centers of Christianity. The founders would then move on to new locations to repeat the pattern. It is through this process that Christianity truly took hold with the people.

Among the most famous of the traveling missionaries on the Continent were Columbanus (c. 540–615) and Boniface (c. 680–754). Columbanus was an Irish monk who spent time in present-day France, Italy, and Germany. Boniface was most closely related to the conversion of the Franks. He was born in southwest England but was called to be part of the evangelization effort on the Continent. In 722 he was ordained a missionary bishop by the pope. He accomplished his goals of converting the people by encouraging other monks and nuns to join his efforts and establish monasteries. Interestingly Boniface and his colleagues were able to establish a level of authority separate from local church

---

13 McNamara, *Sainted Women of the Dark Ages*, 60–105.

leaders, whom he often criticized. Being semi-independent allowed him to ordain his own clergy and gave him great freedom in his evangelization efforts, though the situation inevitably caused conflicts between him and the local bishops.

One of Boniface's closest associates was a nun and later abbess by the name of Leoba (c. 710–782) who was also deeply committed to the evangelization of the Franks. Much of what we know of Leoba is from *Life of Leoba* written by Rudolf of Fulda probably in the mid-830s, about fifty years after her death. Rudolf's aim is theological, but he shows himself to be a careful historian by providing information about his sources, and he makes sure to situate Leoba's life and mission within a larger biblical and theological framework. Leoba's birth and subsequent childhood at a monastery draw parallels to the biblical account of the prophet Samuel. Leoba herself had a prophetic dream that was interpreted by a fellow sister foretelling that Leoba's later mission would be ordained by God.

Leoba was born at the beginning of the eighth century to noble parents but given to the monastery of Wimbourne in Anglia as a child. Rudolf emphasizes her learning and accomplishment as a scholar as well as her holiness. Boniface, to whom Leoba was related on her mother's side, specifically requested that she come and assist his missionary efforts with the Franks. She, along with a number of other nuns, including one named Tecla, heeded his call. Leoba was placed as abbess over the nuns at a double monastery in Bischofsheim. From there she spearheaded evangelistic efforts in the area. As her reputation grew, nobles sent their daughters to live in her monastery, and she became connected with Charlemagne's court. Leoba was particularly adored by Charlemagne's wife, Queen Hiltigard, though it is reported that Leoba despised spending time at court.

When Boniface left for a missionary trip in Frisia, where he would be martyred in 754, he begged Leoba not to leave her adopted homeland. He then left Leoba with his monastic cowl. Through her relationship with Boniface, she became the only woman allowed to pray at his monastery in Fulda. This privilege demonstrates the level of respect both Boniface and the other monks showed toward the abbess.[14]

While Leoba is one of the better-known abbesses of the era, her activities, and those of her monastery, fall within the tradition of respected and influential men and women not only spreading the Christian faith but also acting as agents of culture. Monasteries also played a key role in keeping knowledge and scholarship alive through these long years sometimes referred to as the "Dark Ages."[15] While the number of monasteries for women never reached that of their male counterparts, monastic women still influenced the culture and religion in significant ways. Evidence shows that nuns, like monks, were taught to read and write and had an understanding of scripture, the writings of the church fathers, and at least some level of canon and civil law. Nuns also acted as scribes, or producers of books, a fact that was long dismissed by scholars but is finally now recognized as true.[16]

---

14 Rudolf of Fulda. *Life of Leoba*. Fordham University, accessed April 26, 2022, https://sourcebooks.fordham.edu/basis/leoba.asp.

15 Recent scholarship has shown that the Middle Ages were much less "dark" than many people assume. For example, see Matthew Gabriele and David M. Perry, *The Bright Ages: A New History of Medieval History* (New York: HarperOne, 2021).

16 Sarah Zhang, "Why a Medieval Woman had Lapis Lazuli Hidden in her Teeth," *The Atlantic*, January 9, 2019.

We also know that nuns were sometimes authors, both of theological works and literature. Leoba was one of many nuns who wrote religious poetry, for example.

The relative freedom that religious women enjoyed during the Merovingian period was curtailed during the Carolingian period. Nuns continued to act as scribes, book collectors, and teachers; however, the Carolingian revival of learning, which began under the reign of Charlemagne, largely bypassed women. Also under Charlemagne was the beginning of the effort to cloister women in their monasteries. This cloistering not only limited their access to education but also kept them from their incredibly important missionary involvement. Additional restrictions limiting nuns to the education of girls further reduced their influence. However, as we will see, the later Middle Ages produced a great number of influential women who shaped society.

WOMEN IN BYZANTIUM

While Christians living in the West were adjusting to the changing political situation in a post-Roman reality, Christians in the East were contending with their own political and religious situation. Unlike the fragmenting small kingdoms in the West, the Byzantine Empire in the East remained strong. However, within regions under Constantinople's control, there was a range of doctrinal differences among various Christian groups after the Council of Chalcedon[17] failed to resolve these dogmatic disputes. The reign of co-rulers Justinian I and Theodora highlights this contentious religious situation.

Theodora is one of the more remarkable but also more complicated empresses in Byzantine history, and she has one of the greatest rags-to-riches stories ever. She and her husband were legitimately co-rulers of the empire, and she was arguably one of the most powerful women in Byzantine history. However, unlike the Theodosian augustae, who were born members of the aristocracy, Theodora had humble beginnings—she had been an actress, to be exact. This fact was particularly scandalous because of the association between acting and prostitution at the time, and there were reports that she worked as a courtesan prior to her relationship with Justinian. Theodora turns up in a number of ancient sources, but the most complete picture comes from an account called *Secret History* by a court historian named Procopius, probably written around the year 550. Procopius's other works include an eight-volume military history titled *Wars* and a six-volume work called *Buildings*. Unlike these other writings, *Secret History* was not intended for immediate publication, and it contained scathing criticism of both Theodora and Justinian. Procopius's blatant contempt for Theodora makes this a complicated source since the narrator is unreliable. For example, it is highly unlikely that Theodora and Justinian were

---

17 Justo González, *The Story of Christianity, Volume 1: The Earliest Church to the Dawn of the Reformation* (New York: Harper-One, 2010), 296–301. The Council of Chalcedon was the fourth ecumenical council of the Christian church, held in Chalcedon in 451. It was attended by over 500 bishops or their representatives. The council upheld previous creeds and produced the Definition of Chalcedon, which describes the way in which divinity and humanity are joined in the person of Jesus Christ. An excerpt reads, "This is one and the same Christ, Son, Lord, Only-begotten, manifested in two natures without any confusion, change, division or separation."

actual demons as Procopius suggests. Nonetheless, combined with other sources and a discerning eye, the account does give important information about the empress.[18]

Theodora was born in the year 500. Reportedly her father was a bear keeper at the Hippodrome, and her mother was an actress. While this pedigree may be surprising for a future empress, her husband came from humble roots as well. Justinian, born in 482, came from a peasant family living in the Latin-speaking Balkans. He moved to Constantinople and became an officer of the palace. His fortunes changed dramatically when his uncle Justin, the commander of the imperial guard, was elevated to emperor in 518. Justin's life and career were quite remarkable. He came to Constantinople with nothing, enrolling in the palace guard. He rose through the ranks and finally managed to gain the throne through cunning and a little luck after the death of Emperor Anastasias. His wife's life was probably even more intriguing than his, though we have so few sources that a detailed examination is impossible. What we do know is that Justin's wife, Euphemia, was once a "barbarian slave" named Lupicina who had been her owner's concubine. It seems Justin must have bought her, freed her, and then married her. She appears to have been a capable woman of principle who took her role as empress seriously.

It was sometime after Justin's rise to power that Justinian and Theodora became lovers. They were officially married in 525 after a law was changed to allow a person from the imperial household to marry an actress. In 527, the two were crowned co-emperors. In a society in which status and education meant so much, it must have been alarming to many that Theodora emerged as empress, and the prejudice shown toward her is not terribly surprising. Compared to the virginal Pulcheria of the Theodosian line, an actress and courtesan lacking a formal education sitting on the throne was surely an unpleasant situation for men such as Procopius. It does not appear that accusations of prostitution were fabricated. Theodora did not reject her past, and friends from her days of acting frequented the palace. Even sources who are friendly to her, such as John of Ephesus, who knew and liked her, comment that she was from a brothel. It seems this was simply common knowledge at the time.

Even taking into account prejudices from writers, it appears that Theodora could be ruthless and calculating. She and her husband publicly seemed to oppose each other, though historians believe they were always acting as a team toward the same agenda. This played out regarding religion within the empire. Theodora's husband, Justinian, supported, at least publicly, the Chalcedonian position. Meanwhile one of Theodora's main concerns was advancing the cause of non-Chalcedonian Christians. She was a miaphysite ("one-nature") Christian. In other words, she rejected the formula established at the Council of Chalcedon in 451 regarding the nature of Christ. Miaphysite Christianity is upheld by a number of ancient churches, such as the Coptic Church, the Armenian Church, the Syrian Orthodox Church, and the Ethiopian Orthodox Church, though it was rejected by both the Catholic and Eastern Orthodox churches. The miaphysite position was a minority one

---

18 For a discussion of sources about Theodora, see James Allan Evans, *The Empress Theodora: Partner of Justinian* (Austin: University of Texas Press, 2002), ix–xvi.

in Byzantium, and the population had faced persecution and martyrdom, so the support of the empress was welcomed by the community.

As an example of her support of the miaphysite community, Theodora transformed the Palace of Hormisdas into a monastery of over five hundred monks and nuns who sided with her theological position. Most miaphysite Christians in the city attended Chalcedonian churches, though they distinguished themselves by adding a line ("the immortal God who was crucified for us") to the doxology at the end of the liturgy. It is unclear whether Justinian held his wife's religious beliefs or not. He did pursue a theological compromise by holding a synod of bishops in 533 representing both the Chalcedonian and non-Chalcedonian positions. The synod failed, with both sides unable to reconcile and some Chalcedonian bishops ordering troops to attack several non-Chalcedonian Christians.

While Justinian and Theodora failed to find a compromise to the conflict over the Definition of Chalcedon, Theodora was more successful in her missionary activity, sending non-Chalcedonian missionaries to lands such as Nubia. She also sent the Syrian bishop Jacob Baradeus as a missionary, and his efforts led to the establishment of the Syrian Orthodox Church, or the Jacobite church as it is sometimes called.[19]

Another conflict that plagued the Eastern church was the Iconoclast controversy. This particular conflict can seem strange to Westerners, especially those who grew up in Christian traditions that use few images, such as many reformed denominations. In the Greek East, however, icons—or religious images of Christ, Mary, biblical figures, saints, and martyrs—have long been an important part of Christian worship. An icon is often an image painted on a piece of wood, though it can also be a mosaic in a church or printed on paper. An icon is a symbol, but a powerful one that helps connect the believer with the spiritual truth behind the icon. Believers use icons in their own personal devotion, often keeping icons in their homes. Icons were and continue to be a popular form of religious devotion in the Eastern churches.

In 717, a Byzantine general overthrew the emperor, Theodosius III, and took the throne under the name Leo III. For Leo the veneration of icons was a violation of the second commandment, which forbids the making of idols. It is not entirely clear why he so strongly rejected icons. One theory is that Leo, who was fluent in Arabic, was influenced by Islam, which firmly bans any image. Others have advanced the idea that Leo wanted to limit the power of the monks and nuns, who tended to be strong supporters of icons. Regardless, the ban on icons divided the empire into two camps: the *iconoclasts*, or icon-breakers, and the *iconodules*, or worshipers of icons, though this term is misleading since those who supported the icons did not actually worship the icons themselves. The patriarch of Constantinople was an iconodule, so the emperor replaced him with an iconoclast. Riots broke out when soldiers tried to remove icons from public places. One particular story that speaks to the people's devotion to icons involves a group of women determined to save an icon. The story alleges that when a soldier went to remove an icon

---

19 Dale T. Irving and Scott W. Sunquist, *History of the World Christian Movement, Volume 1: Earliest Christianity to 1453* (Maryknoll: Orbis, 2001), 248.

of Christ from the Chalke Gate, which was the main ceremonial entrance to the Great Palace of Constantinople, a group of angry women killed the soldier. The women were later executed for their act. The story, whether true or not, represents the devotion many women felt toward icons.

Leo's son Constantine V would continue his father's iconoclast policies with even greater fervor after he became emperor in 743. He summoned a church council in 753 that condemned icons. Then came the persecution and martyrdom of iconodules, particularly monks and nuns. Soldiers raided monasteries, seizing icons and arresting all those who opposed them. In 775, the persecutions began to relax with the ascension of a new emperor, another Leo. Leo IV was an iconoclast, but his wife, Irene, was an iconodule.

It is not entirely clear how Irene came to marry Leo, though it is likely Leo's father, Emperor Constantine V, arranged the marriage. Irene came from central Greece and may have lived in Athens prior to her marriage. Historians have noted what an odd choice of a bride she was, some even speculating she was picked in a bride show. However, it seems more likely the emperor was looking for Greek support, and a marriage to an Athenian woman from a prominent family seemed advantageous. She was crowned empress when she married Leo in 769. Like so many royal women before and after her, the most important role for her in the early years of her marriage was to provide a son and heir. On January 14, 771, she gave birth to a son named Constantine. Her husband died in 780, leaving an underage heir; Irene reigned as regent for her son, and she quickly reversed the iconoclast policies. Once her son came of age, they were crowned co-emperors, and they called an ecumenical council in the year 787 to settle the icon affair. The council affirmed the veneration of icons, carefully pointing out that veneration and worship were different in nature, and the icons were to be venerated, though this would not be the end of the controversy. Irene and her son soon fell into a power struggle, and Irene had her son tortured and killed and took sole control over the empire. She only reigned for five years before she was deposed, the iconoclasts once again took control of the empire, and yet more persecutions followed. Despite Irene's quest for power and murder of her own son, she is remembered as a defender of icons, though not a saint, by the Eastern Orthodox Church.

By the year 840, the iconoclast persecutions were dwindling. Throughout the entire affair, the emperor and the military had been the primary persecutors of icons. The church and the people had continued to venerate icons despite wave after wave of violence. In fact, after all of that, icons were as popular as ever. The last iconoclast emperor, Theophilius, died in the year 842, leaving his two-year-old son, Michael, as emperor. His wife, Theodora, ruled as regent and called an end to the persecutions in year 843.[20] This would be the true end of the controversy.

While the lives and actions of empresses are undoubtedly interesting, they tell us little about what life was like for regular believers in the Orthodox East. While evidence is sparse, there are clues as to what life was like for laywomen in medieval Byzantium found in hagiographic texts, monastic archives, donation records, and wills. What can be reconstructed suggests women were active believers who employed a variety of devotional activities.

---

20 Irving and Sunquist, *History of the World Christian Movement*, 361–362.

Few women were literate, even among the elite class, but if they could read, their education was closely tied to religious instruction. Literate women read spiritual and scriptural writings, and everyone, regardless of literacy level, could venerate icons, pray, and attend religious services. If women could afford it, they would often keep an icon in their bedroom. There is indication that urban women and girls went to church, sometimes daily (there is less evidence for women's church attendance in villages). Men and women were segregated at religious services, however, with women often relegated to a narthex, an upper gallery, or a side aisle depending on the church. Women who were menstruating or had recently given birth were not allowed in the church at all.

While the days of long pilgrimages, as seen in the early church, had largely ended by this point in history, it appears that women still made religious journeys and that they largely had access to religious shrines, tombs, and relics. Reasons for making these journeys ranged from participating in feast day activities to looking for cures for medical ailments to seeking help with conceiving a child.

One final note of interest is the close connections between laywomen and monasteries. Just as we saw in the West, the separation between monastery and the world was fluid. Laywomen visited and acted as patrons to monastic communities. It was not unusual for women to enter a convent later in life. In fact, a convent could provide a widowed woman with security and companionship. Poorer widows may have been attracted to the monastic life because participation in a religious community would ensure housing, food, and nursing care toward the end of their lives.[21]

CONVERSION OF KYIVAN RUS

With the rise and expansion of Islam in the seventh century, Islam became the dominant religion south and east of Byzantium, while Latin Christianity was dominant to the west. That meant Orthodox missionary efforts were largely directed to the north, and one of the most significant of these conversion events for Orthodoxy was that of Kyivan Rus.

In the ninth century, a group of Scandinavians moved into the area north of Kyiv and established themselves as the rulers over the already present Slavic people who had lived there for centuries. Over time, intermarriage and alliance merged the two people into one group, called the Rus. The Rus established their capital at Kyiv on the Dnieper River, in what is now modern-day Ukraine. Like many native peoples in Europe, the Rus worshiped a number of gods, and there was a strong element of shamanistic practice as well. It was a patriarchal society, but with age came more authority, so older women did exercise a certain amount of influence over younger women. Upper-class women would have additional authority over servants and slaves as well. All political and religious positions were held by men. The ruling warrior class was often engaged in warfare and trade, but most Rus families were free farmers as opposed to serfs. As long as they paid their

---

21 Alice-Mary Talbot, "The Devotional life of Laywomen," in *A People's History of Christianity, Vol. 3: Byzantine Christianity* (Minneapolis: Fortress Press, 2006), 201–220.

taxes, they were left to a fairly independent existence. There were few large cities within the Rus territory, but Kyiv in particular grew in importance; population estimates range from forty to fifty thousand by the twelfth century. This was the general context for the rather unexpected rise of Christianity at the end of the tenth century.[22]

The story of Princess Olga (c. 916–969), her grandson Vladimir (c. 958–1015), and the conversion of Kyivan Rus is a fantastic tale in which history and· legend are intertwined. While modern readers may question elements of it, it has been a meaningful conversion story over the centuries, and Olga provides an example of a strong Christian leader in a time of instability and change.

The exact date of Olga's birth is unknown, though *The Russian Primary Chronicle*, written in the early twelfth century, states that she was brought to Igor, whom she married, from Pskov in 906. Igor became prince of Kyiv in 913, and he reigned until he was killed in 945 by the Derevlians, an eastern Slavic people he had previously conquered. The Derevlians sent an envoy to Kyiv with the intention of taking Olga for the Derevlian prince named Mal. She agreed to the marriage, feigning pleasure at such a prospect, and the next day had the Derevlian entourage buried alive. She then sent a message to the Derevlians stating that her people would not let her go and to send their best men to collect her, which they did. This group of men she set on fire in a bathhouse. Finally, she agreed to go to Dereva, and there she hosted a funeral feast for her husband. At the feast, the Derevlians apparently got drunk while the Kyivans stayed sober, and Olga ordered her people to slaughter the Derevlians—about five thousand people. She then returned home to gather her son, Svyatoslav, and an army. After a long siege, Olga and the Kyivans took the city and burned it. Some inhabitants were sold into slavery, and others were left so that the Kyivans could later collect tribute from them.[23]

Sometime after these militaristic exploits, Olga went to Constantinople, presumably to negotiate trade agreements with the emperor; however, her trip ended up including a conversion to Christianity. She was reportedly instructed in the faith by the patriarch of Constantinople, and the emperor acted as her godfather at her baptism. *The Russian Primary Chronicle* describes Olga as begging her son to convert to the faith, but he refused, concerned that his warriors would no longer respect him. Considering the constant warfare of Svyatoslav's reign, it would have been devastating to lose the respect of his soldiers. However, even if Svyatoslav did not convert, his son Vladimir later did and initiated the conversion of his entire realm. Olga, who is venerated as a saint the Eastern church, died in 969, and the chronicler had this to write about her:

> Olga was the precursor of the Christian land, even as the day-spring precedes the sun and as the dawn precedes the day. For she shone like the moon by night, and she was radiant among the infidels like a pearl in the mire, since the

---

22 Barbara Evans Clements, *A History of Women in Russia: From Earliest Times to the Present* (Bloomington: Indiana University Press, 2012), 1–4.

23 Clements, *A History of Women in Russia*, 7–9.

people were soiled, and not yet purified of their sin by holy baptism. But she herself was cleansed by this sacred purification.[24]

While Olga's conversion is corroborated by Byzantine sources and her military campaigns are largely recognized, certain elements are likely embellishments. What is certain is that she was regent for her son for about three decades, first while he was a child and later when he was out waging war. She increased the kingdom's revenue, improved relations with other princely families, and strengthened the relationship between Kyiv and Constantinople. This relationship with Constantinople certainly laid the groundwork for her grandson Vladimir to marry the Byzantine princess Anna Porphyrogenita (c. 963–1011).

Anna Porphyrogenita is a somewhat shadowy figure in the history of the conversion of Kyivan Rus. Her husband, Vladimir, is a far more prominent historical figure and is often given sole credit for the conversion of his realm. Anna's marriage to Vladimir was a political one, and politically speaking, her hand was quite a prize. She was the daughter and sister of emperors, and by marrying her, Vladimir gained a level of prestige and legitimacy on the international stage. To say she was a reluctant bride is an understatement—reportedly she commented that she would rather die than marry Vladimir and move to Kyiv. However, her brothers, Emperors Basil and Constantine, convinced her of the match. Of course, a marriage between the princess and a pagan was unacceptable, so Vladimir needed to be baptized, to which he readily agreed.

To what extent Anna participated in the Christianization of Rus is unknown. Once the couple returned to Kyiv, the people were told they would be baptized in the Dnieper River or face Vladimir's displeasure. Although early accounts record the people's great enthusiasm for baptism, one wonders if there was perhaps some elaboration added. There is some evidence that Anna did participate in some church building, but that is about the only available information on her activities in Kyiv. While her marriage to Vladimir undoubtedly prompted the conversion of Rus, it is unclear what, if any, influence she had directly on the new Christians in her adopted land.

The roles of Olga and Anna Porphyrogenita are important in the history of Russian religion. While some elements of their stories are unclear or possibly legend, their influence is real. It is too simplistic to think that the conversion of Kyivan Rus lay solely with these factors—a pious warrior princess and a political marriage do not make a Christian nation. Prince Vladimir was a skilled statesman, and just like Constantine centuries before, his choice to embrace Christianity had many motives. There were already Christians living within Rus, and a warmer political alliance with Byzantium was welcome. It also seems likely that Vladimir sought a religion to unify the many diverse peoples within his realm. In the final analysis, though, a forced baptism does not make a Christian. It was the people who did eventually embrace Christianity that truly made Rus a Christian land.

---

24 *The Russian Primary Chronicle: Laurentian Text*, trans. and eds. Samuel Hazzard Cross and Olgerd P. Sherbowitz-Wetzor, The Mediaeval Academy of America (Cambridge: Crimson Printing Co., 1953), 87.

CHAPTER 4

Monastics and Mystics in the High to Late Middle Ages (1000–1500)

In 1212, on the night of Palm Sunday leading into Holy Week, a wealthy young woman named Clare risked a daring escape. She had been captivated by the teachings of a local wandering preacher ten years her senior by the name of Francis, and she was running from the bonds of wealth and luxury. Her aristocratic family pursued her, but it was in vain. She did not return home; instead, she dedicated her life to a radical vision of voluntary poverty and religious devotion. Soon a small community of women surrounded Clare, and they made their home at San Damiano, outside of Assisi, in close proximity to the Franciscan brothers. Perhaps as early as 1216, Clare sent sisters to establish other monastic houses in Foligno, Perugia, and Florence.[1] Today the Order of Saint Clare, better known as the Poor Clares, has approximately twenty thousand sisters in over seventy countries around the globe.[2] Clare was an important religious visionary and monastic reformer. She was a leader in the religious fervor of her day, and her theology and lifestyle have had a profound impact on the Catholic Church over the centuries. However, Clare, while historically important, is not the only religious woman of the era to make such a mark.

The High Middle Ages, the era in which Clare lived, was a time of theological progress, new monastic orders, and a blossoming of mysticism. Women, including members of traditional monastic communities, beguines, and even laywomen, made profound contributions to religious life and tradition, though their opportunities were unequal. Medieval European society was highly stratified, and access to education and the monastic lifestyle varied depending on class and wealth. Clare, who hailed from the upper echelons of medieval society, had the agency to pursue her religious vocation and the education and political savvy necessary to defend that vocation from powerful ecclesial men who pressured her to conform to a more typical Benedictine monasticism. Most women were not so privileged.

This chapter addresses a variety of issues and movements pertinent to medieval women. After a short historical background and a brief survey of economic opportunities for women in the Middle Ages, we explore the rise of the beguine movement, which was

---

1 Mary Beth Ingham, "The Logic of the Gift: Clare of Assisi and Franciscan Evangelical Life," *The Greek Orthodox Theological Review* 60, nos. 1–2 (2015): 130.

2 "About," Poor Clare Sisters, last modified December 10, 2008, http://poorclare.org/blog/?page_id=36.

75

a lay quasi-monastic movement that began with societal and ecclesial support but was eventually viewed with suspicion by the Catholic Church and later persecuted. Issues of wealth and access to religious vocations directly influenced this important medieval movement. The chapter then moves to a survey of highly influential monastic women including Hildegard of Bingen, Clare of Assisi, Birgitta of Sweden, Catherine of Siena, and Julian of Norwich.

An important theme that runs through this chapter is that of mysticism, and many of these medieval monastics and beguines were indeed mystics. Intimate encounters with the divine have consistently been an important aspect of Christianity since its earliest days, and during the Middle Ages, there were many well-known and influential women mystics who made lasting impacts on theological discourse. Women gained a voice through mystical experiences with the divine. In a sense, they were given permission to act outside of expected gender norms when they had a mandate from God.

The plague arrived in Europe in the middle of the fourteenth century, causing massive death and disruption. Society and religion were inevitably impacted by such an event, and this change in context is evident in the later medieval saints, such as Birgitta, Catherine, and Julian. The chapter ends with a short examination of Joan of Arc, a woman who does not fit easily with the other women in this chapter. Her fame did not rise from written works or the establishment of a religious order. While deeply mystical, she gained her fame on the battlefield.

HISTORICAL BACKGROUND

The flowering of spiritual and intellectual movements that feature prominently in the history of the High to Late Middle Ages follows a time of corruption and decay in Western Christianity within both the Catholic hierarchy and the monastic tradition. In the ninth and tenth centuries, the papacy was plagued by corruption; the various intrigues are complex and beyond our scope, but too often the papacy became a prize for rival parties. Monasteries were plagued by problems as well. Many had been sacked and destroyed by invaders looking for wealth, and those that remained were subject to the corruption of the age. Abbots bought their posts and used the wealth of the monastery for their own purposes, and the *Rule of Benedict* was frequently ignored.[3] For those who were genuinely called to the religious life, the state of the church was scandalous.

To combat the sorry state of religious affairs, a series of different renewal movements was instituted. The Gregorian Reforms, which take their name from Pope Gregory VII (1073–1085), in the eleventh century dramatically changed the structure of the church and were largely concerned with church unity, clerical celibacy, and ending simony, and they did much to centralize authority in the West. Running alongside the papal reforms was the monastic reform movement that had begun in Cluny in the tenth century. Prior

3   Justo González, *The Story of Christianity, Volume 1: The Earliest Church to the Dawn of the Reformation* (New York: Harper-One, 2010), 327.

to this, monastic communities were largely independent houses, but they were gradually transformed into a unified and centralized network integrated into the larger structure of the church. This issue of monastic unification is most pertinent for our study of women monastics and comes to play prominently in the life of Clare of Assisi, who spent most of her adult life fighting to maintain her community's commitment to absolute poverty, and the emergence of the beguine movement, which offered religious women a place outside of convents. Women also were caught up in the attempts to rid the church of corruption. Hildegard of Bingen reprimanded secular rulers for supporting anti-popes, and Birgitta of Sweden and Catherine of Siena encouraged the pope to return to Rome from Avignon.

While leaders in the Western church were attempting to root out corruption and enacting policies of reform, their relationship with Eastern Orthodox Christians was deteriorating. The Great Schism between the Eastern and Western churches is one of the great tragedies of Christian history. There were always linguistic and cultural differences and often tensions between the Catholic and Orthodox Churches; however, gradually over time those differences were exacerbated due to theological disagreements (most notably the issue of the insertion of the *filioque* into the Nicene Creed by the West[4]), variances in church practices, and fundamental disagreements over ecclesial authority.[5] What has long been remembered as the Great Schism between East and West occurred in 1054 when representatives from Rome to Constantinople excommunicated the patriarch of Constantinople; in turn, the patriarch called a church council, which excommunicated the delegates. While not truly the end of East/West relations, it does represent a low point, and it is symbolic of how contentious the relationship between these two great Christian churches had become.

To add to the already declining international relations of the time, in 1095, Pope Urban II called a crusade to claim the Holy Land for Christendom. The immediate reason for the crusade was that the Seljuk Turks had ended Christian pilgrimage to the Holy Land, which had long been an important activity for devout Christians, and many Christians heeded the call to crusade. The soldiers of the First Crusade were largely peasants and rather unorganized. Incredibly this band of makeshift soldiers took Antioch in 1098 and soon after took Jerusalem. Most of the crusaders were men, though there is evidence that women participated in various roles throughout the Crusades to the Holy Land. Hildegard of Bingen, for example, preached her support of the Second Crusade. Eleanor of Aquitaine, who was at that time married to the king of France, took her support of the crusade even further. Dressed as an Amazon warrior, she heeded the call to crusade from Bernard of Clairvaux. She rode with the crusaders as far as Antioch when she apparently was forced back home, against her will, by the French army.

To combat heresies, whether real or only perceived, within Christendom, the church established the Inquisition in the thirteenth century. The church had long been able to call

---

4 One of the major tensions revolved around the *filioque* controversy. The *filioque*, which literally means "and the son," was first inserted into the Nicene Creed at the Third Council of Toledo in the late sixth century. Over time it became standard for Catholics to recite the creed with this addition, but Orthodox Christians were opposed to it, and it became a point of particular contention and played heavily into the Great Schism of 1054.

5 Especially the issue of papal authority.

upon secular leaders to punish those whose beliefs and actions were deemed heretical, but with the Inquisition, the Catholic Church now had a central ecclesial office complete with a special court system, investigators, examinators, security forces, and judges who were known as Inquisitors. The church did not technically kill anyone, though it did employ torture as a method of inquisition. Those found guilty were turned over to secular leaders to be punished or executed.

While the Inquisition represents a low point for Christianity, at least morally, the twelfth through fourteenth centuries also saw a blossoming of spiritual and intellectual developments. Monasteries had long been centers of learning in the West, and their libraries and scriptoriums kept knowledge alive for hundreds of years; however, in the eleventh and twelfth centuries a new type of education emerged—first cathedral schools and then universities. Universities notably were not under the control of bishops or the church in general. Closely related to the rise of the university is the development of scholastic theology. Men such as Anselm of Canterbury, Peter Abelard, and Thomas Aquinas made enormous impacts on Western theology during these years. While women were largely excluded from the scholastic movement, they made important theological contributions outside of institutional learning settings, often influenced by their mystical experiences with God.

The establishment of new and innovative monastic orders, most notably the mendicant orders, is another critical trend in medieval Christian history. The most historically significant of the mendicant orders to emerge, and the two that play into our story, were the Dominicans, or the Order of Preachers, founded by Dominic Guzmán, and the Franciscans, founded by Francis of Assisi. The two orders had similarities, but their emphases and lifestyles were distinct. Dominic was influenced by his experience among the heretical groups of the Cathars and Waldensians. He believed that the most effective ways of combating disbelief and unorthodox thought were evangelization, right living, and correct teaching. He adopted a life of voluntary poverty and itinerancy, quickly gaining followers. By 1215, he was organizing these followers into small bands of preachers. The Dominicans were extremely successful at accomplishing their mission, and many men and women were drawn to the order. The Franciscans, on the other hand, were dedicated to the ideal of voluntary poverty. Their founder, Francis, moved by a profound religious experience, rejected his family's wealth and retreated temporarily from the world. Following a mystical vision, Francis took his message to the world and gained a following. Despite the ban on the establishment of new orders, Francis was able to convince Pope Innocent III to establish the "Order of Lesser Brothers" or the Friars Minor. The order held no wealth, and the brothers spent their time preaching and begging for their basic necessities. The mendicant orders were international and hence under the authority of the pope, not local bishops, and they regularly interacted with secular society. It must be noted that the women's monastic groups that were associated with the mendicant orders were not allowed the same type of freedom and were generally cloistered.

The fourteenth century brought unprecedented challenges to Europe, none more terrifying than the Black Death, a massive outbreak of the plague that is considered to be the deadliest pandemic in human history. While the exact origination point is unknown, scholars speculate that the pathogen arose in the Near or Far East.[6] The plague arrived in Constantinople in 1347, and within a year it had had spread throughout Italy. Within three years the plague had spread throughout all of Europe. It is estimated that one third of Europe's population died within a few years. After 1350 the pestilence storm abated, but Europe continued to see waves of the plague roll through every decade or so for centuries. The ramifications of a mass death event like this were legion both in secular society and in the church. Death seemed like a constant companion in the aftermath, and this fear of disease and death led to horrific consequences. Already marginalized, European Jews were further persecuted, there were labor shortages, and urban centers went into a period of contraction, with recovery incomplete in some areas until the start of the sixteenth century.

While Western Europe was suffering under violence and disease, the Byzantine Empire was coming to an end. Centuries of warfare had chipped away at the once impressive empire. By the fifteenth century, the Byzantine Empire was little more than the city of Constantinople and its surrounding areas. In 1422 the Ottoman Turks, who had come to power around the year 1300, laid siege to Constantinople. Sultan Muhammad II was determined to make Constantinople his capital city. Despite aid from the West, the great Christian city, once called the Second Rome, fell on May 29, 1453. Constantinople was renamed Istanbul. The patriarch of Constantinople was allowed to stay, but he was subject to the Ottoman rulers, who were Muslim. Following the fall of Constantinople, Serbia, Bulgaria, Macedonia, and Greece were all brought under Muslim control as well. The influence of the church in the East became far weaker. In fact, despite Christianity's once global status, by the end of the fifteenth century the only Christian-controlled countries outside Western Europe were Russia and Ethiopia.

WOMEN'S ECONOMIC OPPORTUNITIES WITHIN THE MEDIEVAL CONTEXT

A medieval woman's socioeconomic class and geographic location largely defined her opportunities and experiences. Urban growth took off in the eleventh through the thirteenth centuries, and populations in major European cities increased rapidly. In 1300 London had as many as eighty thousand people, and Paris had two hundred thousand; however, even with the increase in urban populations, Europe continued to be overwhelmingly agrarian with over ninety percent of the population living in the countryside or small towns.[7] Medieval society was land-based, and the lands a family owned largely determined their status.[8] Men were the primary landowners; however, women could and did own

---

6 There has recently been groundbreaking scholarship on the origins of the Black Death. See Monica H. Green, "The Four Black Deaths," *The American Historical Review* 125, no. 5 (December 2020): 1601–1631.

7 Kathryn Reyerson, "Urban Economies," in *The Oxford Handbook of Women & Gender in Medieval Europe*, eds. Judith M. Bennet and Ruth Mazo Karras (Oxford: Oxford University Press, 2013), 296–307.

8 David Herlihy, "Land, Family, and Women in Continental Europe, 701–1200," in *Women in Medieval Society*, ed. Susan Mosher Stuard (Philadelphia: University of Pennsylvania Press, 1976), 24.

property. Inheritance laws varied wildly from place to place, but with a few exceptions, daughters tended to receive a smaller portion than sons, if anything at all.[9] Men and women tended to occupy separate spaces. Women were limited in their movement, though from medieval laws regarding dress, we know women did mingle outside the home.[10] Urban women were largely confined to their own cities since it was not considered safe for women to travel alone.

Most families needed women to engage in some sort of economic activity, whether that be managing a home, working on a family farm or business, or bringing in income through a wage-earning job. The range of occupations open to women was largely determined by changes in supply and demand as well as custom.[11] Rural markets were freer and more competitive than those in towns. However, the work in the countryside tended toward heavy manual labor, which put women at a disadvantage.[12]

Only the wealthiest of families could afford to have women confined to the home, and wealthy women spent considerable time maintaining their households, including managing servants, overseeing food preparation, caring for their children, and placing orders or sending servants to acquire items such as food or other necessities. A limited number of wealthy women, most commonly widows, participated in the larger economy. Some worked as money changers, and others invested in international trade.

Women participated in trades, though they were most represented in industries that were widely considered "women's work," such as textile production and food trades.[13] Women were routinely denied training and were prohibited from joining guilds and working in many craft occupations even if they possessed the skills. This put women at an economic disadvantage, and it also makes it more difficult from a historical perspective to determine exactly how common women artisans were in the medieval period since it was the guilds that kept records.

The poorest women often worked in taverns as servants, wet nurses, peddlers, and prostitutes.[14] While increasingly less common in the later Middle Ages, some women were slaves. Historians have argued that female slaves were more common during this period than male slaves. As in all times, women who were enslaved or poor were more vulnerable to sexual exploitation.[15]

In a rural agrarian setting, both men and women worked hard, and while there was a division of labor along gender lines, both types of labor were critical for the survival of the family. Men spent more of their time in fields, and women tended to milk cows, make

---

9   Jane Whittle, "Rural Economies," in *The Oxford Handbook of Women & Gender in Medieval Europe*, eds. Judith M. Bennet and Ruth Mazo Karras (Oxford: Oxford University Press, 2013), 311–323.

10   Barbara A. Hanawalt, "Medieval English Women in Rural and Urban Domestic Space," *Dumbarton Oaks Papers* 52 (1998): 23.

11   John Hatcher, "Women's Work Reconsidered: Gender and Wage Differentiation in Late Medieval England," *Past & Present*, no. 173 (November 2001): 173.

12   Hatcher, 173.

13   Hatcher, 173.

14   Hanawalt, "Medieval English Women in Rural and Urban Domestic Space," 19–26. There was a tendency to equate tavern work with prostitution.

15   Reyerson, "Urban Economies," 296–307.

butter and cheese, raise poultry, brew beer, make cloth, and take care of children, though there were instances when women worked in harvesting and tending crops as well.

The Black Death caused a massive disruption in the economy and led to widespread labor shortages in the mid-fourteenth century. For those who survived the plague, wages increased, serfdom declined, and the quality of life for the peasantry in general improved. There is ample evidence that women were commonly employed to reap and bind in the field and thresh and winnow in the barns after the Black Death. Women did earn less than men, but it was because laborers were paid by the quantity of work performed. In such physical labor, women were at a disadvantage.[16] The degree of improvement is debated, but peasant women benefited from the increase in material standards of living as real wages rose and food and land became cheaper.[17]

WOMEN'S RELIGIOUS MOVEMENTS OF THE MIDDLES AGES

It should come as little surprise that women became increasingly interested in devoting themselves to a religious life during the years of spiritual renewal in the West. A combination of religious revival, backlash against cultural and economic trends, and the increased influence of mendicant preachers inspired men and women of all social classes to join monastic orders. Unfortunately, there were external factors that made access to monastic life difficult for women. First was the centralization of monastic orders, which brought the semi-independent houses of centuries prior under control of the hierarchy. Second was the decision to separate women's houses from men's houses—the age of the double monasteries where men and women lived and worked together was over. Finally, the cloistering of female houses kept women within the bounds of their monasteries. No longer were nuns allowed to evangelize the countryside as women like Leoba once had. This created a situation where the obligation to care for women's monastic houses was seen as a burden by the men of their religious orders.

This burden of caring for women monastics was seen as so severe that some religious orders tried to remove women from their ranks. One of the most striking examples is that of the Premonstratensians. Norbert, the founder of the order, found enthusiastic reception to his preaching with women, and the order even reestablished the institution of the double monastery in the twelfth century, though it must be noted that unlike the earlier double monasteries run by an abbess, these were run by an abbot. However, once again monks and nuns lived side by side. Despite the popularity of these monastic houses with women, by the end of the century the order began suppressing the double monastery and issuing a decree that women would no longer be admitted. Later Premonstratensian voices were even harsher in their language, claiming that women were a burden to the order and inclined to wickedness and evil and therefore must be rejected.[18]

---

16 Hatcher, "Women's Work Reconsidered," 191–98. (193)

17 Hatcher, 196.

18 R. W. Southern, *Western Society and the Church in the Middle Ages* (Baltimore: Penguin Books Inc., 1979), 312–314.

The struggle between women, the curia, and the Dominican Order provides another fascinating example of the problems of the time. Dominic had originally brought women's houses into the order, though by the end of his life, he showed signs he was beginning to question his commitment to the Dominican nuns. Later Dominicans were much stronger in their rejection of women. Their main complaint was that care for women harmed their ministries. They argued that their primary functions were to preach and spend time in contemplation. Therefore, spending time ministering to women within their order took time away from these main goals. They, like other monastic orders, started limiting the number of women's houses, and some ended up banning women's houses altogether.

The Roman Curia, however, largely supported women's desires to join the religious orders, and indeed there were numerous occasions where religious orders were forced to take on women's houses by papal decree, but this was blatantly going against the stated will of the orders. An interesting example of this is the case of Amicie de Joigny, a widowed countess who established a convent of fifty women in Montargis, France. Her father had been friends with Dominic, and she wished to join the Order of Preachers. Once she realized she would be unable to join directly, she tried to have her monastic house accepted into the order, which they also rejected. Taking matters into her own hands, she met with Pope Innocent IV and personally negotiated for her house at Montargis. She was able to obtain a papal bull incorporating her house into the Dominican Order in 1245 despite the Dominicans explicitly rejecting her house.[19] After this, women increasingly sought incorporation into monastic orders through papal bull.

Unsurprisingly, religious orders did not appreciate the pope forcing them to take on women's houses or, more significantly, forcing upon them the ministry responsibility associated with this. In 1252, Innocent IV promised he would not incorporate any more women's houses into the Dominican Order for another twenty years, but shortly thereafter he released the Dominicans from all pastoral care of the women's houses. The women and their wealthy and well-connected relatives were furious and flooded the curia with complaints.[20] After years of negotiations, the Dominican Order agreed to provide pastoral care to the women's houses within their orders, but it became increasingly difficult for new women's houses to join. There were similar conflicts between the Franciscans and the various women's houses associated with their order as well. In the end, the mendicant orders had to take in women's houses and needed to provide pastoral care to the women, but the number of women's houses was limited.

Even with the incorporation of women's houses into various religious orders, access to a religious life was simply not possible for many women. One issue was that of resources; a women's house needed access to wealth, generally in the form of either money or land or both, to support cloistered women. Influential connections were also important to negotiate incorporation. The average woman was unable to arrange a meeting with the pope to plead her case as Amicie de Joigny had. Even when a religious house was incorporated, it

---

19 Herbert Grundmann, Steven Rowan, and Robert E. Lerner, "The Incorporation of the Women's Religious Movement into the Mendicant Orders," in *Religious Movements in the Middle Ages* (Notre Dame: University of Notre Dame Press, 1995), 89–138.

20 Grundmann, Rowan, and Lerner, "The Incorporation of the Women's Religious Movement," 125.

was generally so full that it would often take in only the richest and most well-connected women. The reasons for this are obvious; aristocratic women brought with them significant wealth, which was needed by the cloistered community, and there was little desire to offend powerful families—not to mention the benefits of these associations. While these practices may have made sense from a purely logistic way of thinking, it left countless devout women unable to join monastic houses.

The situation was untenable. The established church could not provide for the multitude of women seeking a holy life. Out of necessity grew a creative solution: the rise of beguines. The word "beguine," first coined in the 1230s,[21] was originally meant as a slur, taken from the heretical sect the Albigensians, though there seems to be little or no actual association between the beguines and the Albigensian movement. Women throughout Europe began to come together to live a religious life outside of established religious orders. While they were influenced by the general atmosphere of religious renewal, this was exclusively a women's movement. These communities were unregulated, and they did not follow any established monastic rule. They were simply women who pledged to live celibate lives in community and survive off their own labor—these were not wealthy cloistered women living off the income of their lands. In 1216, Pope Honorius III officially permitted women to join these pious communities, thus providing approval of a process that was already occurring.

When the beguine movement first appeared, public opinion seemed to be on the beguines' side. Many people, both in the church and outside, saw them as good and pious women living on alms and hard work. There are numerous contemporary examples of religious men writing complimentary words about the lifestyle of the beguines, though there were also plenty of people who disapproved of the movement. There were beguines charged and executed for heresy even from the earliest days, though there was not widespread persecution.[22] Religious authorities largely viewed the beguines in a positive light until the middle of the thirteenth century, when there seemed to be a shifting of public opinion against these religious communities. Some of the propaganda against the beguines was genuinely biased and based on misogynistic views against religious women living outside strict enclosure or the confines of marriage. However, other criticism seems to speak to some legitimate issues. This loose, unregulated movement did have instances of corruption and heretical thought. Likely there were individual women who were bad actors, as there are in any group. Ultimately, though, it seems the beguines' true crime was being women operating outside of male authority. Certain men came to see the movement as dangerous. Bruno, the bishop of Olmütz, for example, wrote to the pope complaining about the beguines and expressing his desire to see them all either married off or put into an approved order.[23]

Over time the Catholic Church sought greater control over the beguines. In the 1230s, the archbishop of Mainz decreed that women who wore a special habit but did not follow

---

21 Grundmann, Rowan, and Lerner, 139.

22 Southern, *Western Society and the Church in the Middle Ages*, 321.

23 Southern, 329.

a rule—in other words, beguines—were expected to stay in their homes and were barred from traveling between villages. Because a number of women left their beguinages to marry, a 1244 synod in Fritzlar declared only women over forty could become beguines, though it appears this was rarely enforced. It was not only the church hierarchy that struggled with the undefined role of beguines. The beguines appealed to the pope in 1235 for protection against male clergy who were apparently taking advantage of the beguines' unprotected status.[24] The lack of leadership and consistency within the movement legitimately seemed to pose problems both for the beguines and the larger church, though it is also necessary to recognize that negative societal views of women added to the complexity and problems that arose. In reality, women living a holy life in community was not a crime, and even as conflicts between the beguines and the church hierarchy became apparent, the church hierarchy was hesitant to ban the lifestyle altogether. Throughout the fourteenth century, there was a series of decrees from archbishops and popes that brought beguines into established convents and forced them to live under an established rule and submit to enclosure. In 1421, Pope Martin V ordered the archbishop of Cologne to search out and destroy any convents not living according to an official monastic rule. Though it is unknown whether the archbishop complied, the decree demonstrates that the support of the beguine movement was over.[25]

Although the movement was not to last, there was lasting influence from both the movement at large and individual women within the movement. Mechthild of Magdeburg is the most famous of the German beguines. She composed *The Flowering Light of the Godhead*, which has the distinction of being the first collection of mystical writings composed in the German vernacular.[26] She was born sometime around the year 1200, and while it is not entirely clear when she died, she did live to an old age. Little is known of her early life, but we know she experienced her first mystical revelation at the age of twelve and joined a beguine community at Magdeburg in 1230. She openly criticized the clergy and the church hierarchy. During her lifetime, she was considered a saint by many, though she has never formally been canonized. She entered into a Benedictine convent in Helfta, Saxony, around the year 1270. At the time, the community at Helfta was a center of spiritual activity for women and the home of Mechthild of Hackeborn and Gertrude the Great, both known for their mystical writings as well.

Hadewijch of Antwerp (d. 1260), Beatrice of Nazareth (1200–1268), and Marguerite Porete (d. 1310), all beguines, are also known to us through their writings. We know almost nothing about Hadewijch other than that she was active in the first half of the thirteenth century in the Low Countries. From her writings scholars have concluded she was likely the spiritual head of a women's community, probably a group of beguines,

---

24 Grundmann, Rowan, and Lerner, "The Incorporation of the Women's Religious Movement," 142.

25 Southern, *Western Society and the Church in the Middle Ages*, 331.

26 Sara S. Poor, *Mechthild of Magdeburg and Her Book: Gender and the Making of Textual Authority* (Philadelphia: University of Pennsylvania Press, 2004), 1–16.

but at some point was forced to leave due to some sort of opposition. She composed a number of letters, poetry, and visionary prose.[27]

Beatrice of Nazareth, a beguine who later became a Cistercian nun, is known for *The Seven Ways of Holy Love*, a work of mystical writing that describes the seven stages of love. Marguerite Porete is also famous for her writings but in quite a different way from the previous mystics. She was burned to death as a heretic for her book *The Mirror of Simple Souls*.

Marguerite was born sometime around 1260 in the country of Hainaut, and at the time of her death she lived near the town of Valenciennes, which today is in France. Nothing is known of her family, though due to her education and writing abilities, scholars have suggested she was likely upper class. She is called a beguine in the trial records, though it is unclear to which, if any, community she belonged. She probably wrote *Mirror* in the 1290s in the vernacular. She was condemned and her book ordered to be burned by the bishop of Cambrai sometime between 1296 and 1306, though she was not sentenced to execution at this point—merely told not to write anymore or promote her ideas in public. She did not adhere to this sentence and found herself arrested again in 1308. She spent two years in jail, and after the inquisitor had a group of twenty-one theologians read excerpts from her book, she was condemned and sentenced to burning at the stake. Despite Marguerite's unfortunate end, her book continued to circulate as an anonymous work after its condemnation.

Mirror was her life's work and included what she had learned over the years. In some ways, the book fits with the larger genre of mystical writings penned by women in vernacular languages that emerged during this time. She writes about her quest for a mystical union with God, and love plays a central role throughout. There are distinctions that made this text particularly problematic for the church. A recurring theme is that Christians are free from the law and do not need to conform to moral law.[28] Her complete refusal to cooperate with authorities certainly did not help save her life either, but it is also quite possible growing hostilities toward the beguines and the presence of other heretical groups influenced the decision to execute her. As far as we know, she was the first female mystic executed for only her ideas, a disturbing prospect to be sure.[29]

In conclusion, the development of the beguines was in response to widespread religious fervor and offered a religious life for women who were unwilling or unable to join official monastic houses. The solution was not perfect. It is evident that a lack of structure and defined roles did cause difficulties for the beguines and promoted suspicion within the confines of the Catholic Church. Regardless, these beguine communities provided a solution to a legitimate need, and many women were able to live out meaningful Christian lives within this movement.

---

27 Frank Willaert, "Hadewijch," in *Women in the Middle Ages: An Encyclopedia*, vol. 2, eds. Katharina M. Wilson and Nadia Margolis (Westport, CT: Greenwood, 2004), 403–406.

28 Aristoula Georgiadou, "Marguerite Porete," in *Women in the Middle Ages: An Encyclopedia*, vol. 2, eds. Katharina M. Wilson and Nadia Margolis (Westport, CT: Greenwood, 2004), 2:761–763.

29 Sean L. Field, *The Beguine, the Angel, and the Inquisitor: The Trials of Marguerite Porete and Guiard of Cressonessart* (Notre Dame, Indiana: University of Notre Dame Press, 2012).

THE GREAT MONASTICS

The presence of the beguines speaks to larger issues of equality and access during the Middle Ages, but they were not the only women pursuing a holy life. While it is true that entering a monastery could be challenging and that the majority of those who did were members of affluent families, that does not discount the importance and prevalence of the monastic life for women. There are numerous examples of women who became leaders, writers, theologians, and more, all while living a religious life. Through this network, women were active participants in church reform and theological development.

There were a variety of reasons medieval women chose a monastic life. First and foremost was a genuine desire to live a life devoted to God. Some women may have found a life of female community preferable to marriage and child-rearing. In other cases, a monastic life may not have been desired but necessitated by the financial constraints of the family, particularly for members of the lower nobility. For families with numerous daughters, dowries could become a very heavy burden. While convents also required a dowry, it was considerably less than what would be required to make a good marriage match. In cases like these, it was not uncommon for a family to send daughters to a convent instead of contracting a marriage. There were, of course, spiritual benefits to having a nun in the family, and dedication to the faith was generally seen in a positive light.

Monastic women in the early Middle Ages were often not confined to their monasteries, but they were generally cloistered during the High to Late Middle Ages, though exceptions were made. Some women even lived as anchoresses, a position in which they were literally walled into a monastic cell with the expectation that they would never leave. A life of enclosure did not mean giving up all relationships outside of the church, though. Monasteries were active places, and visitors were frequent. Even the position of anchoress could be surprisingly social, with visitors frequently seeking spiritual guidance through a window built into the cell.

It was in this setting that some of the greatest monastic leaders, writers, theologians, and mystics of the Middle Ages lived. Overwhelmingly monastic women were some of the best educated of the era, and it is unsurprising that they left such a disproportionately large legacy.

The Sybil of the Rhine: Hildegard of Bingen

To say Hildegard of Bingen (1098–1179) is one of the most brilliant people of the Middle Ages is no exaggeration. While she firmly fits into the genre of mystic, having received numerous divine visions during her lifetime, she is considered one of the great intellects of the era. Not only did she pen significant theological writings, but she also influenced a wide number of other disciplines, such as music, pharmacy, and literature. She was the first recorded woman to execute a successful public preaching tour. She wrote to and influenced princes, kings, bishops, and popes. She wrote the first morality play and three major works of theology: *Scivias* (*Know the Ways*), *Liber vite meritorum* (*Book of Life's Merits*), and *Liber Divinorum Operum* (*Book of Divine Works*). Fortunately, she also left an unusual amount of information on her personal life for the times. She provides biographical information through her own writings, and since she gained quite a bit of fame throughout her life-time, there are numerous contemporary biographies, including one written by her own secretary, that provide valuable additional information.

Hildegard was blessed with an unusually long life for the twelfth century. She lived for nearly eighty years in a time when the average life expectancy was a little over thirty. She was born in what is now the village of Bermersheim, which is just south of Mainz, Germany. Hildegard was the tenth child of noble parents named Mechtild and Hildebert, and it is often said that she was turned over to the church as a tithe. Of course, this makes for a great story, but the situation was probably more complex than that, especially since she had three older siblings already dedicated to the church. From a young age Hildegard began having mystical visions. To complicate matters, she was a sickly child with long bouts of illness that continued to plague her as an adult. These factors, combined with the expensive reality of a dowry for a tenth child, made dedicating Hildegard to the church a logical choice. It is not entirely clear when this offering was made though. Her *Vita* claims she was offered to God in her eighth year, but it was not until 1112 that she officially joined the Benedictines. She joined with two other women, both named Jutta—Jutta of Spanheim was to be her teacher, and Jutta's niece, also named Jutta, acted as their servant.

Hildegard and the two Juttas made their home at Disibodenberg, which interest-ingly was a men's monastery. The three women were to be anchoresses; the practice of having women anchoresses at a male monastery was not uncommon, and the women were literally walled into a cell with only a small window to allow the passing of food and waste. Jutta of Sponheim practiced extreme asceticism, wearing a hair shirt and uncomfortable chains, eating little, and causing herself other sorts of bodily discomfort. Through this lifestyle, her fame spread, and people flocked to her. Due to her popularity, families asked Jutta to take their daughters. At some point, the anchoress's cell was opened to allow other women to join. Their living arrangement thus became more like that of a double monas-tery than a single anchoress's cell in a men's monastery.

After twenty-four years, Jutta died, and Hildegard finally was able to step out from her shadow. Hildegard was unanimously picked to lead the group of nuns that had gathered there. Five years later, at the age of forty-two, Hildegard had a mystical experience that would completely change her life. Through this vision she gained an understanding of divine revelation, and God commanded her to write what she saw and heard. Hildegard was hesitant. Recording mystical visions was a common activity for women at the time, but it could also be dangerous, especially if her writings were deemed heretical. Therefore, Hildegard sought ecclesial approval before she began to write. First, she discussed it with her superiors at her own monastery; then after receiving permission from them, she took the added step of writing to Bernard of Clairvaux, easily one of the most famous eccle-siastics of his time, who also gave his support to her writing. Still unconvinced, she even wrote to the pope on the subject, though there is no extant reply, so it is unknown if he responded. Either way, she was allowed to write, and write she did.

Her first major text was *Scivias*. She explains in the beginning of the text that God com-manded her to write an intelligible account of her visions because her testimony would help others learn about their creator. A few paragraphs into her works she states:

> Heaven was opened and a fiery light of exceeding brilliance came and perme-
> ated my whole brain, and inflamed my whole heart and my whole breast, not
> like a burning but like a warming flame, as the sun warms anything its rays
> touch. And immediately I knew the meaning of the exposition of the Scriptures,
> namely the Psalter, the Gospel and the other catholic volumes of both the Old
> and the New Testaments.[30]

There are instances where other mystics claim to have received direct knowledge of theo-logical matters from God, so this is not an outlier in the genre, but it is still a remarkable claim nonetheless. Throughout the book she records twenty-six different visions, then breaks down the theological meaning of each vision. *Scivias* is divided into three parts: the first is on the creation and the fall, the second on redemption, and the third on the history of salvation. *Scivias* was her best-known work throughout her life and continues to be her best-known theological work today.

In 1150, while she was writing *Scivias*, Hildegard felt called to found her first monastery. The monks with whom Hildegard and her monastic sisters were living were vehemently opposed to the move (Hildegard was quite famous already and brought prestige to the monastery), but Hildegard felt confident that this was what God wanted her to do. She took twenty nuns and their priest and confessor, named Volmar, and moved to Rupertsburg overlooking Bingen on the Rhine, where she lived for the next thirty-three years.

By the time Hildegard had moved into her new monastery, she was already known for her music compositions, which continue to be played and recorded to this very day. She had neither formal training nor a mentor, though her innate talent is obvious. Likely because of this lack of formal training, her music was incredibly creative. Of course, as an abbess she had ample resources at her disposal to create music, including the monastery's scriptorium and a trained choir within their community. Over half of her songs are anti-phons, nearly a third of her compositions are responsories, and she also wrote fourteen longer works called sequences. While it is impossible to truly represent her musical talents in this written volume, the poetry from one of her antiphons demonstrates her gifts as a lyricist:

> *When the Creator actually spilled*
> *His Blood on the elements,*
> *earth, air, water, and fire*
> *screamed,*
> *collapsed with grief,*
> *shook from sadness.*
> *Now, Father, with this gift*
> *anoint our weaknesses.*[31]

---

30 Hildegard of Bingen, *Scivias*, trans. Mother Columba Hart and Jane Bishop (New York: Paulist Press, 1900), 59.

31 Carmen Acevedo Butcher, *St. Hildegard of Bingen: Doctor of the Church, A Spiritual Reader* (Brewster, MA: Paraclete Press, 2007), 32.

Her mastery of language translated into skills as a preacher. In 1158, she launched a preaching tour, which was unprecedented at the time for a woman. While monks and nuns had a long history of evangelizing, Hildegard lived in the era of cloistered convents—not the time of wandering evangelist nuns. During her first tour, she spoke exclusively in monasteries, but during her second and third preaching tours, she preached in public to lay believers. She would launch a fourth, and final, preaching tour in 1170 at the age of seventy-two.

In 1163, she finished her second theological work, *The Book of Life's Merits*. Around the same time, she wrote an encyclopedia called *Nine Books on the Subtleties of Different Kinds of Creatures*. This included herbal remedies and other medical information, a bestiary, and information on a variety of natural things such as plants, elements, metals, and so on. She followed this up with a handbook called *Causes and Cures*, which as the title suggests was a book of medical knowledge. As can be gleaned from her literary output, Hildegard was highly educated, but it is unknown how she became so. Often Jutta is recognized as Hildegard's teacher, though Hildegard's *Vita* claims Jutta was unschooled. It is very possible Jutta taught her about spiritual matters but Hildegard gained her knowledge elsewhere. Exactly where she gained such an impressive breadth of knowledge remains a mystery.

By 1165, her convent was so crowded, she established a second one. At the age of nearly seventy, she bought a former double monastery at Eibingen, which was east of Bingen. She would cross the Rhine twice a week and visit the nuns in her other convent for the next fourteen years, until her death in 1179.

The final years of her life saw significant conflict with the clergy from Mainz over a burial. A nobleman had died and was buried at her monastery, but the local clergy claimed the man had died in a state of excommunication, so they wanted to exhume his body from consecrated ground. Hildegard said he had received absolution, and she would not allow his body to be dug up. She went so far as to destroy his grave marker so that they would not know where the body was. Conflicts between abbesses and clergy were certainly known to happen, and this final episode demonstrates Hildegard's sheer determination to do what she believed was right. In response to Hildegard's refusal to cooperate, the bishop placed the entire community under an interdict that forbade music at the monastery. This was a profoundly painful punishment for the musician Hildegard. She obeyed the interdict, but she began a fervent writing campaign to get this unjust punishment lifted. Eventually the bishop of Mainz relented and lifted the ban.[32]

Hildegard died shortly after this final conflict on September 17, 1179. In an amusing epitaph to her life, she apparently stayed active in death. According to reports, Hildegard performed so many miracles after her death that the number of faithful seeking her intercession became burdensome for her community. The monastic life was disrupted to the point that the local archbishop had to come and request that Hildegard stop performing miracles from the grave. Despite her incredible life and post-death miracle working, her path to canonization was long and complicated. While there were many who considered

---

32 Honey Meconi, *Hildegard of Bingen* (Urbana: University of Illinois Press, 2018), 72–74.

her a saint early after her death, official canonization hit bureaucratic issues and, in the end, remained incomplete. In the 1800s, there was renewed interest in Hildegard, and her monastery was rebuilt, though in a slightly different location, and the nuns of St. Hildegard Abbey were active in renewing her canonization process. On May 10, 2012, Pope Benedict XVI declared Hildegard a saint, and later that year she was declared a doctor of the church.[33]

Clare of Assisi

Born nearly one hundred years after Hildegard, Clare of Assisi (1193–1253) was one of the great monastic reformers of the High Middle Ages. Clare's story is intertwined with that of Francis of Assisi, and while Francis is the better known of the pair, Clare's story is no less compelling. She founded an order, resisted immense pressure, both from secular and ecclesial forces, to live a holy life of poverty, and holds the distinction of being the first woman to write a monastic rule that was officially recognized by the pope.

Clare was born in 1193 to a noble and wealthy family in Assisi. She lived during a time of social change, which included the birth of modern capitalism, and conflict was a regular occurrence among the nobles and merchant classes in Assisi. It is unknown when Clare first heard Francis preach, but the two developed a friendship, and he was an integral part of her escape from society. On the night of Palm Sunday heading into the Monday of the Holy Week of 1211, Clare fled her home to a small rural church a few miles outside Assisi. There, Francis tonsured her hair, and the next day he sent her to a monastery, where she would briefly stay. A dramatic scene followed when her family showed up with the intent of bringing her home. According to sources, after they saw her tonsured head, she was disowned by her family. This story is quite remarkable when you consider the social conventions of the day. A prominent noblewoman had escaped her wealthy family to join a group of poor men, who were certainly religious but were also living a rather alternative lifestyle. It is no wonder her family was concerned for her well-being, and while it is of little surprise that they chased her down, it *is* somewhat surprising that they did not force her to go back with them. When Clare's sister Catherine, who took the name Agnes, also escaped their family about two weeks after Clare, accounts report the family was even more zealous in their desire to bring her back home, and it took divine assistance to keep Agnes by Clare's side.[34]

Clare and her growing group of followers eventually settled in San Damiano, next to the church that Francis had repaired. Francis wrote up a rule for the women, though it must be noted it was not a church-sanctioned rule due to the ecclesial prohibition on the creation of new orders. The issue of monastic reform came into play in Clare's life in a prominent way. Clare was a devout follower of Francis's teachings on absolute poverty, to which she and her followers were determined to adhere. It is true that all monastics make a vow of poverty, but while an individual could not amass wealth, the orders

---

33 Butcher, *St. Hildegard of Bingen*, 163–165.

34 Joan Mueller, *The Privilege of Poverty: Clare of Assisi, Agnes of Prague, and the Struggle for a Franciscan Rule for Women* (University Park: The Pennsylvania State University Press, 2006), 7–12.

could and very often would—monastic orders could receive large donations and land grants and earn income from their lands. Francis's order, on the other hand, amassed no wealth, and he and his brothers begged for their basic necessities. Clare, too, wanted to run her house in this manner, but they ran into a significant impediment—begging and cloistering are incompatible. It is unclear whether Clare's monastic house was ever out in the world begging and preaching or if they were always cloistered, but it is known that Clare and the church hierarchy did not see eye to eye on this issue and that throughout her life she defended her community from having different monastic rules thrust upon them. One example of this occurred in 1216, when she was given the title of abbess. She resisted titles and reportedly only accepted it out of a sense of obedience to Francis but continued to perform the most menial of jobs and preferred the title of sister. After Francis's death, Clare and her followers faced increased attempts to transform their monastic house into a more traditional Benedictine model, but Clare held fast to Francis's teachings on complete poverty. At the very end of her life, Pope Innocent IV declared that the rule that Clare had written would serve as the governing rule for her community. Clare died one day after receiving the news. Her canonization process was fast, and she was declared a saint in 1255, a mere two years after her death.[35]

Clare is a fascinating woman in Christian history. She was completely committed to the idea of absolute poverty, which put her at odds with the church leadership. She actively resisted any attempt to bring her more in line with typical monastic life, and she demonstrated an incredible adherence to her own beliefs. While Francis certainly inspired and helped her, Clare had clear leadership skills, a spirit of reform, and a dedication to pious Christian living. The writing of her own rule should also not be downplayed. While women most certainly had written up rules for their monastic houses at other points in history, she was the first to have her rule accepted by the pope—a major step indeed.[36]

Birgitta of Sweden

Birgitta of Sweden (1302/3–1373), like Clare, was a reformer, but of a very different variety. She was a wife and a mother, and she became one of the most prominent voices for spiritual renewal in the late Middle Ages. She became a mouthpiece for God, denouncing moral corruption in clerics and kings and gaining international recognition. Her status as a wife and mother made her an unlikely candidate to become "the great mystic of the North," but in other ways, her experience as a married woman and her interactions with the Swedish royal court made her the perfect advocate for reform. Today she is even recognized as one of the co-patron saints of Europe.

Birgitta was born into a powerful Swedish family in the province of Uppland. At the time Sweden was still a small and relatively undeveloped country, considered to be

---

35 Thomas Head, "Clare of Assisi," in *Women in the Middle Ages: An Encyclopedia*, vol. 2, eds. Katharina M. Wilson and Nadia Margolis (Westport, CT: Greenwood, 2004), 194–196.

36 For a more in-depth examination of Clare's rule, see Catherine M. Mooney, "The 1253 Forma Vitae, ca. 1250 to 1253," in *Clare of Assisi and the Thirteenth-Century Church: Religious Women, Rules, and Resistance* (Philadelphia: University of Pennsylvania Press, 2016), 161–196.

on the outskirts of Europe, but urban centers were growing, and the Swedish church was establishing closer ties with continental Europe. Birgitta's father held the powerful position of *lagman*, literally lawman, by which he oversaw the codification of laws and participated in the election of King Magnus Eriksson. In addition to her family's political connections, there were numerous familial connections to the Swedish Church.[37]

When she was around fourteen, her father arranged her marriage to Ulf Gudmarsson, who was also from a prominent Swedish family and would later become the lawman of Nericia. The couple served in the Swedish royal court for some time, and when the king married Blanche of Namur, Birgitta became her advisor, likely instructing her on the customs and language of her adopted land. It is reported that Birgitta was unimpressed with the morality and behavior of Queen Blanche.

Birgitta and Ulf were married for nearly thirty years and had eight children, six of whom would survive until adulthood, including St. Catherine of Sweden. During her time as a wife, Birgitta was recognized for her piousness and works of Christian charity. She educated her children in the Christian faith and encouraged her husband's Christian faith. However, her life would radically transform when her husband died in the mid-1340s. Concerned about her new life of widowhood, she had a particularly intense experience where God communicated directly with her about her future. A few days after her husband's death she heard a voice saying, "I am your God, who wants to speak with you." The voice went on to say:

> Do not be afraid. For I am the creator of all and am not a deceiver. You should know that I do not speak to you for your sake alone, but for the sake of the salvation of all Christians: Therefore, hear what I say. For you shall be my bride and channel, and you shall hear and see spiritual things and heavenly secrets, and my Spirit shall remain with you until your death. Therefore, believe firmly that I am he who was born from a pure virgin, who suffered and died for the salvation of all souls, who rose from the dead and ascended into heaven, and who now with my spirit speaks with you.[38]

This was not Birgitta's first vision, nor would it be her last. Over the course of her life, she recorded some seven hundred visions. From a young age she had had them; at the age of ten, for example, she had a vision of Christ on the cross, and when she asked who had done this to him, he answered, "Those who despise me and refuse my love for them." With the death of her husband, she was able to live out this calling as a prophet in a public way.

For the remainder of her life, she brought divine messages from Christ, Mary, and the saints to the world. She was particularly concerned with the moral failings of the aristocracy, the Hundred Years' War,[39] and the pope's decision to reside in Avignon. In the latter half of the 1340s, she also received direct commands to establish a new religious order

---

37 Claire L. Sahlin, *Birgitta of Sweden and the Voice of Prophecy* (Rochester, NY: Boydell Press, 2001), 14.

38 Sahlin, "Extrav. 47," in *Birgitta of Sweden and the Voice of Prophecy*, 45.

39 The Hundred Years' War stretched slightly longer than one hundred years, from 1337 to 1453.

primarily for women dedicated to the Virgin Mary called the Order of the Most Holy Savior, most commonly known as the Bridgettine Order. The order follows the Rule of St. Augustine and was formally approved by Pope Urban V in 1370, a few years before Birgitta's death. Within a couple of hundred years there were over sixty different monastic houses spread throughout Europe.

In 1349, Birgitta moved permanently to Rome in the midst of the devastating Black Death outbreak. She had two major goals in mind: to get papal approval for her religious order and to persuade the pope to return to Rome. There, she lived a quasi-monastic life, established a center for Scandinavian pilgrims, and cared for the sick and needy. Later in life, she took a pilgrimage through the Holy Land, where she continued to denounce clerics and political leaders who were falling short on their duties to live a faithful Christian life. She died shortly after this final pilgrimage in 1373, her body was returned to Sweden, and she was canonized in 1391.[40] Birgitta was unquestionably a religious leader, but she was arguably a political leader too. As with other mystics, she gained her legitimacy directly from God, but her aristocratic connections undoubtedly helped her interact with Europe's elite.

Catherine of Siena

In some ways, Catherine of Siena's (1347–1380) public presence echoed that of Birgitta of Sweden, though the two were very different saints. So many of the well-known mystics and monastics hailed from the aristocracy, but Catherine, who perhaps ended up being the most influential of all the medieval mystics, was born into the middle class. An important source regarding her life is a hagiographic work that was composed shortly after her death by her confessor, Raymond of Capua. He promoted her cause for sainthood extensively when he succeeded to the generalship of the Dominican Order. As in all hagiographies, there is a level of massaging of facts to fit a saintly narrative. Raymond highlighted Catherine's frail, unlearned nature to explain the authority of her words and actions while also downplaying her very public life.[41] Despite the agenda of the work, it provides valuable information on Catherine's life.

Catherine was the daughter of a dyer of wool. She was also one of twenty-five children, and she had a twin who died shortly after birth. At the age of six Catherine received the first of many visions. She saw Jesus on a throne with the saints Peter, Paul, and John the Evangelist by his side. Raymond highlights this moment as a turning point in her life. It was after this transformative experience that she withdrew to her home and began practicing serious prayer, meditation, and extreme asceticism.[42]

Despite her parents wanting to arrange a marriage for her, she was determined to devote her life to God. She was especially drawn to the Dominican Order, but there was no cloistered Dominican women's house in the area. There was a group of women that

---

40 Maria H. Oen and Unn Falkeid, "Introduction," in *Sanctity and Female Authorship: Brigitta of Sweden & Catherine of Siena*, eds. Maria H. Oen and Unn Falkeid (New York: Routledge, 2020), 2–3; Sandro Sticca, "St. Birgitta of Sweden," in *Women in the Middle Ages: An Encyclopedia*, vol. 2, eds. Katharina M. Wilson and Nadia Margolis (Westport, CT: Greenwood, 2004), 96–98.

41 Thomas F. Luongo, "Introduction," in *The Saintly Politics of Catherine of Siena* (Ithaca: Cornell University Press, 2006), 8.

42 Raymond of Capua, *The Life of St. Catherine of Siena* (Dublin: James Duffy and Co.), 8.

belonged to the Third Order of St. Dominic, and Catherine wanted to join, but they initially refused her because they were older widows who lived in their own homes and provided services to the sick and poor in the community. At the age of sixteen she was allowed to officially join the group, and she then secluded herself in a "cell" within her parents' home. Catherine occupies an unusual space within her context. She was not a beguine, though she functioned more like one than a typical cloistered nun of the era. She was officially involved with the Dominican Order, but she was out in the world. This liminal space proved pivotal for her future influence and fame.

Three years after joining the Dominicans, her biographer tells us she heard a voice urging her into the world against her own protests. This is a point when we should consider Raymond of Capua's agenda in the writings. It is entirely possible this is what happened, but it must be considered that Raymond was using this divine revelation to justify Catherine's entrance into public society while also maintaining culturally accepted gender roles. Catherine began to engage in acts of charity, cultivated a reputation of holiness, and gained a group of followers, both men and women.

To understand the next period of Catherine's life, a brief examination of the state of the papacy during this period is necessary. Due to the political instability in Italy and an increased alliance between the papacy and the French, Pope Clement V moved the location of the papal residence to Avignon in 1308. Technically the city was still located within the papal states, but it undoubtedly put the pope further within the French realm of influence. This relocation lasted through six papacies and seven decades. Unsurprisingly this relocation added to the deteriorating relationships with other countries, which resented the close association between the pope and France.

In 1370, a new pope, Gregory XI, was elected. The same year Catherine had an intense mystical experience where she lay so still for four hours that her followers believed she had died. Upon waking up she set on a campaign to bring the pope back to Rome. In 1376 she negotiated a peace between the pope and the city of Florence, which was critical in creating the circumstances that preceded his return to Rome. It is necessary to highlight how remarkable this moment truly was. A woman, the daughter of a tradesman no less, negotiated a peace between one of the most powerful people in the world and a powerful city. Despite some bumps in the road, eventually the pope did return to Rome in 1377. Unfortunately, the victory was short-lived. Gregory died about a year after his return, which led to a papal schism.

Catherine died a mere three years after the pope's return to Rome. She left behind 380 letters and a devotional work called *Treatise on Divine Providence*. She was canonized a century later, and she was declared a doctor of the church in 1970. Her legacy, however, has been particularly powerful. Not only have her writings remained popular throughout the ages, but she has also frequently been a powerful witness and example for other religious women. Her ability to occupy both a religious and a political space is also significant. One cannot merely look at Catherine as a Catholic mystic—she was an influential political figure of her day, and this is intrinsic to understanding her as a historical figure.

Julian of Norwich

We do not even know the real name of the anchoress and mystic known as Julian of Norwich (1343–after 1416), who was born four years before Catherine of Siena in far-off England. The name by which she is known was taken from the church where she lived as an anchoress: St. Julian's in Norwich, England. Yet Julian produced some of the most interesting and enduring writings of the Middle Ages. Julian is considered one of the premier mystics, and to this day people are moved and comforted by her writings. During a time in Christian history when scholastic men were dominating the creative and theological output in Europe, Julian provides a powerful and mystical alternative. She is the first known woman writer in the English language, and she and her writings have grown increasingly popular over the past hundred years or so.

Much of her life is unknown, and historians are left largely with conjecture based on her writings and her historical context. Of the few things we can confidently state from her writings, she was born in 1342 or 1343, and she was probably raised around Norwich, England. Judging from her level of education and social connections, it seems reasonable to assume she came from an affluent background. Julian lived during a very difficult point in history. She was a child when the Black Death ravaged Europe, and she lived during the Hundred Years' War between England and France. There is insufficient evidence as to what Julian's life was like prior to her revelations, but it has been the subject of scholarly debate. Some historians have argued that she had been married and had children, and others argue that she was already a Benedictine nun at the time of her visions. It is certainly plausible that she had been married, and considering the plague and wars, it is entirely possible she lost her husband and any children she may have had. It is also equally plausible that she devoted her life to God at a young age and entered a monastic house instead of marrying; we simply do not have enough evidence to say definitively either way. What we do know is that when she was thirty years old, she experienced an intense illness, which she had prayed for in her youth, that precipitated sixteen visions or "showings." The visions were primarily about God's love for humanity, and she wrote two texts concerning them: the first is a shorter text titled *A Vision Shown to a Devout Woman*, and the second is titled *A Revelation of Love*, which is a longer expanded version of the visions. The overarching themes of Julian's visions are love and comfort. One better-known example occurs in the fifth chapter of *A Revelation of Love*. God shows her something the size of a hazelnut lying in the palm of her hand. He explains that *it is all that is made*. When she wonders how something so small could last, God explains, "It will last forever for God loves it. And so shall all things that are loved by God."[43]

Evidence suggests Julian became an anchoress later in life, probably around the age of fifty. There are a number of extant wills leaving Julian money, which suggests she was enclosed for twenty years or so; these bequests also suggest something of Julian's reputation and fame as an anchorite. While she was enclosed in her cell, she was also located in a

---

43 Julian of Norwich, "A Revelation of Love," in *The Writings of Julian of Norwich: A Vision Showed to a Devout Woman and a Revelation of Love*, eds. Nicholas Watson and Jacqueline Jenkins (University Park: The University of Pennsylvania, 2006), 139. I translated the phrase from Middle English for ease of reading.

busy neighborhood in one of England's larger cities. She received guests, and she was likely more exposed to the world than one would assume from her description as an anchoress. Outside of the wills and her own writings, there is a fascinating reference to Julian in *The Book of Margery Kempe*. Kempe was a married mother who also experienced divine visions around the same time as Julian. Kempe visited Julian around 1413 to discuss her visions with the famed anchorite. According to the book, Julian was a source of encouragement for Margery.[44]

Julian was never canonized, but she remains an influential and inspirational figure. What is so remarkable about her writings is how beautiful and hopeful they are despite the suffering that Julian experienced in her own life. She lived during an age defined by violence and disease, yet her words showcase God's love and care for creation. She preached a message of comfort and reassurance in the darkest of times. By far her most famous quote speaks to those sentiments: "All shall be well, and all shall be well, and all manner of things shall be well."[45]

Joan of Arc

Joan of Arc (d. 1431) is unlike any of the other women covered in this chapter; in fact, she is quite unique in history. She was neither a nun nor a beguine—she won fame on the battlefield. Burned as a heretic, she is a canonized saint. She is one of the most famed heroes of France, she has been the subject of many histories, stories, and works of art, and she has long captured the imaginations of countless people. She was born in one of the more tumultuous periods in French history. France was at a low point in the Hundred Years' War with England, and the country was pushed into a civil war when the king, Charles VI, also known as Charles the Mad, died without a clear heir apparent—the claimants were his son, the dauphin Charles, and his grandson, the infant English king Henry VI. While his supporters declared him king and he took the name Charles VII, the dauphin was not crowned and had little chance of claiming the throne—that is, until he met the teenage girl claiming to be on a divine mission.

Joan of Arc was born around 1412 to a peasant family in Domrémy in northwest France. At the age of thirteen Joan had started hearing voices she claimed were Archangel Michael and Saints Catherine and Margaret, and these voices told her she had a mission to save France from the English. She said that she would have the dauphin crowned at Rheims (the traditional place of crowning French kings). She faced a theological inquiry, and the bishops who examined her determined the voices to be authentic. Shortly thereafter, she joined the French army, where she soon served as a commanding officer. She is credited with breaking the English siege at Orleans, which turned the tide of the war. Joan stood nearby as the dauphin was crowned king in Rheims. The French, tired of civil war, rallied to their new king.

---

44 Nicholas Watson and Jacqueline Jenkins, eds., *The Writings of Julian of Norwich: A Vision Showed to a Devout Woman and a Revelation of Love* (University Park: The University of Pennsylvania, 2006), 4–6.

45 Julian of Norwich, "A Revelation of Love," 209.

The king continued to have Joan fight in the army, and she was captured by the English the following year. She was turned over to an ecclesiastical court in the English-controlled region of France called Rouen. This court found her guilty of heresy based on her claims of religious visions and for dressing as a man (she wore full armor into battles as any soldier would). She officially repented for her alleged heresy but then recanted because she said had been rebuked by Catherine and Margaret for recanting. In the end, she was burned at the stake in 1431 for the crime of wearing men's clothing. It was the end for Joan, but it was not the end of her story. Twenty-five years later, the pope reopened her case, and she was found to be innocent. Over time, she became a national hero in France, and in 1920 she was canonized, though it is worth noting that she was considered a saint by many long before her canonization.

Like many of the other women in this chapter, she used divine guidance to step outside of her prescribed gender role. However, her call was unique. Saints rarely claim divine inspiration for a military mission. She won an important battle in a long and grueling war and is credited with having the dauphin finally crowned king of France, but the fascination with Joan goes beyond simply what she was able to accomplish in her short life. There are many military commanders who have successfully broken sieges and not claimed a prominent place in history or become national heroes. She did not bring an end to the Hundred Years' War, which raged on until 1475, nor did she bring an end to the civil conflicts within France. It was her unexpected status (a young woman of peasant class) combined with her success on the battlefield and her tragic and unjust death that propelled her to the level of fame she now has. Much is often made of the criminal charges leveraged against her style of dress to prove the misogyny of her captors. It is true that sentencing a woman to death for wearing men's clothing is a ridiculous charge. However, it must be considered that she was charged by her enemies—not her allies. Most of her captors were indeed French, but they were enemies of Charles VII, whom she had helped crown king. She was tried as a heretic because the theologians at the University of Paris, who had turned against Charles VII, had requested it. The benefits of a heresy conviction were twofold for her enemies: it would undermine her claims at direct communication with God, and it would also discredit Charles VII. In many ways, she was a victim of the circumstances of her times: the civil unrest in France, the endless wars with England, the unjust process of Inquisition trials, the intertwining of religion and politics, and cultural assumptions of what a successful military commander should look and act like. Regardless, there is little doubt future generations will continue to be fascinated by the Maid of Orleans.[46]

---

46 Francois Michaud-Fréjaville, "St. Joan of Arc," in *Women in the Middle Ages: An Encyclopedia*, vol. 2, eds. Katharina M. Wilson and Nadia Margolis (Westport, CT: Greenwood, 2004), 96–98.

CHAPTER 5

Women in the Protestant and Catholic Reformations (1500s)

> Then with many tears, we took off their veils and belts and the white skirts, and put little shirts on them and worldly belts, and headdresses on their heads. I led them with a few sisters into the chapel, where we waited probably an entire hour before the wild she-wolves rode up in two carriages. . . . They sent the two men to me, Sebald Pfinzing and Endres Imhoff, who had been ordered by a councilor as I had bid to serve as witnesses. I did not want to do it; I did not want to treat the matter secretly. I said that if they were in the right, then they should not be ashamed. I would not give the sisters back at any other spot than where I had taken them in, that was, through the chapel door.
>
> —Pirckheimer, "Denkwürdigkeiten"

Abbess Caritas Pirckheimer of the Klarakloster in Nuremberg penned these words to describe the moment she returned three of her sisters to their families who had embraced Reformation sentiments. What would have been unimaginable when Pirckheimer became abbess years earlier had become a reality. Nuns were leaving the monastic life, sometimes of their own free will; other times they were forcibly taken by their families, who no longer supported the Catholic Church. When contemplating the emptying of convents during the Reformation, it is easy to gloss over the human experience of leaving a life behind that one never expected to leave—whether for good or ill.

The Reformation era is rightfully remembered as a time of theological creativity, but as demonstrated by the above quote, it was also a time of disruption and uncertainty. New ideas, both religious and secular, were rocking society, and the world was changing. There are always points of hardship in a massive societal transformation such as this. These changes and disruptions influenced the lives of women just as much as they influenced the lives of men, the only difference being that women had less control over the direction in which the world was headed. Some women embraced Reformation ideas, and others rejected them, but all were influenced by them.

This chapter focuses on the varying ways in which women participated in, influenced, and were influenced by the Protestant Reformation. After a brief section of pertinent historical background, the chapter begins with a survey of women who were public defenders of Reformation ideas. This includes women who wrote public defenses and engaged in the theological debates of the day. This is an admittedly small group of women, which makes their voices all the more important when constructing a historical picture of women's experiences.

Next is an exploration of the two primary roles available to European women in the sixteenth century, both nun and wife, including the newly reinstituted position of pastor's wife as a legitimate religious vocation. A closer examination of two women, Katharina von Bora and Teresa of Ávila, one a Protestant wife and mother and the other a Catholic nun, allows us to see how these roles played out in reality and how these women influenced the religious landscape around them. The final section of the chapter focuses on Mary I and Elizabeth I, sisters who were both queens but took radically different approaches to religious policy in England during the sixteenth century. Mary would be reviled in history, and Elizabeth would be critical in the shaping of the Anglican church as we know it today.

HISTORICAL BACKGROUND

The sixteenth century stands as a turning point in Western history—a moment of transition when the medieval period started giving way to modernity. There were aspects of European society that still resembled the Middle Ages, but new ideas and changes were blossoming. The Renaissance, with its focus on cultural, political, and economic "rebirth," was in full swing. Scientific discoveries, technological advances, and masterful works of art and literature were shaping a new society.

The most notable invention of the era was that of the printing press in the mid-fifteenth century. Prior to this invention, books were expensive and unobtainable for most. Now for the first time in history, books, including Bibles, became available to the people. Literacy rates climbed, in great part thanks to the Protestant Reformation's emphasis on access to scripture, which led to further technological and intellectual progress. The printing press and the printing of polemic pamphlets also made it possible to launch a *popular* revolt against the Catholic Church.

The rise of humanism put humans at the center of the universe, thus changing our relationship with the world and the divine. It was a time of global exploration, and newly discovered goods originating from the New World were making their way to Europe; the insidious transatlantic slave trade was thriving, and wealth taken from the Americas was filling the coffers of the European elite. Economically speaking, the sixteenth century predates the Industrial Revolution, but the period has been termed the "industrious revolution" by economic historian Jan de Vries to refer to the European phenomenon of "increased labor toward commercially orientated production in the 16th and 17th centuries," a move that recognizes the resonance between the eras.[1]

Despite these significant changes and advances, for most everyday Christians, life in the sixteenth century was not radically different from that in earlier centuries. Europe was a

---

1 R. Bin Wong, "Early Modern Economic History in the Long Run," *Science & Society* 68, no. 1 (2004): 86.

stratified society; peasant uprisings speak to the desperation of the times. Infant and child mortality rates were tragically high, and the plague still ravaged Europe regularly, generally killing more children than adults. Transportation from region to region was certainly possible, and people did indeed travel; however, we are still many years from the invention of trains and other methods of mass transportation. Politically, it was still the era of kings and queens, the introduction of democratic systems of government still centuries away.

Militarily, European monarchs worried about the Ottoman Turks. Their steady advancement since the fall of Constantinople in 1453 into historically Christian lands threatened the European stronghold of Christendom. By the sixteenth century, the Ottomans had inched dangerously close to Vienna. The Ottomans, while rarely primary characters in the story of the Reformation, quietly sit in the background of this tale, influencing European decisions. Charles V, the Holy Roman emperor who would contend with the Luther affair, always needed to be mindful of his constant warfare with the French and the Ottomans when making deals over religion within his realm.

The year 1517 is often viewed as the beginning of the Reformation era because it was in the fall of that year that Martin Luther, an Augustinian monk and professor of the Old Testament at the relatively new university in Wittenberg, posted his *Ninety-Five Theses*. These theses, originally meant as discussion points among the faculty, set off a series of events that would lead to the fracturing of the Western church. There had been attempts at reform both within and outside of the Catholic Church prior to 1517. John Wycliffe (1330–1384) is largely seen as a precursor to the Reformation, though he was not declared a heretic by the church until after his death. Jan Hus (1370–1415), an influential Bohemian priest, was burned at the stake after being condemned for his beliefs, but his ideas continued to influence religious affairs. Within the Catholic Church, the priest and humanist Desiderius Erasmus (1466–1536) publicly advocated for reform and an end to abuses. It would be Luther who provided the most significant challenge to the Catholic Church and Luther who would pave the way for many others to do the same.

Luther excelled at rhetoric, and the printing press allowed him to lead a popular reformation by writing to and for wide audiences, often in the German vernacular of the day. Any hope for a unified Protestant church, however, was soon dashed. As a result of the church's first mass media war, and with the doors to reform flung wide open, people armed with scripture and zeal began to question the Catholic Church *and* Luther's theology.[2] Huldrych Zwingli (1584–1531), an early Reformer in Zurich, came to different conclusions than Luther, especially regarding the sacrament of Communion. The Anabaptists questioned infant baptism, among other things, and were reviled by Catholics and most other Protestant groups alike. John Calvin (1509–1564), a second-generation Reformer, was critical in providing clear and systematic theological thinking to the Reform movement.

Despite the counterefforts of the Catholic Church and various pro-Catholic governments, Protestantism continued to grow. Eventually the divisions would lead to armed

---

2 For an in-depth examination of printing in the Reformation, see Andrew Pettegree, *Brand Luther: 1517, Printing, and the Making of the Reformation* (New York: Penguin Press, 2015).

conflicts and the dreaded wars of religion in the seventeenth century, though with centuries of secular animosity between European nations, one cannot blame these conflicts on religion alone.

WOMEN AND THE REFORMATION

In 1976, American historian Joan Kelly asked a critical question: *Did women have a Renaissance?*[3] It is reasonable to ask the same of women in the Protestant Reformation: *Did women have a Reformation?* The answer is complex. In a time that is heralded as such a pivotal point in history, all the well-known Protestant Reformers were men, and historical scholarship has focused almost exclusively on men's contributions. Recently scholars have begun to seriously look at women's impact on the Reformation, and there were some notable contributions from women despite the fact that women and men were not on equal footing at the time.

Women, however, were unquestionably *impacted* by the Reformation despite their tenuous involvement in leadership. It has been a point of scholarly debate whether the impact of the Reformation was positive or negative. On the one hand, it offered new radical theological developments: the priesthood of all believers, spiritual equality, and justification by faith alone. The Reformers wrote theological tracts in the vernacular, which meant more women could access theology at a time when Latin made access difficult for anyone but the most educated. The Reformers' attention to literacy had enormous positive ramifications for women, and women did indeed read and engage with these questions.

On a societal level, the roles of wife and mother were elevated with the rise of Protestantism. Within medieval Catholicism, monks, nuns, and priests were considered to have chosen the holier path than their married counterparts. However, Luther argued that marriage and motherhood were equally important religious vocations. Eventually he came to reject the monastic life altogether.[4] Despite those positive changes, there were losses for women when Western Christendom fractured. The rejection of the veneration of the saints and the Virgin Mary removed important female representation from the faith. Mysticism and prophecy, two areas in which women consistently had a voice, were largely rejected in favor of a faith that relied heavily on the preaching of the Word, an area that was dominated by men. The most jarring change for women, though, was the closing of monastic houses.

In the early years of the Reformation, many monks and priests embraced the reforms. It was relatively easy for these men to go out and become pastors and continue their religious vocation, albeit in a different manner. In a similar vein, there were nuns who also embraced the reforms and fled their convents. However, there was also a significant number of nuns who strongly rejected the reforms and refused to leave their convents. Some of the most vigorous protests against the Reformation came from convents.

---

3 Joan Kelly, *Women, History, and Theory* (Chicago: University of Chicago Press, 1984), 19–50.

4 Kirsi Stjerna, *Women and the Reformation* (Malden, MA: Blackwell, 2009), 23.

What caused the radically different reactions from women? It likely had to do with how they had come to live in a convent and their individual sense of religious vocation. There were instances in the late medieval age when children were forced into a monastic life by their family. For girls, perhaps the family was unable or unwilling to contract a marriage, or a dowry was too much of a financial burden. Monasteries sometimes became the dumping ground for the aristocracy's unwanted children. Katharina von Bora, who was dropped off at a convent by her father at age five, is a perfect example. It is likely she never felt called to the monastic life, and her story was that of many women living in convents.

There were women who genuinely wanted to be nuns, though. Nuns were generally better educated and better fed, and while there is no feasible way to definitively measure life expectancy between groups, it has been suggested that monastic women lived about twenty years longer than married women.[5] They would never have to deal with an abusive husband, dangerous childbirths, or the abysmal infant mortality rate. Enclosure in a monastery did not provide freedom in any modern sense of the word, but it did offer a type of lifestyle to which some women were drawn. As in previous times, nuns were still able to live in a community of women, they had modest access to education, and abbesses enjoyed a certain level of leadership and authority within their communities. The wealthier convents could be quite luxurious, and some had rather loose ideas of cloistering. Teresa of Ávila, for example, who often left her convent to visit friends and family and to work to reform her religious order, had a remarkable amount of freedom for a woman of her era.

When territories embraced Protestantism in its various forms, many nuns did not find the closing of their convents liberating—they saw the devaluation and destruction of their lifestyle. Sometimes the conflicts over closing a convent became heated. An example of a particularly ardent defender of female monasticism is that of Caritas Pirckheimer (1467–1532), whose quote opened this chapter. Pirckheimer had been sent to the Klarakloster in Nuremberg at the age of twelve. The convent was a wealthy institution that was well known for both its piety and learning. Pirckheimer, who became abbess in 1503, was an accomplished Latinist and an able administrator of her convent. Once Reformation sentiment swept Nuremberg, she was a capable defender of her community's right to continue to live as nuns. When local Protestants interrupted deliveries of basic supplies to the convent and physically assaulted the nuns, she mounted a vigorous defense. When the Protestants demanded she release the nuns from their vows, she refused, arguing that they made the vows to God and not her. Finally, the Reformer Philip Melanchthon was called in to deal with Pirckheimer's convent, and a compromise was agreed upon.[6] The convent would stay open until the last nun died (which did not happen until 1590), but they could not accept any new nuns. This deal came at a high cost to the nuns, though; they were not allowed to attend Mass, receive Communion, or make confession, which are

---

5 Ruth A. Tucker, *Katie Luther, First Lady of the Reformation: The Unconventional Life of Katharina von Bora* (Grand Rapids: Zondervan, 2017), 19.

6 Gwendolyn Bryant, "Caritas Pirckheimer," in *Women Writers of the Renaissance and Reformation*, ed. Katharina M. Wilson (Athens: University of Georgia Press, 1987): 287.

all essential parts of Catholic life.[7] Interestingly, there were some monastic women who did accept Reformation teachings but still refused to leave their convents.

In areas that embraced the Reformation, the fate of nuns varied. Some women were forced out of their convents, and others chose to leave freely. The available options for them were to return to their family of origin, move to another territory that remained Catholic, or marry. Of those who chose to marry, a number married pastors and took on the role of pastor's wife—a revived position in Western Europe for which they were exceedingly qualified. This position did not come without baggage. It had been centuries since priests had been allowed to marry in the West, and therefore, early pastor's wives dealt with an image problem—many saw them as concubines rather than wives.[8]

One of the earliest women to embrace the role of pastor's wife as a new type of ministry was Katharina Schütz Zell (1498–1562), who viewed her position as a true calling and saw herself as a ministry partner. She was also the most published female lay theologian of the era.[9]

Schütz Zell was born in 1498 in Strasbourg to a middle-class family. Her father was a craftsman, and the family was comfortable but not wealthy. Interestingly, it appears that two of her maternal relatives had been beguines in Strasbourg.[10] Schütz Zell received a basic education as a child, and then she was self-taught as she grew older. She learned the basics of Latin, and she read the lectionary, the Bible, and later many of Luther's writings. From a young age, she decided to carve out a unique path for herself. She did not want to enter a convent or marry, so she learned a trade—specifically she learned to produce tapestries and was even part of a guild. It has been suggested that she would have considered a monastic life if her family had been able to afford it, but regardless her plans changed when she converted to Protestantism, likely in 1521 or 1522. After her conversion, she decided to marry a former priest named Matthew Zell, who had become one of the pioneer Reformers in Strasbourg, in December of 1523. Significantly, this was a year and a half before Martin Luther and Katharina von Bora married. Schütz Zell was twenty years younger than her husband, but they reportedly had a good marriage, though it was not without controversy. Her husband's enemies spread rumors that he was abusive and unfaithful, but Schütz Zell defended him against these charges and wrote that he loved her and held her in great honor.

It was during their first year of marriage that Schütz Zell published two booklets: one was a letter of consolation to women in the city of Kentzingen who were suffering for their Protestant faith, and the other was a defense of clerical marriage. The following section outlines her reasons for entering into a marriage with a pastor:

---

7   Stjerna, *Women and the Reformation*, 28–29.

8   For a further examination of that, see Marjorie Elizabeth Plummer, *From Priest's Whore to Pastor's Wife: Clerical Marriage and the Process of Reform in the Early German Reformation* (Burlington, VA: Ashgate, 2012).

9   Mark Sidwell, "Did Women Have a Reformation?: The Case of Katherine Zell," *Puritan Reformed Journal* 10, no. 1 (January 2018): 140–153; Charlotte Methuen, "Preaching the Gospel through love of neighbour: the ministry of Katharina Schütz Zell," *Journal of Ecclesiastical History* 61, no. 4 (October 2010): 707–728.

10 Methuen, "Preaching the Gospel through love of neighbour," 711.

This is also a reason why I have helped the priests to establish [clerical] marriage. And the very first one here at Strasbourg occurred with God's help, for I had made up my mind not to marry. But then I witnessed the great fear, the raging opposition, and the great lewdness. When I nevertheless took a husband, I meant to give heart to and show the way to all Christians, as I hope to have done. Therefore, I also wrote a little book, in which are displayed the grounds of my faith and the reason for my marriage. Which surprised not a few people, for no one had a clue in word or deed that I intended to marry, for which reason I had the idea that I needed to offer my reasons, so far as I have learned and knowing nothing to the contrary, also moved by my husband, namely, that he entered this marriage for the honor of God and the salvation of himself and all men. I find no trace of dishonorable desire or other such feelings in him. And I have been granted neither great wealth nor other gifts that might have motivated him.[11]

She continued to write throughout her life, and over the course of thirty-four years, Schütz Zell produced prayer books, an autobiographical work, and devotional writings, and she edited a book of hymns. In addition, she wrote letters that are still available. She kept up correspondence with an impressive network of individuals, which included both John Calvin and Desiderius Erasmus; she even maintained a friendship with Caspar Schwenckfeld, an Anabaptist leader, which caused some conflicts but also speaks to her open and ecumenical spirit.[12] Notably, she also hosted other leading Reformers within her home, including both Luther and Zwingli.

During her marriage, Schütz Zell had two biological children who died very young, which caused her tremendous suffering. She strongly identified as a mother, but she did not believe that motherhood had to be tied to the immediate household or biological children. She therefore saw herself as a mother to the church at large. It is clear that she viewed her role as a mother and her vocation as a ministry partner as intertwined. As a ministry partner and the wife of one of the most prominent pastors in Strasbourg, Schütz Zell played an important role in ministering to the people of her husband's parish, a role that included caring for refugees, the sick, prisoners, and those who had been condemned to death. She was very pastoral, especially to other women, and she saw her role as a genuine calling. Even after the death of her husband, she continued her ministries, though as a widow, life was more difficult.

Another woman who embraced the life of a pastor's wife was a former nun by the name of Marie Dentière (c. 1495–1561). Her background was typical for medieval and early modern nuns—she was born into an aristocratic family and entered an Augustinian convent in Tourni, Belgium, and some sources suggest she eventually became the abbess. As a nun, she became interested in Luther's writings and converted to Protestantism

---

11 Katharina Schütz Zell, *Defending Clerical Marriage* (1524), *German History in Documents and Images*, accessed April 26, 2022, https://ghdi.ghi-dc.org/docpage.cfm?docpage_id=5313.

12 Sidwell, "Did Women Have a Reformation?," 151–152.

around 1524. According to sources, four years later she was married to a former priest of Tourni named Simon Robert with whom she would have five children. The couple lived in Strasbourg from 1520 to 1528 and likely knew a number of the key Strasbourg Reformers, and from 1525 to 1533 they lived in an area outside of Geneva where they supported William Farel's reforms. In 1533, Robert died, leaving Dentière a widow, but she married another Reformer named Antoine Froment, and the family moved to Geneva in 1535.[13]

Dentière not only embraced the role of pastor's wife but was also a fierce and vocal supporter of the Reformation. In Geneva, she led an active campaign to encourage nuns to reject celibacy, leave their convents, and embrace the Reformation just as she had years prior. Her actions led her into open conflict with the local Sisters of St. Clare. In 1535, she and some other Protestants "invaded" the convent to make sure no one was being held captive, which was not well received by the nuns who lived there. Dentière became engaged in a heated and personal battle with Jeanne de Jussie, a nun who lived in the convent. Both women penned frustrated accounts of the encounter. The truth of the matter is, they simply could not understand each other's positions, and they represent two different but prevalent positions for women during the Reformation. Dentière embraced Protestant ideas and found freedom and happiness in her life outside of convent walls, and she could not understand why women would fight to remain as she had once been. Theologically Dentière was Reformed, though not necessarily fully in line with Calvin. The Gospels were at the heart of her theology, and she believed in their liberating power for women.

In her letter to the queen of Navarre, the king of France's sister, who had evangelical leanings, Dentière writes an enthusiastic defense of women's engagement with the religious debates of the day:

> Why then is it necessary to gossip about women? Seeing that it was not a woman who sold and betrayed Jesus, but a man, named Judas. Who are they, I ask you, who have invented and contrived the ceremonies, heresies, and false doctrines on the earth, if not men? . . . If God has given graces to some good women, revealing to them something holy and good through His Holy Scripture, should they, for the sake of the defamers of the truth, refrain from writing down, speaking, or declaring it to each other? Ah! It would be too impudent to hide the talent which God has given to us, we who ought to have the grace to persevere to the end. Amen![14]

One can get a feeling for Dentière's strong personality in this short excerpt, but it also shows a thoughtful and engaged mind who was confident in her call to defend her religious beliefs.

---

13 Sujin G. Pak, "Three early female Protestant reforms' appropriation of prophecy as interpretation of Scripture," *Church History* 84, no. 1 (March 2015): 90–123.

14 Marie Dentière, "A Most Beneficial Letter, Prepared and Written Down by a Christian Woman of Tournai, and Sent to the Queen of Navarre, Sister of the King of France, Against the Turks, the Jews, the Infidels, the False Christians, the Anabaptists and the Lutherans," in *Women Writers of the Renaissance and Reformation*, ed. Katharina M. Wilson (Athens: University of Georgia Press, 1987), 278.

Despite her support of reforming, Dentière ran afoul of local leaders such as John Calvin, who seemed to find her frustratingly independent and far too vocal. However, in 1561, he asked her to write a preface to his sermon on female apparel, which she did. She remains one of the few published women Reformers, especially among the French-speaking Reformers. She chronicled firsthand accounts of the happenings in Geneva and was not afraid to criticize male Reformers. More significantly, she was one of the first women to defend Reformed theology in French.[15]

Not all women who made a mark on the Protestant Reformation were married to pastors. In fact, Argula von Grumbach (c. 1492–1568), a Protestant lay pamphleteer, was married to a Catholic. While much of her life remains unknown, historians have been able to piece together a fascinating individual who wrote bravely despite experiencing significant personal suffering as a result.

Von Grumbach was born into the wealthy and aristocratic von Stauff family in Bavaria. She lived a privileged childhood, receiving a private education, including a solid religious education. As a testament to her high-born status, at the age of fifteen or sixteen, she served as the maid-in-waiting to Kunigunde, Emperor Maximilian's sister. Despite her privileged position in society, she experienced hardships. Both of her parents died of the plague in 1509. Her uncle Hieronymus von Stauff, who became her guardian after the death of her parents, was executed for alleged political plotting in 1516. Around this time, she married Friedrich von Grumbach, a northern Bavarian landowner with whom she would have four children. Not much is known about Friedrich, but their marriage was stormy, and sources indicate he may have been physically violent. There was immense political pressure put upon him to bring her in line with Catholic teachings.

Theologically, she identified with Luther and had contact with both him and Philip Melanchthon. In 1523, she stated that she had read all that Luther had published in German.[16] She was committed to the Reformation and particularly the notion of "sola scriptura." As for her written defenses of the Reformation, there are eight surviving publications, all from 1523 and 1524, though she is best known for her open letter to the faculty of the University of Ingolstadt.

What would inspire an aristocratic woman with no formal theological training to challenge a university faculty? The Ingolstadt theologians had arrested and interrogated an eighteen-year-old student named Arsacius Seehofer who had "evangelical" tendencies. Seehofer had come to campus with new ideas and pamphlets coming out of Wittenberg. Unfortunately for the student the faculty was strongly Catholic, and Johann Eck, Luther's famed opponent at the Leipzig Debate, was even on it. In a turn of events that would never happen on a modern university campus, the student was sentenced to be executed by burning. Afterward his father stepped in, and the student's execution sentence was converted to a public recanting of his beliefs. Through this whole affair, there was shockingly little opposition to the faculty's actions, and von Grumbach, who found the situation horrifying, traveled to meet the Reformer Andreas Osiander to discuss it. In September

---

of 1523 she wrote an open letter to the university faculty publicly challenging them to prove Seehofer's heresy.

This was no fluff piece. The letter was laced with biblical references and sound arguments, and she wanted the faculty to respond to her personally. She boldly states at the end of her letter, "What I have written to you is no woman's chit-chat, but the word of God; and [I write] as a member of the Christian Church, against which the gates of Hell cannot prevail."[17] Her final lines hint that she fears they will not take her seriously because she is a woman, yet she also shows remarkable boldness in her beliefs. One certainly has to credit her for standing up for what she believed was right.

Unsurprisingly, she did not get a debate with the faculty; nor did they give any sort of public response. However, her letter was printed and caused quite a stir. In retaliation her husband lost his position, and she was the victim of slanderous tirades by a number of clergymen. However, one theologian who gained significant appreciation for her was Martin Luther. They, too, began to write letters to each other, and they even met in person. Luther viewed her as a most pious and noble woman.

Little is known about her life after her infamous letter. We know she attended the Diet of Augsburg, and after the death of her first husband, she married a man with Lutheran sympathies. There are some sources that suggest she continued to be a champion for the Reformation, though it appears she never took such a public role again.[18]

KATHARINA VON BORA LUTHER

Katharina von Bora (1499–1552), also known as Katie Luther, had an eventful life. She became a nun, and then she became a wife and mother. She was at the center of the Wittenberg Reformation, but we do not have a single one of her own thoughts on the events that unfolded. Unlike the other women discussed in this chapter, Katharina von Bora was not a religious or political leader; nor was she a Reformer. She is remembered not for her own accomplishments, though she was a capable woman, but mainly because of who she married: the most prominent and influential of all the Protestant Reformers, Martin Luther. Because of her husband, historians have a good amount of information on her life. Therefore, in our context here, she is the perfect representative for women who were inclined toward reformation and how that played out in a society where women had few options outside of a monastery or marriage.

Von Bora was born into a family of lesser nobility in Saxony. Her mother died when she was five years old; shortly thereafter her father placed her in a Benedictine cloister, which also served as a boarding school for girls. As a teenager, von Bora was moved to a Cistercian monastery where her aunt was a nun. It is a seemingly obvious point, but one

17 Argula von Grumbach, "To the University of Ingolstadt," in *Argula von Grumbach: A Woman's Voice in the Reformation*, ed. Peter Matheson (Edinburgh: T & T Clark, 1995), 90.

18 Peter Matheson, *Argula von Grumbach: A Woman's Voice in the Reformation* (Edinburgh: T & T Clark, 1995), 4–39.

worth explicitly mentioning—it was her father who chose a monastic life for his daughter; young Katharina had no choice in the matter.

There is little documented evidence as to the state of her mind while living in the Cistercian monastery, but it seems unlikely she was content with her situation. Somehow she and some of her fellow nuns gained access to Reformation ideas, and she was influenced by this new and exciting religious movement. Of course, a nun cannot simply abandon her vows, and the escape from her convent was carefully planned. She and about a dozen other nuns left monastic life behind tucked into herring barrels on a cart normally used for transporting goods to market. They arrived in Wittenberg, home to Luther and the center of the German Reformation, in April of 1523, and the Reformers suddenly found themselves in the positions of matchmakers for this group of runaway nuns.

It proved difficult to find von Bora a husband. She had been engaged to a man whose parents decided that a runaway nun was not an acceptable choice for their son; thus the engagement was called off. She later rejected at least one other suitor. Meanwhile, she had been living and serving in local households, including that of the artist Lucas Cranach. It was von Bora who suggested the match to Luther—apparently, she said she would be willing to marry either him or another Wittenberg professor by the name of Nicolaus Amsdorf. Luther and von Bora married in a small ceremony on June 23, 1525. Von Bora was twenty-five years old, and Luther was forty-one. They hosted a larger public celebration of their wedding a few days later on June 27.

It does not appear that the marriage was a love match, at least not at first. Luther claimed he married von Bora because he wanted to provide his father with more grandchildren and to spite the devil and the pope. We know nothing of von Bora's own thoughts regarding the marriage. At the age of twenty-five she was an older bride for the times, though still younger than her husband. While Luther proved to be a faithful and loving husband, he was certainly not an easy man to be married to. He was heavily involved in the Reformation, thus leaving her to run their household and finances independently. In fact, he was notoriously bad with finances, and at the beginning of their marriage, money was tight. He also suffered from health problems, especially in his older age, which likely caused von Bora stress. Not to mention, there was some serious apprehension about their marriage on the part of others.

In truth, their marriage was highly controversial. To understand how shocking the marriage between a former monk and a former nun really was at the time, a quote from Thomas More brings much, albeit biased, perspective: "Luther not only teaches monks, friars, and nuns to marry, but also being a monk, has married a nun himself and with her lives under the name of wedlock in open, incestuous lechery without care or shame." Erasmus, always one to demonstrate considerable wit, commented that the entire Luther tragedy had turned into a comedy.[19] Even Luther's own friends and allies were concerned by the turn of events. Luther's friend and co-Reformer Philip Melanchthon hoped the marriage would temper Luther; it did not. There is no indication of how von Bora's

---

19 Hans J. Hillerbrand, *The Division of Christendom: Christianity in the Sixteenth Century* (Louisville: Westminster John Knox Press, 2007), 147.

friends or family felt about the match, though it is doubtful they were much happier. Despite this rather ominous start, their marriage proved to be successful.

At the time of the marriage, Luther was still living in the Augustinian monastery, called the Black Cloister, with one other remaining monk—all of the other brothers had since left. So, it would seem von Bora was trading one monastery for another. Von Bora, however, proved to be a highly efficient and capable businessperson. She ran the Black Cloister as an inn, and soon their home was filled with students, paying guests, and, of course, guests who did not pay because Luther told them they did not have to do so. One can easily imagine the business-minded von Bora frustrated with her husband's generosity on occasion. In addition to the income from housing guests, the Black Cloister had livestock and a brewery. Luther had much to say about von Bora's skills as a brewer in particular. She also acquired farmlands and an orchard. Through their various holdings and Martin's salary, the Luthers were one of the more affluent families in Wittenberg at the time.

Together, the couple had six children: Hans in 1526, Elizabeth in 1527, Magdalene in 1529, Martin in 1531, Paul in 1533, and Margaret in 1534.[20] However, infant and child mortality rates were abysmal during the sixteenth century, and like so many other couples, von Bora and Luther lost children. Elizabeth died as an infant, and Magdalene died as a teenager; both events caused the couple tremendous heartache. From Luther's writings, we know he took an interest in caring for the children, and it seems von Bora had her husband's support in raising them. It is also clear from his writings that he loved and respected her, though he was unquestionably the head of the household and the marriage functioned within typical sixteenth-century gender roles.

Luther died in 1546, leaving von Bora a widow in her mid-forties. The time following her husband's death was difficult, and she faced financial and personal hardships. Luther, in opposition to Saxon law, explicitly stated he wanted von Bora to administer her own estate and remain in charge of their children. His wishes fell on deaf ears, and a court named guardians for both her and her children. Even more ruinous, however, was the outbreak of the Schmalkaldic War (1546–1547), in which the Protestant and Catholic states finally resorted to war over their religious differences, only months after Luther's death. Von Bora and her children had to flee Wittenberg when troops advanced on the city. In her absence, most of her holdings were destroyed, except the cloister itself, which she continued to run as an inn after she was able to return to Wittenberg. As a widow, she barely made enough to survive. Finally, in the year 1552, with the plague ravaging Wittenberg, she and her two youngest children fled south for the city of Torgua. She sustained injuries in a wagon accident and died three months later at the age of fifty-two.

Interest in von Bora is a somewhat recent phenomenon. During her marriage to Luther, many of his friends and colleagues found her domineering, and even scholars did not take much of an interest in her until the twentieth century. There are many reasons for this lack of interest in von Bora, but the most obvious may be Luther's own contradictions

---

20 James M. Kittelson and Hans Wiersma, *Luther the Reformer: The Story of the Man and this Career*, 2nd ed. (Minneapolis: Fortress Press, 2016).

toward women and marriage. In his writing, Luther was very much a man of his time. To him, the primary function of a woman was to bear children. Wives were helpmates, and they were to submit to their husband's authority.[21] While there is no doubt that he held these deeply rooted beliefs about women, his relationship with von Bora complicates this picture. Their marriage was a surprisingly equal one for that day and era. In a letter from 1534, he addressed von Bora as his dear "Lord Kethe," playing with the masculine title to address his wife. Later in a letter he complains about some bad beer he has drunk, and he says, "And I thought what good wine and beer I have at home, and in addition a beautiful lady, or should I say lord."[22] Even taking into account the somewhat teasing tone of the letters, Luther recognizes that his wife is not the typical helpmate that he lifts up in his writings. His will is an even better example of this. He trusted von Bora to run her own estate and raise their children, while society did not. For others surrounding the Luthers, von Bora's independence seemed like too much. She was not as quiet or submissive as she should have been. In today's world, these seem like positive qualities to many, but this has not always been the case.

One other complication regarding von Bora is the lack of her own writings. Von Bora is now largely seen as a female icon of the Reformation, yet we do not have any written evidence as to her own religious thoughts and beliefs. Yes, there is plenty of biographical information on von Bora provided by her husband and other legal documents, but we do not have any of her own words regarding the dramatic and world-changing events that were happening in her own home and community. It is her associations and life that speak to her beliefs, and we are left with conjecture without clear evidence from her own life. Presumably, reform propaganda influenced her escape from the monastery. It is also a reasonable assumption to say she would not have married Martin Luther had she not held reform sentiments. She was at the center of reform, and it is unimaginable that she would not have been at least a little swept up in it.

TERESA OF ÁVILA

Born in the city of Ávila in the old Spanish kingdom of Castile, Teresa de Ahumada y Cepeda (1515–1582), better known to history as Teresa of Ávila, was two years old when Martin Luther nailed his *Ninety-Five Theses* on the door in faraway Wittenberg. Her story is starkly different from Katharina von Bora's exodus from monastic life to Protestant wife and mother. Teresa instead became one of the leading figures in the Catholic Reformation. She was a monastic reformer, a writer, and a mystic. She has inspired many to lives of religious devotion, but she has also been the subject of intense debate. While many see a pious saint (and indeed she is canonized), others see a symbol of Spanish national pride, and still others question her sanity.

---

21 Susan C. Karant-Nunn and Merry E. Wiesner-Hanks, *Luther on Women: A Sourcebook* (Cambridge: Cambridge University Press, 2003), 89.

22 Karant-Nunn and Wiesner-Hanks, 188.

To understand Teresa and her life, one needs at least a basic understanding of her context and her family history. Under the reign of Ferdinand and Isabella, the Catholic Monarchs, the last Moorish stronghold of Granada fell, and the reconquest of the Iberian Peninsula was complete. Alongside this victory came an increase in the power and activity of the Inquisition. Normally the Inquisition was a tool of papal authority, but in Spain, it was placed under the authority of these zealous monarchs. In 1492, the same year Columbus landed in the Caribbean, all Jews living in territories controlled by Isabella and Ferdinand were told to convert to Catholicism or be exiled. Most Spanish Jews refused baptism, and although exact estimates are impossible to know, likely two hundred thousand Jews were forced to flee Spain. Some stayed and converted, likely tens of thousands of people. This group was called *conversos* or "new Christians." Legally they had the same rights as any other Spanish Christians, but they were under particular scrutiny from the Spanish Inquisition. There was a perennial fear these new Christians would backslide into their old ways, and therefore they had to be watched vigilantly.[23]

While this all may serve as interesting background in general, this history had a profound impact on Teresa's own family. Teresa's mother, Beatriz Dávila y Ahumada, was from an Old Christian family that happened to be one of the leading families in Ávila, but Teresa's father, Alonso Sánchez de Cepeda, had a more complicated family history. Alonso's grandfather had been a *converso*, and his father, Juan, had been convicted by the Inquisition as a Judaizer in Toledo. Because he had confessed to his alleged crimes, he was given a pardon and a relatively lenient punishment of public shaming. After the ordeal, Juan moved his family out of Toledo to Ávila, and the family began to use his wife's name of Cepeda (an Old Christian family name). Juan obtained a court document to affirm his nobility, and the family hid their Jewish roots and entered fully into the Old Christian society of Ávila without suspicion. It has been a point of scholarly debate whether or not Teresa knew about her family history, but many believe she did and that it influenced her choices in life.[24]

Teresa was the fifth of twelve children. Her two eldest siblings were from Alonso's first marriage, and she was from his second. Teresa's mother died at the age of thirty-three after the birth of her tenth child. Most of Teresa's brothers left home and headed to the Americas to make their fortunes. Teresa seemed like an unlikely candidate for the holy life despite her incredibly famous childhood attempt at martyrdom. At the age of seven she convinced one of her brothers to accompany her journey to the land of the Moors, where they could die as martyrs. They did not get far before their uncle found them and brought them home. While this tale is often told as a demonstration of her piety, it might better be used as a demonstration of the take-charge attitude that would serve her so well in life.

23　Cathleen Medwick, *Teresa of Avila: The Progress of a Soul* (London: Duckworth, 2000), 8–19.

24　Carlos Eire, *The Life of Saint Teresa of Avila* (Princeton: Princeton University Press, 2019), 4–5. I am less convinced that Teresa knew this history. Her grandfather and father had gone to great lengths to hide this, so I believe it likely they took this secret to their graves.

As a young woman she was apparently a handful. She loved romance novels and fashion. One can look at her early life and see that perhaps she was just a little too beautiful, rich, and adventurous for her own good in this society. Exasperated, her father sent her off to an Augustinian convent when she was fifteen. While she had little desire to become a nun, she did enjoy her time there. Unfortunately, after a year and a half she became very sick and had to return home. After she recovered, she entered the Carmelite Convent of the Incarnation in Ávila against her father's wishes at the age of twenty. Life at the convent likely provided her with more freedom than had she decided to marry. The Incarnation was a wealthy convent that was not strictly cloistered, and Teresa was able to come and go, visiting friends and family. She would receive visitors, and she had friends who were already nuns at the Incarnation when she joined. For a Spanish woman in the sixteenth century, this was about as much freedom as one could hope for. She entered into religious life in November of 1536 and took her final vows a year later. Again, she became ill, and by the following fall, her father had removed her from the convent and brought her to her older sister's house. By 1539 she was so sick that he took her home to Ávila to die. Seemingly, on August 15, 1539, she did indeed die. Her father was so distraught, he delayed the burial, and the family kept a vigil by her body. On the third night, one of her brothers accidently set a curtain on fire, and during the commotion, Teresa regained consciousness. While she was alive, she was bedridden and paralyzed—needing constant care. Four long years later, she was finally well enough to resume regular life, though certain ailments would plague her for the rest of her life. She spent the next twelve years in a state of rather lukewarm religiosity, until she had a radical conversion experience in 1555. From this point on, she would be a force to be reckoned with.[25]

Teresa's story is intertwined with her mystical experiences, and today this is the aspect of her life that is best known. She had miraculous encounters with the divine. She had intellectual visions that imparted her with theological knowledge. She saw Jesus, angels, demons, and the dead. She spent an excruciating few moments in hell, and she had visions of heaven. There were reports of her levitating—something she found deeply embarrassing. These levitations stopped after she prayed to God to cease this inconvenient miracle. Her most well-known mystical experience was the transverberation, which has been brought to life through various works of art, the most famous being *Ecstasy of St. Teresa* by Gian Lorenzo Bernini. During this vision, an angel pierced her heart with a flaming lance, causing her both incredible pain and pleasure. All this activity brought Teresa a good deal of fame, but it also brought concerns from the Inquisition.

She wrote her first book—her autobiography, or her *Vida*, known today as *The Life of Teresa of Jesus*[26]—because various clerical authorities wanted to examine her prayer life, her theology, and her mystical experiences in detail. Despite suspicion, the church deemed her theology orthodox and her mystical experiences legitimate. Concerned about what others would do with her writings, the Inquisition tried to keep the autobiography from

---

25 Eire, *The Life of Saint Teresa of Avila*, 15–16.

26 Teresa of Ávila, *Autobiography of St. Teresa of Ávila*, trans. and ed. E. Allison Peers (Mineola, NY: Dover Publications, Inc., 2010).

the public. Eventually, though, her autobiography was widely read and became a Catholic classic. She also wrote *The Way of Perfection* and *The Interior Castle*, both of which are important contributions to Spanish Renaissance literature.

Teresa was not just a mystic; she made her mark as a religious reformer as well. Teresa believed God was calling her to return the Carmelite Order back to its original strictness, which included a return to enclosure, poverty, and commitment to silent prayer. The nuns were to be discalced, which meant wearing sandals instead of shoes to show their commitment to poverty. One other important aspect of her reforms was to accept women of all social classes. Dowries were welcomed, but not required, and a faithful woman seeking a monastic life would not be turned away due to lack of funds. There was considerable opposition to her first monastic house in Ávila. Her commitment to absolute poverty was also a concern. However, Teresa opened the Convent of St. Joseph in 1562. After this she would spend the rest of her life establishing fourteen new Discalced Carmelite convents and two monastic houses for men. After a full and active lifetime, Teresa died at the age of sixty-seven in October of 1582. She was canonized in 1611, which extended the influence of her writings. Teresa has remained a popular saint throughout the centuries and was declared a doctor of the church in 1970.

Katharine von Bora and Teresa of Ávila make for a fascinating comparison. Both entered a life of monasticism as young women, but their paths could not have been more different. Von Bora in her German setting had access to and was influenced by Reformation literature. She fled her convent and married Luther himself. She made a life for herself, supporting herself through business ventures and raising her family. Teresa, on the other hand, became a true icon of the Catholic Reformation. It is unlikely Teresa had any direct access to any Reformation writings. However, she did pity and pray for the Lutherans, whom she believed had lost their way.

Another interesting comparison is how history has remembered each of these women. Interest in Von Bora has recently spiked, but for many years she was little more than a footnote to her much more famous husband. Her dominant personality made people uncomfortable, and her business-mindedness was perhaps too worldly. Teresa also had detractors during her lifetime and after. While she established a series of enclosed convents, she was frequently out in the world—a highly energetic and influential woman who crossed boundaries of what a proper sixteenth-century nun should be doing. On the other hand, her popularity consistently surpassed that of her detractors. An examination of her devotees throughout the years shows a winding and sometimes bizarre path. From social activist Dorothy Day to Fascist leader General Franco, her supporters are an eclectic group indeed.

In some ways, these two women were atypical of the era, but they also represent the two choices that women had in that particular time and place: marriage or monastery. For better or for worse, Protestant women lost the option of monastic life, but monasticism would continue as an important part of women's Christian history in the Catholic Church.

QUEENS OF THE ENGLISH REFORMATION

The English Reformation was remarkably different from the German one. Incredibly it had everything to do with one man's desire to annul his marriage. Henry VIII, the man who would go down in history as one of the most influential English kings, was born the spare heir. His wife, Catherine of Aragon, was the daughter of Isabella and Ferdinand of Spain. She came to England in 1501 to be married to Henry's older brother, Arthur. Five months later, Arthur died. Catherine was left a sixteen-year-old widow, and Henry found himself the heir apparent. Arthur and Catherine's marriage had been political in nature—an English–Spanish alliance cemented by marriage—and it was advantageous for both countries. This desire for an alliance did not end with Arthur's death, so it was decided that Catherine should marry Henry. There was a problem, though. Canon law forbade marriage between a widow and her brother-in-law. However, it was possible to get a papal dispensation under certain circumstances. The papal dispensation was reliant on Catherine and Arthur never having consummated their marriage. Whether they consummated their marriage is unknown. Arthur apparently bragged of his sexual exploits with his wife, but Catherine maintained to her dying day that she never slept with Arthur.

The dispensation was granted, though it seems that Henry never wanted the marriage and felt forced into it. The couple did not marry until 1509 when Henry became king at eighteen years of age. Eighteen years later, Henry would shock his wife by telling her they had never been truly married in the eyes of God and that they must separate. Proof of their marriage's cursed nature could be seen in Catherine's inability to produce a male heir. Catherine had eight pregnancies and only one surviving child, a girl named Mary. Henry had an illegitimate son, so the blame of not producing a male heir was put on Catherine, who was now past her child-bearing years.

Henry was in a tricky position in 1527, and his request for an annulment was complex. He was allowed to marry in 1509 through a papal dispensation. Eighteen years later, Henry wanted the pope to state that according to canon law there was an impediment on the marriage. Therefore, the original dispensation had to be rescinded, thus rendering his marriage invalid. There are issues that made it difficult for the pope to comply with Henry's request. First, Henry's case for why the marriage should be annulled was not particularly convincing. Second and much more seriously, he was asking the current pope to declare that his predecessor had been in error by giving a dispensation in the first place. Added to these theologically murky waters, there were some political events working against Henry's request. Charles V, the Holy Roman emperor, was Catherine's nephew, and he put political pressure on the pope to deny Henry's request. Catherine had no intention of getting out of the way either. It is worth noting that Henry never again married another woman with such powerful connections.

Pope Clement procrastinated on this decision for as long as he could, thinking this might just be a middle-aged man's infatuation with a "girl"—the girl being Anne Boleyn, the doomed young lover of the king. Henry became increasingly impatient with the pope. In 1532 he decided to deprive the pope of any English revenue; the message was clear—no annulment, no money. Then, through a series of parliamentary acts, England broke from

Rome completely, and the king became the head of the English Church. Henry and Catherine's marriage was declared invalid, and one week later a pregnant Anne Boleyn was crowned queen. Unfortunately for her, she carried a girl and not the son Henry so desperately wanted. Anne was later accused of adultery (which was almost certainly a false charge) and executed. Henry would go on to marry four more times, with his third wife finally giving birth to a son named Edward.

Henry died on January 28, 1547. He left a nine-year-old son as heir. During Edward's reign, there was a movement toward Continental Protestantism. *The Book of Common Prayer* was published, clergy were allowed to marry, the Communion cup was offered to the laity, and the government removed and/or destroyed Catholic paintings, sculptures of saints, stained glass windows, music, vestments, and so on from countless churches. Edward died at the age of fifteen, ushering in a dramatically different type of ruler: his older sister Mary.

Before we dive into the life of Mary Tudor (1516–1558), it must be noted how unusual her and later Elizabeth's ascensions to the throne were in English history. Mary and Elizabeth certainly were not the first women to have a legitimate claim to the English throne, but generally, royal daughters were married off and their claims to the throne were then transferred to their male children. This had even been the case with Mary and Elizabeth's great-grandmother, who had passed her royal claim to her son Henry VII.[27] This put both women in an unprecedented position in English history, and they each faced specific challenges to their authority because they were women.

History has not been kind to Mary Tudor. Her reign is often depicted as backward-looking and oppressive. England's last Catholic queen is remembered as a failed monarch and a cruel one at that. The story is not so simple, however. A more nuanced look at her life and reign reveals a complicated ruler who deserves a more prominent place in history. She and her government undoubtedly made mistakes, and that should be recognized, but the level of criticism leveled has been disproportionate compared to that of other monarchs of the same era. She was a fascinating person, and the study of her life and reign has much to add to the understanding of Reformation history. She was also the first woman in England to rule in her own right; that fact alone makes her a worthy subject.

Mary was the only surviving child of Henry VIII and Catherine of Aragon, but Henry was slow to acknowledge her as his heir, always hoping for the son who never came. When discussing the historic ramifications of the "king's great matter" it is easy to gloss over the child that Henry was so desperate to keep from the throne, but understanding her childhood and early adulthood provides invaluable information by which we can analyze her later choices as queen. While she was still a child, there had been marriage negotiations for Mary's hand—first to the French dauphin and then to Charles V, the Holy Roman emperor—but those agreements had fallen apart, and Mary remained single until after she became queen.

27 J. L. McIntosh, *From Heads of Household to Heads of State: the Preaccession Households of Mary and Elizabeth Tudor, 1516–1558* (New York: Columbia University Press, 2013), loc. 16 of 415, EPUB.

Interestingly, on a personal level, Henry demonstrated significant affection for Mary, but his affections did not persuade him from his determined plans for a male heir. Mary was about eleven years old when her father began to fight for an annulment, and she was seventeen when Henry finally divorced Catherine, married Anne Boleyn, and had Mary declared illegitimate. This meant that Mary went from being the recognized heir to a status of the king's "natural" child. Once Elizabeth was born, Elizabeth was immediately declared the heir to the throne. This may seem odd since Henry had just replaced one girl for another at this point, but there was a political reason. The Catholic Church did not recognize Elizabeth, or any future children of Anne's, as legitimate, and neither did many Catholic countries. Therefore, it was imperative that Henry establish any children of Anne as the legitimate heirs, anticipating the future birth of a boy. Of course, Anne fell victim to Henry's wrath and would have no more children. Soon Elizabeth would join Mary in her designation as illegitimate in 1536.

Throughout her trials, Mary found comfort in her Catholic faith. Her devotion to Catholicism went beyond personal preference, though. The Catholic Church maintained that she was the true heir to the English throne, and rejecting the faith made little sense for any future ambitions to become queen. In addition, there was inevitable resentment toward Protestantism, the faith that had allowed her father to divorce her mother and declare her illegitimate. This commitment to Catholicism would become one of the major criticisms of her reign.

Despite declaring them illegitimate, Henry did reestablish both Mary and Elizabeth as heirs to the throne with the Third Act of Succession in 1544 behind his son Edward. Edward tried to subvert this by removing his two sisters once again from the line of succession and designating a Protestant cousin, Jane Gray, as his heir. However, following Edward's death, support for Mary grew very quickly, and she was able to seize the throne, and Gray was later executed. Mary rode into London with Elizabeth at her side and became queen at the age of thirty-seven.

Mary saw her foremost task as queen to be the reestablishment of Catholicism in England. Her partner in her quest was Cardinal Reginald Pole. An accomplished man, Pole had presided over the opening sessions on the Council of Trent;[28] he had been active in the Italian Catholic Reformation, and he was nearly elected pope in 1549.[29] He had been exiled during Henry's reign but returned to England once Mary became queen. He became Mary's trusted confidant and later the last Catholic to hold the position of archbishop of Canterbury. After decades of Protestantism, though, the English were not enthusiastic about once more embracing the Catholic faith.

One of the biggest issues in England's return to Catholicism was that of the church lands that had been seized under Henry's reign. The Catholic Church wanted the lands returned to the church, but this proved complex, and once it was established that formal

---

28 The Council of Trent was the nineteenth ecumenical council of the Roman Catholic Church and was held in three parts between the years 1545 and 1563. The council was prompted by the Reformation and is well known for its decrees of self-reform and for its dogmatic definitions that clarified points of Catholic theology in response to Protestant challenges. It is considered one of the most important church councils in history.

29 Eamon Duffy, *Fires of Faith: Catholic England under Mary Tudor* (New Haven: Yale University Press, 2009), 9.

restitution of Catholicism did not depend on the return of the church lands, Parliament and wealthy landowners were amenable to an official return to Catholicism. In November of 1554, England officially rejoined the Catholic Church. This, however, did not mean a popular acceptance of Catholicism, and soon after, the persecutions began.

More than 280 Protestants were burned in under four years from 1555 to 1558.[30] In the sixteenth century, when executions were common and religious differences were often punished by burning, her persecutions were not entirely unusual, though they were intense. Burning someone alive for their religious beliefs is never a defendable action, though unfortunately in this era it was far too common. Both her father and sister had more people executed during their reigns, but their reigns were also significantly longer. There were prominent victims, such as Thomas Cranmer, but most of the executed were regular people. Unsurprisingly, the persecutions did little to endear the English people toward Catholicism. John Foxe brought these persecutions to life with a history of Christian martyrs, including those killed under Mary, called *Foxe's Book of Martyrs*.[31] This book was wildly popular and kept the horrors of the persecutions fresh in people's minds long after they ended.

After a reign of only five years, Mary died in November 1558 at the age of forty-three. There were few who mourned her death or the end of her reign. It is interesting to note that Reginald Pole died the same day. Since she never had the children she had so desperately wanted, Mary proclaimed, rather reluctantly, Elizabeth as heir.

Without question, Mary made blunders during her reign. It seems likely Mary did not understand how Protestant England had become in the years since her father broke with Rome. Perhaps if she and Pole had accepted help from the Jesuits and instigated an active Counter-Reformation effort on the ground, they would have been more successful in changing the hearts and minds of the people. Instead, it was Catholicism that was enforced from the top down, and the people were not interested. Another problem with her reign was simply the length of it. While her father and sister had long reigns, she held the throne for a mere five years, and those five years were simply not long enough to truly make a difference. Elizabeth would be the one to steer England to its Protestant future, and Mary would become known to future generations as "Bloody Mary."

Elizabeth (1533–1603) came to the throne in 1558 at the age of twenty-five, and over the next forty-five years she would prove to be one of England's greatest monarchs. Like her older sister, she faced hardships in her childhood, but unlike Mary, she rose to the demands of ruling, and England became a stronger nation under her reign. Her religious leanings were Protestant, but she was a politician, not a religious zealot. After decades of religious turbulence, this proved to be what the country desperately needed.

The most pressing problem Elizabeth faced when she came to power was that of religion. During Mary's reign she had acted as a good Catholic, even going as far as requesting Catholic books and engaging Catholic theologians in conversation. Her true religious

---

30 Duffy, *Fires of Faith*, 7.

31 John Foxe, *Foxe's Book of Martyrs Or A History of the Lives, Sufferings, and Triumphant Deaths of the Primitive Protestant Martyrs* (Chicago: The John C. Winston Co.), 204–298, https://www.gutenberg.org/files/22400/22400-h/22400-h.htm.

intentions became apparent as soon as she became queen. She had largely been raised by Protestants, and this was probably her natural inclination, but just as it was politically necessary for Mary to be Catholic, it was necessary for Elizabeth to be Protestant. As Anne Boleyn's daughter, the Catholic Church considered her illegitimate. Then there was the simple fact that Catholicism had not reestablished itself during Mary's reign. Mary's persecutions had soured the public even further against the faith. Simply put, after decades of religious turmoil the people were tired of it. Protestantism seemed the best path forward, but what type of Protestantism remained the question.

The intricacies of Parliament and the various acts that brought about England's return to Protestantism are beyond the scope of this investigation, but by 1559, the Act of Supremacy undid Mary's repeal of all of Henry VIII's ecclesial legislation. Mary's submission to Rome was also rescinded—once again England was Protestant. There were some changes to Henry's legislation, most notably regarding the role of the monarch. Elizabeth was to be the "Supreme Governor, as well in all spiritual causes, as in temporal," whereas Henry had been the "Supreme Head on Earth under Christ of the Church."[32] Functionally speaking, they were acting in a similar capacity, but the new title lacked the theological significance of the old. The obvious reason for such a change was that England was not ready to have a woman be declared the head of the church. The implication of Elizabeth's title was that she was a partner with Parliament in spiritual matters.

The introduction of the Thirty-nine Articles in 1563 added definition to the settlement in 1559. Elizabeth appointed Matthew Parker as the archbishop of Canterbury; incredibly Parker had survived the winds of religious change through the reigns of Henry, Edward, and Mary. The Church of England embraced a moderate form of Protestantism. Above all else, the religious direction Elizabeth took the Church of England in can be seen as practical, and it proved to be a successful solution to the problem of religion. Though Catholics and more Reformed Protestants would both object to the settlement, there was a flexibility and moderation that appealed to most English people.

Elizabeth was a successful queen, a fact even her political enemies conceded. Interestingly we have a remarkable comment from Pope Sixtus V that speaks volumes about her abilities: "She certainly is a great queen and were she only Catholic she would be our dearly beloved. Just look at how she governs; she is only a woman, only mistress of half an island, and yet she makes herself feared by Spain, by France, by the Empire, by all."[33] As a Protestant, she may not have been their beloved, but it is clear they respected her nonetheless.

---

32 Hans Hillerbrand, *The Division of Christendom: Christianity in the Sixteenth Century* (Louisville: Westminster John Knox Press, 2007).

33 Walter Walsh, *The Jesuits in Great Britain: An Historical Inquiry into their Political Influence* (New York: George Routledge and Sons, 1903), 111.

CHAPTER 6

Women in Colonial America (1500–1750)

At the end of the fifteenth century, a certain Genoese sailor approached Isabella and Ferdinand of Spain, styled as the Catholic Monarchs, with a plan to reach Asia without having to use Muslim-controlled trade routes. His plan to sail west seemed dubious, but the zealous queen took a chance on him and his plan. Columbus never found a direct water route to Asia, but he did stumble upon the Americas—a moment that marks the beginning of centuries of exploration, exploitation, and colonization; a moment that would have a profound impact across the globe.

Soon other European nations joined in the scramble to control these distant lands. The cost of the conquests was high. Countless lives were lost, and cultures were destroyed. Much of European interest in the Americas was based in economic endeavors, but some European migrants made their way to spread Christianity, create new religious communities, or seek out religious freedom.

This chapter examines women and religion in the New World in the colonial era; however, experiences varied widely depending on social and physical location. All over the Americas there was a profound mixing of cultures, and race, social class, and status of either free or enslaved had deep impacts on how a woman experienced the world. In Latin America, Catholicism quickly became the dominant religious expression. In religiously diverse North America, especially the territories that became the United States, a variety of Christian faiths came together to create a predominantly Protestant society.

Due to the profound differences in life between Latin America and what would later become the United States and Canada, the chapter is broken into two sections based on location. In the first part, Latin America, with its strongly Iberian influences, is considered. Beginning with the impact of Columbian contact, themes include the emergence of a uniquely American form of Catholicism; life and experiences for women in a variety of social locations including Indigenous women, Black women, and European women; the emergence of Latin American monasticism; and the impact of lay leaders called *beatas*.

In the second half of the chapter, North America, particularly the English-controlled Eastern Seaboard, is examined. After a brief section of historical background, the experiences of American Indians, Puritan, and Quaker women are explored. General themes include colonization, the clashing of cultures, religious freedom, gender inequality, women's leadership, and religious persecution within the British-controlled colonies.

LATIN AMERICA

Historical Background

The world profoundly changed that day the Spanish landed in the Americas. There was a massive transference of agriculture and disease and a mass migration of peoples following Columbian contact. There was also a transference of religion, specifically Christianity from Europe to colonial Latin America. It was no gentle evangelism that brought Christianity to the Americas. The Spanish and Portuguese arrived with the cross *and* the sword. They brought a particular type of Christianity—a brand of Catholicism that had been profoundly shaped by the *Reconquista* in which faith, violence, and nationalism became intertwined in unprecedented ways. The church and state were unusually connected; the agreement known as *patronato real* or royal patronage gave the Spanish and Portuguese almost complete control over the Catholic Church in their conquered lands. The brutality by which Christianity was brought does not mean that the Spanish soldiers and friars were not sincere in their desire to convert; many were profoundly religious. However, sincerity cannot be confused with benevolence; nor does sincerity in motive make an action good or life-giving. There were far too many brutal wrongs committed in the name of religion during and following the conquest of the Americas.

The story of colonial Latin America is a story of contradiction—faith and violence; gospel and oppression; the hierarchical church and the faith of the people. Yet through this contradictory process, Christianity took root in the Americas. It was transformed from its Iberian form into something uniquely American. Today 40 percent of the world's Catholics live in Latin America, and Protestant and charismatic forms of Christianity are spreading quickly. A testament to the influence and importance of the Latin American Church can be seen in the election of the first Latin American pope, Francis, in 2013. The creation and expansion of liberation theology on a global scale is further proof of the profound influence Latin American Christianity has had on the world. Any serious study of Christianity today must include Latin America, and for us here, that means an examination of women in the Latin American context.

Columbian Contact

There is no easy or simple way to summarize the experiences and faiths of the numerous and disparate groups of peoples who lived in Latin America prior to Columbian contact. Indigenous societies ranged from nomadic tribes to large and complex empires. Religious expression varied immensely, though most societies were polytheistic. The arrival of the Spanish was devastating to the Indigenous populations of the Americas, and the Iberian conquest was swift. The Spanish came to control large swaths of land in South and Central America and a significant portion of the Caribbean, and their influence reached into North America. Portugal, which focused much of its colonization efforts on Africa and Asia, claimed what would become Brazil.

Europeans did have superior weapons, but the biggest factor in their military success was pestilence. Europeans brought with them a host of diseases, such as smallpox, influenza, measles, and malaria, that decimated the native population. Without any sort of scientific understanding of disease, many people, both Indigenous and European, believed the pestilence was divine punishment for the native populations.

The loss of life, caused by a combination of disease, enslavement, overwork, and mass suicide, was so severe that Europeans began transporting enslaved Africans to the Americas as early as the beginning of the sixteenth century to replace the lost Indigenous labor. Thus began the transatlantic slave trade, one of the most devastating and tragic events of human history. What emerged in Latin America was a diverse but highly stratified hierarchy based on race. Europeans born in Europe, called *peninsulares*, were at the top of this social hierarchy and Indigenous people and Africans on the bottom. This hierarchy permeated all aspects of society, including the church.[1]

The religious structure in colonial Latin America was unique. Ondina and Justo Gonzalés describe the Latin American Church as having two faces. The dominant church face justified the conquest and exploitation of the American Indian peoples in the name of evangelization. The other face of the church was one of protest against these injustices.[2] Often, though not always, these two faces were segregated by church function, the secular (parish priests and church hierarchy) and the regular (clergy belonging to religious orders such as the Franciscans, Dominicans, Jesuits, and so on).[3] Through royal patronage, the church hierarchy was appointed by the Spanish and therefore was overwhelmingly loyal to the Spanish crown. The friars, who primarily came to evangelize, lived and worked more closely with the American Indian and African populations and tended to be more sympathetic to their suffering. Two prime examples of this side of Christianity are Dominican Bartolome de las Casas, who spent a significant portion of his life crisscrossing the Atlantic fighting for American Indian rights, and Jesuit Pedro Claver, who devoted his life to serving enslaved Africans in the port city of Cartagena in what is now Colombia. The tension between the two faces of Christianity permeates this history.

A Uniquely American Catholicism

As is the way when missionizing a land, there was transference and then *transformation* of both belief and culture. European missionaries, understanding the necessity of presenting Christianity in an accessible manner, went about learning the language and culture of the Indigenous peoples. Already by the mid-sixteenth century, missionaries had written books on native languages, cultures, and history. Missionaries also began a process of translating alien Christian concepts into more relatable language for those they were wishing to convert. Through this process, new converts made Christianity their own. The Virgin of Guadalupe is one of the most prominent symbols of this new Latin American Catholicism.

---

1   The racial hierarchy was broken into roughly five categories: *peninsulares*, Creoles, mestizos, American Indians and mixed-raced peoples, and people of African descent. Generally, the darker one's skin, the lower they sat on the societal hierarchy.

2   Ondina E. Gonzalés and Justo Gonzalés, *Christianity in Latin America: A History* (Cambridge: Cambridge University Press, 2008), 3–5.

3   To avoid confusion on these terms, it is helpful to understand the root of each. The term "regular" does not mean ordinary, but rather it derives from the Latin word *regula* or set of rules—so regular clergy lived according to the particular set of rules provided by their order. "Secular" comes from the Latin word *saeculum*, which means to be in the world—secular clergy lived in the world, not in monasteries.

The legend goes like this: On December 9, 1531 (about ten years after the Spanish conquered the Aztec capitol city of Tenochtitlan), the Virgin Mary appeared to a native man named Juan Diego on Tepeyac Hill, which is just outside Mexico City. She spoke to Juan Diego in his native language of Nahuatl and told him to go to Bishop Zumár-raga and tell him that she wanted a shrine built in her honor. The bishop did not believe Juan Diego and refused to build the shrine. The Virgin appeared two more times to Juan Diego, and eventually the bishop told Juan Diego that he needed a sign if he were to comply with this request. In the early morning of Tuesday, December 12, 1531, the Virgin made her fourth appearance to Juan Diego. This time she ordered him to collect roses, which were out of season, in his tilma (a type of cloak made of cactus fibers). Juan Diego took the roses to the bishop, and when he opened his cloak, dozens of roses fell to the floor, and his cloak had an image of the Virgin Mary imprinted on the inside. The image incorporated both Catholic and Aztec symbols, and Mary's skin was notably dark. The bishop had the shrine built, right on the hill once dedicated to the Aztec mother god-dess. For the Spanish, the Virgin's appearance affirmed their evangelization efforts, and for the Indigenous communities, her appearance demonstrated her commitment to them.[4] The Virgin of Guadalupe is not just a religious symbol; she has become an icon in Mex-ican history, art, literature, and popular culture. In 1808, Father Miguel Hidalgo carried her image into battle at the outbreak of Mexico's struggle for independence. In the 1970s César Chávez carried her image as he and his movement fought for basic economic and political rights for migrant farm workers. In the words of Octavio Paz, "the Virgin is the consolation of the poor, the shield of the weak, the help of the oppressed. In sum, she is the Mother of orphans."[5]

Interestingly, Guadalupe is not the only important Marian image in the Americas. The Virgin of Caridad del Cobre is an important symbol in Cuba; Our Lady of Copacabana became the patroness of Bolivia; and Our Lady of Aparecida is the principal patroness of Brazil. Each of these appearances signifies a moment of a uniquely Latin American expression of the faith.

Women in Latin America

The experiences of Latin American women varied based on race, class, and location, though some generalizations can be made. Life for Indigenous women during conquest and colonization was disruptive. Everywhere in the Americas there were dramatic declines in population. The original inhabitants of the Caribbean islands disappeared almost com-pletely, and an estimated 50 to 90 percent of the Indigenous population in Mexico died. In Peru, eighty-two million people died from about 1540 to 1800.[6] The deaths were largely a result of the disease, overwork, and general brutality inflicted upon them by the Europeans.

4 Gonzalés and Gonzalés, *Christianity in Latin America*, 55–56.

5 Octavio Paz, "The Sons of La Malinche," in *Labyrinth of Solitude*, trans. Lysander Kemp (New York: Grove Atlantic Press, 1994), 88.

6 Teresa A. Meade, *A History of Modern Latin America: 1800 to the Present* (Malden, MA: Wiley-Blackwell, 2010), 27.

In addition to the profound loss of life, European invaders began to enforce Christian beliefs and fundamentally restructure society. Some women were killed, others were enslaved, and some were able to successfully integrate into this new European-dominated society. Countless Indigenous women were indeed victims of sexual violence, but others had consensual relations with Europeans. The most famous early relationship between a Spanish man and an American Indian woman is that of Hernán Cortés and Malintzin (also known as La Malinche), who was enslaved and acted as one of his advisors during Cortés's conquest of Mexico. She was also his lover and the mother of his firstborn son. Her legacy has been complicated to say the least.

There were numerous American Indian women who actively fought against the conquest and colonization, some through resistance efforts and others through military force. Micaela Bastidas (1744–1781) was an active military leader against Spanish rule in South America and is considered a martyr for Peruvian independence. As a testament to the involvement of women in the resistance, when the Spanish finally defeated the rebel troops in Peru and Bolivia in 1782, they found that out of the seventy-three rebel leaders, thirty-two were women. All thirty-two were executed.

Like Indigenous women, women of African descent were marginalized in colonial Latin America. Most were brought to the Americas as slaves, generally from West Africa, and they took with them a variety of different cultures and religions that would come to influence Latin American society. It is critical to understand that this was a society that was built on slave labor and that millions of people were forcibly taken to the Americas. A slave's experience varied depending on location. In the Caribbean women worked side by side with men on plantations. In South and Central American cities, they largely had domestic roles, such as those of cook, servant, and laundress. They frequently ran errands in public, acting as the contact between their enclosed female owner and the world. Like enslaved women in so many times and cultures, they were at much higher risk of sexual violence, and they had few protections from abuse from their owners.

The story of European women is different from that of their Indigenous and African counterparts. Most of the initial conquest and colonization of Latin America was done by European men, though there are some notable exceptions. Inés de Suárez (1507–1580), a famed *conquistadora*, came to the Americas looking for her husband only to find he was already dead. She was able to procure a small *encomienda*, and she worked as a baker and a water finder.[7] She later became the mistress of a high-ranking officer in Pizarro's army and accompanied him on the exploration and conquest of Chile. Suárez gained a reputation as a skilled fighter and eventually married the royal governor of Chile.[8] Another notable *conquistadora* was Cataline de Eruaso (1492?–1560), who at the age of fifteen escaped her convent in Spain, disguised herself as a man, and made her way to America. She lived an anonymous life as a mercenary and adventurer until she was arrested for killing a man in a duel and it was discovered she was a woman. However, instead of being punished, she

---

7 An *encomienda* was a grant by the Spanish Crown to American colonists giving them the right to demand tribute and forced labor from Indigenous peoples. While technically not slavery, it functioned similarly.

8 Teresa A. Meade, *A History of Modern Latin America*, 26.

became quite famous and even had an audience with the pope, who did remind her of the commandment not to kill.[9]

Suárez and Eruaso are fascinating examples of women who participated in the conquest, but they are the exception—not the norm. It is estimated that women constituted no more than 6 percent of Spanish immigrants to the Americas in the first decade and only 10 percent of all colonists who came in the first thirty years. Of the few women that did come, most were traveling with their families, though a significant portion were servants.[10] Over time, the number of Iberian women immigrating to the Americas increased. By the 1550s, European-born women were a substantial presence in the Spanish colonies. By the end of the sixteenth century women made up 28 to 40 percent of immigrants, though this number again dropped in the eighteenth century. It is estimated that about 2,900 Spanish women immigrated each year between 1500 and 1700. Brazil had only about five hundred Portuguese women arriving each year during the same period.[11]

Why would Iberian women leave their homes in Spain or Portugal for the Americas? Many were wives or relatives of the initial conquistadors and settlers. Because the church and culture equated marriage with a stable society, colonial governments encouraged European men to call their wives to the colonies; however, this had varying success, with some men opting to conveniently forget about certain attachments back in Europe. For women, the possibility of marriage in a setting where men greatly outnumbered women increased their odds of making an advantageous marriage match. We also should not discount a sense of adventure.

Visibility in society and business generally increased as women went down the socioeconomic ladder. Wealthy white women were the most secluded—either in the home or in a convent. This seclusion did not prevent them from engaging in business, though wealthy women may have had a male relative act for them within the public sphere. It was also not unusual for wealthier women to open their homes to boarders or send slaves to earn wages if they needed additional income. This was especially common in the case of widows. Middle-class women also tried to stay out of public life, but they often worked with their spouses in family businesses or, in the case of widows, continued the family business after their husband passed. Women who lacked financial resources generally worked and supported themselves.

Monastic Houses for Women in Colonial Latin America

Since monasticism was such an important element of European Christianity, it did not take long for the Spanish to establish convents in the Americas. The process of approval was long and difficult, involving permission from both the pope and the Crown (a process made only more arduous considering the distance of the Americas), so often colonists went ahead and established the convents before getting approval. This was the case with the first convent built in the Americas, Nuestra Señora de la Concepción in Mexico City,

---

9 Susan Migden Socolow, *The Women of Colonial Latin America*, 2nd ed. (Cambridge: Cambridge University Press, 2015), 174.

10 Socolow, *The Women of Colonial Latin America*, 57.

11 Socolow, *The Women of Colonial Latin America*, 62–63.

which was founded in 1540–1541 under the direction of Bishop Zumárraga. Cuzco's first convent, Santa Clara, was founded in 1551; the first convent in Guatemala was established in 1578, and the first convent in Havana was established in 1574. Portuguese-controlled Brazil was a different story. Because there were far fewer women in Brazil compared to the Spanish colonies and the Portuguese colonial government restricted the establishment of convents to encourage women to marry, the first Brazilian convent did not open until 1677.

Convents were overwhelmingly established in cities. The countryside was considered dangerous, and an urban setting kept nuns closer to family, friends, and spiritual advisors. While nuns were technically removed from the world, they were still very much part of busy urban life—the fact that some nuns even managed to run successful businesses from within their convent walls is a testament to their integration with the larger society.

There were two types of convents: the discalced and the calced.[12] Regardless of whether a woman entered a discalced or calced convent, she was expected to live the rest of her life within the monastery walls. The discalced convents were strict and closely followed their vows of poverty and cloistering. These orders typically did not demand a dowry upon entry, so in theory they were open to more women. At discalced convents, women lived a communal life, eating simple meals, praying, attending Mass, and doing chores. They strove to obey the rules as their founders envisioned them. They had limited interaction with the outside world, and they took their vows of poverty seriously. There was a tendency toward more extreme asceticism, and the austerity of these monastic houses limited their appeal, with likely only about thirty or fewer nuns in residence.

Calced convents, on the other hand, were more lenient in their observance of their vows and lifestyle. Because of this laxity, calced convents grew to be far more numerous and tended to have far more nuns than their discalced counterparts. Some of these convents, known as *conventos grandes*, could house hundreds of nuns. The women in these convents overwhelmingly came from wealthy families, and they frequently brought servants and slaves to live with them within the convent walls. A good example of a *convento grande* was La Concepción in Lima, which housed a little over 1,000 inhabitants, including 318 nuns, at the beginning of the eighteenth century.[13] To accommodate so many residents, these convents needed to be large. La Concepción's property, for example, took up a block and a half. At one point in the late sixteenth century, the convents in Lima were the largest property owners in the city.

Society's rigid social structure was present in these convents, and even nuns were segregated into different tiers: the black-veiled nuns and the white-veiled nuns. Both tiers had to be of European descent, but the black-veiled nuns sat at the top of the convent's social structure. These women came from elite families and brought considerable wealth with them into the convent. They were the only inhabitants allowed to profess full vows,

---

12 The terms calced and discalced derive from the Latin word for shoe. Within monastic orders, calced religious wear shoes, while discalced religious go barefoot or wear only sandals. For example, Teresa of Ávila's reformed Carmelite order, the Discalced Carmelites, went barefoot or wore sandals.

13 Socolow, *The Women of Colonial Latin America*, 111.

vote, or hold office. The white-veiled nuns were women who came from families that were lower down on the social scale and brought more modest dowries. They were considered lay sisters and did much of the domestic work, leaving more leisure and prayer time for the black-veiled nuns. Below the white-veiled nuns were servants and slaves who worked in the kitchens and performed other menial labor. There were also secular inhabitants such as unchaste daughters of the city's elite, abandoned or divorced women, women needing protection, or even friends or relatives of the nuns. If a convent was a teaching institution, which they often were, there were girls within the walls receiving an education. Even if a convent was not a teaching institution, it likely had some orphaned girls and housed the illegitimate children of the city's elite. Outside of the servants and slaves, the rest of the residents would typically be white. There were some exceptions to this rule, such as Juana Esperanza de San Alberto, an African slave who lived within the convent for decades and was allowed to become a nun shortly before her death. However, these instances were extremely rare.

Colonial Latin America was a place that offered women few options outside of marriage or monastery. Undoubtedly, many women entered the monastic life out of genuine religious piety, but there was a segment of nuns whose religious vocations were questionable. Over time, many of the calced convents deteriorated in their commitment to pious living, and some grand convents were instead places of wealth and frivolity. There were parties and plays, frequent contact with the outside world, and even refusals to live communally. As an example of the excesses, in 1755, the bishop of Lima reprimanded nuns for keeping bulls within convent walls so they could stage their own bullfights.[14] It was not unheard of for nuns to adorn their habits with fancy silks and jewels, and some nuns refused to wear monastic garb at all. The attempts to reform convents by the church hierarchy were met with varying degrees of success. While some reform efforts worked, often nuns simply refused to comply with the new directives from the bishop.

The most prominent and well-known nun of the colonial era is Sor Juana Inés de la Cruz (1648–1695). In fact, Sor Juana, as she is generally known, is likely the most famous woman in all colonial Latin America—recognized in a surprising number of disciplines from academic to literary to theological. She produced poems, essays, letters, plays, and complex theological works. She has become an icon of Mexican identity, and she was even featured on the two hundred–peso bill for decades, with a fragment of one her most famous poems, "*You Foolish Men*," written in defense of women's pursuit of learning, printed on the bill (albeit in very tiny print):

> *Foolish men, who accuse,*
> *Women without reason,*
> *Without seeing that you create,*
> *The very faults that you identify.*[15]

---

14 Gonzalés and Gonzalés, *Christianity in Latin America*, 121.

15 Leigh Thelmadatter, "An unlikely modern icon, Sor Juana's celebrity cuts across age and class," *Mexico News Daily*, February 13, 2021, Mexico Life, https://mexiconewsdaily.com/mexicolife/sor-juanas-celebrity-cuts-across-age-and-class/. Sor

Sor Juana's rise to prominence was unlikely considering the circumstances of her birth. She was born in a small town in New Spain around the year 1650 to a Creole mother and a Spanish father; her parents were unmarried. As a child she showed both brilliance and a deep desire for learning, but as a girl she was limited in her ability to receive a formal education. She even asked her mother if she could dress as a man to attend the University of Mexico—she was told no. She had to settle for self-teaching in her grandfather's library until she was sent to Mexico City around the age of ten. There, she continued to teach herself, and she caught the attention of the viceroy Antonio Sebastián de Toledo (the marquis of Mancera) and his wife. Sor Juana won a position as a lady-in-waiting in the viceregal court, and she long counted this powerful couple as close friends and allies. Having a complete disinterest in marriage, Sor Juana decided to become a nun in 1667. Likely she understood this to be her best chance at continuing a life dedicated to scholarship and learning. She first tried a discalced Carmelite convent, which proved far too restrictive, and she left within months because of illness. In 1669, she entered a calced convent, the Hieronymite Convent of Santa Paula, with a dowry given to her by her grandfather and the requirement of legitimate birth waived, likely due to her political connections.

At this convent she lived a comfortable existence. Her monastic "cell" was a two-story apartment that housed her personal library—with thousands of volumes, it was one of the largest in New Spain. The breadth of her intellectual pursuits is stunning, though she is best known for her literary works. She had a surprising level of freedom in her scholarship through most of her life, with the church hierarchy largely tolerating this independent nun. Although technically cloistered, her convent had a rather loose interpretation of this requirement, and she was able to exchange ideas with many of the leading intellectuals of the day and continue her friendship with the viceroys and other prominent figures. She became famous within her lifetime in both New Spain and Spain, and in many ways, she symbolized the height of culture and education in colonial Mexico.

Eventually her constant pushing against both gender norms and expectations for nuns caught up with her. In 1691, Sor Juana published a defense of a woman's right to knowledge and study in her now famous *Respuesta a Sor Filotea de la Cruz*. Utilizing the genre of letter writing, Sor Juana crafted a careful defense using personal narrative, historic learned women, and works of the church fathers to argue her case. Although the reaction was not immediate, by 1694, the Inquisition had moved to silence her. She was forced to renew her monastic vows and sell both her library and scientific instruments. It is unknown how effective these measures would have been in the long term because Sor Juana died the next year when an epidemic swept through the convent. From an inventory of her cell after her death, it appears she was already beginning to replace her library.[16]

While Sor Juana most certainly does not represent a typical nun, she is an important figure in Latin American history. Her collected works are largely considered prominent

---

Juana was removed from the two hundred–peso bill only to be put on the one hundred–peso bill in 2021.

16 Kathleen Ann Myers, *Neither Saints Nor Sinners: Writing the Lives of Women in Spanish America* (Oxford: Oxford University Press, 2003), 93–115.

examples of literature of the Spanish Golden Age. Modern feminist scholars have been attracted to her defense of women's rights for good reason. Had she been born in a different time, when women had more opportunities, she might not have entered the monastic life, but within her context, this was the most logical choice. That being said, she did pen significant theological works in addition to her more secular writings, and one should not completely question her religious vocation.

Beatas

Considering how few women were allowed to enter monastic life, compounded by the excesses and lax lifestyles of some nuns, it should come as little surprise that some of the most respected religious women of the era were found outside of convent walls, specifically in a group called *beatas*, or religious laywomen. *Beatas* took simple vows and often lived secluded lives. There were various reasons a woman may have chosen the life of a *beata* over that of a nun; since entrance into a convent was costly and only open to women of European descent, monastic life simply was not an option for many women. Other women did not want to be cloistered. Even the laxest of the grand convents, while allowing people to come in, did not allow nuns to leave. Other women believed that they could best follow God by being present in the world serving others.

The first of the colonial *beatas* arrived in Mexico in the mid-1520s at the request of Bishop Zumárraga. He specifically wanted religious women to instruct the daughters of high-ranking American Indians in the Christian faith. Therefore, the women would be primarily concerned with mission work—something cloistered nuns could not do. The arrangement did not work particularly well. This was a group of women who were adventurous enough to sail to the other side of the world, and unlike nuns, they had not made any formal vows to the church. Therefore, they were not *required* to be obedient to the church, and the bishop found them to be frustratingly independent. They soon found other things to occupy their time and tended to wander off from their obligation to the bishop. While this initial experience with *beatas* teaching and acting as missionaries failed, soon America was producing its own *beatas*. They still tended to be independent, though in different ways than the initial group of Spanish *beatas*.

The most renowned of the colonial *beatas* is Rosa de Lima (1586–1617), the first canonized saint in the Americas. In many ways Rosa follows in the footsteps of ascetic saints before her, but in other ways she is uniquely American. Rosa was born Isabel Floras de Olivia in 1586 in the city of Lima, which had been founded a mere fifty years prior. Her parents were Creoles of modest means. When Isabel was a baby, a servant saw her face transform into a rose, and she was called Rosa from that point forward. At the age of five, Rosa heard about the life of Catherine of Siena and began to emulate her. At some point Rosa experienced a mystical marriage to Christ, and she chose to live a religious life, going by the name Rosa de Santa María. She began a life of prayer and penance in a hut she built in her yard, again emulating the popular Italian saint. Her choice proved unsatisfactory to both her mother and her confessor. Rosa's beauty is well documented, and her mother believed an advantageous marriage would ease the family's financial troubles, while Rosa's confessor wanted her to live a life of enclosure at a convent. But Rosa had no desire to be confined by either a marriage or a convent, and she actively fought against and undermined any attempt to bring her in line with their desires. Eventually she became a tertiary, first to the Franciscans and later to the Dominicans, which involved simple vows of chastity, poverty, and obedience but did not require enclosure in a convent. She surrounded herself with a group of laywomen who also wanted to devote their lives to God.

According to documents from her canonization process, she worked ten hours a day, prayed for twelve, and slept for only two. In addition to this apparent sleep deprivation, she practiced extreme asceticism, which included hanging herself by her hair, wearing a metal crown with nails on her head under her habit, and whipping herself; she also tried to survive by eating only the Communion host. Her family and her confessor were understandably concerned about her fanatical forms of penance; her confessor even admonished her on the evils of self-mortification, but she was determined and frequently went to great lengths to hide her fanatical behavior. It must be noted that while her family and confessor believed these behaviors to be excessive, many of her contemporaries were exceedingly impressed, and she was considered by many to be a living saint. Because of this reputation for holiness, she advised Jesuit and Dominican friars, visited with prominent women in the city, established a circle of followers, and organized prayer groups in the city. There are numerous miracles associated with Rosa. It is said she was blessed with the divine gifts of intercessional powers and prophecy. Legends credit her with saving the city from pirates, earthquakes, and disease-carrying mosquitoes, and she is particularly well known for praying for people of Indigenous and African descent in the city. Despite all this, she lamented that she was a woman and could not evangelize outside of her own city.

She died at the age of thirty-one, and the canonization process began immediately. A group of her followers reportedly experienced flights of spirit right after her death, and even people living in faraway Europe testified to her miraculous intercessions. Despite the initial enthusiasm, her case faltered. Her cult in Lima was suspended by the Dominican Order, her writings were examined by the Inquisition, and some of her followers had their writings examined and censured. Interestingly while she and her followers were being examined in Lima, her cause was being promoted in Europe. King Philip IV of Spain was so enthusiastic about her canonization that he named her the patron saint of his armed forces—before she was even declared a saint. Finally in 1671, over fifty years after her death, she officially became a saint in the Catholic Church. While Rosa gained international recognition and canonization, most *beatas* were known locally as holy women but never received such fame.

Because women of color were largely barred from entering convents, a number gained their reputations as holy women as *beatas*. One such case was Catarina de San Juan (1607–1688), who lived in the city of Puebla. Like Rosa de Lima, Catarina was beloved by her local community. At her death in 1688, she was given an elaborate funeral mass attended by prominent religious and secular leaders within the city, the room where she had lived was transformed into an altar, and within four years of her death, two hagiographic accounts had been written. Then the tide of support suddenly changed. The Inquisition banned the displaying of her picture and one of her biographies. Within eight years of her death, her altar was boarded up. She continued to be a popular local religious figure, but she was never considered for sainthood.

Catarina's biography, like many other hagiographic accounts, is steeped in legend, and it is difficult to disentangle fact from fiction. According to these accounts, she was born a princess in the Mogul Empire with the name Mirrha. Although her family was not Christian, she began receiving miraculous favors from the Virgin Mary as a child. Due to local wars, her family fled to the coast where she was kidnapped by Portuguese pirates. She was taken first to Cochín and then Manila, where she converted to Christianity after meeting Jesuit missionaries. In 1619, she was taken to New Spain, where she was bought by a childless couple as a domestic slave. After her owner died and his wife entered a convent, Catarina became a servant for a local priest. Despite Catarina's decision to devote herself to a life of chastity, Suárez forced her to marry his slave, who was abusive. By the 1640s, both the priest and Domingo were dead, and Catarina was free to devote her life to God as a lay holy woman.

A wealthy local couple became her benefactors and bought her a room across the street from a local church run by the Jesuits. She supported herself by sewing and making chocolate, and she spent her time praying, doing works of charity, and practicing forms of penance. She was under the guidance of a local Jesuit named Miguel Godínez who considered her a genuine Christian mystic. She had significant contact with the city's religious elite, and she was well respected in the community, with many seeking her out for her charity and her holiness. Despite the respect she received in her lifetime, the suppression of her legacy is not entirely surprising. She was closely associated with the Jesuits, a group that ran into trouble in the Americas not long after Catarina's death. The hagiographic account of her life, which was banned, is filled with highly sensational tales of men pursuing Catarina for her beauty, including an eroticized encounter between Catarina and Jesus. The Inquisition deemed the account indecent, unbelievable, and nearly blasphemous.[17]

Another famed *beata* was Ursula de Jesús (1604–1668), a contemporary of Catarina de San Juan and a woman of African descent who became well known as a mystic in Lima, Peru. Born into slavery, she was sent to live in the home of a prominent mystic in 1612, where she spent the next five years. In 1617, she was sent to serve a young novice in the convent of Santa Clara. Therefore, much of her childhood was dominated by mystical religious fervor. Following a near-death experience, Ursula underwent a dramatic conversion and devoted her life to obedience and poverty. She was particularly well known for her fervent prayers for souls suffering in purgatory.

After forty-one years as a slave, the nuns of Santa Clara purchased her freedom. She decided to remain in the convent, working as a servant, but she was now able to devote considerable time to spiritual practices. She, like many other women of the era, practiced extreme asceticism, wearing hair shirts and wrapping sharp metal studs around her arms and waist; she regularly whipped herself and wore a crown of thorns. While she was never canonized, she gained a reputation locally as a mystic and holy woman.[18]

---

17 Myers, *Neither Saints Nor Sinners*, 44–68.

18 Myers, 116–139.

It should be noted that the boundary between nun and *beata* was not always a firm one. Ursula de Jesús lived as a *beata* within the walls of a convent, and had she had the opportunity to take the veil, one suspects she would have. Another well-known holy woman, by the name of María de San José, lived many years as a *beata* but became a nun when the opportunity arose. María was born in 1656 on a *hacienda* outside of Puebla, New Spain. When she was ten or eleven, she had a vision of the devil claiming her as his own, after which she devoted herself to spiritual practices and extreme mortification. Throughout her life she would continue to be tormented with visions of the demonic.

She employed dramatic self-harm in the name of God, and even considering the cultural differences, her actions were extreme. Her health suffered terribly, and there is little doubt her lifestyle influenced her ailments. She spent two decades living this solitary life of a *beata*—emulating the saints and following the Rule of St. Clare. She even built a hut in her backyard like Rosa de Lima. Unlike Rosa de Lima, however, María longed to enter a convent, but her family's financial constraints made it impossible until she was accepted into an Augustinian convent that had just been built for women who were virtuous but poor in Oaxaca. She struggled with the convent schedule after living so many years on her own, but eventually she settled into her new role, and she was even the instructor of novices for the last two decades of her life. She became recognized by both the clergy and community as a powerful intercessor and mystic.[19]

Many of the religious women in Latin America practiced self-mortification. In fact, of all the women examined in this chapter, Sor Juana is the only one to have rejected these extreme practices completely. In a modern context, these practices are distasteful at best and horrifying at worst. That women and girls harmed themselves in the name of Christ in such dramatic ways is indeed disconcerting. This form of extreme asceticism, while prominent among the most famous of holy women, was not necessarily the norm. María de San José was ridiculed by her fellow nuns for her practices, and Rosa de Lima hid her self-harm from her family and confessor. Regardless, there was unquestionably a tendency toward these practices, and Christian history has more than its fair share of extreme women ascetics.

In conclusion, the colonial period in Latin America was a time of intense religious piety but also a time of violence and extreme social stratification. Unfortunately, this stratification bled into all areas of society, including religious life. The monastic life was generally open only to wealthy women of European descent, though women of color and women of lower economic status could and did gain reputations as *beatas*. Women, while limited by cultural norms and expectations, participated in and contributed to the spread and development of a uniquely American Catholicism that continues to be influential today.

---

19 Myers, *Neither Saints Nor Sinners*, 69–89.

NORTH AMERICA

Historical Background

The spread of religious ideas was remarkably different in North America compared to Latin America. Early Catholic missionaries made headway through both Spanish and French holdings in North America, and their influence would long be felt in Canada, Mexico, the American Southwest, Louisiana, and Florida. If one were to glance at a colonial map in the year 1776, it may have been assumed that North America would become largely Catholic. However, the most impactful religious movements in what would become the United States were forming along the English-controlled Eastern Seaboard, and it was Protestantism, not Catholicism, that would become the main Christian expression in the United States.

Jamestown, established in 1607, was the first permanent English settlement in North America. Around the same time, permanent French settlements were being established in the Acadia region of Canada, and Plymouth Colony was established in what would become Massachusetts in 1620. Like in Latin America, the colonists brought disease that decimated the Indigenous populations. Unlike South America, the settlers in North America were largely privately organized and funded—there was no English equivalent of royal patronage. Some settlers were economically motivated, and others were religiously motivated, but by and large, settlers were independent agents. Therefore, immediately the British-controlled American colonies demonstrated a remarkable diversity of religious thought and practice.

In the American colonies, the four largest Christian groups were Puritans, Quakers, Anglicans, and Catholics. Geographically speaking, the Puritans, with their vision of a new Zion, settled in the New England area. There were various Quaker pioneers throughout the colonies, though eventually a good number settled in the Pennsylvania area. There were Anglicans in most colonies, but they were especially prominent in the Southern colonies. There was a substantial minority of Roman Catholics, but mass immigration for Catholics largely did not occur until the nineteenth century. Starting in 1619, European slave traders began bringing African slaves to the colonies. An estimated 15 percent of slaves were Muslim, and the rest practiced indigenous African religions. There were also small numbers of other religious groups, including Jews, Lutherans, and Baptists, all present from the early to mid-1600s.

There are difficulties when trying to piece together the experiences of American Indian women living in the colonial period. Like with Indigenous tribes in Latin America, there was great diversity of belief and lifestyle prior to European contact; in fact, there were more than four hundred different tribes, bands, and confederacies. Far more problematic, though, is that much of our historical documentation about American Indian women during this era was written by European men. American Indian tribes were largely oral cultures; therefore, the documentation of culture and events was often recorded by outsiders. Even when Europeans were sympathetic to Indigenous cultures, which was certainly not always the case, they still often carried issues of superiority and cultural blindness, not to mention a lack of knowledge of the language. Despite these limitations in sources, a picture emerges that is both similar and different from experiences in Latin America. While the Spanish and the Portuguese brought the church and a plan to convert the Indigenous peoples of Latin America, there was little organized effort to convert American Indians, at least in the colonial period, in the American colonies. There were certainly zealous missionaries, but by and large the efforts were far less coordinated, and the missionaries represented a wide variety of different Christian denominations.

Efforts to convert American Indians had limited results in the colonial period. There was general distrust and a belief that the missionaries posed a threat to traditional culture and leadership—a concern that was not unfounded. Language and cultural differences proved a significant hurdle, and the inability of many early missionaries to converse fluently with potential converts limited both the effectiveness of their evangelization and the commitments of convents who may have only received a superficial explanation of the Christian faith. One group in which early missionaries found some success was younger females, notably girls, teenagers, and women in their childbearing years, especially within native groups that lived a more sedentary lifestyle, particularly those living in towns.[20]

One of the few sustained Protestant efforts to convert Native Americans was a mission in Martha's Vineyard. Thomas Mayhew Jr. began missionary work in the 1640s among the Wampanoag population, which is estimated to have numbered somewhere between 1,500 and 3,000 people at the time, while there were about sixty-five English people living on the east end of the island. Euro-Americans did not become the majority on the island until the 1720s. Mayhew's efforts had little effect until an epidemic prompted a wave of conversions. It is of particular note that this mission did not insist on sudden cultural change for the converted Wampanoag, which likely added to its unusual success.[21]

Experience Mayhew compiled biographical sketches of American Indian converts in Martha's Vineyard in his book *Indian Converts*, which included a number of women, most notably Jerusha Ompan.[22] He provides some biographical information, though the purpose of this sketch is to highlight her spiritual qualities. Ompan was born to Christian converts who taught her to read and instructed her in the catechism. Even as a child she demonstrated intellectual prowess, which continued into adulthood. Mayhew gives an account of her regular study, and if she did not have time during the day, she would read at night. Most intriguing, though, is Mayhew's description of her theological curiosity:

> She used to ask serious Questions in Matters of Religion, as particularly of
> one she enquired, Whether Adam had Free-Will before his Fall, and how his Sin

20 Jaqueline Peterson and Mary Druke, "American Indian Women and Religion," in *Women and Religion in America, Volume 2: The Colonial Period and Revolutionary Periods*, eds. Rosemary Radford Ruether and Rosemary Skinner Keller (Cambridge: Harper and Row, 1983): 1–14. (9)

21 James P. Ronda, "Generation of Faith: The Christian Indians of Martha's Vineyard," *The William and Mary Quarterly* 38, no. 3 (July 1981), 369–394.

22 Experience Mayhew, *Indian Converts: Or, Some Account of the Lives and Dying Speeches of a Considerable Number of the Christianized Indians of Martha's Vineyard, in New England, by Experience Mayhew* (London: printed for Samuel Gerrish, bookseller in Boston, 1727), excerpted in *Women and Religion in America, Volume 2: The Colonial Period and Revolutionary Periods*, eds. Rosemary Radford Ruether and Rosemary Skinner Keller (Cambridge: Harper and Row, 1983), 34–36.

came to be imputed and propagated to his Posterity, and how we might be delivered from it? And, lastly, how she ought to order her Prayers with respect to it?[23]

The most coordinated efforts among Christian missionaries in North America in the early colonial period were among Catholic religious. Communities of Christian American Indian women were found in New France after missions were established by the Jesuits and the Ursulines. Much of our understanding of these converts comes from the writings of priests who chronicled stories of faith and miracles among these groups. For example, most of what we know about Kateri Tekakwitha (1656–1680), who is likely the best known of the American Indian converts to Catholicism, is found in the writings of two Jesuit priests named Claude Chauchetiére and Pierre Cholenec, which were based on oral testimony provided by two Christian Iroquois women, Anastasia Tegonhatsiongo and Marie-Thérèse Tegaiaguenta, who knew her.[24]

Kateri's father was a Mohawk chief, and her mother was an Algonquin Catholic convert, but they both died during a smallpox outbreak when Kateri was young that left her scarred and partially blind. At the age of twenty, Kateri was baptized by a Jesuit priest, and she took a vow of virginity and practiced extreme asceticism, including walking on hot coals, sleeping in thorns, and other forms of self-mortification. Kateri was not allowed to take vows as a nun, but she lived in a community of Christian women who also practiced forms of extreme asceticism.[25]

She died at the age of twenty-four, and there are numerous accounts of miracles associated with Kateri after her death. She was beatified in 1980, and she was canonized in 2012, though her canonization was not without controversy due to the history of abuses of native peoples by the Catholic church.[26] Kateri, however, is an outlier, and most American Indians were far more resistant to the missionary efforts during the colonial period.

One final interesting episode features American Indian women calling out the hypocrisy of white missionaries. Willian Savery, a Quaker missionary, recorded an encounter between American Indian women who were inspired to speak at the Indian Council of the Six Nations at Canandaigua in 1794 after hearing Jemima Wilkinson, better known at that time as the Public Universal Friend (who will be discussed further in chapter 7), preaching. Savery described the women's message like this:

> The substance of this was, that they felt a deep interest in the affairs of their
> nation, and having heard the opinions of their sachems, they fully concurred
> in them, that the white people had been the cause of all the Indian's distresses;
> that they had pressed and squeezed them together, until it gave them great pain
> at their hearts, and that the whites ought to give them back the lands they had

---

23 Mayhew, 35.

24 Mónica Díaz, "Native American Women and Religion in the American Colonies: Textual and Visual Traces of an Imagined Community," *Legacy* 28, no. 2 (2011): 213.

25 Díaz, 213–214.

26 "Mixed Reactions to First Native American Saint," NPR, last modified February 10, 2012, https://www.npr.org/2012/02/10/146695395/mixed-reactions-to-first-native-american-saint.

taken from them. That one of the white women had yesterday told the Indians
to repent; and they now called on the white people to repent, for they had as
much need as the Indians, and that they should wrong the Indians no more.[27]

The women fully grasped the message the Christians were preaching—perhaps better
than the missionaries understood it themselves. These three women, whose names are not
known, were inspired enough to demand that white Christians live according to their own
religious principles.

A New Zion

As far as cultural influence on American ideals, the Puritans in New England left a disproportionate legacy. The first Puritan colony at Plymouth fared poorly through its first
winter and was later absorbed into the larger Massachusetts Bay Colony, which was char-
tered in 1629 and founded in 1630. These colonies were a religious experiment, a New
Zion, in a wild land. While it has been long been part of the American imagination that
these first European colonists to New England were committed to freedom of religion, the
reality of the situation proves more complex. The Puritans were dedicated to creating
what they believed to be a perfect religious society, which most certainly did not involve
pluralism as we understand it today. The colony was not truly a theocracy, though the
Puritans did sometimes characterize their society as such—they were too hesitant of
state churches, like those they had fled in England. However, neither could their state
be considered secular either, and there was a considerable cooperation between church
and state in New England.[28] A commitment to the Puritan religious experiment was
essential, and those who threatened it were considered problematic for the success of
the community. Therefore, the first of the heresy trials began in 1635, only five years
after the community's founding.

Puritan society, like many others of the same era, had definitive views on gender
roles. The most important role, for both women and men, was *believer*, but beyond that,
women and men each had their prescribed familial and societal roles based on gender.
Marriage was a fundamental component of Puritan society, and a woman's primary function was as a wife and a mother. She was to be subordinate to her husband, but the husband should not be a tyrant. Women were largely occupied with traditional domestic tasks
such as caring for the home and nurturing children, and they were also largely responsible
for educating children in religious matters. Therefore, it was important for women to
receive some sort of religious education. The high literacy rates for both men and women
demonstrate the community's commitment to education.

Within the church, women were not allowed to preach, teach men, or even question
male leadership. However, they were not required to stay completely silent either. There
is evidence that women shared their conversion stories, and women were full church

---

27 William Savery, *A Journal of the Life, Travels and Religious Labors of William Savery* (London: C. Gilpin, 1844), 69–70.

28 Philip Gorski, *American Covenant: A History of Civil Religion from the Puritans to the Present* (Princeton: Princeton University Press, 2017), 44–45.

members. One should also not assume that marginalized formal power meant that women were powerless within their communities and churches. As in the case of Anne Hutchinson, who will be examined in more detail below, it was quite possible for women to gain influence despite the limitations put on them.

As in many other times and places, Puritans generally believed that women were weaker spiritually and more prone to sin. Eve's shadow has been long indeed. Despite this belief, churches tended to have more women members than men, and church leaders were left trying to understand why these supposedly weaker beings seemed to be more pious and devout. Within a hundred years, societal views on women would fundamentally change, with women being viewed as naturally more inclined to faith, more spiritual, and less carnal than men. However, at this time, pastors attributed women's piousness to their experiences. It was argued that women's experiences as submissive wives and mothers, compounded by the dangers of childbirth, led to a more pious disposition despite their inherently sinful nature.

Regardless of the definitive gender roles, there were Puritan women who left their marks on history. Anne Bradstreet (1612–1672), who was a young wife at the founding of the Massachusetts Bay Colony, left her legacy through poetry. Born in 1612 in Northamptonshire, England, she married at sixteen and two years later took the arduous journey to Massachusetts to be part of the Puritan experiment. When she arrived in the New World, she was distressed by the rough living, sickness, and death that were prevalent in the small colony. Her first known extant poem, "Upon a Fit of Sickness, Anno 1632," was written when she was facing a severe illness at the age of nineteen. The poem demonstrates themes of the brevity of life, the certainty of death, and the Christian hope in eternal salvation. A short excerpt from the poem shows both her mastery of language and her theology:

> O bubble blast, how long can'st last?
> that always art a breaking,
> No sooner blown, but dead and gone,
> ev'n as a word that's speaking.
> O whilst I live this grace me give,
> I doing good may be,
> Then death's arrest I shall count best,
> because it's Thy decree;
> Bestow much cost there's nothing lost,
> to make salvation sure.[29]

Bradstreet was the first woman in the New World to be recognized as an accomplished poet, and she is still considered one of the most important early American authors. Through her writings, she offers glimpses of life for a wife, a mother, and a faithful Christian in the difficult early days of the colony.

---

29 Anne Bradstreet, "Upon a Fit of Sickness, Anno 1632," lines 17–26, https://www.findinganne.org/blog-1/2019/2/6/on-deaths -door.

A woman who left a more complicated legacy is Anne Hutchinson (1591–1643). Now hailed by some as a feminist hero, she was called an American Jezebel and an instrument of Satan by Governor Winthrop during her lifetime. Her father, an Anglican minister who was critical of the Anglican Church, provided her with an unusually good religious education for the time, and she used this theological knowledge to her advantage later in life. She married William Hutchinson in 1612, with whom she would have fifteen children. In England, the Hutchinsons were influenced by the preacher John Cotton and became Puritans. Hutchinson believed that she had the ability to distinguish between true and false preachers, and according to her, there were only two true preachers in all of England: John Cotton and her brother-in-law John Wheelwright. When Cotton left for the Americas, the Hutchinsons followed in 1634.

Once in the colonies, it did not take long for Hutchinson to run afoul of the authorities. She held weekly Bible studies and sermon discussions for women, which in theory would have been fine had these meetings stayed just for women. However, a second mixed-gender meeting began sometime later, and it appears she both gave her own insights and criticized various clergy, which was perceived as overstepping her role as a listener and a woman. By 1636, the colony was divided between people who supported Hutchinson and those who opposed her. The conflict was about more than her theological insights—this represented a major division within the community. Her supporters included John Cotton, the new colonial governor Henry Vane, and most of the members of the Boston Church. Her opponents included former governor John Winthrop, most of the local ministers, and many of the colonists outside of Boston.

She accused her opponents of preaching a covenant of works, and her opponents accused her of being an antinomian,[30] argued that she and her supporters were immoral, and charged that she was going to destroy their entire religious experiment. Tellingly an opponent said this to her: "You have stept out of your place, you have rather bine a Husband than a Wife and a preacher than a Hearer, and a Magistrate than a Subject."[31] Her crime was social as well as theological, for she had stepped outside of her appropriate gender role. In the end, she was tried and convicted of heresy; she and her supporters were excommunicated and exiled. The Hutchinson family moved to Rhode Island, which had been recently founded as a haven for religious freedom. Unfortunately for the Puritans, Hutchinson was not the last woman to challenge their religious experiment.

Women and the Society of Friends

While the Puritans preached a rigid separation for men and women in both society and the church, the Society of Friends, more commonly known as the Quakers, offered a radically different take on gender and equality during the colonial era. The group originated in England, but Quakers quickly migrated to the American colonies. Their founder was

---

30 Antinomianism (literally meaning "against law") is a belief that Christians are exempt from the obligations of biblical law, moral law, and church-prescribed behavioral norms. Considered heresy, very few people would ever call themselves antinomians, so the term is generally used as an accusation against someone else, as in the case of Hutchinson.

31 John Winthrop, *The History of New England from 1630 to 1649*, ed. James Savage (Boston: Phelps & Farnham, 1825), 201.

a gifted and charismatic man by the name of George Fox, and central to Fox's theology was the Light of Christ. The general idea is that every human being is enlightened by the divine Light of Christ. If people follow this inner light, they will see their sinful nature and come to Christ. If they fail to follow the light, they will be lost. Therefore, one does not need to have access to scripture or even knowledge of Christ to be saved. Conversely, those claiming Christian belief who do not follow the light will not be saved. Fox also taught that humans did not need an intermediary to God. Since God speaks directly to humanity, there was no need for a priestly class. Fox's theology was radical: everyone had access to God; everyone had inner light; and ultimately a priestly class and even the Bible were unnecessary for salvation. Religious leaders saw potential for chaos in his message.[32]

Fox's teaching attracted quite a following. Throughout the 1650s, Quakerism spread throughout England, Wales, and, in a limited capacity, Ireland. Meanwhile opposition also grew largely due to their social and theological positions, but many also protested the prominent position women held within the movement. While gender norms of the day were typically maintained within Quaker society, there was a fundamental equality between men and women. Indeed, there were prominent women in leadership, and these woman leaders were actively engaged in mission work. In early Quakerism, the most prominent woman was Margaret Fell (1614–1702), who is commonly known as the "mother of Quakerism." She famously penned an early women's rights tract in 1666 using scripture and reason to argue for women's leadership within Christianity. She pointedly remarks in response to those who believe women are to be silent, "Mark this, you that despise and oppose the Message of the Lord God that he sends by Women; What had become of the Redemption of the whole Body of Mankind, if they had not cause to believe the Message that the Lord Jesus sent by these Women, of and concerning his Resurrection?"[33]

The Quakers brought their egalitarian views with them when they arrived in the Americas, and women were some of their earliest missionaries on American soil. The first Quaker to arrive in the American colonies was a woman by the name of Elizabeth Harris; she traveled in the Chesapeake area around 1655 or 1656. Six years later, there were nearly sixty Quakers who had visited Maryland and Virginia. In 1656, two women named Mary Austin and Mary Fisher arrived in Massachusetts to preach their message. In response, the Puritans arrested them, examined them for witchcraft, burned their Quaker books, and put them on a ship headed to Barbados. Subsequent Quaker missionaries had similar experiences in Massachusetts. Between 1656 and 1659, at least thirty-three Quakers arrived, and they were all expelled, often first enduring physical violence or torture. Puritan converts to Quakerism were treated harshly—generally their property was seized and they were exiled. In 1659, the Puritans went a step further and passed a new law imposing the death penalty on Quakers.[34]

---

32 Thomas D. Hamm, *Quakers in America* (New York: Columbia, 2003), 15–16.

33 Margaret Fell, *Women's Speaking Justified, Proved, and Allowed of by the Scriptures, All Such as Speak by the Spirit and Power of the Lord Jesus* (1666). The full text can be found here: http://www.qhpress.org/texts/fell.html.

34 Hamm, *Quakers in America*, 21–22.

It was a convert to the Society of Friends who caused the Boston Puritans significant headaches. Mary Dyer (d. 1660), whose statue now sits outside the Massachusetts State House, is celebrated today as a martyr for religious liberty, but during her lifetime she faced persecution and finally death for her missionary work. It is unknown where or in what year she was born, though she was married to a man named William Dyer in London in 1533. The couple were English Puritans and moved to Boston in 1535—right during the Hutchinson affair. Mary Dyer was a supporter of Anne Hutchinson and was excommunicated and exiled in 1538 when Hutchinson was condemned. Dyer and her husband moved to Rhode Island; then in the 1650s they returned to England, where they joined the Society of Friends. Eventually the couple returned to New England, and Dyer felt called to minister to her former neighbors and friends in Boston.

The Puritans in Boston believed her to be a heretic, inspired by the devil, and acting outside of her appropriate gender roles. More than likely they also found her incredibly frustrating because she absolutely refused to adhere to their numerous banishments. After her initial banishment in 1538 for supporting Hutchinson, she was again banished in 1657 for being a Quaker. She was then exiled from New Haven, Connecticut, in 1658. She returned to Boston in the summer of 1659 to visit two imprisoned Quakers and was banished once more. In the fall of the same year, she returned yet again; this time she was sentenced to death along with two other Quakers, both men. She was literally on the scaffold, her two companions hanged, when she was given a last-minute reprieve and once again banished. Finally in the spring of 1660, she returned to Boston, and the Boston leadership had had enough. This time Dyer was indeed executed. She was one of only four Quakers to be executed for their beliefs in Boston.

If one were to describe Dyer in one word, it would certainly be *persistent*. While her story is the most dramatic, she was just one of many Quaker women to have an impactful influence on early American society. Indeed, elsewhere, Quakers achieved a level of religious freedom, and women became missionaries, preachers, and social activists. Since Quakers had no formal clergy, women were neither priests nor pastors, but they had influence within the church and society. Most notably, all marriages needed to be approved by the women's meeting, which was a mighty power indeed.

CHAPTER 7

Women in the Time of Reason, Revolutions, and Awakenings (1700–1850)

In the year 1792, an English servant by the name of Joanna Southcott had the first of many visions that would begin her career as a prophetic and religious leader. She claimed to be the second Eve, the bride of Christ, and the woman clothed with the sun. When she was sixty-four years old, she declared she would soon give birth to a second messiah.[1] Southcott was a prolific prophet, publishing sixty-five visions and prophesies between 1801 and 1814, and there are estimates that a total of 108,000 copies of her works were circulated—though most of her writings were given away for free.[2] While she gained a following, especially among peasants, domestic servants, and factory workers, many in English society deemed her mad.[3] While she was fairly influential within her lifetime and certainly well known, her celebrity and religious impact faded over time, but she stands as a fascinating figure from the late eighteenth and early nineteenth centuries—a time that is generally associated with reason and progress.

For students of secular history, the eighteenth century is remembered for the Enlightenment, the philosophical movement originating in Europe that uplifted reason as *the* societal ideal. In many ways, we, especially those living in the West, are still living in the Enlightenment's long shadow. The Enlightenment had some positive effects on religion—witch trials began to decline, and commitments to equality within some denominations increased—but one can also see the current era of disenchantment and waning belief as heirs to this worship of rationalism. The eighteenth century, however, held more than the Enlightenment. It was a time of social instability, the Napoleonic Wars, revolutions, and religious experimentation.

As secular society embraced reason, forms of religion emerged that were more emotional, incorporated a greater role for the laity, and allowed women a larger role within churches. Major religious developments included in this chapter are the blossoming of the Pietist movement and the Methodist movement, the founding of global Protestant

---

1 Roger Robins, "Anglican Prophetess Joanna Southcott and the Gospel Story," *Anglican and Episcopal History* 61, no. 3 (September 1992): 277.

2 Robert William Rix, "Joanna Southcott and the Strange Effects of Printing: Publishing Prophesies in the Early Nineteenth Century," *History of Religions* 55, no. 1 (August 2015): 65–66.

3 Rix, 68.

missions, the First Great Awakening, and the emergence of religious prophets, some of whom even established their own utopian communities.

These events and movements seemingly contradict the overarching themes of the era, which are rationalism and Enlightenment. While there were undeniably tensions—tensions between rationalism and emotionalism, tensions between ideals of freedom and equality and the oppression that so many felt—these dichotomies are not altogether unexpected. The flattening of the hierarchy within many popular religious traditions speaks to the messaging of equality. The emergence of more emotional forms of religious expression can be seen as a reaction against the rationalism that was making such gains, especially in wealthier and more educated circles. The civil unrest and revolutionary activity of the era lent themselves to increased reliance on and devotion to God but also to an increase in apocalyptic fervor.

HISTORICAL BACKGROUND

In many ways, the modern world as we know it was shaped by the events of the eighteenth century, particularly looking at history from a Western perspective. Rapid developments in a variety of sectors, including transportation, agriculture, manufacturing, and construction, were fundamentally changing life. These advances in science and technology gave human beings a newfound confidence in their ability to control their environment. For some, especially among the West's intelligentsia, the growing reliance on science and progress reduced their perceived need for God. This trend has not lessened with time.

The Enlightenment played out in a variety of disciplines, including philosophy, the arts and sciences, politics, and even theology. One of the lasting impacts on society was the questioning of long-standing notions of sovereignty by philosophers and other intellectuals of the era. While most were not yet ready to eliminate the monarchies that ruled Europe, they began to argue for a different view of government: namely government as a contract between those who ruled and those who were ruled. They addressed issues of freedom and equality, although these concepts rarely included women, the peasantry and working classes, slaves, or people of color. That does not mean that these marginalized groups were not influenced by rhetoric of freedom and equality. In fact, there are numerous instances where individuals spoke out to claim those universal rights, such as the French revolutionary Marie Gouze, who penned *Declaration of the Rights of Women and the Female Citizen* in 1791. In a telling series of events, she was later executed in part for her relentless crusade for women's rights.[4]

Most prominent figures associated with the Enlightenment were men. Generally speaking, women were not seen as intellectual equals, and they were actively discriminated against in higher education and various trade guilds. Yet women still contributed to the overall era of advancement. There were wealthy salonnières who hosted leading intellectuals in their

---

4   Jerry H. Bently and Herbert F. Ziegler, *Traditions & Encounters: A Global Perspective on the Past, Volume II: From 1500 to the Present* (Boston: McGraw Hill, 2003), 807.

own homes, women novelists (the novel genre grew in popularity during this time), and women who were sought-after artists, musicians, and leaders in the sciences.[5]

As we approach the beginning of the nineteenth century, these radically different views of government, freedom, and liberty led to real-world resistance to European monarchies. The American Revolution (1775–1783) and the French Revolution (1789–1799) in the latter half of the eighteenth century and the revolutions for independence in Latin America at the beginning of the nineteenth century (by 1826 all of Latin America had gained independence except Cuba and Puerto Rico) rocked the status quo. These revolutions promoted general ideas of liberty and justice, yet they fell short in a variety of ways. In France, the revolution quickly devolved into the Reign of Terror, and within a decade Napoleon Bonaparte, a military dictator, had assumed control of France. In North America, the crafters of the new American government continued to support slavery and extended voting rights only to landed white men. The revolutions in Latin America produced varied results. After Simon Bolívar's dream of creating a vast republic failed, he expressed his disappointment most poetically: "America is ungovernable. Those who have served the revolution have plowed the sea."[6]

The Haitian Revolution (1791–1804) was the largest and most successful slave rebellion in the Americas; it also ended French rule of the island. It brought inspiration to some and struck fear into the hearts of slaveowners all around the Americas. Three years after Haiti's triumph, the British passed the Act for the Abolition of the Slave Trade, which ended the trading of enslaved peoples within the British Empire, and in 1833, they passed the Abolition of Slavery Act, which ordered the gradual emancipation of slaves in all the British-controlled colonies. In 1808, the United States passed a federal law making it illegal to import enslaved peoples, though slavery did not end until 1865 with the conclusion of the American Civil War. In 1811, Spain abolished slavery both in Spain and in its American colonies while the empire was fragmenting in the revolutionary impulse that was permeating Latin America. The last of the slave-holding countries were Cuba, which abolished slavery in 1886, and Brazil, which did so in 1888. Reading a list of emancipation dates simply does not convey the long and hard struggle for freedom that drove these changes (which is discussed in more detail in chapter 10).

All this attention to philosophical movements, revolutions, and activism provides a critical background to understanding eighteenth-century religious movements. The Age of Reason saw critical developments in religion, namely the blossoming of Pietism and creative advancements in Spiritualist thought. It was a time of revival and renewed personal piety on both sides of the Atlantic. It was the era of the First Great Awakening that set both the British Isles and the American Eastern Seaboard on fire with religious zeal. This event, or rather series of events, would prove particularly important in the American colonies, setting the precedent for popular religious revivals in the future United States.

---

5 For a more detailed examination of women in the arts and sciences, see chapter five in Jennine Hurl-Eamon, *Women's Roles in Eighteenth-Century Europe* (Santa Barbara: Greenwood, 2010), 89–110.

6 Simón Bolívar, *Obras completes*, vol. 3 (Havana: Lex, 1950), 501, quoted in González, *The Story of Christianity*, 365.

While global missions would not explode until the nineteenth century, the eighteenth saw the beginnings of Protestant missions, most notably among the Moravians.

Meanwhile women were making modest gains in both leadership and increasingly participating in religious life in various religious traditions. Other women established their own sects or religious communities. Both the creativity and disruptions of the era, compounded by American religious freedom, influenced the religious experimentation of the age, which would continue, especially in the United States, from that point forward.

In many ways the Enlightenment era was one of contradiction. Rhetoric of freedom and equality gained traction, but few people outside of landed men benefited from these concepts. The time is remembered for its commitment to rationalism, though we simultaneously see incredible movements of more emotional forms of Christianity. While women were still viewed as inferior and limited in their options, there were nonetheless advancements in a variety of fields, both secular and religious.

PIETISM

Trying to define pietism is a surprisingly complicated endeavor. The term is used to refer to German Pietism, which arose in the seventeenth century but flourished in the eighteenth. It can also be used as a more general term that describes a variety of different faith traditions that emphasize personal faith and individual piety. Complicating this matter even more is the fact that Pietists (whether you are using the term in a more general sense or even in the stricter sense of German Pietism) were never a homogenous group, though there were general tenets most shared. To quote church historian Jonathan Strom, "Pietists sought to revivify Christianity and emphasize godly living, biblical devotion, regeneration, millennialism, and new forms of religious association. Pietists remained, however, theologically heterogeneous and varied significantly."[7]

There were Pietists that operated within established churches, often called churchly or ecclesial Pietists, such as Philipp Jakob Spener or August Francke. There were also those who operated outside of the established churches for a variety of reasons—this group is often referred to as the radical Pietists. It is important to keep in mind that these divisions could be quite fluid. Added to this already fuzzy definition is transatlantic immigration and the subsequent transference of culture and belief. Pietism arrived in the Americas in 1694 and became prominent throughout the Atlantic region during the eighteenth century. American varieties of Pietism were inevitably distinct from their European counterparts.

This section will focus primarily on women in the German and Norwegian Lutheran traditions, the Moravians, and the Methodists. It is important to remember that the Moravians, who are often considered part of a more radical branch of Pietism, are a religious tradition whose founding preceded Martin Luther by at least sixty years. Their

---

7   Jonathan Strom, Hartmut Lehmann, and James Van Horn Melton, eds., *Pietism in Germany and North America 1680–1820* (Burlington, VT: Ashgate, 2009), 2.

particular form of Protestantism was forced underground for a many years, but they have a distinct history and theology that differ from those of Lutheranism. John Wesley, the founder of the Methodist movement, was influenced by both the German Pietists and the Moravians, but he never left his Anglican tradition. It was Wesley's version of piety that was most influential in what would become the United States. It may be helpful to view Pietism as a web with strands in different places influencing different people, each distinct but sharing certain commitments.

The individual elements of Pietism were not new developments in the eighteenth century. Activities such as personal piety, Bible studies, and attention to godly living were radical but also . . . not. Pietism was directly influenced by both the dogmatic debates within Lutheranism and the rationalism that was becoming increasingly prominent in the European and colonial intelligentsia. The development of religious movements that reacted against such rigidity is understandable, and when looking at the larger picture of the history of Christian thought and movements, one could view it as even expected. The attention to *personal* piety should also not be overlooked. This is a more individualistic form of Christianity, even though there was emphasis on community through Bible studies, small group prayer meetings, and the like.

Philip Jakob Spener (1635–1705) is largely considered the father of German Pietism. After receiving his doctorate, he took a post as a pastor in Frankfurt, where he founded small Bible study groups that he called "colleges of piety" to encourage faithful living. In 1675, he published *Pia Desideria*, which further explained the development of piety. Spener emphasized the Word of God, the development of a more spiritual priesthood, and Christian love and encouraged other clergy to focus less on doctrinal differences, and he even stressed sanctification, which led to criticism that he was more of a Calvinist than a Lutheran.

Spener's view on gender roles within the church is a helpful investigation into what the "father of Pietism" believed regarding women, which of course influenced the movement in general. Through his writings, he argued for an equality between men and women based on Galatians 3:28, though he also held to the scriptural ban on women teaching in public congregations outlined in Corinthians 14:34 and I Timothy 2:11–12. He seemed to support the gender norms of the era, whereby women should indeed use their gifts but within their proper domestic sphere. The issue of Christian small groups of course complicates this situation since these offered leadership positions within the home. Spener seemed to generally oppose women leading these groups, but on the other hand, there were instances where he defended women when they did.[8] While his positions may seem confusing to a modern reader, the ambivalence suggests he saw the radical equality present in scripture yet was still a man of his time and bound by societal expectations.

Historically, much of Pietistic scholarship focused on male leadership of the various movements, but newer scholarship has added immensely to the picture of gender within eighteenth-century Pietism. With an emphasis on pious living and more lay involvement

---

8   Denise D. Kettering-Lane, "Philipp Spener and the Role of Women in the Church: The Spiritual Priesthood of All Believers in German Pietism," *The Covenant Quarterly* 75, no. 1 (2017): 50–59.

in the movement, Pietism often allowed women increased leadership opportunities, and women were particularly attracted to it. There are examples of women who held prominent leadership roles within a number of Pietistic traditions, but often women's leadership was curbed by the social conventions of the time. However, when women were denied official leadership roles (which often was the case), there were other ways in which they participated as active members of their Pietist traditions.

One way in which women were able to express their religious beliefs and experiences was through the written word. There are numerous women authors, from a wide range of social classes and education levels, associated with the Pietist movement. These writings include biographical writings, religious reflections, religious poems, and hymns. Henriette Catharina von Gersdorff (1648–1726), who was notably the grandmother of Nikolaus von Zinzendorf and played an active role in his young life and education, was a particularly prolific writer. She was highly educated in literature and the arts, and she knew at least five languages. Gersdorff published her first book, called *Meditations on the Passion of Jesus*, in 1665 when she was seventeen. In 1729, her nearly nine-hundred-page book titled *Songs and Poetic Observations* was published and included both hymns and songs.[9]

Another prolific writer of the era was Johanna Eleonora von Merlau Petersen (1644–1724). She was well known within her life and is still one of the best-known female Pietists. She was born in Frankfurt to an impoverished noble family. Her mother died when she was nine, and she was sent to the court of the counts of Solms-Rödelheim at the age of twelve. In 1661, she became a lady-in-waiting to the dukes of Schleswig-Holstein-Sonderburg, and in 1664, she moved to Wiesenburg in Saxony.[10] She found court life difficult because of her religious devotion—she faced mockery and criticism, but her requests to leave were denied for many years. In 1675, she moved to Frankfurt where she lived with Maria Juliana Baur von Eyseneck, a widow and a friend of Spener's. There she taught girls and would be among a group that founded a new Pietistic circle in Saalhof.[11]

In 1680, she married a Lutheran pastor named Johann Wilhelm Petersen (1649–1727), with Spener acting as officiant. Her husband was the superintendent of the city of Eutin, though he would eventually lose his position due to his belief in the Millennial Kingdom, which became a dominant theme in his preaching. They moved to an estate in Magdeburg, where they were supported by various wealthy patrons. It was there that Johanna and her husband both wrote extensively. Between 1689 and 1719, she wrote fifteen books on various topics, including prayer, meditation, biblical exegesis, theology, and her life. There are aspects of her writings that were condemned by contemporaries, including her millenarian views and her belief in universal salvation, which were both

---

9   Ulrike Gleixner, "Pietism and Gender: Self-modeling and Agency," in *A Companion to German Pietism, 1660–1800* (Leiden: Brill, 2015), 433–435.

10 Ruth Albrecht, "Johanna Eleanor Petersen in the Context of Women's and Gender Studies," in *Pietism in Germany and North America 1860–1800* (Leiden: Brill, 2015), 71–84.

11 Gleixner, "Pietism and Gender: Self-modeling and Agency," 443.

considered unorthodox.[12] Regardless, her contributions are significant, and she represents an important voice in the earlier years of German Pietism.

Prophecy was another way in which women asserted some leadership within the community, particularly in the more radical wings of Pietism. Johanna Eleonora von Merlau Petersen experienced visionary dreams. Rosamunde Juliane von Asseburg (1672–1712) prophesized in the Petersens' house in 1691–1692. Her prophesies offered a message of both hope and consolation for the group but also confirmed the Petersens' millenarian views. Swiss Pietist Ursula Meyer's (1682–1743) prophesies were published in her book *A Heavenly Evening Glow* in 1781. Her message included expectations of the Millennial Kingdom, universal salvation, and love.[13]

While chronologically later than the beginnings of the German Lutheran Pietist revivals, the Hauge movement, a notable Norwegian Pietist revival, was significant for its large number of women in leadership and preaching roles, and their status within the church was generally higher than that in society of the time. The movement was founded by Hans Nielsen Hauge (1771–1824) after he had a dramatic spiritual conversion event in 1796 and felt called to lead a revival movement as a lay preacher. He also developed a number of businesses that helped to revitalize the flagging Norwegian economy.[14]

One of the primary reasons women held leadership roles within the movement was that Hauge supported it. He encouraged women to actively participate in meetings and speak in public. He believed that if women had the gift to speak, then they should use it.[15] Women were critical to the movement's formation and growth—they recruited others to the movement, especially through their familial networks, and they acted as preachers and leaders.

Taking on the life of a traveling preacher was a far more difficult task for women than men, and often, women preachers tended to travel together for both practical reasons and issues of safety. Between vagrancy laws and the Conventicle Act of 1741, which forbade any religious meeting not authorized by the state church, many itinerant preachers, including women preachers, were arrested. Despite the risks, there are numerous women recorded as Haugean preachers, such as Randi Andersdatter Løvaas (1776–1859), who held meetings and traveled with Hauge in 1801, and Pernille Christensdatter Void (1776–1821), who held meetings and traveled all over southern Norway, often with her friend Marthe Gabestad (1781–1841).[16]

Women were also leaders. In 1802, Hauge named thirty-three leaders around the country, and six of them were women.[17] One particularly well-known leader was Sara Oust (1778–1822). She joined the movement probably in 1799 and began speaking, reading, and singing for members of her local community and soon became a local group leader. Her group became the center of a local revival in North Osterdalen, and it appears she and

---

12 Gleixner, 443–444.

13 Gleixner, 455.

14 Thomas E. Jacobson, "St. Hans Nielson Hauge," *Lutheran Forum* 48, no. 3 (Fall 2014): 33.

15 Inger Furseth, "The Role of Women in the Hauge Movement," *Lutheran Quarterly* 13, no. 4 (Winter 1999): 396. (395–422).

16 Furseth, 400–401.

17 Furseth, 402.

about ten friends lived in community under her leadership. If this was not problematic enough to religious authorities, she was known to speak out against local clergy. At one point, a local pastor came and physically assaulted her—slapping her, yelling at her, and throwing her Bible into the fire. It was the clergyman who ended up leaving in tears after his actions.[18] Even after Sara married, she continued to lead, and her husband assisted.

The role of women declined after Hauge's death in 1824. Without his leadership and advocacy, women were pushed out of the public aspects of leadership. There are other factors that led to this decline, including general male opposition to women's leadership and the movement's shift from more rural to an increasingly urban setting. As the movement became more organized, women lost leadership opportunities, which is a common occurrence as new religious movements become more established.[19]

The above Lutheran Pietist examples are not an exhaustive look at women in these traditions, but they do demonstrate a tendency for women to gain leadership roles in a movement that is more fluid and less controlled by ecclesiastic hierarchies. Importantly, the tendency to see a person's gift and religious call as justification for a public ministry was a critical development in women gaining more voice in Protestant denominations in future centuries.

THE MORAVIANS

Often considered part of the radical branch of Pietism, the Moravian Church has a distinct history and theology that separates it from Lutheran Pietism. The Moravians descend from the fifteenth-century Bohemian martyr Jan Hus (1369–1415). About fifty years after his death, the Moravian Church, or the Unity of Brethren as it was officially called, was founded by a group of Hus's followers in eastern Bohemia. By 1517, the year Martin Luther posted his *Ninety-Five Theses*, the Moravian Church had at least two hundred thousand followers, four hundred parishes, and its own hymnal and catechism. However, in the mid-sixteenth century, a persecution began, and the Moravian Church was forced underground. It was during the eighteenth century that the church saw renewal. Moravian families fleeing persecution in Bohemia and Moravia found shelter on the estate of Count Nicholas Ludwig von Zinzendorf (1700–1760), who proved to be an important patron and ally. They built the community of Herrnhut, to which even more Moravians came. Zinzendorf, although a Lutheran, became so attracted to the Moravians that he resigned his post in Dresden and joined the community. In 1727, the community experienced a spiritual revival, and in 1732, the first Moravian missionaries were sent to the Caribbean. Within a few years, there were missionaries in the West Indies, Africa, India, South America, and North America.[20] Moravian settlements sprang up in Europe and North

---

18 Furseth, "The Role of Women in the Hauge Movement," 404.

19 Furseth, 415–416.

20 For more information on the history and theology of the Moravian Church, their website provides resources: "A Brief History of the Moravian Church," *The Moravian Church*, accessed June 1, 2021, https://www.moravian.org/2018/07/a-brief-history-of-the-moravian-church/.

America. There were numerous prominent women within the Moravian Church through the eighteenth century—leaders, writers, and missionaries.

At Herrnhut, conventional gender norms and concepts of womanhood were questioned and modified, though traditional views of wifely submission remained. Moravian theology of love between true believers emphasized a more egalitarian community regarding gender but also class and wealth.[21] A unique aspect of Herrnhut and later Moravian communities was the separation of believers into groups called choirs, which sorted believers according to their age, gender, and marital status. Believers worshiped and studied with their choirs, and notably many single believers lived in dormitory-style housing together. Therefore, while there may have been a level of equality, there was also significant separation between groups.[22] In fact, it is likely that this choir system allowed for the advancement of women into leadership roles—it was up to women to guide other women.

Within Moravian communities, women served as elders (called "congregational Judges"[23]), teachers, and overseers. One such woman who exercised considerable leadership was Anna Nitschmann (1715–1760), who was a missionary and poet and served as a formal leader within the community. She was elected to the position of general elder, a role that made her the spiritual mentor and guide to all women in the Moravian community, beginning in 1730, at the age of only fourteen. At the age of twenty-two, she wrote her autobiography, which recounts the persecution her community faced in Bohemia, her spiritual awakening at the age of eight, and her move from Bohemia to Herrnhut at the age of ten.[24] Nitschmann traveled extensively and became a missionary to the Iroquois in the 1740s. She was ordained as a deacon and became the first female presbyter in the Moravian Church. Despite the titles, it is unclear whether women presided over Communion.[25]

Regarding other instances of women's leadership, there is evidence that women sometimes contributed to the discussion at synods and conferences, though it seems unlikely they had equal status. Women did hold their own meetings and conferences, occurring mostly on the congregational levels. Women were allowed to speak, pray publicly, and give their testimonies.[26]

Like other groups of Pietists, women were frequently writers, and both women and men were encouraged to write hymns and religious poetry. Beginning in the 1750s, Moravians, again both women and men, took up the custom of writing spiritual autobiographies,

---

21 Peter Vogt, "A Voice for Themselves: Women as Participants in Congregational Discourse in the Eighteen-Century Moravian Movement," in *Women Preachers and Prophets through Two Millennia of Christianity* (Berkeley: University of California Press, 1998), 228–229.

22 Jon F. Sensbach, *A Separate Canaan: The Making of an Afro-Moravian World in North Carolina, 1763–1840* (Chapel Hill: University of North Carolina, 1998), 26.

23 Craig Atwood, "Five Centuries of Women's Leadership in the Moravian Church" (presentation, 12th Moravian Women's Conference, Sandy Cove, Maryland, June 2015), 4, https://moravianwomen.files.wordpress.com/2015/06/five-centuries-of-womens-leadership.pdf.

24 Gleixner, "Pietism and Gender: Self-modeling and Agency," 445–446.

25 Atwood, "Five Centuries of Women's Leadership in the Moravian Church," 5–7.

26 Vogt, "Moravian Women as Speaker, Preachers, and Writers," 234–235.

which interestingly would be read aloud at a believer's funeral as a final testimony.[27] The question of whether women were allowed to preach is complicated, and the practice likely varied by location. Opponents repeatedly accused Zinzendorf and the Moravians of allowing women to preach, but Zinzendorf claimed that women did not. Yet there is evidence that some women, like Rebecca Protten, who will be discussed further below, did indeed preach.

Global missions are another area in which Moravian women demonstrated leadership. The enterprise came about in an interesting way. Zinzendorf met a Black, Dutch-speaking Christian man named Anton Ulrich in 1731 while visiting the Danish court. Ulrich returned to Herrnhut with Zinzendorf, where he told the Moravians about the enslaved Africans in the West Indies and asked them to send missionaries. Two men by the name of David Nitschmann and Leonard Dober were so inspired, they left for Saint Thomas, arriving there in 1733. Apparently, they sought to become slaves as Ulrich had suggested, but because the two men were white, Danish law forbade them from doing so. Regardless, the mission was a success in relation to converting, though it brought criticism from whites on the island who believed the missionaries' message was subversive. Quickly the driving force of evangelism was not the white missionaries but Black converts who became dynamic preachers.[28]

One such individual was Rebecca Protten (1718–1780). While some aspects of her life are shrouded in mystery, there is enough information about her to give us a decent picture of her remarkable life. According to her reports she had been born with the name Shelly in Antigua but was kidnapped, taken to the island of St. Thomas, and sold as a slave to a wealthy plantation owner when she was a child. St. Thomas, a holding of Denmark, was an island where slaves outnumbered whites five to one. To control the slave population the ruling elite established draconian slave laws and a culture of brutality and terror.

Protten grew up as a slave but somehow managed to gain an education. She learned how to read and write in at least two languages, and she spoke at least five. When she was a young teenager, she converted to Christianity and was freed around the same time. It was a Catholic priest who baptized her and gave her the name Rebecca. It is unknown whether her conversion influenced her manumission, but from the records it appears that the women of the household were instrumental in her freedom. There were few freed Black people on the island, and she continued to work for her former owners but with elevated status and wages.[29]

When she was eighteen, she became connected with the Moravian missionaries that had come to St. Thomas. She became an enthusiastic evangelist, teacher, and itinerant preacher, particularly to the island's enslaved women, though she taught and preached to men as well.[30] To be clear, this calling was not without risk. The island planters, always

---

27 Vogt, 237.

28 Sensbach, *A Separate Canaan*, 31–39.

29 Jon F. Sensbach, *Rebecca's Revival: Creating Black Christianity in the Atlantic World* (Cambridge: Harvard, 2005), 28–44.

30 Sensbach, *Rebecca's Revival*, 77.

fearful of rebellion, made life difficult and often dangerous for missionaries, especially the Moravians, who they considered particularly odd. It was not unheard of for missionaries to be physically attacked or restricted in their movements. Yet she persevered and became the most influential woman evangelist on the island.

When Protten was twenty, she married one of the white missionaries, a man named Matthäus Freundlich. The marriage was arranged, and it is unknown how the two felt about each other. Later that year, they both were imprisoned on trumped-up charges, though it is likely their true crimes were evangelism and interracial marriage. Protten was released from jail somewhat shockingly by Count Zinzendorf's unexpected arrival on the island.

After their ordeal, the couple headed to Germany, but Protten's husband died on the way. She joined the community of Moravians, living in the widow's choir. While there, she and another Afro-Caribbean woman were both ordained as deaconesses. The importance of this cannot be glossed over. These two likely were the first Black women ordained in Western Christianity in the modern age. After four years, she married a Moravian missionary named Christian Protten. While this was likely another arranged marriage, the two seemed to be fond of each other. Eventually the two moved to the Gold Coast in Africa, where they ran a school for mixed-race children. It is unclear how Rebecca spent the last years of her life, but she died in 1780, a widow still living on the African coast.[31]

THE WESLEYAN TRADITIONS

Around the time Rebecca Protten was first meeting Moravian missionaries on St. Thomas, another group of Moravian missionaries was heading to Georgia, in the American colonies, on a different mission. On the way, this group met a young Anglican priest by the name of John Wesley (1703–1791), who was heading to his post in Savannah. It is unknown how these missionaries perceived Wesley, but they left a profound impact on him. Wesley failed as a pastor in Savannah, and back in England he sought the advice of a Moravian. Following this exchange, Wesley had a conversion experience—a strange warming of his heart. After visiting the community at Herrnhut, Wesley knew the Moravian life was not for him, but he did unleash a new and transformative movement that would profoundly influence Christianity from that point forward.

Wesley's influence on modern Christianity has been undeniably immense. Wesley never intended to establish a new denomination. He worked under the assumption that Methodist meetings would prepare and enrich believers for worship within the Anglican Church, and he remained an Anglican priest until the day he died. However, the Methodist movement broke away from the Anglican Church, and in the United States, the new denomination was in the hands of Francis Asbury. The Methodist movement and later

---

31 For an in-depth look at both her life and an examination of Moravian missionary activity on the island of St. Thomas, see Sensbach, *Rebecca's Revival*.

Methodist denominations had a structure and theology that was conducive to women's leadership even in the early days.

Wesley was unsuccessful in his romantic relationships, and this sometimes colors how people have viewed his relationship with women. However, he was deeply influenced by his very capable mother, Susanna Wesley (1669–1742). While Susanna is most often associated with her famous reforming sons, John and Charles, she was an energetic and devout woman who pushed boundaries and is a genuinely interesting religious figure in her own right.

Susanna was the daughter of a Presbyterian minister who held a religious appointment until the Restoration when, refusing to subscribe to the Book of Common Prayer, he was removed. This is of particular interest because despite Susanna's upbringing within the Nonconformist streams of English Christianity, she joined the Church of England. In 1688, she married Samuel Wesley, who, like Susanna, was the child of a Presbyterian minister but also joined the Church of England. In 1689, Samuel was ordained an Anglican priest. The two had a large family, and finances were tight. Susanna spent much of her time educating her many children, both the boys and girls, despite it being irregular for girls to receive a thorough religious education at the time.[32]

In a move that was perceived as both overstepping her role and foreshadowing the Methodist movement, Susanna held irregular prayer services in her own home on Sundays during the winter of 1711–12. These evening gatherings were so popular (with likely about two hundred people in regular attendance) that her husband, who was in London at the time as a delegate to the Church of England convocation, got word of her activities. Her detractors accused her of conducting clandestine conventicles and usurping the authority of her husband. Samuel wrote a letter to his wife rebuking her, but she was not so easily dissuaded. She responded with a vigorous defense of her activities. Still unconvinced, Samuel wrote her again telling her stop. Her response was stunningly defiant:

> If you do, after all, think fit to dissolve this assembly, do not tell me any more than you desire me to do it, for that will not satisfy my conscience; but send me your positive command in such full and express terms as may absolve me from all guilt and punishment for neglecting this opportunity of doing good to souls, when you and I shall appear before the great and awful tribunal of our Lord Jesus Christ.[33]

Her husband relented. As an adult, John Wesley, who replicated this small group model with his own Methodist societies, read over this correspondence between his parents and recognized his mother's gift as a "preacher of righteousness."[34]

The respect Wesley felt for his mother certainly influenced his progressive views on women's involvement in leadership. While he never endorsed women's ordination, he did

---

32 Charles Wallace, ed., *Susanna Wesley: The Complete Writings* (New York: Oxford University Press, 1997), 4–11.

33 Susanna Wesley, "To Samuel Wesley Sr., 25 February 1711/12," in Wallace, ed., *Susanna Wesley: The Complete Writings*, 13.

34 Wallace, ed., *Susanna Wesley: The Complete Writings*, 14.

believe that women held an important role in the church, and when talks were held about limiting the role of women, he enthusiastically defended their right to pray, sing, and read the scriptures in public.[35]

Wesley organized his followers into societies, first meeting in homes and later in their own buildings. When societies grew too large, he broke them into classes, with eleven members and a leader. These classes met weekly to read Scripture, pray, discuss religious matters, and collect funds.[36] This proved an ideal situation for women to lead, and lead they did. Another unique feature of Methodism was the use of laypeople in preaching, which was first and foremost practical. Wesley's movement became popular, yet Anglican priests were rarely willing to join. After heeding the advice of his mother, he approved of lay preachers, though they were not to take the place of clergy and were not to offer Communion. This space of public preacher yet not ordained clergy became another area where women exercised religious leadership and influence.

The move to women's preaching was somewhat gradual in the early Methodist tradition. The first women to speak publicly for their faith prayed or utilized the practice of exhorting, which resembled preaching but was considered a unique activity, at least in name. The first Methodist woman formally authorized to preach was Sarah Crosby (1729–1804). Crosby heard Wesley preach in 1750 and shortly after joined the movement, becoming a class leader two years later. It seems her husband left her in 1757, and she found companionship living with a group of Methodist women, including Mary Bosanquet Fletcher (1763–1815). This group worked among the poor in London, and soon their activities became well known. In 1760, Crosby experienced a profound conversion experience and felt the call to preach, at which she was apparently remarkably gifted. She sought council from Wesley, and he supported her public preaching.[37] Soon there were a number of women preaching, including Ann Gilbert, the first Cornish woman to preach; Elizabeth Hurrell in Yorkshire, Lancashire, and Derbyshire; and Margaret Davidson in Ireland.[38] While women made up a minority of preachers in the early Methodist movement, their presence and influence cannot be exaggerated.

It was in 1769 that the first Methodist preachers, recruited by Wesley, arrived in the Americas.[39] However, it wouldn't be until after the American Revolution that Methodism would explode under the capable leadership of Francis Asbury, the first American bishop. Once Methodism was established in the Americas, the early tradition of women playing an active role in the faith continued.

Racial prejudice quickly led to a split within the movement. In 1787, a small group of African American Methodists, fed up with ill treatment from white Christians at St. George Methodist Episcopal Church in Philadelphia, walked out in protest. The

---

35 Paul Wesley Chilcote, *John Wesley and the Women Preachers of Early Methodism* (Metuchen, NJ: The American Theological Library Association and the Scarecrow Press, Inc., 1991), 21–24.

36 Gonzáles, *The Story of Christianity II*, 269.

37 Chilcote, *John Wesley and the Women Preachers of Early Methodism*, 118–123.

38 Chilcote, 145–161.

39 J. Gordon Melton, *A Will to Choose: The Origins of African American Methodism* (Lanham: Rowman & Littlefield Publishers, Inc., 2007), 43.

protesting Christians formed a mutual aid society called the Free African Society. Within the Free African Society, there were women included in the original charter, such as Jane Ann Murray and Sarah Dougherty. Dougherty, a well-known widow in the area, opened her home to the newly formed society,. and it was their regular meeting place until December of 1788. Also significantly, women were voting members of the organization, so they had a voice in how the organization's money was allocated.[40]

The community desired to be a Christian church, not just a mutual aid society. There were some disagreements on structure and denomination affiliation. Some members left to form an Episcopalian denomination, but others stayed and organized the Bethel African Methodist Church. Other African American Methodist organizations were forming in other cities in the United States as well, and in 1816 sixteen representatives from five different states met at Bethel Church and formed the African Methodist Episcopal Church (AME) under the leadership of their first bishop, Richard Allen. While women did not act as representatives at the meeting, we know there were women in attendance, including Allen's second wife, Sara Bass Allen (1764–1849), who acted as hostess for the event.[41]

Bass Allen was born into slavery in 1764 in Virginia but brought to Philadelphia when she was eight years old. While there is little available information on her early life, we know she had obtained her freedom by 1800. Like many women of the era, her primary work was maintaining her household and raising her children, but she was also actively involved in supporting the work of the AME.[42] During that critical founding meeting in 1816, the men discussed denominational affiliation, while the women gathered in another room. The task at hand was mending the clergy's clothing so that they would look their best as representatives of their new denomination. This event was a preview of the continued efforts that women's groups provided their congregations in the form of raising funds, mending garments, and providing itinerant clergy with meals and housing. In 1828, the local women's groups were officially designated the Daughters of Conference. Others women's groups in the AME included the Independent Daughters of Hope, United Daughters of Tapaico, Sisters of the Good Shepherd, Daughters of Sharon, African Female Tract Association, and Daughters of Samaria.[43] The foundation of these women's aid societies became critical in the functioning of the denomination.

In addition to the critical support roles women provided, some women associated with the AME, such as Jarena Lee and Amanda Berry Smith, made names for themselves as talented preachers and evangelists, a topic to which we shall return in chapter 9. Indeed, throughout the nineteenth and twentieth centuries, Methodist women continued to be influential preachers, missionaries, and reformers.

40 Jualynne E. Dobson, *Engendering Church: Women, Power, and the AME Church* (Lanham: Rowman & Littlefield Publishers, Inc., 2002), 10.

41 Dobson, *Engendering Church*, 11–16.

42 "Sara Allen," *Africans in America, Part 3: Brotherly Love*, PBS Online, accessed February 3, 2022, https://www.pbs.org/wgbh/aia/part3/3p246.html.

43 Dobson, *Engendering Church*, 46.

THE FIRST GREAT AWAKENING

After considering Lutheran Pietism, Moravian missions, and the growth of Methodism, the First Great Awakening, which is a term that describes a series of religious revivals that occurred in both the British Isles and the American colonies in the 1730s and 1740s, makes sense. In the American colonies, this series of revivals led to an all-around greater commitment to faith and conversion. Its reach was not as immense as that of the Second Great Awakening (which will be discussed in chapter 9), but the First Great Awakening established patterns of popular religion that would come to dominate in the United States. With leading figures such as Jonathan Edwards and George Whitefield, key features of the First Great Awakening included calls to conversion, itinerant preaching (often outdoors), media use to promote revivals, ecumenical interests, and an emphasis on approachable preaching, often using the vernacular. Other lasting legacies include the establishment of colleges and a greater commitment to missions. One can also argue that this revival led to a tradition of undermining clerical authority.

Outside of the fledgling Methodist circles, women had a limited leadership role in the First Great Awakening, but their participation within the revival atmosphere was evident. The role of women in the church was on the cusp of change. These new religious methods, including but not limited to religious experiences outside of churches, would eventually lead to an atmosphere where women were more involved in church leadership and parachurch organizations.

Despite limitations, there were women who managed to carve out leadership roles for themselves. One of the most remarkable examples is a Puritan woman by the name of Sarah Osborn (1692–1674), who left an autobiography and other letters and writings through which we can understand her active ministry.

Osborn was born in England but moved to the American colonies in 1722, married at eighteen, and was widowed with a young son before she was twenty. To support herself she became a schoolteacher. She married again in 1742, but her husband's business failings forced her to return to teaching once again. She was converted in 1737, and in the 1740s she led a young women's religious society called the Female Society in her home that met for decades.

In the 1760s, when revival hit Newport, her Female Society experienced revival as well, and Osborn felt driven to expand her leadership roles to other areas. At one point Osborn held religious meetings in her home six days of the week. She also began teaching a group of African Americans on Sunday evenings that included a young men's society. It was this activity, teaching men, that became a point of concern for her spiritual advisor, Joseph Fish. He believed that she was stepping out of her appropriate gender role. Through a series of letters between Osborn and Fish, she vigorously defended her actions through a detailed argument that includes God's call, her ability to care for her family despite her ministry work, and a less than subtle mention that no men were willing to engage in this work.[44] It does appear that her defense was successful because she continued with these

---

44 Sarah Osborn, "My Resting and Reaping Times: Sarah Osborn's Defense of her Revival Activities, Written to her Spiritual Adviser, Revered Joseph Fish," in *Women and Religion in America, Volume 2: The Colonial Period and Revolutionary Periods*,

activities. Interestingly, a few years later, Osborn and her Female Society were influential in calling pastor Samuel Hopkins to First Church Newport. This simple fact demonstrates that women did indeed have influence over which pastors were being called. Hopkins, who had been a disciple of Jonathan Edwards, respected Osborn so much that he published her memoirs[45] and edited some of her writings on biblical and other religious topics.[46]

While not a religious leader in a traditional sense, Phillis Wheatley (c. 1753–1784) was a deeply religious and skilled poet who lived in Boston during the Revolutionary War era. Scholarly treatment of Wheatley has been mixed. For example, scholar Eleanor Smith criticized Wheatley for her lack of attention to enslaved Black people. She argues that "Wheatley did not help herself by following all the dictates of Whites nor did she contribute to the well-being of Black people of her time."[47] However, Sondra O'Neale argues that any evaluation of Wheatley must consider her status as a slave and that Wheatley did indeed wage a subtle war against slavery.[48]

Wheatley was kidnapped from Africa as a young child and sold to John Wheatley, a white tailor, in Boston in 1761. Wheatley became a personal slave to John's wife, Susannah, and they taught her to read and write, and she was educated in scripture, Latin, and classics. While still a teenager, she began to write poetry.[49] Her book, *Poems of Various Subjects, Religious and Moral*, was the first published book written by a Black woman in America. She was also only one of three Americans who were able to publish while they were still enslaved, which is an important point to note. After Susanna died, Wheatley was freed in 1774. That same year, Wheatley penned a letter to Reverend Samson Occum, an Indian American Presbyterian preacher, in which she states:

> Otherwise, perhaps, the Israelites had been less solicitous for their Freedom from Egyptian slavery; I do not say they would have been contented without it, by no means, for in every human Breast, God has implanted a Principle, which we call Love of Freedom; it is impatient of Oppression, and pants for Deliverance; and by the Leave of our modern Egyptians I will assert, that the same Principle lives in us.[50]

After her manumission, Wheatley faced financial hardships, and she even worked as a washerwoman to support herself while still writing poetry. In 1778, Wheatley married

eds. Rosemary Radford Ruether and Rosemary Skinner Keller (Cambridge: Harper and Row, 1983), 348–351.

45 Samuel Hopkins, *Memoirs of the Life of Sarah Osborn who died at Newport (Rhode Island) on the Second Day of August, 1796 in the Eighty-third year of her Age*, 2nd ed. (Catskill, NY: N. Elliot, bookseller, 1815).

46 Susan Hill Lindley, *You Have Stept Out of Your Place: A History of Women and Religion in America* (Louisville: Westminster John Knox Press, 1996), 45–46.

47 Eleanor Smith, "Phillis Wheatley: A Black Perspective," in "Black English and Black History-Continuing Themes," special issue, *Journal of Negro Education* 43, no. 3 (Summer 1974): 407.

48 Sondra O'Neale, "A Slave's Subtle War: Phillis Wheatley's Use of Biblical Myth and Symi," *Early American Literature* 21, no. 2 (Fall 1986): 144–165.

49 Smith, "Phillis Wheatley," 403.

50 Phillis Wheatley, "Letter to Reverent Samson Occum (1774)," *The Connecticut Gazette*, March 7, 1774, https://www.learningforjustice.org/classroom-resources/texts/hard-history/letter-to-reverend-samson-occum.

a man named John Peters, but her financial situation did not improve. His business ventures were unsuccessful, likely victims of the political and economic instability of the Revolutionary War. Wheatley died in 1784 while her husband was in jail for being unable to pay off a debt. Their last surviving child died in time to be buried with Wheatley.

REVOLUTIONARY-ERA UTOPIAN EXPERIMENTS

While some women were making small but steady gains in religious leadership within more traditional Christian churches and movements, other women were carving out a place for themselves in new and experimental religions, particularly in North America. Situated within the disruptive Revolutionary era, these religious leaders, generally styled as prophets, helped establish the long tradition of American creativity in religious and utopian experiments. Unlike ecclesial leaders, prophets receive authority from God alone—not institutions. Many of these Revolutionary-era prophets were espousing ideas relating to end times, an unsurprising fact considering the social disruption.

Mother Ann Lee

The Shakers were one of the most successful and longest-lasting of the communal religious experiments in American history. Today largely remembered for their high-quality furniture, in the eighteenth and nineteenth centuries, they were a radical religious sect, engaging in communal living that dismantled traditional family structures. Remarkably, they were led by a woman who claimed to be the second coming of Christ, and they believed that the millennial dispensation had begun with their small society.

The story of the Shakers is inevitably bound to the life of their founder, Mother Ann Lee, though the entire affair is somewhat shrouded in mystery. Neither Mother Ann Lee, who was illiterate, nor any other founding members wrote any of their beliefs down. This leads to difficulty in analyzing the evolution of early Shaker history and theology. However, the basic details of Lee's life are available, from which we can piece together a story of both her life and the founding of the Shakers.

While her exact birthdate is unknown, Lee was baptized on June 1, 1742, in Manchester, England, which was a manufacturing town. Her father was a blacksmith, and in 1762, she married another blacksmith named Abraham Standerin. She had four children, but none would survive past early childhood. At some point during this time, she became increasingly fearful of sexual intercourse, and in 1770 she had a vision of Adam and Eve having sex. From this vision she came to believe that this act had caused the fall of humanity and the entrance of sin into the world. Following this vision, Jesus came to her and told her to preach this message to the world, which she did.[51] There has been no shortage of speculation on Ann Lee herself through the years. Wild assertions have been thrown out on the origins of her belief in celibacy, and Lee's own sex life has been

---

51 Lawrence Foster, *Women, Family, and Utopia: Communal Experiments of the Shakers, the Oneida Community, and the Mormons* (Syracuse: Syracuse University Press, 1991), 22.

thoroughly analyzed. Although her teachings on celibacy were looked at with suspicion within English, and later American, society, Lee is hardly the first religious woman who rejected sex after the tragic loss of her children.

Lee gained a small following, but considering her radical message, her group faced persecution in England. In 1774, Lee, her husband, and a few other Shakers decided to leave England and try their luck in the American colonies.[52] During Lee's lifetime, the Shakers grew modestly and again faced persecutions from their neighbors on American soil. The movement was not highly organized, and there was still a fluidity in ideas and practices. Lee died in 1784, to be replaced by James Whittaker, who died in 1787. It was Joseph Meacham, an American recruit to the Shakers, who took over leadership next. One of his first acts was to appoint a woman named Lucy Wright (1760–1821) as co-leader. This pattern of a man and a woman in co-leadership positions would continue from this point on. It was under their leadership that the Shakers were gathered together in communal living on self-sustaining farms. The gathering had several practical advantages, such as protection from external threats of persecution, economic stability for members, and a strong sense of unity and common purpose.[53]

When Meacham died in 1796, he was replaced, but Wright became the effective head of the Shaker society, and it was under her tenure that the Shakers began their great expansion. Wright was a gifted leader, but her path to the Shaker community had been anything but assured. Her life started in a conventional manner. Wright was the daughter of middle-class farmers, and she married Elizer Goodrich, a Revolutionary War vet, in 1779. For whatever reason, the couple, though fond of each other, found themselves to be incompatible in marriage. It was Goodrich who wanted to join the Shakers, not Wright. It is unclear exactly what her feelings were toward the religious movement, though she displayed hesitancy. While it was possible for her to have sued for a divorce, likely the easiest solution was for her to join the community along with her husband, which she did. Despite any initial reservations, she proved to be a devoted member and an effective leader.[54]

The Shakers were bound by many rules and regulations to ensure celibacy. These rules were designed to keep the sexes as separate as possible while they continued to cohabitate. Men and women were not permitted to talk, walk, or ride together in private. They were not allowed to give each other gifts or eat at the same tables. Men were not allowed to provide medical treatment to a woman unless a female nurse was present. There were rules about who would go up and down stairs first and what side of the church they would sit on, and children were raised only by their same gender. Women were not allowed to walk alone in fields or in barns, nor were they allowed to sit cross-legged.[55] Despite all

---

52 Foster, 27.

53 Stein, *The Shaker Experience*, 43.

54 Glendyne R. Werland, "The Short Marriage of Mother Lucy Wright," in *Sisters in the Faith: Shaker Women and Equality of the Sexes* (Amherst: University of Massachusetts Press, 2011), 29–41.

55 Louis J. Kern, *Ordered Love: Sex Roles and Sexuality in Victorian Utopias—the Shakers, the Mormons, and the Oneida Community* (Chapel Hill: The University of North Carolina Press, 1981), 94–95.

the regulations, men and women lived in the same Shaker community and interacted with each other on a regular basis.

The Shakers are an interesting example of a community that was committed to radical egalitarianism during the eighteenth century. Their founder was a woman, and their leadership structure was set up in such a way that both women and men shared power. Alas, celibacy for all members of a religious community inhibits the growth and longevity of a movement. The Shakers gradually declined in number. As of the writing of this book, there are a mere three Shakers left living in Sabbathday Lake Shaker Village in New Gloucester, Maine.[56]

Public Universal Friend

The Public Universal Friend is currently having a moment in both historical and popular circles. For roughly 250 years the Friend served as a curiosity or a footnote to Revolutionary-era history, but it is likely that the Friend is now better known than at any point in history. Major news outlets, such as the *Washington Post* and *NPR*, have both run stories about this "genderless" prophet.[57] As non-binary identities have grown in visibility, the Friend has been seen as an important historical figure who rejected traditional gender norms and embraced a gender-fluid identity. Historians have long struggled with pronouns when discussing the Friend. It is believed that the Friend's followers at least occasionally used male pronouns, but the Friend avoided using any pronoun at all—instead choosing to be called the Public Universal Friend or simply the Friend—because the Friend was neither male nor female. When asked directly about gender identity, the Friend answered with a simple "I am what I am." As is evident, the Friend cannot simply be seen as a "woman preacher" or "lady religious leader," though in the past, the Friend was often categorized that way. The Friend defied traditional gender norms, but the importance of this figure led me to include the Friend's story in this chapter. The Friend was a charismatic and effective prophet in a tumultuous era, and studying this figure helps us better understand the religious atmosphere of the era.

The Universal Public Friend was born as Jemima Wilkinson in the American colonies in the year 1751. Wilkinson was a fourth-generation American of European descent, and her family were members of the colonial Rhode Island elite. Her father was a Quaker, and Wilkinson was influenced by that religious tradition. Around the turn of the Revolutionary War, a series of incidents pushed the Wilkinson family out of their local meeting. Wilkinson, inspired by George Whitefield, joined the New Light Baptists and was then kicked out of the Quaker meeting in 1776. Her sister was kicked out for becoming pregnant outside of marriage, and some of her brothers were kicked out for fighting in the war. Compounded by the highly stressful political situation (going to war against the British), Wilkinson became ill and claimed to have died.

---

56 A link to the community's website: https://www.maineshakers.com/.

57 Samantha Schmidt, "A genderless prophet drew hundreds of followers long before the age of nonbinary pronouns," *Washington Post*, January 5, 2020, History, https://www.washingtonpost.com/history/2020/01/05/long-before-theythem-pronouns-genderless-prophet-drew-hundreds-followers/. Throughline, "Public Universal Friend," produced by Rund Abdelfatah, March 5, 2020, podcast, 48:00, https://www.npr.org/2020/03/04/812092399/public-universal-friend.

From this point on the person of Jemima Wilkinson was gone. In her place was the Public Universal Friend, a messianic figure who was believed to be using Wilkinson's body after her spirit departed. The Public Universal Friend said the Friend's mission was to preach to a sinful and dying world. Although the Friend's personal claims were radical for the time, the Friend's theology and preaching were surprisingly mundane. In many respects the Friend's theology was similar to Quakerism, and the Friend taught an interesting blend of practical teachings and biblical teachings, along with some mystical interpretations of dreams, prophesies, and faith healings, though the Friend would later abandon the faith healings. The Friend taught that celibacy was preferred but not mandatory. Simply put, it was the figure of the Friend who was controversial, not so much the Friend's message.

Immediately after rebirth, the Friend went out and began preaching and amassing a following that became known as the Universal Friends. While the Friend's supporters grew, so did detractors. The Friend was accused of a variety of crimes that ranged from hiding a secret pregnancy to blasphemy. In 1790, the Friend decided to retire from public preaching and create a place of refuge—a utopian community in western New York named Jerusalem.[58] By 1800, the settlement had about 260 inhabitants, and the Friend was deeply involved in local affairs including mediating disputes between local whites and American Indians.[59]

The Public Universal Friend died in 1819 at the age of sixty-seven. The community of Jerusalem did not last long after their prophet and leader's death. Within twenty years, the entire experiment had unraveled. It appears that without the charismatic figure of the Friend, there was little motivation to continue as a community.

---

58 Susan Juster, *Doomsayers: Anglo-American Prophesy in the Age of Revolution* (Philadelphia: University of Pennsylvania Press, 2003), 221–222.

59 Juster, 223.

CHAPTER 8

Women and Global Missions

As a historian who teaches the history of Christianity at a seminary, I have covered global missions on numerous occasions, and it is a subject that students consistently find challenging. On the one hand, they understand as divinity students that the Great Commission is part of their faith. They know that the church was able to expand from a tiny sect in Israel to a global faith because of missions. On the other hand, we are living in a post-colonial world where imperialism and colonialism have had a profound impact (often in the form of significant harm), particularly in the areas of the world often termed the "Global South." It is not just seminary students who are struggling to sort out the relationship between missions and imperialism/colonialism. This has been an important question in historical studies, and historians, too, link missions with Western imperialism. The connection is made for obvious reasons—the rise of Protestant missions coincides with ambitious imperialist policies designed to carve up the world for European (and later American and Japanese) powers. Missionaries often had access to mission fields because of these policies, and they did frequently carry with them beliefs, either consciously or subconsciously, of their cultural superiority.

However, it would be false to assert that missionaries were uncritically supportive of imperial powers. There were numerous occasions when Western missionaries were vocal opponents of imperialistic governments. Missionaries' primary concern was to spread the gospel, not act as political agents for their home countries. That being said, there have been too many instances when Christianity came to a new land with both the cross and the sword and too many instances when missionaries confused faith and culture and imposed Western cultural norms alongside teaching about the Christian faith. While it is appealing in our modern era to deem individual acts or movements "good" or "bad," this is rarely a good idea when dealing with history, and it is especially unhelpful when contending with this particular topic. One hundred years ago, most Westerners viewed missions as "good." Now there is far more nuanced reflection on what was gained and what was lost through missionary activity—and there is increased pessimism in general. Regardless of where someone falls in their assessment of missions, they are important aspects of history to wrestle with. These questions have a profound impact on how Christians should conduct missions today.

Compounding the already complex history of global missions is that there are a multitude of different stories. Missionaries hailed from a plethora of different denominations and missionary societies, founded in different countries, and they worked in a multitude of different mission fields. For example, how a Catholic brother conducted his ministry in sixteenth-century Mexico is going to look different from how an American Baptist woman conducted her ministry in Burma in the nineteenth century. One cannot simply lump all missionaries, missionary societies, or mission fields together.

To more specific issues regarding the history of missions, often historians will pinpoint the eighteenth century as the rise of global missions. This is of course only part of the story—specifically the Protestant part. The Christian church in its varied forms has been involved in missions from its earliest days. There was a renewed effort toward global missions with Columbian contact in the Americas (discussed in more detail in chapter 6) and increased interaction between Europe and Africa and Asia around the same time. These missions were conducted primarily by Catholic religious, and their impact varied depending on when and where missionaries were sent. The first part of this chapter is devoted to women who interacted with Catholic missionaries in Africa and Asia. These are also stories of resistance and reclaiming. The second part of this chapter is devoted to the global missions that blossomed in the nineteenth and twentieth centuries. This will be the more familiar section to many readers, covering women's missionary societies and the ecumenical work that came to be so important in that movement.

Due to the incredibly complex history of missions, this chapter does not attempt a systematic analysis of all missions. A historian would need to write volumes to complete such a task. This chapter instead gives glimpses and stories from the perspectives of both women missionaries (and missionary societies) and the women receiving (or rejecting) the message. These stories are fragments, parts of a complicated and unruly whole. But through these glimpses, you can see determined women shaping their own destinies and the world around them.

KOREA AND COLUMBA KANG WANSUK

We begin our look in Asia, the birthplace of Christianity. People often forget that Jesus and his first followers lived their entire lives in western Asia. Despite its beginnings and consistent presence in Asia, today Christianity is largely a minority religion within the region, though the number of Christians is indeed growing. One of the most successful Christian communities in East Asia is South Korea. Today approximately 30 percent of South Koreans are Christian—about 11 percent Catholic and the rest Protestant. These numbers include the largest Pentecostal church in the world, Yoido Full Gospel Church in Seoul, which incredibly has close to half a million members and over five hundred pastors.[1] The success of Korean Christianity is surprising considering in the year 1900, only about 1 percent of the population was Christian.[2] Conversely, in North Korea, estimates

---

1   Yaqoido Full Gospel Church, "About us," Yoido Full Gospel Church, accessed April 23, 2022, https://english.fgtv.com/a01/01 .asp.

2   Phillip Connor, "6 Facts about South Korea's growing Christian population," *Pew Research Center*, last modified August 12, 2014, https://www.pewresearch.org/fact-tank/2014/08/12/6-facts-about-christianity-in-south-korea/.

of Christian adherence are low, and stories of Christian persecution are harrowing; it is one of the most dangerous places to be a Christian in the world.[3]

Despite the incredible growth of South Korean Christianity in the twentieth century, Korea has a much older relationship with Christianity.[4] It is likely that Korea had some interaction with Christianity, particular its Eastern forms, long before the first permanent Christian communities in the 1700s, but the primary religions in Korea until that point included indigenous Korean religions, Buddhism, and Confucianism. In 1777, a group of Korean scholars organized a seminar to study Chinese writings about Catholicism, which had been brought to Korea from China through diplomatic missions. By the 1780s this group was looked at with suspicion within society. It must be emphasized that foreign missionaries did not bring Christianity to Korea in a typical missionary outreach. It was Koreans who initiated the study of Christian writings and the adherence to this new faith. The initial believers were not Catholic in a traditional sense. Because there were no priests in the earliest days of the Christian movements, there was no Mass or administration of the sacraments. Believers studied, prayed, and held discussions, but they could not fully participate in the Catholic faith until the arrival of a Chinese priest named Zhou Wen-mo in 1795. Like the Korean-led introduction of Christianity, the priest was not sent but requested by the Christian community in Korea to come and serve.[5]

From its beginnings, women played a large role in the Korean Church. In some interesting parallels to the early church, the Christian faith was largely practiced within the home and therefore largely within the domain of women. Likewise, because it was underground, much of the evangelistic efforts happened within the home, within families, and within the private sphere of women. Women were therefore critical in the spread of the faith. Of the women in this early Christian movement, Kang Wan-suk (1761–1801; commonly referred to as Columba in Western sources) was one of the most important and influential. We know of her through both Catholic and government sources, and her importance in the church is undisputed—she was one of the key leaders in the movement.

Kang Wan-suk was from the Tŏksan (now Yesan) district in southwestern Ch'ungch'ŏng province, which, along with Seoul, was an active area in the early Christian church. She was from a semi-noble family and married into a family of a similar status, probably when she was a teenager. She married a widower who had a son, and she gave birth to a daughter in 1781. It seems she was Buddhist or at least interested in Buddhism before she converted to Catholicism. We do not know exactly when she converted, but it must have been sometime before 1791 because that year she was arrested and briefly imprisoned during a large roundup of Catholics. She began evangelizing for her new faith, and her earliest converts included her parents, her mother-in-law, and her stepson. Her

3 It must be noted that these are merely estimates. Due to Christianity's illegal status and North Korea's closed nature, more accurate numbers are simply not possible.

4 Korea was divided into North Korea and South Korea in 1945.

5 Sebastian C. H. Kim and Kirsteen Kim, *A History of Korean Christianity* (New York: Cambridge University Press, 2015), 28–29.

husband refused to convert, and eventually they divorced. Interestingly, when Kang left, her mother-in-law and stepson left with her.[6]

Without a husband to slow her down, she left for Seoul, where she played numerous important roles in the church. She lived in a house with several other Catholic women, in a sort of makeshift celibate monastic community. Since she was literate and well versed in doctrine, she oversaw catechesis for women, encouraged women to evangelize and start their own congregations, and also ministered to women in need. In a society with separate spheres for men and women, she was central to the lives of Catholic women. This separateness was also a key reason she became the perfect protector for Korea's one and only priest.

Shortly after Father Zhou's arrival, his presence was betrayed, and he had to flee. He found safety for the next six years with Kang. Her home would be his home, office, and church. Kang coordinated his schedule, worked as his liaison, and most importantly became responsible for his safety. His presence in her home was an absolute secret, even among most of the Christians in the community, and she was the sole person who knew of all his movements and travels among this underground community. With Kang's help, Zhou was able to focus on establishing the church, teaching doctrine, performing the sacraments, and training leaders. Her presence and protection made his role possible.

In 1801, following the death of her husband, the dowager queen of Korea declared a formal prohibition on Catholicism. The persecution was severe and largely targeted the leadership. Some Catholics were beaten and tortured to make them renounce their faith; if they did not, they were killed. Other Catholics were exiled. During this persecution, Kang was forced to move Zhou to the residence of two other women: Maria Song and Maria Sin. Kang was arrested and tortured horrifically but never gave up Zhou's position, and she was finally executed. To Kang's credit, Zhou was never caught. In the end he turned himself over to the authorities, hoping that it would stop the persecutions. It did not. In fact, the persecutions intensified when it was realized how close a relationship the priest had with noblewomen. Zhou, like Kang, was executed by beheading.[7] With most of the male leadership and the only priest dead, Catholicism returned to its former lay-led status for a number of decades before more priests were sent to Korea in the 1830s. Women continued to exercise leadership within this underground movement, including preserving the memories of the martyrs.[8]

It is safe to say that without Kang, the Christian community in Korea would have been far less successful. Her bravery in the face of persecutions and even death has inspired many and is a testament to her faith. Unfortunately, we do not have any of her own writings on faith, so we do not know the extent of her theological reflection; nor do we know how or why she decided to embrace the faith in the first place. She emphasized chastity and a virginal life. Due to her close contact with Zhou, it is likely she had more Catholic

6 Gari Ledyard, "Kollumba Kang Wansuk, an Early Catholic Activist and Martyr," in *Christianity in Korea*, eds. Robert E. Buswell and Timothy S. Lee (Honolulu: University of Hawai'i Press, 2006), 38–71, http://www.jstor.org/stable/j.ctt6wr2rg.7.

7 Kim and Kim, *A History of Korean Christianity*, 31–36.

8 Kim and Kim, 38.

knowledge than most. As for her general character, we can assess that she was a highly capable person who acted outside the expected sphere based on her gender and status. She became a leader of an illegal faith knowing full well what could, and eventually did, happen to her.

It should be noted that once Protestant missionaries began to appear in Korea later in the 1800s, there were certain similarities between how Catholic and Protestant women functioned within their respective churches. Like Catholicism, Protestantism in its varying forms, including Methodism, Presbyterianism, Anglicism, and so on, offered women more agency and leadership opportunities than traditional Confucian culture. Women were encouraged to learn to read so that they could study the scriptures, which in turn led to more women being literate in general. Women were active in evangelism, especially among their families and through networks of other women, and they proved to be capable evangelists indeed. One early convert, Chun Sam-deok, for example, is credited with leading six hundred people to Christ. Another evangelist, a Methodist convert by the name of Kim Gang, became an itinerant preacher with a circuit of over 1,450 miles, and she faced various forms of opposition and hardship, including imprisonment, but continued with her mission. Korean Protestant women also benefitted from the community provided by their church networks. These networks provided women with both social and spiritual companionship but also aid. Protestant women also participated in various reform efforts, including those for literacy for women and temperance, and they publicly fought against the practice of concubinage.[9]

WALATTA-PETROS AND VITA KIMPA – OPPOSITION TO CATHOLIC MISSIONARIES

It was Koreans who instigated their relationship with Christianity, but that was not the case in many other contexts around the world. In the case of Ethiopia, which was already Christian when Jesuits arrived, the interactions between the people and Catholic missionaries could not have been more different from the experience of the Korean Catholic Church.

This is ultimately a story of resistance, a story about women who defied European powers to preserve their own form of Christianity in the seventeenth century. To understand Walatta-Petros and her resistance to the European Catholicism that was brought to Ethiopia by Jesuit missionaries, one must understand a little about the Ethiopian Orthodox Church. It is one of the ancient churches, and the story of the baptism of the Ethiopian eunuch in Acts 8 establishes a connection that traces back to the apostles. It was administratively tied to the Coptic Orthodox Church throughout most of its existence but has been independent since 1959. Like the Coptic Church, the Ethiopian Church rejected the Council of Chalcedon in the fifth century and is miaphysite.

---

9 Kim and Kim, *A History of Korean Christianity*, 75–76.

From its beginning the Ethiopian Church was distinctly African. Ethiopia was beyond the reach of both Rome and Persia, and Ethiopian Christianity grew and developed in its African context. Inevitably, an ancient church that was born and developed in Ethiopia is going to look different from one that grew and developed in Europe. There is variance in practice and customs; for example, Ethiopians do not eat pork due to Old Testament prohibitions against it, and they celebrate the Sabbath on both Saturday and Sunday. There is agreement between the two faiths on fundamental issues of Christianity, like the Trinity. However, when European Catholic missionaries arrived in Ethiopia in the 1500s and 1600s, they wanted to convert the Ethiopians to their version of European Catholic Christianity. Instead of seeing a rich and ancient Christian faith, the missionaries just saw that it was different from how they practiced and declared the Ethiopians heretics. For the most part these missionaries were unsuccessful until 1607 when a new king by the name of Susenyos took the throne. He converted to Catholicism in 1621 and invited more Jesuits into the country. What is interesting is many men of the court were willing to accept Catholicism for reasons of state, but by and large women were not. They resisted Catholicism vigorously, and it was through their resistance that Catholics were finally banished from the country.

Much of this story comes from a biography written in 1672 of an Ethiopian woman named Walatta-Petros, who lived in the highlands of Ethiopia. She was a leader in a successful nonviolent campaign against the Europeans and then founded and led a monastery. The account, firmly in the genre of hagiography, was written by her disciples, and the book was recently translated into English for the first time.[10] This is a story that turns the traditional view of global missions on its head and brings an important perspective to the conversation.

Walatta-Petros was born into a noble family and married to a man named Malkiya-Kristos, a military commander and one of the king's counsellors, when she was about sixteen. They had three children, all of whom died in infancy. Compounding the devastating loss of her children, her husband decided to convert to Catholicism along with the king and other noblemen. This prompted Walatta-Petros to leave her husband and take up the life of a nun at the age of twenty-three. Her husband reportedly threatened to destroy an entire town to bring her home, so she returned to him to spare their lives. However, once she learned that her husband had participated in the murder of the head of the Ethiopian Orthodox Church, she stopped eating and wearing any sorts of adornments, and she refused to sleep with him. Only then did her husband allow her to leave.

Shortly after, she met a woman by the name of Eheta-Kristos, who became her lifelong companion. Walatta-Petros became an itinerant preacher and publicly spoke out against the Catholic clergy and all those who had converted to Catholicism, including the king and the court. She was arrested and brought to face the king. On three different occasions Walatta-Petros's husband had to beg the king to spare her life. She endured an intense attempt to convert her to Catholicism, and finally, when that was unsuccessful, she was

---

10 Galawdewos, *The Life and Struggles of Our Mother Walatta Petros: A Seventeenth-Century African Biography of an Ethiopian Woman*, trans. and eds. Wendy Laura Belcher and Michael Kleiner (Princeton: Princeton University Press, 2015), 1–48.

exiled and imprisoned for three years. Quite remarkably she managed to convert her jailer, who had previously tried to seduce and murder her. When she returned from her imprisonment, she established a monastic community around Lake Tana, where she was the head of both the monks and nuns. Not long after, the king returned the country to the Ethiopian Orthodox Church three months before his death in 1632. His son assumed the throne and kicked the Catholic missionaries out of the country and began a persecution of the Catholics. Walatta-Petros spent the rest of her life establishing monastic houses around Ethiopia.[11]

Another example of a strong African leader is Kimpa Vita (1684–1706), also known as Dona Beatrice. She was born into a time of political turmoil and cultural conflict in what was then known as the Kongo Kingdom. The Portuguese had arrived about two hundred years earlier, bringing with them both Christianity and the slave trade; the slave trade caused both depopulation and social disorder within Kongo. By the year 1700, the number of Kongolese being sold into the slave trade had reached seven thousand people every year. Added to this already difficult context were civil wars, food shortages, and general political disorder. It was also a time of religious decline and corruption. Kimpa Vita emerged a prophet, and she openly challenged imperial powers and their version of Christianity. For these challenges, she would pay for her life, but she continues to be an important early voice of resistance against Western imperialism and religious superiority.

Most of what we know of Kimpa Vita comes from European sources, specifically a Capuchin priest by the name of Bernardo de Gallo who interviewed Kimpa Vita. Despite the limitations of this European source, we can still grasp many basic elements of her story. Kimpa Vita was a member of a noble family born in 1684, and it is believed that prior to her baptism, she was a traditional healer called a *nganga*. In 1704, she became ill to the point of death. It was then that she said St. Anthony appeared to her and told her he would preach through her. Kimpa Vita was convinced that she was to bring about the restoration of the Kongo Kingdom, and she set out to meet with the king, Pedro IV, at Kibangu, where he held court.

Her theology was uniquely African, and it criticized European Christianity. She argued that Jesus had actually been born in São Salvador and that Jesus and Mary were Black Africans—not white Europeans. She opposed the idea that all saints were European. She also minimized the importance of the sacraments, but at the heart of her message was a call to conversion that would unite the nation.

There were aspects of her theology that were unorthodox. According to sources, every Friday she would die and ascend to heaven, where she would plead the cause of Africa to God. It is unclear whether or not this dying was taken literally or figuratively, but either way, it was a powerful witness and demonstrated Kimpa Vita's importance as a prophet and leader for her people. She reportedly could also levitate and speak in unknown

---

11 Galawdewos, *The Life and Struggles of Our Mother Walatta Petros: A Seventeenth-Century African Biography of an Ethiopian Woman*, concise ed., trans. and eds. Wendy Laura Belcher and Michael Kleiner (Princeton: Princeton University Press, 2015), x–xiii.

languages. She continued to work as a healer, and many came to believe in her miraculous healing abilities, and soon she was regarded as a living saint. She amassed a large following of people who were called "Little Anthonies."

In late 1705 she discovered that she was pregnant, and while she had been married twice before, she was currently unmarried. Wanting to hide the pregnancy, she and her lieutenant Barro, who was presumably also the child's father, went into hiding so that she could deliver the baby. Shortly after the birth, she was found, arrested, and taken to Pedro IV. She was tried by the Kongolese, though the Capuchin priests were also involved. Both she and Barro were burned at the stake, and Pedro IV marched on her followers, many of whom were sold into slavery.

Her death was not the end of her movement or her story. There are myths and legends associated with the prophet. It is believed that two springs appeared at the place where she was killed. People started incorporating her memory in folk beliefs, and she has long been remembered as a religious leader. Her ministry was cut short by violence and oppressive powers, but she is one of the earliest founders of an African-initiated Christian movement, and she imagined a uniquely African Christianity stripped of much of the European culture that was brought with the missionaries.[12]

RISE OF PROTESTANT MISSIONS

Much of the reason for the expansion of Protestant missions in the nineteenth century was the expanding role of Western governments in Africa and Asia. Just as global Catholic missions accelerated in the sixteenth century with the colonization efforts of the Spanish and Portuguese in the Americas, the expansion of imperial and colonial activities of other Protestant countries in turn increased global Protestant missions. The relationship between colonial powers and missionary societies was complex, and their goals were not always aligned in the ways people often assume. However, even the most sympathetic Westerners tended to bring with them a sense of cultural superiority that has had long-lasting ramifications.

The founding of missionary societies, largely in the nineteenth century, pushed Protestant missions to explode in popularity in the West. There were some early forerunners of the movement, such as the Society of Promoting Christian Knowledge founded in 1698 and the Society for the Propagation of the Gospel in Foreign Parts founded in 1701, which were both Anglican. But it was the work of British missionary William Carey through the Particular Baptist Society for Propagating the Gospel Amongst the Heathen (for obvious reasons the name was later shortened to the Baptist Missionary Society) founded in 1792 that started the popular wave of missionary societies that

---

12 Slightly different versions of her story can be found in various sources, including the following: Dale T. Irvin and Scott W. Sunquist, *History of the World Christian Movement, Volume 2: Modern Christianity from 1454–1800* (Maryknoll: Orbis Books, 2012), 215–217; Frederick Quinn, *African Saints: Saints Martyrs, and Holy People from the Continent of Africa* (New York: A Crossroads Book, 2002), 193–194; Teresia Mbari Hinga, introduction to *African, Christian, Feminist: The Enduring Search of What Matters* (Maryknoll: Orbis Books, 2017).

dominated foreign missions throughout the nineteenth and early twentieth centuries. Soon there were missionary societies being formed throughout Europe and the United States.[13] What is particularly interesting about the development of these missionary societies was their independence from government authorities. Prior to this, missionaries were often sent either by the state or with official support of the state (think of the friars in Latin America, for example). These new mission boards had their own agendas, which may or may not have aligned with government goals, and most governments adopted a neutral or even slightly hostile stance to the missionary societies. If the governments had a neutral stance, the general populations of Western countries did not. Supporting missionary societies became wildly popular for European and American Christians. It was generally lay believers who were funding missionary activity overseas with the belief that they were contributing to the expansion of the gospel throughout the world. In turn, the missionary societies brought stories back from the mission fields—Westerners were learning about the world through these missions.

From the beginning, women played an important role in global missions. Women formed their own missionary societies, either independently or within their denominations, which often excluded men from membership. Already in the year 1800, a woman named Mary Webb founded the Boston Female Society for Missionary Purposes, which was a group that included both Congregationalist and Baptist women. This particular group gave money to both American home missions and the British work in India. Once the American Board of Commissioners for Foreign Missions (ABCFM) was founded, this group, and countless other women's "mite societies,"[14] began donating to global missions. It is important to note the role of race in this discussion about missions. While the majority of total foreign missionaries and missionary boards were white, there were African American missionaries, who were sent to Africa in particular. Sometimes white missionary boards sent Black missionaries out, but other times, it was Black denominations that sent their own missionaries. In 1876, for example, the African Methodist Episcopal Zion Church began its missionary efforts in Liberia. The majority of Black missionaries were men, but there were both Black missionary wives and single women missionaries who were sent to Africa as well.[15]

A moment must be spent on motivation because women living in the West put significant time and money into foreign missions. There is scholarly debate as to exactly why women became so invested in this movement. One needs to consider the social situation in the West—women were gaining more rights and participating in more church and parachurch organizations in general, which logically would expand to the field of global missions. However, there was a particular interest in sending missionaries abroad that was fueled by more than just an expanded role in society. In Lisa Joy Pruitt's book on American women missionaries in Asia, she states that women were motivated by a genuine desire

13 Gonzáles, *The Story of Christianity*, 418.

14 Mite societies collect funds for charity by small contributions. This can be a very effective form of fundraising if enough people give.

15 Sylvia M. Jacobs, "The Historical Roles of Afro-Americans in American Missionary Efforts in Africa," in *Black Americans and the Missionary Movement in Africa*, ed. Sylvia M. Jacobs (Westport, CT: Greenwood Press, 1982), 10–11, 18.

to improve the lives of women abroad, and she bases this observation on a wide variety of missionary literature. In my own research on women's missionary societies, I observed similar motivations expressed. Through foreign missions, Western women gained knowledge about the world, and along with this knowledge came a legitimate concern for their "sisters" abroad.[16] In addition to the general evangelism that one would expect from missionaries, ending foot binding in China and the practice of sati in India and providing education and medical care to women were important issues. From our perspectives today, we can see the limitations of such an approach, but that does not change women's motivations at the time.

Why women felt the need to form their own missionary societies separate from the men's boards is another question worth exploring. Women were largely excluded from male-dominated missionary boards, and while their fundraising skills were always welcome, they were not the ones to make the decisions on how those funds were to be spent. Women consistently believed male-run mission boards were not providing adequate financing for women missionaries; nor were they attentive enough to the needs of foreign women through their ministries. Generally speaking, they believed women missionaries were better equipped to work with foreign women, and they wanted missionary programs that put women first. Nineteenth-century Western women were by and large a civically engaged group, and there were numerous social issues they cared about, many of which directly related to women and children. This concern for women and children extended to women and children living abroad. By the later part of the nineteenth century, a common phrase had emerged to describe women's mission work: "women's work for women."

Considering their perspectives and lived experience, it is unsurprising then that there were fundamental differences in how male-run and female-run boards believed that missions should be run, and the influence of these missionary boards cannot be over-emphasized. For example, by the start of the twentieth century, nearly every single Protestant denomination in the United States had some sort of women's missionary society, and these societies experienced rapid growth.[17] Between 1873 and 1909, the northern Woman's Baptist Foreign Missionary Society expanded from 255 to 5,000 auxiliaries, and Presbyterian women's auxiliaries expanded from 100 to over 10,000 from 1870 to 1909. Methodist women were contributing nearly a million dollars annually by 1910.[18] With this number of auxiliaries working together and so much money being raised, there were men who expressed concern about the independence and influence these boards gave women. Despite platitudes from the women that they were not intending to challenge male authority in any way, these mission boards did just that. Through these and other social reform groups, Western women learned valuable skills in organization and leadership.

---

16 Lisa Joy Pruitt, *A Looking Glass for Ladies: American Protestant Women and the Orient in the Nineteenth Century* (Macon, GA: Mercer University Press, 2005), 1–2.

17 Lindley, *You Have Stept Out of Your Place*, 70.

18 Pruitt, *A Looking Glass for Ladies*, 178.

It was the phenomenal success of women's missionary boards that became the source of their biggest challenge. Through these boards, women carved out power and influence within their faith traditions. They also raised *a lot* of money, and by the twentieth century, many denominations were trying to gain greater control over these women's missionary societies. Optimistically one could view the attempt to merge mission boards within denominations as an attempt to make missions more efficient. Having two separate mission boards, one run by men and the other run by women, understandably could cause issues for a denomination. More pessimistically, one can see the attempt to take over the women-led boards as a combination of wanting to curtail women's influence and control their finances. In theory, having one board to run missions, if it were run in an egalitarian fashion with both men and women equally represented, could provide a more efficient system; after all, it was women's exclusion that partially prompted the women's boards in the first place. And there were instances of equal boards that emerged, such as the Disciples of Christ's newly formed United Christian Missionary Society of 1919, which gave women equal representation.[19] Other women's mission boards did not fare as well. For example, difficulties arose several times over women's ability to control the money they raised in the Norwegian Lutheran Church of America's Women's Missionary Federation, which was the result of a denomination merger and thus mission board merger. Women were granted minimal representation on the board, and their operating budget was repeatedly cut despite fundraising an astonishing amount of money. In 1922 they were allotted $5,303 for operating costs, and in 1926 they were given $3,500. Compare that to the $272,063.32 that they raised in 1927, which they did not control. The Federation's president, Delia Davison Ylvisaker, wrote a letter that indicated her complete frustration with the situation:

> We raise money which we give to the church and do not have a word to say as to its distribution. Individually and collectively the statements made by us about our work have been challenged. The church has given the Federation representation on its Boards "in order that we may learn the work." . . . Can we as self-respecting women continue to work in the conditions in which we are not situated? Can we give our best to the work of our beloved church, as things are now?[20]

Needless to say, the experiences of women varied depending on their denominational association. One interesting suggestion that scholars have made is that the curtailing of women's mission boards' independence prompted women to start asking larger questions about their status within their church bodies, thus adding urgency to the question of women's ordination.

---

19 Lindley, *You Have Stept Out of Your Place*, 301.

20 WMF Minutes, 1 September 1919, WMF Papers (ELC), ALC Archives, St. Paul, quoted in DeAne Lagerquist, *From My Mother's Arms* (Minneapolis, Augsburg Fortress, 1991), 77–78.

WOMEN MISSIONARIES

While issues of power and funding were playing out on mission boards, missionaries were being sent off across the globe. The first Protestant women sent out were "missionary wives," who were, as the name suggests, women who were married to male missionaries. There are many biographies of missionary wives, and nearly all include some sort of conversion experience followed by a desire to be "useful." In more modern terms, we may understand this longing as their sense of call to ministry. With societal limits to women's engagement in ministry in the West, the emerging field of global missions provided women with an opportunity to engage abroad in ways that would have been nearly impossible at home.

From the beginning, missionary boards understood the importance of missionary wives. They were needed to support and help their husbands so the latter could concentrate on their work. They took on the traditional roles of wife and mother in an unfamiliar land. But they also had an added task that cannot be overlooked: they were to provide critical evangelism in the field. Fashioned as assistant missionaries, they were expected to minister to other women because male missionaries generally did not have access to women. Without converting the wives, mothers, and daughters, the entire operation was doomed to fail, and both missionaries and mission boards understood this. We can look back at this and see that missionary wives were given a nearly impossible task. They were to care for their home and family and also be full-time missionaries to other women, but many women were excited to head out to foreign lands to spread the gospel in this capacity.

One particularly famous early missionary wife was Ann Hasseltine Judson. Born in 1789, she experienced a spiritual struggle of sorts in 1806 that resulted in a greater commitment to the Christian faith, after which she began a period of theological study. She married Adoniram Judson, who was to be a missionary, in 1812. The decision to become a missionary wife was a serious choice indeed and one that Ann, who hardly even knew Judson when he proposed, did not take lightly. Ann debated a great deal after the proposal, trying to decide if this marriage represented God's will for her life. She understood that if she accepted his proposal, she was taking on a particular vocation. Because the role of missionary wife was one of the few socially acceptable ministry positions for women, there were women who actively sought out such marriages. It is not always clear what role love played in these missionary partnerships. Of course, there are worse reasons to marry than the desire to embark on a joint ministry overseas, and a dedication to missions could have provided a foundation for a partnership.

The Judsons sailed for India shortly after their marriage with six other missionaries—they were some of the first missionaries sent out by the ABCFM. During their long boat journey, they became convinced of adult baptism, which caused difficulties for their association with the Congregationalists. Once they arrived in Calcutta, they were baptized by an associate of Willian Carey, but they were forced to leave India by the East India Company. They eventually ended up in Burma (now Myanmar), where they served as American Baptist missionaries. While in Burma, Ann took her role as a missionary seriously. She and her husband both committed themselves to the study of languages, and she translated the Gospel of Matthew into Thai and the books of Daniel and Jonah into Burmese, and she wrote a Burmese catechism. She also participated in direct ministry with Burmese women. For the general advancement of missions, she wrote letters home to be published in missionary journals, which were widely read. The importance of these journals must be highlighted. When she returned to the United States in 1822 and 1823, she continued to write and speak about foreign missions, adding to their popularity.

While she did much to promote foreign missions, Ann struggled with personal tragedy and political instability. Her first pregnancy ended in miscarriage, and her son Roger died within a year of his birth in 1815. Their daughter Maria outlived her mother by only about six months. In 1824, war broke out between the British and the Burmese, and Adoniram was arrested along with a number of other foreigners. Ann spent the next two years caring for her imprisoned husband and other missionaries while simultaneously working for her husband's release through political means. Both she and her husband survived the war, and he was released in October of 1826. Unfortunately, she died shortly thereafter at the age of thirty-six. Her death made her even more famous—she was considered a martyr for Christian missions. Within three years a biography was published, based on many of her own writings, and many subsequent biographies followed.[21]

There undoubtedly was a level of idealism that many missionaries held prior to their arrival in their mission field, but the reality of their situation was generally much more difficult than they had anticipated. Disease, overwork, and, too often, early death were the fate of many missionary wives. A particularly well-known early death in the mission field was that of a friend and colleague of Ann Judson who sailed with her on that original ship to India. Nineteen-year-old Harriet Newell died of consumption shortly after her newborn baby died of exposure at sea in 1812. News of her death caused such a stir that Westerners even debated whether women should be sent abroad, but she also became a powerful symbol of self-sacrifice and inspiration for other missionary wives.[22]

For the women that survived, life was undoubtedly hard; as women, maintaining a household and caring for and educating their own children fell largely on their shoulders while their husbands focused on their missionary work. It was generally accepted that their duties to their own family were more important than their mission work, but when women had to step back from mission work, that largely meant that the missionary efforts to women then stalled. The demands on women were simply too much.

Due to these conflicting requirements placed on missionary wives, it became apparent to missionaries in the field that single women, who were not burdened with caring for a family, were needed. Running parallel in Catholic missions, Catholic sisters were fulfilling this need, but in Protestant traditions, there was greater concern about sending single women. There was some mission work done by Protestant deaconesses, but the prospect of sending single women to foreign lands as missionaries was met with doubt and

---

21 Dana L. Robert, *American Women in Mission: A Social History of their Thought and Practice Mission* (Macon, GA: Mercer University Press, 1996), 43–46.

22 Robert, *American Women in Mission*, 40–42.

opposition by many male leaders, who questioned whether these women could meet the demands of travel and ministry without the support and oversight of a husband.

Regardless of concerns, single women, either unmarried or widowed, were sent overseas. Charlotte White, a widow, was the first single woman to be sent abroad by the ABCFM in 1815, though she ended up marrying another missionary before she even arrived in Burma.[23] Slowly but surely more single women made their way abroad, though often single women were connected in some way with a missionary family.

Whether married or single, missionary work provided women an opportunity to engage in activities that were largely unavailable to them in the West. Some women missionaries engaged in large-scale public preaching, though most women's evangelism was directed primarily at other women and was more informal and personal. Protestant missionaries were generally concerned with education so that everyone had access to scripture, and women missionaries in particular placed a high value on literacy for both women and children, so teaching was a common activity for women. Women founded day schools and boarding schools, wrote catechisms, completed Bible translations, and generally worked to promote literacy. Medicine was another opportunity for women missionaries. While women doctors were fairly uncommon in the West, they became increasingly common among missionaries. For example, in 1905, one third of the three hundred medical missionaries stationed in China were women.[24]

Women missionaries became increasingly common throughout the nineteenth century, and by the 1870s, there were more women foreign missionaries than men in some places.[25] While there are far more well-known missionaries than can possibly be covered in this short chapter, two of the best-known single women missionaries are Lottie Moon (1840–1912) and Katharine Bushnell (1855–1946). They were both sent to China, but Moon spent her entire life there, while Bushnell returned to the United States within a few years and transitioned to a career primarily in social reform.

Lottie Moon was born to a wealthy slave-owning family in Virginia, though her family lost their fortune in the Civil War. She was intelligent and independent from a young age, and she was one of the first Southern American women to earn a master's degree. In 1873, she followed her sister Edmonia to China to work as a missionary for the Southern Baptist Convention (SBC). Officially she did women's work abroad—she was a teacher at a girls' school—but she excelled at personal evangelism. Her grasp of Chinese was excellent, and she preached to women (and whatever men may have been listening) and taught children Bible stories and hymns. She was fiercely independent, and she took to wearing traditional Chinese dress instead of Western clothing. In 1885, she moved to the town of Pingtu, and it is believed that she was the first woman to establish an in-land mission by herself. There, she had little interaction with other Westerners and had no protection through

---

23   Lindley, *You Have Stept Out of Your Place*, 75.

24   Li Ma, *Christian Women and Modern China: Recovering a Women's History of Chinese Protestantism* (Lanham, MD: Lexington Books, 2021), 5.

25   Ma, 5.

government treaties. Her work proved successful, and Pingtu became one of the SBC's most successful mission fields.

The final years of her life were filled with tragedy. The Chinese Revolution of 1911 compounded with drought and famine brought widespread suffering to her region of China. Concerned about others, Moon gave all her food away and faced physical and psychological ailments and starvation. It was decided that she needed to be sent home to the United States, but she died on the ship in a Japanese harbor before she ever made it back.[26]

While Lottie Moon was certainly an important figure in mission history, her legacy has been shaped by the success of the Lottie Moon Christmas Offering, which she had nothing to do with in reality. In 1918, six years after she starved to death, the Women's Missionary Union began using Lottie Moon's name for the organization's Christmas Offering for Chinese missions. By 1924, the SBC was in financial ruin, and the Foreign Mission Board called back many of their missionaries from the field. Today this story is well known in the SBC: women saved the day by pouring money into the Lottie Moon Christmas Offering. In 1923/24, before the financial crisis, the fund raised $49,000, but the next year, in 1924/25, the Lottie Moon Christmas Offering raised $306,000. Soon, the annual Lottie Moon Christmas Offering funded approximately anywhere from 40 to 50 percent of the Foreign Mission Board's budget each year. Amazingly what had been a struggling missionary society was transformed into one of the largest Protestant missions in the world.[27] As of 2021, the Lottie Moon Christmas Offering has raised an incredible five billion dollars for global missions for the Southern Baptists, a fact that is even more remarkable since Moon herself struggled to get the support and help she needed during her lifetime.[28]

Katharine Bushnell provides an interesting contrast to Lottie Moon. Bushnell's time in China was temporary, and the two women had wildly different career trajectories. While Moon was careful to adhere to prescribed gender roles established by her denomination (at least publicly), Bushnell became an important early feminist voice. In addition to being a foreign missionary, she was an ardent supporter of temperance and the social purity campaign. Bushnell was born in Evanston, Illinois, and attended Northwestern University, where she met Frances Willard. She studied medicine and began her career as a medical missionary for the Woman's Mission Board of the Methodist Episcopal Church in China in 1879. She only stayed in China for three years, during which she was plagued by sickness and exhaustion. She returned to the United States in 1882, and she established her own medical practice in Denver, Colorado. Bushnell was not to stay in medicine, however. She became the head of the western Women's Christian Temperance Union's Social Purity Department, and she moved to Chicago, where she founded the Anchorage Mission, a shelter that served thousands of women a year.

---

26 Catherine B. Allen, "The Legacy of Lottie Moon," *International Bulletin of Mission Research* 17, no. 4 (October 1993): 146–152.

27 Elizabeth H. Flowers, "The Contested Legacy of Lottie Moon: Southern Baptists, Women, and Partisan Protestantism," *Fides et Historia* 43, no. 1 (Winter/Spring 2011): 14–15.

28 "Lottie Moon Christmas Offering: Your 2020 Gifts at Work," imb, accessed April 23, 2022, https://www.imb.org/generosity/lottie-moon-christmas-offering/.

Bushnell is best known not for her missions or her reform work but for her book *God's Word to Women*. While she personally considered her time in China the greatest mistake of her life, her work abroad and her observations of non-Western women's oppression propelled her to see the oppression within her own culture, which had a significant impact on her future scholarly work. She believed the Bible to be inspired and infallible; however, she had genuine misgivings about Bible translations. She believed that men's prejudice was influencing their Bible translations and that the root of women's oppression stemmed from these sex-biased translations. She found that the Bible was a powerful means of resistance, and her knowledge of both Hebrew and Greek allowed her to create a profound critique of her own cultural and religious inheritance.[29]

NINETEENTH-CENTURY CATHOLIC WOMEN'S MISSIONARIES

Catholics dominated global missions in the sixteenth and seventeenth centuries, but their activities were largely contracted by the end of the eighteenth. This changed after the tumultuous times of the French Revolution and Napoleonic Wars. Once Napoleon was defeated, a popular religious movement in France arose in reaction against the anti-religious mentality of the previous decades. Along with this religious revival came a Catholic commitment to foreign missions once more. In 1822, the Society for the Propagation of the Faith was established in France by Pauline Jaricot (1799–1862). Jaricot was a devout Catholic laywoman who felt called to help revive religion in France and engaged in works of charity. Both she and her brother became attracted to the idea of foreign missions after hearing about some of the British missionary societies, and they wanted to create a similar organization in France. Despite opposition from some laymen and clergy, Jaricot persevered, and her society was formed. Jaricot emphasized that almsgiving for missions should be accompanied by prayer to the Sacred Heart of Jesus. The Propagation of the Faith supported missions throughout Africa, Asia, the Americas, and Oceania and continues as one of the Pontifical Mission Societies today. As for Jaricot, her role in the society, especially as a laywoman, is of particular interest.[30]

While the Society for the Propagation of the Faith was similar to Protestant missionary societies, there were a number of new Catholic women's religious orders founded in the nineteenth century to take on the work of global missions. Euphrasie Barbier, a Catholic nun, founded the *Religieuses de Notre Dame des Missions* in 1861 under the direction of the priests belonging to the Society of Mary after she was unable to embark on foreign missions within her first order. The Holy Spirit Missionary Sisters were founded by

---

29 Kristin Kobes Du Mez, "Reorienting American Religious History in the Age of Global Christianity: The Case of Katharine Bushnell," in *American Evangelicalism: George Marsden and the State of American Religious History*, eds. Darren Dochuk, Thomas S. Kidd, and Kurt W. Peterson (Notre Dame: University of Notre Dame Press, 2014), 180–198. (189–190); Dana Hardwick, "Man's Prattle, Woman's Words: The Biblical Mission of Katharine Bushnell," in *Spirituality & Social Responsibility: Vocational Vision of Women in The United Methodist Tradition*, ed. Rosemary Skinner Keller (Nashville: Abingdon Press, 1993), 165.

30 Susan E. Smith, *Women in Mission: From the New Testament to Today* (Maryknoll: Orbis, 2007), 136.

Father Arnold Janssen in Holland in 1889. His hope was that these sisters would help his male missionaries in the Society of the Divine Word. In 1910, however, the Holy Spirit Sisters, frustrated with their "helper" role, became independent financially and administratively from the Society of the Divine Word. The sisters soon engaged in healthcare, social reform, and educational missions in the United States, Brazil, Papua New Guinea, China, and Japan.[31]

The best known of the nineteenth-century women's missionary orders is the Maryknoll Sisters founded in 1912 in the United States by Mary Rogers. Rogers came from a wealthy Irish American family and was profoundly influenced by the Society for the Propagation of the Faith. She first worked to spread the word about Catholic foreign missions among American Catholics, and when Father James Walsh founded the Catholic Foreign Mission Society of America, more commonly known as the Maryknollers, she founded the Foreign Mission Sisters of St. Dominic, also known as the Maryknoll Sisters, which was the first order of American Catholic sisters to devote its work to foreign missions. Despite common opinions that nuns should only assist male missionaries, the Maryknoll Sisters found they were effective missionaries and could reach places and people, especially other women, that men could not. Roger's theology is of particular interest. Initially, she viewed the Virgin Mary as the one who prepared Christ for ministry, but her Mariology developed to a point where she saw the Virgin as the one who *gave* Christ to others. This shift in theological thinking has profound theological implications. Women are no longer helpers to men's work but the ones who bring Christ to the world.[32]

Another shift in Catholic women's missions, which was Catholic sisters engaging in medical care, occurred in the first half of the twentieth century. Prior to the twentieth century, Protestants were building successful medical ministries around the world, while Catholic religious were barred from studying medicine—obstetrics was a particular point of contention. By 1925, the Catholic Medical Mission Board had recognized the need for medical missionaries. A medical doctor by the name of Anna Dengal, who had been working in Pakistan, established the Pious Society, which evolved into the Society of Catholic Medical Missionaries in 1936; this was also the year that the Vatican decreed that women religious could train as physicians, surgeons, and obstetricians. The Society of Catholic Medical Missionaries was the first group founded for women religious to work as medical professionals.[33]

CONSEQUENCES

Western women, both Protestant and Catholic, benefited from engaging in foreign missions. Participating in mission boards gave women control over resources and gave them a sense of purpose. Women missionaries were able to engage in a variety of ministries,

---

31 Smith, 140–141.

32 Smith, *Women in Mission*, 142–144.

33 Smith, 147.

including education and healthcare, to a degree that would have been nearly impossible in their own countries. An argument could be made that through engagement in foreign missions (and various other reform movements), Western women were able to improve their own social situation, promote causes like suffrage, and generally gain more rights.

But what about the women to whom they were ministering? Were women missionaries engaged in cultural imperialism? Did they better or worsen the lives of the women they were sent to serve? As with all things relating to global missions, the answer is complicated. Women and girls did benefit from medical assistance brought by missionary doctors. Missionaries also provided educational options for women, which often did improve their circumstances. As we will see in chapter 11, sometimes Indigenous women were even able to make careers for themselves as doctors and preachers. That being said, women missionaries did engage in cultural imperialism whether they intended to or not. In fact, it has been argued that women were more effective as agents in this cultural imperialism than male missionaries.

Some missionaries were more culturally sensitive than others, but there was undoubtedly a lack of appreciation and respect for the cultures they were stepping into. Missionaries brought with them the ideals of the Western middle class, including their own moral and cultural values. These included firm ideas of prescribed gender roles, marriage, family structure, child-rearing practices, and education. This transference of cultural ideals could even include imposing Western styles of music and dress, which perhaps seems the least defensible because they are so frivolous.

Once the political imperialism of the nineteenth and twentieth centuries began to decline, some countries reacted strongly to the presence of foreign missionaries. China, for example, kicked out all foreign missionaries once the People's Republic of China was established, and interestingly, it was after Western missionaries left that Christianity began a period of significant growth there. In Africa, great Christian growth, especially among women, occurred in the African-initiated churches, which flourished without Western intervention.

Today there are interesting and exciting trends in global missions. Despite the long tradition of missionaries being sent from Europe and North America, the portion of long-term missionaries hailing from the Global North is declining. In 2021, 227,000 missionaries, who make up about 53 percent of total missionaries, came from the Global North. This is down from 88 percent in 1970. However, missionaries from the Global South now make up 47 percent of the total—203,000 in 2021. This shift has happened in a remarkably short time. In 1970, for example, only 31,000 or 12 percent of missionaries hailed from the Global South.[34] While the United States still sends out the most missionaries in total, South Korea, Brazil, India, South Africa, the Philippines, Mexico, China, Colombia, and Nigeria are all now major senders of Christian missionaries.[35]

---

34 Gina A. Zurlo, Todd M. Johnson, and Peter F. Crossing, "World Christianity and Mission 2021: Questions about the Future," *International Bulletin of Mission Research* 45, no. 1 (December 2020): 16–17.

35 Melissa Steffan, "The Surprising Countries Most Missionaries are Sent From and Go To," *Christianity Today*, July 25, 2013, https://www.christianitytoday.com/news/2013/july/missionaries-countries-sent-received-csgc-gordon-conwell.html.

CHAPTER 9

Enter the Evangelist and the Prophetess

Before most women could become ordained pastors or even vote in church elections, there were women pioneers who were preaching, teaching, and sometimes beginning their own denominations or even separate religions. It must be recognized that the women discussed in this chapter faced pushback for their public ministries and that they were the exception, not the norm, for their era. Regardless, each of the women represents an important step in the fight for women's involvement in ministry, women's ordination, and women's engagement in theological studies. This chapter looks at the lives and ministries of numerous women who changed the face of public ministry, beginning during the Second Great Awakening (c. 1795–1835) and leading into the start of the twentieth century. What unites all these women is their call to public ministry. Many of these preaching women engaged in social reform ministry or other forms of practical ministry, but ultimately it is their preaching and leadership that have come to define their historic legacy.

As seen in chapter 7, women began to carve out more leadership roles during the eighteenth century in a variety of Christian traditions, but these leadership roles were still extremely limited, especially in more public forms. It was during the era of the Second Great Awakening, especially in the United States, that women became more visible in public ministry. This awakening, which truly transformed American religion, emphasized free will and personal conversion and incorporated more social reform efforts. Large revivals, first in the frontier and later in urban centers, became a hallmark of this movement. Women participated in these revivals, prayed aloud and gave their testimonies, and as we will see, some preached, some organized revivals, and some wrote religious autobiographies or even theological texts.

As time moved on, women became increasingly accepted in public leadership roles. For example, by the beginning of the twentieth century, individuals like Aimee Semple McPherson filled stadiums and used modern media to reach thousands of people who were never able to make it to her Angelus Temple in California. Amazingly all this happened long before women gained ordination rights in most mainline denominations. In fact, it is an easy assumption to make that women's leadership, or even women's ordination, occurred in more progressive faith traditions. The idea of the steady march of progress and equality is a story that is easy to accept—but the reality is more complex. Most women included in this chapter were associated with the Holiness and Pentecostal traditions and not more progressive mainline denominations. These traditions emphasize both personal experience and the work of the Holy Spirit in opposition to church bodies that hold up hierarchy, tradition, or even scripture as their guiding principles. The theology in both these movements encouraged believers to exhort their faith, which prompted more lay believers, both women and men, to speak publicly—whether preaching or not—about their faith. Believers generally recognized that the Holy Spirit worked through both women and men, and therefore, it was possible for a woman to be called to various public ministries. There is a tension in these histories between socially accepted gender roles and a theological understanding that anyone can be called. Each woman in this chapter had difficulties thrust upon her because of her gender, race, and/or class, but their success in evangelism demonstrates that a significant number of people were willing to accept their message despite the dominant societal expectations.

While the preachers and evangelists discussed below were in many senses the exception, not the norm, their public ministry is critical for understanding the progress women made in the nineteenth and early twentieth centuries. They were demonstrating to the world that women could preach, lead, and run church organizations. Their primary motivation was not advancing women's rights, however. Their primary goal was preaching the gospel. It is true that many did support various social causes as a secondary focus of their ministries, but it was the call to preach that brought them into the world, and it was that sense of call that pushed them to defend themselves to a world that was not quite ready for them.

HOLINESS PREACHERS

> Between four and five years after my sanctification, on a certain time, an impressive silence fell upon me, and I stood as if some one was about to speak to me, yet I had no such thought in my heart. But to my utter surprise there seemed to sound a voice which I thought I distinctly heard, and most certainly understood, which said to me, "Go preach the Gospel!" I immediately replied aloud, "No one will believe me." Again the same voice seemed to say, "Preach the Gospel: I will put words in your mouth, and will turn your enemies to become your friends."[1]

Thus begins Jarena Lee's (1783–1864) explanation of her call to preach that she outlines in her autobiography. At first, she did not trust this call; she feared it was Satan, so she went to pray for confirmation. Having received confirmation from God through prayer, she went to see Richard Allen, and he responded that women could not preach in the AME. Her first reaction was relief, but soon she felt the call to preach regardless of denominational restrictions. Eventually she would become a well-known itinerant preacher and author, but it was a long and difficult road that brought her to that point. It was exceedingly uncommon for women to preach publicly at the time, so much so that she is considered the first African American woman to do so.

---

1 Jarena Lee, *Religious Experience and Journal of Mrs. Jarena Lee, Giving an Account of her Call to Preach the Gospel* (Philadelphia: 1849), 11.

There is little information about Jarena Lee's early life; she does not even tell readers what her family name was before her marriage. Her autobiography is overwhelmingly focused on her spiritual journey, but throughout it she does provide a basic biographical framework. Lee was born on February 11, 1783, in Cape May, New Jersey. She was free but poor, and as a child of seven she was sent out to work as a maid for a white household, and when she was about eleven, she moved to Philadelphia, where she continued to work as a domestic servant. In her autobiography, she comments that her parents were not religious and that it was in Philadelphia that she began attending church. First, she attended a Presbyterian church, but soon she started attending a Methodist church, where she was converted shortly after hearing Richard Allen preach. Sometime later, after wrestling with her faith, she achieved entire sanctification.[2] It was about four or five years after her sanctification that she first felt the call to preach.

In 1811, she married a Methodist pastor by the name of Joseph Lee and moved to Snow Hill, Pennsylvania, about six miles outside of Philadelphia, where he led a congregation. She was discontented in Snow Hill, but after much prayer she was convinced that she needed to stay so that her husband could minister to his congregation. She did not pursue her own call to preach while she was married. After six years her husband died, leaving her a widow with two small children. It was after his death that her call to preach was renewed in a most dramatic fashion. She was at Bethel Church in Philadelphia, and Richard Allen was supposed to be preaching on Jonah 2:9. According to Lee, Allen lost the Spirit in that moment, and she jumped up and preached a sermon instead. Remarkably, instead of censuring her, Allen publicly affirmed her call, and from that point on he supported her as a preacher. Unfortunately, the AME still did not ordain or license women preachers at the time, so officially Lee did not preach—she "exhorted and taught." This distinction is mainly semantic, and she saw herself as a preacher and defended her right to preach vigorously. One of her arguments, which is particularly convincing, is based on her results:

> In my wanderings up and down among men, preaching according to my ability, I have frequently found families who told me that they had not for several years been to a meeting, and yet, while listening to hear what God would say by this poor female instrument, have believed with trembling—tears rolling down their cheeks, the signs of contrition and repentance towards God. I firmly believe that I have sown seed, in the name of the Lord, which shall appear with its increase at the great day of accounts, when Christ shall come to make up his jewels.[3]

This was not her only defense of her ministry. In fact, her autobiography is filled with arguments for why women should preach that range from the practical to the mystical

---

2 Sanctification is as a theological concept that can mean (1) to make something holy or (2) to be purified or freed from sin. In the case of the Holiness movement, "entire sanctification" or the "second blessing" refers to being granted deliverance from both inward and outward sin, which leads to "Christian perfection." Within Pentecostalism this idea of "second blessing" refers to the baptism of the Holy Spirit (often with the subsequent gift of speaking in tongues).

3 Lee, *Religious Experience and Journal of Mrs. Jarena Lee*, 12.

to the theological. For example, at one point, she asks rhetorically whether Mary preached the resurrection at the very climax of Christianity. Her answer is yes, Mary obviously did, and that very act is precedent for women preaching.

Lee went on to have a successful public ministry. She preached at various house meetings and occasionally from the pulpit at different AME churches. Her career coincided with the Second Great Awakening, during which camp meetings and revivals were major events for the faithful or for those looking to be faithful. She became an itinerant preacher in various places within the United States and Canada. She preached to both men and women, to people of various racial backgrounds, and to ecumenical groups. It is clear from her writings that she was an engaging preacher and that people were being slain by the Spirit and called to a more holy life while listening to her. Her career spanned two decades until sickness began to slow her down. It is not entirely clear when she died, though the mid-1850s seems likely. It is unknown how many people she preached to or how many people she converted, though it is likely those numbers are significant considering her lengthy career. She was undoubtedly a pioneer and an inspiration to other women who desired to preach.

Lee was not the only woman of color of the era who engaged in a career of evangelism. Nor was she the only African American woman evangelist to pen her own autobiography. Her close friend and sometimes preaching companion Zilpha Elaw also felt the call to go out into the world and preach. She also penned her life story, titled *Memoirs of the Life, Religious Experiences, Ministerial Travels, and Labours of Ms. Zilpha Elaw, an American Female of Colour; Together with Some Accounts of the Great Religious Revivals in America [Written by Herself]*, in 1846. Unlike Lee, who waited until she had the support of her denomination before preaching, Elaw began preaching without that support. Slightly younger than Lee, Elaw was born free in 1790 in Pennsylvania and raised in Philadelphia. Her evangelistic career was hindered by her husband, who was neither a Christian nor a supporter of his wife's evangelistic efforts. However, after his death, she went on to have a preaching career both in the United States and in England. In direct defiance of the Black Codes, which were enacted in the American South to restrict the movement of African Americans, Elaw held prayer meetings throughout Maryland.[4]

Amanda Berry Smith

Of all the women in this chapter, Amanda Berry Smith may have led the most fascinating life. She was a leader in the Holiness movement and one of the most important evangelists of her generation. She was also a talented singer, a social reformer, and a well-traveled missionary. Her ministries took her all around the world—she would travel from the United States to England, to India, to Africa, and finally back to the United States again. Her personal story is filled with hardship and loss, but from these tragedies she was able to rise up and become an influential Christian leader.

---

4 Jualynne E. Dobson, *Engendering Church: Women, Power, and the AME Church* (Lanham: Rowman & Littlefield Publishers, Inc., 2002), 27.

Berry Smith was born into slavery in 1837. While her parents were enslaved at two different though adjacent farms, her father was able to work enough overtime at night, in addition to his regular work, to purchase his freedom and then that of his family. The family continued to live on the land of her father's previous owner, but they were free. Their situation was not entirely unusual at the time. Between 1810 and 1865, Maryland had the largest free Black population in the country, with about one quarter of Black people free. This led to a highly competitive job market between free Black people and poor whites, and the state created numerous restrictive laws that could force free Black people into slavery.[5] Eventually the Berry family moved out of the South to Pennsylvania and settled on a farm, where Berry Smith did domestic work for the family that owned it. While there, the Berry family would hide runaway slaves escaping from the South. When Berry Smith was thirteen, she went to live with a wealthy white widow to work as a domestic servant. It was there that she encountered a religious revival that made an impression on her. She joined the church and attended a class, but it interfered with her work, and she eventually had to quit.[6]

In 1854, she married a man named Calvin Devine, but it seems to have been a difficult marriage. They had two children, and only one survived, a girl named Mazie. Devine had a drinking problem, and the only insight she provides in her autobiography about her first husband is the following: "He could talk on the subject of religion very sensibly at times; but when strong drink would get the better of him which I am very sorry to say was quite often, then he was very profane and unreasonable."[7] He joined the Union Army during the Civil War and never returned home.

In 1856, shortly before the birth of her daughter, she had a dramatic conversion experience, which she described as such:

> There seemed to be a halo of light all over me; the change was so real and so thorough that I have often said that if I had been as black as ink or as green as grass or as white as snow, I would not have been frightened. I went into the dining room; we had a large mirror that went from the floor to the ceiling, and I went and looked in it to see if anything had transpired in my color, because there was something wonderful had taken place inside of me, and it really seemed to me it was outside too, and as I looked in the glass I cried out, "Hallelujah, I have got religion; glory to God, I have got religion!"[8]

As an example of Berry Smith's character and bravery (and the precarious position of free Black people in the American South at the time), she rescued her sister from slavery in Maryland during the Civil War. When Berry Smith was young, her aunt had asked their

---

5 Adrienne Israel, *Amanda Berry Smith, From Washerwoman to Evangelist* (Lanham, MD: The Scarecrow Press, Inc., 1998), 12.

6 Amanda Berry Smith, *An Autobiography. The Story of the Lord's Dealings with Mrs. Amanda Smith: The Colored Evangelist; Containing an Account of her Life Work of Faith, and her Travels in America, England, Ireland, Scotland, India, and Africa, as an Independent Missionary* (Chicago: Meyer & Brother, Publishers, 1893).

7 Smith, *Mrs. Amanda Smith*, 42.

8 Smith, 47.

family for one of the girls because she had only one child and wanted a companion for her. Berry Smith's sister, Frances, went to live with her aunt and cousin. The aunt proved to be a harsh woman and would beat Frances, so Frances ran off and ended up being sold into slavery even though she had been born free. Berry Smith went to Maryland, hoping the presence of the Union soldiers would protect her, and purchased the freedom of her sister, which put her into debt.[9]

Berry Smith married again, this time to a man named James Smith, who was significantly older. He was a local preacher and an ordained deacon in the AME. Prior to their marriage he told her that he wanted to be an itinerant preacher, but after their marriage he admitted that he had lied to get her to marry him. This came as a huge disappointment to Berry Smith because she had wanted to be a minister's wife, believing that was a position in which she could do ministry herself. Added to this, the couple lost all their children in infancy, and her husband died in 1869. These tremendous tragedies, however, allowed Berry Smith the freedom to engage in religious life. In fact, in the same month that her husband died, she received a direct commission from God to go out and preach in New Jersey—she was gone for seven months. By 1870, she was preaching and singing at camp meetings sponsored by the National Association for the Promotion of Holiness. Like Lee before her, Smith preached to racially and religiously diverse audiences. As recognition of her talent as both a preacher and a singer increased, so did the number of people coming to see her. It is believed she preached to crowds of about eight thousand in 1875.

Berry Smith identified primarily as an evangelist, and her first and foremost concern was spreading the gospel, but like many other preachers of the era, she became involved in social reform efforts—most significantly temperance. Berry Smith joined the Women's Christian Temperance Union (WCTU) in 1875, a choice that would dramatically influence her life going forward. The WCTU's membership was primarily white, and when women of color joined, they were often segregated into their own chapters. Berry Smith, though, was appointed an evangelist by the Evangelistic Department, which sponsored religious events. It was through these activities that she met the head of the British WCTU and was invited to go on a temperance preaching tour through Great Britain. She stayed in Britain for two years, then went to India for eighteen months, after which she went to Africa, where she stayed for eight years. She returned to the United States in 1890, where she settled in a suburb outside of Chicago. It was there that she built an orphanage called the Amanda Smith Industrial School for Girls, which was the only Protestant institution for African American children in Illinois at the time. She died in 1915, leaving a tremendous legacy of both evangelism and reform.

Phoebe Palmer

When Amanda Berry Smith lived in New York, she regularly attended Holiness meetings called Tuesday Meetings for the Promotion of Holiness at the home of Phoebe Palmer (1807–1874).[10] Like Smith, Palmer was one of the great evangelists and revivalists of

---

9 Smith, 50–54.
10 Smith, *Mrs. Amanda Smith*, 139.

the nineteenth century. Not only did Palmer preach and lead hundreds of revivals in the United States, Canada, and the British Isles, but she was also a theologian, writer, and social reformer. The story of her path to ministry is a fascinating journey of a young wife and mother who embraced public ministry due to a deep sense of call. Palmer, née Worrall, was born in 1807 in New York City. She was the fourth of sixteen children.[11] Her parents were devout Methodists, and church life was an important part of Palmer's youth.[12]

She met Walter Clarke Palmer, a young physician and a Methodist, in 1826.[13] By all accounts, the Palmers had a strong and happy marriage. They worked together as partners in ministry, and Walter supported Phoebe in her career as a preacher and writer. Sadly, the Palmers suffered tragedy in their early marriage, and these heartbreaking events would deeply influence both Palmer's call and theology. Three of her six children died as babies. In Palmer's intense grief, she had a mystical experience. She heard God telling her to stop blaming herself and others for the deaths. The trials came from God, and she was assured that good would come of her suffering.[14]

After a long struggle, Palmer received sanctification in 1837. Afterward she developed her "shorter way" for others who were seeking it, which is explained in her best-known book, *The Way of Holiness*.[15] Palmer was not trying to create a new theology of sanctification. She was instead offering help to others who were struggling as she had. The shorter way involves three different steps: entire consecration, faith, and testimony. The first step is that a believer needs to put everything on the "altar," which is Christ himself. You cannot hold anything back—believers need to be a living sacrifice. The second step is faith in the sanctification regardless of outward signs or personal emotions. To doubt God and his promise is a sin itself. The final step then is one of testimony. A believer cannot keep this blessing private; the gift of sanctification is meant to be shared with the world.[16] This last step in the process, that of testimony, is critical to understanding Palmer's life following her sanctification.

Once Palmer had committed herself to ministry, she was all in. Her weekly Tuesday Meetings for the Promotion of Holiness were ecumenical prayer and Bible groups that drew in both men and women, including Amanda Berry Smith, from a variety of denominations. These were so popular that hundreds of people came each week, and eventually the Palmers needed to construct an addition to their house to accommodate the sheer number of participants. She wrote extensively about holiness as well. Her best-known books are *The Way of Holiness* published in 1842, *Entire Devotion to God* published in 1845, *Faith and Its Effects: or, Fragments from my Portfolio* published in 1848, and *The Promise of the Father*

---

11 Elaine A. Heath, *Naked Faith: The Mystical Theology of Phoebe Palmer* (Cambridge, UK: James Clark & Co., 2010), 3. About half of her siblings died before reaching adulthood, though the exact number varies from source to source.

12 Charles Edward White, *The Beauty of Holiness: Phoebe Palmer as Theologian, Revivalist, Feminist, and Humanitarian* (Eugene, OR: Wipf & Stock, 1986), 1–3.

13 White, 4.

14 White, 7–8.

15 Phoebe Palmer, *The Way of Holiness* (New York: Piercy and Reed Printers, 1843).

16 Heath, *Naked Faith*, 22–26.

published in 1859. *The Promise of the Father* is of note for its carefully constructed argument defending women's role in public ministry.

Palmer was truly one of the great revivalists of the nineteenth century. For the first twenty years or so of her ministry she generally attended revivals alone while Walter stayed home to work and take care of their children. However, Walter also had a gift for ministry, and eventually he was able to retire from his medical profession to dedicate his life to ministry full time. The Palmers put significant planning into their revivals. They considered a revival an attack against Satan, so they believed "it requires as least as much planning and preparation as a battle between nations."[17] While they would need to adapt certain aspects depending on the situation, they followed a general revival outline. First, the Palmers would decide where to go. They only went where they were officially invited—they would never hold a revival where they did not have the full support of the minister. The second condition was that the people of the congregation had to be willing to make sacrifices for the revival; in other words, the people needed to devote their time and energy to the revival work while the Palmers were in town. The Palmers argued that they did not bring the revival; they were co-laborers with the people. After arriving in the location of the revival, they would preach about entire sanctification. Reports of Phoebe's preaching style indicate she was calm, deliberate, and logical in her ministry.[18] Often the Palmers stayed in one place for several weeks, holding nightly services. However, depending on the work of the Spirit, there could be up to five services a day.[19] After a revival began to bear fruit, the Palmers would form "Christian vigilance bands." These groups agreed to make business or domestic vocations "subservient to Christ"; devote at least a half hour a day to evangelism; work to encourage other Christians to engage in evangelism; meet weekly, pray for each other, and report progress; and finally meet monthly with the other bands and the minister.[20] Through these groups, the Palmers ensured the seeds of the revivals would be tended to long after they left.

Again like Berry Smith, Palmer was also engaged in a number of social reform movements, especially the temperance movement. However, it was her writings and preaching that had the most impact on society. Her theology became critical in the blossoming Holiness movements, and her preaching reached thousands upon thousands of people in numerous countries.

Catherine and Evangeline Booth

In 1859, Phoebe Palmer brought her revivals to the British Isles, where she stayed for the next four years. The tour was considered a success, but it certainly was not without controversy. This vocal American woman prompted English clergy to speak out against her tour. One such minister was a man named Arthur Augustus Rees, who wrote a tract titled *Reasons for Not Co-operating in the Alleged "Sunderland Revivals"* in which he explicitly forbids

17 White, *The Beauty of Holiness*, 171.

18 White, 171–173.

19 Margaret McFadden, "The Ironies of Pentecost: Phoebe Palmer, World Evangelism, and Female Networks," *Methodist History* 31, no. 2 (January 1993): 70.

20 White, *The Beauty of Holiness*, 175.

women from preaching and argues that women must remain subject to men. His pamphlet did nothing to stop Palmer's revivals, but it did find its way into the hands of a particular Englishwoman by the name of Catherine Mumford Booth (1829–1890). Booth, who would later go on to have a successful preaching career and cofound the Salvation Army, was furious when she read the tract from Rees and set out to write her own tract defending women's role in public ministry. In December of 1859, she published a response to Rees in the following tract: *Female Teaching: or the Rev. A. A. Rees versus Mrs. Palmer Being a Reply to a Pamphlet by the Above Named Gentleman on the Sunderland Revival.* She wrote her parents later, saying, "I should like to have given him more *pepper* but being a Lady I felt I must preserve a becoming dignity!" It was not just pepper she threw at him in her defense though; she offered up a cohesive argument based on the created order, scripture, call, and prophecy.[21] Despite her vigorous defense of women in ministry, at that time Booth had never preached in public or engaged in any sort of public ministry outside of her role as a pastor's wife. This would soon change.

The next year, in 1860, Booth began her preaching career. Booth's husband, William, was a Methodist pastor and itinerant preacher. He could not preach due to illness, so she stepped in and then continued his work. Over time, between Booth's writings and preaching, she gained both notoriety and celebrity. She led her own preaching campaigns, spoke to large congregations, and eventually came to receive more invitations to preach than she could manage. She did all this while balancing life as a mother of eight. In 1865, the Booths moved to London and established a home mission that was called the Christian Mission; this would later be renamed the Salvation Army. It is through this effort that Booth would come to be known as the "mother of the Salvation Army."

One cannot see the Salvation Army simply as a home mission. It was, and continues to be, a complex organization that in reality gave birth to a spiritual movement. The theology of the Salvation Army, often called Salvationism, was a "culturally engaged and engaging spirituality, which incorporated a rich variety of means of spiritual formation and expressions of the spiritual disciplines."[22] Booth was critical in establishing both the mission and the theological emphasis of the organization. The Army sought to bring salvation to the poor through meeting both their physical and spiritual needs. In a time of growing urbanization and industrialization, the Army was uniquely suited to meeting the needs of the people.

One key aspect of the Salvation Army was its inclusion of women; they preached, led, held office, spoke, and voted in official meetings. In other words, if a woman had the skills and desire to engage in public ministry, she was encouraged to do so. In fact, in the 1880s, the Army had a growing number of women officers called the Hallelujah Lasses who preached in the streets and provided services to the poor.[23] While they were undoubtedly

---

21 Pamela J. Walker, "A Chaste and Fervid Eloquence: Catherine Booth and the Ministry of Women in the Salvation Army," in *Women Preachers and Prophets through Two Millennia of Christianity*, eds. Beverly Kienzle and Pamela J. Walker (Berkeley: University of California Press, 1998), 291.

22 John Read, *Catherine Booth: Laying the Theological Foundations of a Radical Movement* (Cambridge, UK: Lutterworth Press, 2013), 3–4.

23 Walker, "A Chaste and Fervid Eloquence," 296.

progressive for the age, there was not complete equality between the sexes. The Salvation Army affirmed female submission in marriage, and women preachers were paid less than men for many years. Regardless, women had opportunities within the Army to engage in a ministry career that otherwise would have been impossible.

The opportunities available through the Salvation Army are abundantly clear in the life of Catherine Booth's daughter, Evangeline, who served as fourth general—a position her father had held—and first woman general of the organization.[24] An obituary from *Christian Century* from 1950 describes her as "a great woman, a great orator, and a great Christian leader . . . and all Booth."[25] Born on Christmas Day in 1865, the year the Salvation Army was founded, she grew up immersed in the culture of the Army. In 1896 she was sent to America to deal with an intra-organizational schism and was appointed temporary Army commander of the United States and Canada. The position, which she would hold until 1934, would be made permanent in 1904. Soon the New York office became the central headquarters of the organization. During World War I, she organized the Army's presence among the Allied troops. Her preaching drew enormous crowds. She insisted the Army be democratized—a battle she won against her older brother Bramwell. She was elected General in 1934 and held the position until her term ended in 1939, at which point she moved home to upstate New York, where she remained until her death in 1950.

PENTECOSTAL PREACHERS

There were two major events that rocked California in the year 1906. One event was a literal shaking—the great San Francisco earthquake. The other event could be described as a spiritual earthquake, an event that would profoundly change the religious landscape around the globe—the Azusa Street Revival. This revival, under the leadership of William Seymour (1870–1922), lasted for three years. It was characterized by ecstatic worship, glossolalia (speaking in tongues), healings, and other miraculous spiritual gifts. It is largely considered by historians to be the start of the modern Pentecostal movement, and various Charismatic and Neo-Pentecostal movements are traced back to this event as well.

In some ways all this attention given to Azusa is misleading. The revival did not occur in a vacuum, and there were many precursors to this event. The Holiness movement, and its emphasis on the second blessing, affirmed a spiritual conversion event. In fact, it was from the Holiness tradition that Pentecostalism would emerge. Types of ecstatic worship were present at revivals before this. Jarena Lee, for example, spoke of people being slain by the Spirit during her services, and people were speaking in tongues, which would become a hallmark trait of Pentecostalism, at revivals prior to Azusa. There was an incident of glossolalia five years before Azusa at Charles Fox Parham's Bible school, but the event petered out instead of exploding. Seymour was introduced to the concept of speaking in tongues

---

24 General is the title given to the leader of the Salvation Army.
25 "Another General Booth Enters Heaven," *Christian Century* 67, no. 31 (August 2, 1950): 909.

as evidence of the baptism of the Holy Spirit in Houston, Texas, by his pastor, Lucy Farrow, in 1905, prior to his own revival. The elements of Pentecostalism were there, but Azusa was the spark to ignite the movement. The initial inclusion of all people regardless of race, ethnicity, or gender was a critical aspect of the event and helps to explain the leadership roles of many women within the Pentecostal tradition.

In 1906, Seymour, an ordained evangelist, felt called by God to head to California. He arrived in Los Angeles on February 22, 1906, and began preaching at Julia Hutchins's Holiness church two days later. In his first sermon, he preached on Acts 2:4 and the necessity of speaking in other tongues as proof of the Pentecostal experience. Outraged and shocked by Seymour's claims, Hutchins locked the doors to the church, and Seymour was without a job or a place to stay. Hutchins would later become a convert to Pentecostalism and join the revival.

Despite these setbacks, Seymour continued preaching. He began leading prayer meetings in the home of Richard and Ruth Asberry, located in a small but lively African American community. Seymour's first attendants were primarily African American domestic servants and other laborers. The small group grew larger as visitors, both Black and white, from a variety of denominational backgrounds began to visit. There were so many visitors that they could no longer fit in the house, and it became clear the group needed a larger space.

The group began to meet at the former Stevens AME Church on April 15, 1906. The church had been abandoned after a fire and eventually came to be used as a warehouse and stable. A group of over one hundred "prayer warriors" prayed for a revival that would shake the nation. The great San Francisco earthquake on April 18, 1906, set the stage for a spectacular revival with apocalyptic overtones. Shortly thereafter people began to experience healings—the first being a man healed of a club foot. The racial and ethnic diversity continued to grow. Members of Azusa included immigrants from Mexico, Sweden, Ireland, England, Russia, and China among others.

The worship schedule for Azusa was incredibly busy. Seymour or another associate would preach three times a day, seven days a week. Often the services would go on so long that they would blend into each other. Baptisms of the Holy Spirit, healings, and exorcisms reportedly happened on a regular basis. All the music during worship was spontaneous and often without instruments. On April 6, 1906, Seymour led the prayer group on a ten-day fast. Three days later the Azusa Street Revival officially began on April 9 when Seymour laid hands on a member of the group named Edward Lee and prayed for him to receive baptism of the Holy Spirit. Lee began to speak in tongues. Three days later, Seymour received the gift as well. Jennie Evans Moore, who would eventually marry Seymour, became the first woman to speak in tongues. Reportedly she was also able to suddenly speak in Spanish, French, Latin, Greek, Hebrew, and Hindustani; she apparently also miraculously gained the ability to play the piano.[26]

---

26 Jennifer Hornyak Wojciechowski, "William J. Seymore," in *The World's Greatest Religious Leaders: How Religious Leaders Helped Shape World History*, eds. Scott Hendrix and Uchenna Okeja (Santa Barbara: ABC-CIO, 2018).

Women were active participants in the revival. There were seasoned preachers involved like Lucy Farrow, Julia Hutchins, Anna Hall, Ardella Mead, Mabel Smith, Lillian Garr, and Ivey Campbell. These women worked alongside newly empowered novices such as Jennie Evans Moore and Florence Crawford. Women preached, they prayed with seekers, they received spiritual gifts, they were on the administrative board, they helped publish the Pentecostal newspaper that was established, and they were missionaries for the Pentecostal cause.[27] Eventually, women's leadership would be curtailed from its initial inclusive levels, but even then, Pentecostal denominations tended to have more women in leadership than mainline denominations. Considering the emphasis on experience and the Holy Spirit, this is unsurprising. Therefore, there are many women who led and taught within this movement, and we will focus on a few who were particularly influential.

One of the most influential leaders at Azusa was Lucy Farrow, Seymour's previous pastor and mentor. Little is known about Farrow's early life—there are no reliable sources on her family (outside a report that she was the niece of famed abolitionist Frederick Douglass), her religious experiences, or her education. It is believed she was born in 1851 either into slavery or free but later sold into slavery. By 1890, she was living in Houston with her son and his wife while she pastored a small Holiness church. In Houston she met Charles Parham and returned to Kansas with him, where she received the gift of speaking in tongues. She later returned to Houston, where she taught her congregation, including Seymour, that speaking in tongues was a necessary expression of baptism of the Holy Spirit. It was also Farrow who recommended Seymour be invited to Los Angeles.

The exact timing of her own arrival at Azusa is disputed, but she arrived prior to the outbreak of revival, and she was, with her own experience of Spirit baptism, an important voice in bringing about the revival. She stayed on at Azusa to work as a pastor and a teacher and became a central figure early in the movement, but after a few months, she felt called to bring the message to the world. She embarked on a preaching tour that included stops in Texas, Louisiana, North Carolina, Virginia, New York, England, and Liberia, where she stayed for about seven months. After that she headed back to the United States, where she led additional revivals in the American South. She died in 1911 back in Houston at the age of sixty.[28]

Another leader at Azusa worth noting is Florence Reed Crawford (1873–1936), who is significant for her work associated with Azusa but also her founding of a Christian denomination after her contentious break with Seymour. Crawford was born to atheist parents but embraced religion when she was young. She came to Los Angeles in 1890 and married Frank Mortimer Crawford, though they separated in 1907. She was involved in various social reform movements, such as the WCTU and the National Congress of Mothers. She went looking for a spiritual home and found Azusa in the early days of the revival, where she spoke in tongues and also reportedly miraculously gained the ability to write in seven or eight different languages and was healed from an assortment of physical ailments that had plagued her for years.

---

27 Estrelda Alexander, *The Women of Azusa Street* (Cleveland: Pilgrim Press, 2005), 37–38.

28 Alexander, *The Women of Azusa Street*, 39–46.

She sat on the Azusa Street administrative board and served as coeditor (along with Seymour and Clara Lum) and staff writer on the Azusa Street newsletter, *The Apostolic Faith*. She became a gifted preacher and faith healer who went on the preaching circuit in California, where she led revivals and drew such crowds that often law enforcement would be called to keep the peace. She received invitations to preach in various parts of the United States and Canada. She was named state overseer of California, a post in which she directed teams of evangelists to hold revivals throughout California, Oregon, and Washington. She did all this in about a year's time; then her relationship with Seymour deteriorated.

It is unknown exactly what caused the break, though historians have speculated that it may have been related to personal relationships or a limiting of women's leadership within the mission. Regardless, the fallout was severe. Crawford left the mission in 1908 and moved to Portland, Oregon. Following her departure, Clara Clum followed and took the mailing list for *The Apostolic Faith*, which was a blow for Seymour and Azusa, and Crawford and Lum continued to produce the newsletter from Portland. In Portland, her ministry grew, and she founded her own denomination, the Apostolic Faith Mission, which was Pentecostal in nature but also highly sectarian. The denomination is still in existence today, making Crawford one of the earliest women to found her own Christian denomination.[29]

Though she did not have a direct connection with Azusa, Aimee Semple McPherson, née Kennedy (1890–1944), was one of the great evangelists of the twentieth century and likely the best-known woman in the Pentecostal movement. She was a larger-than-life figure who intertwined the gospel message with the glamour of classic Hollywood. She died in 1944 of what was determined to be an accidental overdose at the age of fifty-three. Unfortunately, the scandals that plagued her later years, included an alleged kidnapping hoax, have clouded her legacy as a Christian leader. An emphasis on her troubled years ignores the fact that she was a passionate and talented evangelist, a master at using new media, a coordinator of numerous charitable outreaches, and the founder of a Christian denomination.

McPherson was born in Ontario, Canada, in 1890. Her father was a Methodist, and her mother was part of the Salvation Army. At seventeen she experienced a conversion after hearing a Pentecostal preacher by the name of Robert Semple. They were married shortly after and became missionaries to China. Semple died two years after their marriage while McPherson was eight months pregnant with their daughter, Roberta Star Semple. McPherson returned to the United States and began working with the Salvation Army. She married Harold McPherson in 1911, which proved an unhappy marriage but produced a son named Rolf who would carry on his mother's evangelism. Throughout this difficult time in her life, she felt God calling her to preach, and she became an itinerant preacher. Her husband joined her for a short time, but they divorced soon after, which freed her to travel to revivals with her mother assisting her.

She settled in Los Angeles, the home of Pentecostalism, in 1918. At that time, Los Angeles was a tourist hub, and instead of traveling all over the country, McPherson

---

29 For more information on Crawford, see Alexander, *The Women of Azusa Street*, chap. 5.

believed she could preach to tourists there instead, which would in turn spread her message throughout the United States and further. She built her Angelus Temple in 1923 with the vision that it would serve this ecumenical purpose. It is a beautiful and massive church that is still functioning today and can seat over five thousand people for a service.

One aspect of McPherson's ministry, which is critical for understanding her success as an evangelist, was her penchant for glamour and spectacle. McPherson fused that aesthetic with her ministry. When she preached, she wore dresses that resembled vestments but incorporated elements of fashion and drama. Her services were larger than life, with people in costume and dramatic faith healings and salvations. She was no plain-clothed preacher letting the Word speak for itself. She brought in an element of entertainment that spoke to a nation that was in the midst of a massive media and entertainment shift. She predated televangelism (though she would have made a good televangelist); she did, however, utilize the newest media at the time, which was radio. In fact, she was one of the first women to commission her own radio station in the United States. Unfortunately, because of her aesthetic, her status as both divorced and a woman, and her media presence, she was the focus of criticism from other preachers.

Her ministry was not all glitz and glamour, however. She genuinely reached many with her message, and she founded myriad charitable missions. She was active in numerous relief efforts and war efforts, and she was committed to helping the poor. She was engaged in creating food kitchens, free clinics, and other outreaches, particularly during the Great Depression, when need was particularly high. Eventually her church became the center of a new denomination that she established: the Foursquare Church. Her denomination was founded on the four-fold ministry of Jesus as the Savior, baptizer with the Holy Spirit, healer, and coming king. There are now tens of thousands of Foursquare churches around the world.[30]

LIMITED ORDINATION

After examining all these examples of women who created public ministries, the obvious question is, Did the increase in women's preaching lead to ordination and an increased participation in church leadership? The answer is complex. There was limited ordination in the nineteenth and early twentieth centuries, though not necessarily in the Holiness and Pentecostal denominations that loom so large in the history of women's evangelism. Some of the earliest pastoral appointments were within Congregationalist and Unitarian churches, though these appointments were few and far between. It was not until the second half of the twentieth century that it became more common for mainline Protestant denominations to ordain women, though the activities of preaching, evangelizing, and early ordination within the nineteenth century started these conversations.

---

30 The Foursquare Church, *A Simplified Guide to Foursquare Belief* (Los Angeles: International Church of the Foursquare Gospel, n.d.), https://s3.amazonaws.com/foursquare.org/wp-content/uploads/sites/2/2019/11/08165309/SimplifiedGuideBrochure_WEB_FINAL.pdf.

The long-cited first woman to be ordained was Antionette Brown. Born in 1825 to a New England family with Puritan roots, she grew up in the "burned-over district" of New York—so called because of the sheer number of religious revivals that had swept the area. From a young age, she wanted to be a minister—not a woman missionary, not a teacher, but a minister. The odds seemed stacked against this pious young woman. She applied to Oberlin, which was a liberal coed college, to get a theological education. Despite Oberlin's liberal leanings, accepting a woman for theological studies proved too radical. After an initial refusal and additional protest by Brown and her friend Lucy Stone, Brown and Oberlin came to a compromise. She would take theological classes, but she would not receive a degree or a license to preach. This undoubtedly seems like a poor deal today, but Brown was able to get a theological education even if it was not formally recognized. Over the next couple of years Brown occasionally preached, generally at the request of a liberal male pastor, and she became involved in temperance, abolition, and the women's rights movement. In 1852, she was invited to become the pastor of a small Congregationalist church in South Butler, New York. Brown was appointed by the congregation itself and did not have the consent of the larger Congregationalist denomination. What made her ordination possible was the highly individual nature of Congregational churches. This represents a larger trend of early cases of women's ordination. While a generalization, the more hierarchical a church, the more difficult the path to ordination. Conversely individual churches with a high level of autonomy inevitably had more freedom to ordain whomever they wanted.

Unfortunately, this appointment was not the moment of triumph that Brown had been longing for. The job was exhausting, and she had little support. Many Christians were critical of a woman pastoring a church, and many of her more progressive friends were critical of Christianity in general. She stepped down in 1854, a mere two years after her historic appointment, to concentrate on public speaking and raising a family; perhaps more significant is that she was becoming increasingly wary of identifying with a particular church.[31] Eventually she left the Congregationalist denomination altogether and joined the Unitarians though was unable to find a full-time ministry position. To compound the dubious success of her appointment, by the year 1900, nearly fifty years later, there were fewer than forty women ministers in Congregationalism. Brown's appointment was a first, but it did not signify any real and lasting change in church leadership.

The first woman to be ordained with the full consent of her denomination was Olympia Brown (1835–1926). She, too, had difficulties pursuing a theological degree, but eventually she enrolled at St. Lawrence University in New York and was ordained by the Universalists in 1863. Brown went on to have a successful ministry career, serving in a number of churches over the next twenty-five years. In addition to her ministry, she became a successful leader in the women's rights movement. Due to her longevity, she was one of the few early suffrage leaders who lived long enough to finally vote after the passing of the Nineteenth Amendment.

---

31 Bill. J. Leonard and Jill Y. Crainshaw, *Encyclopedia of Religious Controversies in the United States*, vol. 1 (Santa Barbara: ABC-CLIO, 2013), 107.

Within the Methodist tradition, which produced many women preachers and evange-lists, the Methodist Episcopal Church (MEC) granted Anna Howard Shaw (1847–1919) a preaching license in the 1870s. After she completed a theological degree at the Boston Theological Seminary in 1878, she was hired at a church in East Dennis, Massachusetts, but the MEC refused her application for ordination because she was a woman. Two years later, she was ordained by the Methodist Protestant Church and able to continue her post at East Dennis. Interestingly she also became a medical doctor, but by the mid-1880s, she had completely devoted her career to temperance and women's suffrage. Fif-teen years after Shaw's appointment as the first ordained white woman Methodist, Julia Foote (1823–1901) became the first woman ordained as a deacon and the second to be appointed as an elder in the African Methodist Episcopal Zion Church.

If the appointment of these women into ministry did not open a floodgate, it at least started a trickle of other ordinations. According to Frances Willard's 1889 book, *Woman in the Pulpit*, denominations had ordained women at the time. At that time the Quak-ers, Methodists, Baptists, Free Baptists, Congregationalists, Universalists, and Unitarians were all ordaining women.[32] There were also women officers in the Salvation Army that Willard does not mention. The number of ordained women was not great in any of these denominations. For example, the Unitarians, whom Willard lists, had only ordained 539 women between 1863 and 1959. The Congregationalists, who ordained Antionette Brown, had only ordained about one hundred women by the 1920s.[33] Ordination did not mean equality in church leadership either. Women tended to be paid less; they had fewer desirable appointments, and they were less involved in the church hierarchy throughout the nineteenth century.

THE PROPHETS

By and large this book examines women who participated in the Christian church, in any of its multitude of expressions. However, not all women fit comfortably in the established church, and there were some who rejected the core tenets to participate in alternative reli-gious movements or even establish their own religion. In past times, they may have been declared heretics and persecuted, but in the nineteenth century these women were able to carve out new paths and establish their own religious movements, including a variety of Spiritualist traditions and Christian Science. There were also women who remained within more orthodox traditions but ran afoul of authorities or brought in unique theo-logical aspects that pushed their movements outside of the mainstream.

---

32 Frances Willard, *Woman in the Pulpit* (Chicago: Woman's Temperance Publication Association, 1889), 94. The inclusion of Quakers in the list is a bit misleading since Quakers did not have any sort of formalized clergy.

33 Lindley, *You Have Stept Out of Your Place*, 309.

Spiritualism and Theosophy

In 1848, the same year the first women's rights convention in the United States was hosted in Seneca Falls, NY, two teenage sisters were creating quite a sensation. Maggie (1833–1893) and Katie Fox (1837–1892) claimed that they could communicate with the dead through "rappings," which they later admitted to being a noise they produced by cracking their toe joints, but people were ready and willing to believe that they could communicate with the dead. The Fox sisters functioned as mediums; they held public séances, and they sparked a popular sensation. Soon the Spiritualist movement was much bigger than the sisters. In 1851, there were seven Spiritualist periodicals in the United States; six years later, there were sixty-seven.[34]

Spiritualism played into traditional views of women at the time. Women, who were seen as more pious, passive, and receptive, suddenly became the perfect mediums because they were merely channeling spirits. Spiritualism was of course a decentralized movement with no hierarchy or church authority other than whatever the spirits may have directed a medium to do. Despite the emphasis on passivity, Spiritualism did provide women with a public religious position.

Another related religious theme that became popular during the nineteenth century was "knowledge from the East." One such religious movement, the Theosophical Society, founded by a woman named Helena Blavatsky (1831–1891), emphasized esoteric knowledge in a sort of quasi-universalism. While the movement largely died out after Blavatsky's death, it had a surprising amount of influence in society, and some prominent individuals studied it. Part of the allure of Theosophy was in the mystery of its founder. Little concrete information is known about Blavatsky's life prior to her arrival in New York in the early 1870s. But is it believed that she was born in 1831 in Ukraine, and her family was minor German/Russian aristocracy. She was married at the age of seventeen to a much older Russian governor in the Caucasus. She soon ran away from him and began her travels in the East. She arrived in New York in the early 1870s, allegedly from Tibet. She said she was instructed in the esoteric wisdom of the ages in Tibet by the "masters"—gifted seers who stood in succession to Moses, Krishna, Lao-tze, the Buddha, and Christ.

Her teachings combined traditional Spiritualism with aspects of Eastern religions. For example, she agreed that Spiritualists could commune with spirits but argued that these were not true spirits. They were merely shells left behind by the deceased. All the world's religions became a single "ancient wisdom." Officially, the Theosophical Society based itself upon the following three objectives: to form a nucleus of the Universal Brotherhood of Humanity, without distinction of race, creed, sex, caste, or color; to encourage the study of comparative religion, philosophy, and science; and to investigate the unexplained laws of nature and the powers latent in man.

---

34 John Corrigan and Winthrop S. Hudson, *Religions in America: An Historical Account of the Development of American Religious Life*, 7th ed. (Upper Saddle River, NJ: Pearson, 2004), 213–214.

Mary Baker Eddy and Christian Science

Around the same time Madam Blavatsky was founding the Theosophical Society, Mary Baker Eddy (1821–1910) was bringing forth a different type of worldview. Mary Baker Eddy's church, Christian Science, is an important nineteenth-century movement that does not conform to orthodox Christian principles but still operates in a Christian space. Whether or not people understand it to be a Christian movement, Eddy herself saw it that way. Christian Science also provided women with an important opportunity to participate in hierarchal leadership and in healing practices, especially in the late nineteenth and early twentieth centuries.

Christian Science does not just teach that connecting to the spiritual realm is possible—Christian Scientists believe that reality is purely spiritual, not physical, and that the world is an illusion. Therefore, sickness and death are also an illusion or, perhaps more accurately, a mental or spiritual failing of sorts. The establishment or, as Eddy preferred to call it, the "discovery" of Christian Science was intertwined with Eddy's own life. She was born in New Hampshire in 1821 to a Congregationalist family. She had health problems from a young age, which would play significantly into her religious journey. She married and moved to the American South in 1843, but her husband died within a year, leaving her a pregnant widow without any resources. She returned home and, due to health problems, had to give up her son. She married again, to an itinerant dentist, but the marriage was unhappy, and her health declined even further. Then she met Phineas Quimby, an advocate for mental cures for ill health.

Eddy was highly influenced by Quimby and began lecturing on his teachings. In 1866, Eddy was in crisis. Quimby had died, and Eddy was suffering from tremendous back pain as a result of a fall. After reading Matthew 9:2 (the verse reads, "Some men brought to him a paralyzed man, lying on a mat. When Jesus saw their faith, he said to the man, 'Take heart, son; your sins are forgiven'"), she claimed to have been miraculously cured. This was a monumental moment in her life, and she spent the next decade refining her theology. In 1875, she published *Science and Health*, to which she added *Key to the Scriptures* in 1883. This book has literally sold millions of copies. In 1877, she divorced her second husband and was married for a third time, to Asa Gilbert Eddy. The Church of Christ, Scientist, as her movement is officially called, was formally established in 1879. The church grew rapidly through both her writings and her own skills as a teacher.

Christian Science provided opportunities for women. The theology was egalitarian, and Eddy viewed God as both male and female—both father and mother. But these opportunities for women extended far beyond merely intellectual views of God as mother. Women had concrete leadership paths within the organization. Each Christian Science society was established under parallel leaders—one man and one woman as the official readers. Their task was to read from the Bible and *Science and Health*, though no sermons were permitted by either men or women. Women could also work as missionaries or as healing practitioners.

The position of "healing practitioner" needs some additional background to be understood correctly. This was a time when the medical field was being professionalized. There were many necessary reasons for this professionalization, including the much-needed oversight of doctors and healers, who may or may not have had a patient's best interest at heart. But this professionalization increasingly made medicine a man's field, and women, who had worked as healers for millennia, were being pushed out.

Because Christian Science teaches that reality is spiritual, believers viewed traditional medicine as misguided at best. Therefore, healing should be a mental discipline. Christian Science healing practitioners would not have done things traditionally associated with medicine, such as setting bones and treating infectious diseases. They would have offered prayer and guidance on the mental and spiritual practices needed to overcome an (ultimately not real) ailment. In the nineteenth century, considering the still primitive state of medicine, prayer may have sometimes offered a somewhat comparable outcome. However, as time has passed and medicine has advanced, faith in Christian Science healing has understandably lessened.

Interestingly, although Eddy was a public religious leader and her organization offered leadership positions to other women, men occupied much of the higher levels of leadership within the organization. Eddy was traditional when it came to gender roles even though she rejected them herself. Any forays into social reform, such as suffrage, were secondary to her primary identity as a religious leader.

Ellen G. White and the Seventh-Day Adventists

In the 1820s, a Baptist by the name of William Miller predicted the second coming of Christ sometime in 1843—this was later changed to October of 1844. He figured this out using scripture, particularly the book of Daniel, and he tentatively started telling people. By 1840, belief in his predictions had become a large movement that included itinerant preachers promoting end times. There were tracts printed and even children's books produced. First 1843 passed; then October of 1844 passed; Jesus had not returned, and the world had not ended. These non-events came to be known as the Great Disappointment. The Great Disappointment proved inconvenient for many true believers. Miller himself was excommunicated and died in obscurity, but his ideas continued on in a number of new religious movements, which include Jehovah's Witnesses and, more importantly for our study here, Seventh-day Adventists.

How does someone respond when they truly believe the world is about to end and then it does not? Most Millerites, as the believers in Miller's predictions were called, returned to their regular lives. However, some could not give up the belief. A certain number of followers decided that Miller had misinterpreted some of his predictions. Christ was not returning to Earth in 1844, but 1844 did mark the beginning of God's judgment of the world. They believed that while the end was imminent, no one could know the exact time of Christ's return. This is the context of Ellen Harmon White's entrance into religious life. Her parents were Millerites, and she was about seventeen during the Great Disappointment. In 1846, she married a Millerite preacher named James White.

Shortly after Judgment Day failed to occur, White had the first of hundreds of visions. She is considered by many a modern-day prophet, and like the mystics of old, it is through this direct communication with the divine that White gained her religious authority. A vision from 1847 shows the importance of the Sabbath for White and the religious denomination she cofounded along with her husband and Joseph Bates:

> I saw an angel flying swiftly to me. He quickly carried me from the earth to the Holy City. In the city I saw a temple, which I entered. . . . In the Ark was the golden pot of manna, Aaron's rod that budded, and the tables of stone which folded together like a book. Jesus opened them, and I saw the Ten Commandments written on them with the finger of God. On one table were four, and on the other six. But the fourth, the Sabbath commandment, shone above them all; for the Sabbath was set apart to be kept in honor of God's holy name.[35]

Theologically speaking, the Adventists are Trinitarian Christians, but their emphasis on the end of days and Sabbath separate them from more mainstream forms of Christianity. The Adventists also emphasize healthy living and a vegetarian diet. Interestingly, despite having a woman as a founder and prophet, the denomination still does not ordain women to the ministry today.

Teresa Urrea

Teresa Urrea (1873–1906?) did not establish her own religion, though she was a famed healer and was hailed as "la santa de Cabora" by those who believed in her powers. She ran afoul of both ecclesial and secular authorities, but she always maintained that she was a Catholic and instructed believers to worship God and not her. She also communicated with spiritual beings, though hers were firmly within the Catholic framework of saints and angels.

Urrea was born in 1873 in Sinaloa, Mexico, to a wealthy landowner and a fifteen-year-old American Indian servant who worked for him. As a child, Urrea learned herbal remedies from an American Indian *curandera* and acted as her assistant. In her later teens, Urrea began suffering from seizures, and after one episode where she reportedly lay unconscious for several days, she recovered and subsequently believed that she had a mission to help people. She lived out this belief zealously, and when the *curandera* died, Urrea took over her work. She acquired a following and a large reputation. By the end of 1891, she was being credited with various miracles, and Cabora, where she lived, started to resemble a pilgrimage site. Urrea believed that she was in direct contact with God and the saints. She was anticlerical in her beliefs, and she even routinely performed sacraments—activities that clearly did not make the Catholic Church particularly fond of this folk saint.

It was during these years as a successful healer that Urrea became involved in American Indian rebellions against the Mexican government under the regime of Porfirio Díaz, though to what extent is debated. Regardless, the government believed she was directly involved and exiled both Urrea and her father. The two moved to the United States, where her cult continued—and according to the Mexican government, so did her involvement in

---

35 Ellen G. White, "Ellen Harmon White, Seventh Day Adventist Prophetess," in *Women and Religion in America, Volume 1: The Nineteenth Century*, ed. Rosemary Radford Ruether and Rosemary Skinner Keller (Cambridge: Harper and Row, 1981), 80–81.

inciting rebellion. In 1900, convinced by wealthy entrepreneurs, she began a healing tour around the country. It was something of a mash-up of medical healing, entertainment, and religious revival. Within a couple of years, she was disillusioned and moved back to Arizona and continued her ministry there. Unfortunately, her health both physically and mentally declined at this point, and she died in either late 1905 or early 1906 at the age of thirty-two.

Urrea demonstrates an interesting instance of a woman who established a successful healing ministry and achieved the status of local saint (though she was never recognized as such by the Catholic Church). There is no reason to believe she was insincere in her ministry; she believed strongly in her own abilities and her mission, even when it ran contrary to what the established church taught.[36]

---

36 Matt S. Meier, Conchita Franco Serri, and Richard A. Garcia, *Notable Latino Americans* (Westport, CT: ABC-CLIO, 1997), 389–392; Gonzales, *Christianity in Latin America*, 156–157.

CHAPTER 10

Women and Reform

> Why should not a woman seek to be a reformer? If she is to shrink from being such an iconoclast as shall 'break the image of man's lower worship,' as so long held up to view; if she is to fear to exercise her reason, and her noble powers, lest she should be thought to 'attempt to act the man,' and not 'acknowledge his supremacy': if she is to be satisfied with the narrow sphere assigned her by man, nor aspire to a higher, lest she should transcend the bounds of female delicacy, truly it is a mournful prospect for a woman.
>
> —Lucretia Mott, "Why Shouldn't a Woman Be a Reformer?"

Lucretia Mott, who worked tirelessly for both abolition and women's rights, spoke these words in December of 1849 in response to criticism aimed at women who were fighting for more rights. While Mott, who was active in the Society of Friends, was an exceptionally vocal advocate for change, her commitment to social reform centered in her Christian faith was not unusual among religious women of the era.

Christian women have always engaged in acts of charity, hospitality, and care of the sick, the poor, and the marginalized. There is nothing new about women trying to offer comfort or improve their society through acts of Christian charity. The nineteenth century, however, saw an enormous increase in the number of Christian women who were actively *organizing* to meet the needs of their communities and influence societal change all over the globe. This engagement in religiously inspired social activism continued through the twentieth century and into our current era. Considering the recurring theme throughout history, it is doubtful this impulse will end.

There was a deep thread of optimism that ran through the nineteenth-century reform movements. Despite glaring problems in society like massive wealth inequality, corruption, poverty, and a slew of societal issues deemed evil by the church, technological and scientific advances made anything seem possible, and there was undoubtedly a general air of social engagement in many places in the world, both inside and outside of the church. This was the era of global missions, temperance, and the beginning days of the women's rights movement. The era when a vast network of social services was being built by both religious institutions and governments and fights against corruption and unchecked capitalism reigned supreme. The rise of the Social Gospel looked at salvation on a larger societal scale. It considered systems and how to improve them, and a more complex understanding of social problems came into being.[1]

---

1 For a more in-depth examination of the Social Gospel, see Christopher Evans, *The Social Gospel in American Religion: A History* (New York: New York University Press, 2017).

The twentieth century was markedly different from the nineteenth. The unprecedented loss of life caused by the two world wars compounded by countless other tragedies led to a sense of disillusionment in both society and religion. By the end of the Second World War, in light of the Holocaust and other mass death events, many people questioned whether human beings were indeed born good or whether we were truly capable of ever making a just world. The concept of ushering in Christ's return through perfecting society seemed naïve, to say the least. Regardless of this disenchantment, women continued to work for systemic changes within their communities and society at large. In other words, they never gave up the fight.

CATHOLIC WOMEN

By and large the first women who were active in works of Christian charity and various aspects of social reform efforts were Catholic sisters. Though cloistered throughout much of the medieval and early modern eras, nuns provided services from their convents including taking in orphans, providing healing care, and running schools. In the early seventeenth century, the Daughters of Charity were founded by Vincent de Paul and Louise de Marillac, a pious aristocratic widow, in Paris, France. Unlike other religious orders, this group made vows annually, so they could leave the order without ecclesiastical permission, and they were the first non-cloistered religious institute of women devoted to charitable works. This group of French women, who were technically not nuns, served the poorest of the poor, and they organized hospitals, built schools, offered job training, provided free meals, and worked to improve prison conditions. Quickly, the Daughters of Charity spread throughout the world, and inspired by their success, it became increasingly common for nuns to be out in society providing critical services in a variety of contexts including education, healthcare, and foreign missions.

In Chile, for example, nuns and Catholic laywomen took on a pivotal role in providing social services to the people. When a new liberal government took control of the country, they realized providing social services was more complex than they had anticipated, and they turned to women to fill that role. In 1854, the Chilean government signed contracts with four different groups of nuns. It was these religious women who first provided such assistance and then legitimized nursing, teaching, and other social service professions for Chilean women in general. Soon laywomen became active in the work of the nuns by raising funds and acting as administrators. As social services gradually became more secularized, women still dominated these careers.

Similarly, in nineteenth-century Argentina, the government established the female-run Beneficent Society to oversee charitable efforts for women and children. The popularity of this society among wealthy women inspired the creation of other female associations designed to assist the poor and new immigrants. One of the most successful groups, the Conferences of the Ladies of St. Vincent de Paul, boasted thousands of members and spread throughout the country. The women of the various conferences raised money for those in need, provided basic services, and propagated the Catholic faith.[2]

In the United States, Elizabeth Seton (1774–1821) founded the Sisters of Charity, which oversaw hospitals, schools, and orphanages. Seton, a high-society Episcopalian, traveled to Italy with her husband and daughter in 1803, hoping the warmer climate would cure her husband's tuberculosis. Her husband died in Italy, but Seton was introduced to the Catholic faith while she was there. Once she returned to New York, she was formally received into the church in 1805. In 1808, she accepted an invitation from a French Sulpician priest by the name of William DuBourg to open a Catholic school for poor girls in Baltimore—it was the first of its kind in the United States. In 1809, Seton, now known as Mother Seton, gathered a group of women and founded the Sisters of Charity of St. Joseph and built a permanent headquarters in Emmitsburg, Maryland; the group adopted the rules of the Daughters of Charity. Seton died in 1821 of tuberculosis, but the order she founded was critical in launching the tradition of Catholic community service within the United States. A few years after Seton founded the Sisters of Charity, Mary Rhodes, Christina Steward, and Nancy Havern established the Sisters of Loretto in Kentucky in 1812, which was the first American sisterhood without ties to European religious communities; this group founded schools in Kentucky, Missouri, and other parts of the American Midwest and Southwest.[3]

DEACONESS MOVEMENT

The nineteenth century brought a renewal of an ancient order that allowed women a larger role within Protestant churches—that is, the modern deaconess movement. This is a different although connected story than that of women's ordination within church bodies because today many deaconesses are indeed ordained. Some historians have viewed the diaconate as a transitional position between Protestant lay leadership and ordinated women clergy. Historically, deaconesses straddled a line that was not quite ordained ministry but not quite lay involvement. However, viewing this position as merely transitional is an incomplete analysis, and it devalues the vocational calling of deaconesses both past and present.

The ancient and modern movements are distinct and should not be confused, though the modern movement undoubtedly found inspiration in both the biblical figure of Phoebe and the ancient diaconate. The modern deaconess movement provided a space for Protestant women to pursue ministry full time in a way that was reminiscent of Catholic sisters but was and continues to be distinct. Modern deaconesses were unmarried women (though today there are married deaconesses) who worked in ministry, often as nurses or in other areas of social services and missions. They were associated with a number of different Christian traditions, and they were particularly visible in the Lutheran and

---

2 Gonzalés and Gonzalés, *Christianity in Latin America*, 148–149.

3 James T. Fisher, *Catholics in America* (Oxford: Oxford University Press, 2000), 38–41.

Methodist denominations. They were often misunderstood—inaccurately called Protestant nuns—but their contributions were and continue to be significant for the church.

From the Reformation on, Protestant women were limited in their options regarding ministry. With the abolishment of convents in Protestant lands, marriage became the norm for women. While some women found very meaningful lives as a pastor's wife, that ministry role was completely dependent on marriage. For women who did not want a marriage and a family, there were few viable options over the next 250 years. This would change with the founding of the first German deaconess institution in Kaiserswerth, Germany, in 1836. Theodore and Frederike Münster Fliedner, the two founders of the institute, were inspired by a variety of different movements including a men's deacon movement, Catholic sisters, and Mennonite deaconesses. The general atmosphere of religious awakening undoubtedly influenced the founding as well.

The Kaiserswerth Deaconess Institute was incredibly successful. Single women entered the institute and were trained as nurses while immersed in an atmosphere of religious devotion with frequent worship services. The community became a tight-knit surrogate family for the women, and through their association with this movement, they were able to engage in activities that were largely seen as inappropriate for single women, such as holding a job and engaging in full-time ministry. Within fifteen years, Kaiserswerth ran a deaconess motherhouse, a hospital, a center for the rehabilitation of women convicts, a teacher training school, a girls' high school, a kindergarten, an orphanage, a home for "female invalids," a farm, and the school for deaconesses. By the nineteenth century, there were nearly fifteen thousand women associated with Kaiserswerth, and other deaconess houses began showing up all over Germany.[4]

Around the same time, another movement was brewing in England—the Oxford Movement. This was a movement within the larger Anglican Church that encouraged a return to a more Catholic understanding of the faith, which included renewed attention to both the early and medieval churches. From this, the Anglican sisterhoods emerged. The first Anglican woman to take the vows of poverty, chastity, and obedience was Marion Hughes in 1841, and in 1845 the first sisterhood was founded.[5] Due to the sisterhoods' association with Catholicism, Low Church Anglicans opposed them and encouraged the development of a diaconate for women inspired by the German example. In 1862, after spending months at Kaiserswerth, an Englishwoman by the name of Elizabeth Ferard was ordained as the first Anglican deaconess. In England, the deaconess movement was not limited to the Anglican Church. In fact, one of the most influential deaconess homes and training centers, Mildmay, was ecumenical. Unlike the German deaconess movement, the English movement tended to focus more on outreach rather than nursing, likely

---

4 Jenny Wiley Legath, *Sanctified Sisters: A History of Protestant Deaconesses* (New York: New York University Press, 2019), 9–10.

5 Sisterhoods, which were confined to the Anglican and Episcopal traditions, were distinct from the diaconate, though there was some fluidity between the movements. Sisterhoods required vows, whereas deaconesses were not required to give vows—in fact, vows seemed much too Catholic for most Protestants!

because English women were already more engaged in nursing at this time due to more liberal English views of women's roles in society.[6]

Seeing these European successes, not to mention the advocacy of Florence Nightingale, the famed nurse and social reformer who trained at Kaiserswerth, American Protestants became increasingly interested in the deaconess movement.[7] The first American deaconess institute was founded in Pittsburgh in 1850. Despite a slow beginning in the United States, by the turn of the twentieth century, American denominations rapidly began establishing deaconess orders. While not a complete list of all denominations to establish a deaconess program, the following demonstrates the proliferation of the office around the turn of the twentieth century:

> Norwegian Lutherans, 1883; Methodist Episcopal Church, 1888; Protestant Episcopal Church, 1889; Evangelical Synod, 1889; Presbyterian Church (USA), 1892; German Reformed Church, 1892; German Methodist Episcopal Church, 1896; Church of the United Brethren in Christ, 1897; Evangelical Association, 1898; African Methodist Episcopal Church and General Conference Mennonites, both 1900; Methodist Episcopal Church, South, 1902; Danish Lutherans, 1903; United Evangelical Church, 1906; Methodist Protestant Church, 1908; and Lutheran Church—Missouri Synod . . . , 1919.[8]

Although numerous denominations consecrated deaconesses, it is hard to assess exactly how many deaconesses there were. While only one of numerous Methodist denominations in the United States, in 1897 the Methodist Episcopal Church, North Church's yearbook listed 303 deaconesses working at that time within the country and 630 in total if you counted those working internationally.[9]

The relationship between deaconesses and ordained ministry is complex. Deaconesses, at least in their early stages, were not ordained, and some deaconesses were explicitly forbidden from preaching. Deaconesses did often engage in evangelism, though, and there is a fine line between evangelism and preaching.[10] Regardless, deaconesses were not ordained clergy.

By the mid-twentieth century, many of the denominations that had established deaconess programs were beginning to ordain women. There were some women who left the diaconate for ordained ministry, but most did not. Some denominations began to phase out their deaconess programs during this time, but numerous such programs have continued until the present day and have adapted with the times. Some historians write of the diaconate as a thing of the past, but indeed it continues as evidenced by the current

---

6 Legath, *Sanctified Sisters*, 11–12.

7 Nightingale trained for a number of months at Kaiserswerth, and she viewed the experience as a turning point in her life, but she did not become a deaconess. She wrote about Kaiserswerth in Florence Nightingale, *The Institution of Kaiserswerth on the Rhine for the Practical Training of Deaconesses, etc.* (London: London Training Ragged Colonial Training School, 1851).

8 Legath, *Sanctified Sisters*, 18.

9 Arthur Benton Sanford, *Methodist Yearbook, 1897* (New York: Eaton and Mains, 1897), 99.

10 Legath, *Sanctified Sisters*, 153–155.

global and ecumenical deaconess association, DIAKONIA World Federation. It includes deaconesses from Africa, Asia, the Caribbean, Europe, North and South America, and Oceania. The deaconesses come from diverse denominations including Lutheranism, Methodism, Anglicanism, and many others. The work and sense of community among deaconesses should not be overlooked, nor should the office be seen as merely a transition between lay and ordained ministry.[11]

LAY PROTESTANT WOMEN ORGANIZE

Unlike Catholic sisters or even Protestant deaconesses, lay Protestant women had fewer opportunities to engage in works of public charity. The alternative to monastic life was marriage, and marriage brought children, increased responsibility in the home, and less free time for works of charity. In fact, before the nineteenth century, you see little organization among laywomen and far fewer laywomen engaged in any sort of social activism. This begins to change by the end of the eighteenth century, and organization is in full swing during the nineteenth.

There were numerous factors that led to the increase in organization and an engagement in social activism. Industrialization led to more free time, though it also ironically emphasized a separation between men and women and their respective "spheres of influence" as compared to families that worked closer together in an agricultural society. While they were once considered to be more wicked and more likely to fall into sin, women, at least in many Western countries, were now largely seen as more pious and more spiritual. The ideal woman tended to her husband and educated her children at home, especially in spiritual matters.[12] Women were to operate within their domestic sphere—they were too good, too pious to be dealing with ugly worldly matters like politics or business. The legacy of women being seen as more pious has had long-lasting ramifications, especially regarding modern purity culture, but nineteenth-century, women were able to use this to their advantage. Because mothers needed to raise the next generation, they had to be educated, and throughout the nineteenth century, women were increasingly able to access education, including college degrees—though they were still a small minority of the total college-educated population. This access to education gave women additional skills that proved useful in organizing.

It is easy to forget now that the prospect of women organizing, or even being engaged in the larger world, was seen as controversial. Religious institutions were the one place in the public sphere in which women could freely move with little questioning of their activities. Therefore, the earliest women-led organizations tended to be directly associated with a church (or synagogue since there were parallel movements happening in Judaism as

---

11 Diakonia World Federation, http://dwfmembers.org/.

12 This concept of ideal womanhood popular in the West pertains primarily to white middle- to upper-class women. This idea did not represent reality, however. Many women worked out of the home, oftentimes in factories or as domestic laborers, to survive. For a closer examination of this concept, see Nancy M. Theriot, *Mothers and Daughters in Nineteenth-Century America: The Biosocial Construction of Femininity* (Lexington, Kentucky: University Press of Kentucky, 1996), 62–76.

well) and often called ladies' aid societies.[13] This association gave the organizations more legitimacy since they were doing work for the church.

Originally the ladies' aid societies gained prominence during the American Civil War (ladies' aid as in *aiding* the war effort). However, the societies quickly lost their association with war and became a regular part of congregations. Their function was to support the mission of the congregations, though the reality was a bit more complex. These humble church groups were surprisingly revolutionary. In a time when few women were taught leadership skills, these societies are where women learned how to lead and how to organize. Typical activities included buying organs, paying for various building projects like putting in basements, parking lots, electricity, and so on, or even paying staff and pastors' salaries if necessary.

Over time, some small, local women's groups expanded their activities outward to their communities. These activities largely fall under the umbrella term of "home missions," and they ran parallel to foreign missions—oftentimes women would engage in both home and foreign mission groups and boards within their congregations. Common home mission causes included care for women, children, and the elderly. Women's charitable groups supported hospitals by making surgical dressings and visiting patients. They provided the poor with rent and food assistance and clothing. Some women's groups took on large-scale city missions, like settlement housing or housing for single working women. They created rescue homes for women and orphanages for children.[14]

A few reform issues rose to national prominence and had massive support among women, most notably temperance, but other prominent areas of reform included civil rights and other forms of anti-colonial resistance and women's suffrage. What follows is an examination of these reform areas in the nineteenth and the early twentieth centuries. The breakdowns may be slightly misleading because most reform movements transcended a single issue and many issues overlap. However, some method of organization is necessary, and despite its limitations, this does emphasize key areas of reform in the aforementioned centuries.

ABOLITION / CIVIL RIGHTS

While abolition, the fight for civil rights, and resistance against imperial and colonial forces include different movements and activities from a variety of contexts, there are connections and common themes that emerge. As older forms of oppression established in the sixteenth and seventeenth centuries, like slavery, were outlawed in the nineteenth century, they were replaced by other forms of imperialistic oppression like inequitable political laws and economic exploitation. In each of these oppressive systems, women were marginalized

---

13 Not all church-associated women's groups were called this, but it was common enough that I will use the term for all of these types of organizations.

14 I deal extensively with religious women's organization and engagement with social reform in Jennifer Hornyak Wojciechowski, "Bringing the Kingdom: Religious Women's Engagement in Social Reform in Minnesota from 1880 to 1920" (PhD diss., Luther Seminary, St. Paul, 2019).

and offered up forms of resistance—sometimes as part of organizations, sometimes through mass movements, and sometimes through individual forms of resistance.

One of the first mass movements for social change against oppressive systems in which women were active participants was abolition. There was limited Christian opposition to slavery from the very beginning of the transatlantic slave trade, but unfortunately, these voices were too few and far between. The insatiable need for labor in the Americas and the obscene wealth being made by the elite few overshadowed any meager attempt to end such a horrific system. By the late eighteenth century, there was active resistance to both the institution of slavery and the slave trade internationally, but it was during the Second Great Awakening that some groups of American Christians became actively invested in bringing an end to slavery. It must be clearly stated that not all Christians supported abolition—unfortunately there were many who claimed a Christian faith that actively promoted slavery. There was, however, a shift, especially in the American North, to a greater engagement with the movement among Christians.

Anti-slavery societies were formed, abolitionist newspapers were published, speaking tours were organized, and books that argued against the evils of slavery were published. There was debate on the how emancipation should be carried out—gradually versus immediately. There was variance in the methods used to bring about change—moral persuasion versus a more militant approach. An example that highlights each of these approaches is Harriet Beecher Stowe compared to John Brown. Beecher Stowe, of the well-known Beecher family, wrote *Uncle Tom's Cabin* after being influenced by both the passing of the oppressive Fugitive Slave Act in 1850 and the tragic death of one of her children. *Uncle Tom's Cabin* was controversial when it came out in 1852 and has been criticized for using racial stereotypes and being patronizing.[15] In the nineteenth century, it was also a best-selling novel, with over three hundred thousand copies selling in the first year, and it undeniably galvanized the abolitionism movement.[16] On the other side of the spectrum was John Brown and his raid on Harpers Ferry, Virginia, in 1859, which he hoped would spark a slave revolt. The raid was unsuccessful, and Brown was tried and hanged for treason. However, the event heightened animosities between the North and South, and Brown was viewed as a martyr for the cause. Despite this variance, the abolitionist cause became more popular in some circles, and the fusion of abolition and Christian belief can be seen in the leaders of the movement. Many of the most outspoken abolitionists were indeed Christians including Frederick Douglass, Sojourner Truth, Harriet Tubman, Nat Turner, Lucretia Mott, the Grimké sisters, Harriet Beecher Stowe, William Lloyd Garrison, and even John Brown.

One of the more remarkable leaders in the abolitionist movement was Sojourner Truth (1797–1883), who knew firsthand the horrors of slavery. She was born Isabella Baumfree, but she changed her name to Sojourner Truth in 1843 when she felt the Holy Spirit calling her to speak the truth. She was born in New York state, which had begun the process of emancipation in 1799 but would not completely end slavery until the year

15 Lindley, *You Have Stept Out of Your Place*, 111–113.

16 Library of Congress, "Books that Shaped America: Harriet Beecher Stowe, Uncle Tom's Cabin (1852)," accessed April 24, 2022, https://www.loc.gov/exhibits/books-that-shaped-america/1850-to-1900.html.

1827. Her owner had promised to free her in the year 1826 but then refused when the time came. Fearing for her safety, she fled with her youngest daughter and hid with an abolitionist family who then purchased her freedom. In the meantime, her former owner illegally sold her son to a slaveholder in Alabama. To reclaim her son, Truth took her case to court. She had no legal training, but she was determined to get her son back. Throughout her trial she was able to raise money to help fund her case, and she became one of the first Black women in American history to successfully sue a white man.

In the 1830s, Truth started attending religious revivals and eventually became an itinerant preacher herself. It was in this capacity as a preacher that she met Frederick Douglass and William Lloyd Garrison, who encouraged Truth to give speeches against slavery. She soon became a regular public speaker on the subject. As a Black woman she faced additional danger in her quest. At one point an angry mob nearly attacked her, though she was amazingly able to calm them by singing. In addition to abolition, she also took up the causes of women's rights and temperance. A line from her famous "Ain't I a Woman" speech highlights her commitment to women's rights and how it was intertwined with her strong religious faith: "And how came Jesus into the world? Through God who created him and woman who bore him. Man, where is your part?"[17] In fact, she came into conflict with other abolitionists over the issue of women's suffrage. Some leaders believed that suffrage for African American men should take priority over women's suffrage—Truth believed they should occur simultaneously.

Her biography, *The Narrative of Sojourner Truth*, published in 1850, brought her national recognition.[18] Around the same time, she moved to Battle Creek, Michigan, where some of her daughters lived. From there she continued to speak nationally for abolition, and she assisted escaped slaves in reaching freedom. During the Civil War, she worked as a nurse and raised funds and supplies for Black soldiers. After the war ended, she continued her activism by focusing on women's rights, fighting against segregation, and working for civil rights. She campaigned the American government to give land to former slaves—even bringing it up with Lincoln himself when she met him, though Congress failed to act.

Truth lived up to her name, speaking the truth about a host of injustices in the world—just as her younger contemporary Harriet Tubman did. Their flights to freedom were different, but they ended up committing themselves to similar reform movements throughout their lives. After Harriet Tubman (born Araminta Ross, 1822–1913) escaped slavery herself, she was a conductor on the Underground Railroad and led thirteen dangerous missions down South to rescue slaves. She never once lost a passenger. During the Civil War she was first a nurse and later a scout and a spy; she was the first woman

---

17 Sojourner Truth, "Ain't I a Woman?," speech, Woman's Rights Convention, May 29, 1851, Akron, OH. This line is from the 1851 version transcribed by Marius Robinson, who was in attendance at the convention and published the speech on June 21, 1851, in the *Anti-Slavery Bugle*. The more commonly known version of the speech, which was published in 1863 by the *New York Independent*, is inaccurate. The 1863 version, which was updated by Frances Gage, embellished Truth's original speech with an overtly racist rendering of a Southern slave dialect—a particular dialect that Truth, who lived her life in the American North, did not have. For more information, see "Compare the Speeches," The Sojourner Truth Project, accessed April 24, 2022, https://www.thesojournertruthproject.com/compare-the-speeches/.

18 Sojourner Truth, *The Narrative of Sojourner Truth*, ed. Olive Gilbert (Boston: printed by the author, 1850). A complete version of the book is available at https://digital.library.upenn.edu/women/truth/1850/1850.html.

to lead a military raid in American history. She was an outspoken social activist, and she was aligned with the more radical edge of abolitionists—for example, she supported John Brown's raid on Harpers Ferry. After the war, she was a vocal supporter of women's rights. Both Tubman and Truth were Methodists and profoundly religious, which inevitably influenced their activism.

Much younger than either Truth or Tubman, Ida B. Wells (1862–1931) was born a slave during the Civil War. While slavery ended shortly after her birth, Wells did not live in an equal society. Despite advocacy by people like Truth and Tubman, slavery was replaced not with equality but with a slew of restrictive laws targeting African Americans, and hate crimes and mob violence became increasingly common. Wells is best known for her tireless work in the anti-lynching movement, though like many other reformers, she worked for numerous causes. She was a devout Methodist and profoundly influenced by her faith. She was active during the era of the Social Gospel, and she embodied many of the ideals of the movement. She faced opposition for being both Black and a woman, yet she became one of the best-known African American women of her era.

She was the oldest child of Elizabeth and James Wells, who were politically active during Reconstruction. She was able to get an education, but at the age of sixteen she needed to leave school to care for her younger siblings following the death of both of her parents. She took a job as a teacher to support her family and moved them to Memphis, Tennessee, where she became a journalist. By 1891, she was a regular correspondent for three newspapers, a regular contributor to another eight publications, and an editor for yet another. She became a co-owner of *Free Speech* and devoted herself to turning it into a successful and profitable paper.[19]

Wells was propelled into the campaign against lynching when her close friend, Thomas Moss, was lynched along with his two business partners in 1892. They ran a successful grocery store, and when local whites came to attack their store, they defended it. It was the defense of their own property that led to their murder. There was no attempt to charge any of the perpetrators despite the fact that the mob participants were known. The Black community in Memphis was devastated and shaken, and Wells refused to be silent.

Wells used her platform as a journalist to investigate aspects of lynching, particularly the persistent myth of Black men raping white women, which was frequently used as justification for mob violence. In response, Southern whites broke into the offices of *Free Speech* and destroyed the property. Thankfully, Wells was out of town during the attack, so she was not harmed; however, the threats became so bad that she had to relocate to Chicago, Illinois, shortly thereafter. In 1895, she married attorney Ferdinand L. Barnett and decided it was time to retire from public life and raise a family. Her retirement was short-lived, and she was soon back to speaking, writing, and fighting against injustices while balancing the demands of motherhood.

---

19 Emilie M. Townes, "Because God Gave Her Vision: The Religious Impulse of Ida B. Wells-Barnett," in *Spirituality & Social Responsibility: Vocational Vision of Women in The United Methodist Tradition*, ed. Rosemary Radford Ruether (Nashville: Abingdon Press, 1993), 145.

In Chicago, she formed the Alpha Suffrage Club, which was Illinois's first Black women's suffrage organization. She fought for equal education for Black children by helping to block the establishment of segregation in Chicago schools. She was a founder of the National Association for the Advancement of Colored People. She even ran for the state senate as an independent in 1930, one year before her death.

ANTI-COLONIAL RESISTANCE

While women in the United States were fighting first against slavery and later for civil rights, women of color around the globe were resisting oppressive colonial forces. In South Africa, women became an active voice against the growing apartheid system. In 1890, a "pass law" system was established in British-controlled South Africa that ordered all African women to carry government registration cards, and the government, police, and employers used this system to restrict these women's movements and economic activities. In 1913, a group of African women petitioned the governor with a list of grievances. They marched against the policy, held demonstrations, and even publicly burned their passes. Unfortunately, their voices were ignored by the colonial government, and the scheme was expanded and evolved into the horrifically oppressive apartheid system. Yet this women-led resistance movement established a tradition of women protesting against the British and Boers.[20]

Like in colonialized Africa, women in India were active in resisting colonial rule and improving the lives of other women. They edited Indian newspapers and joined the Indian National Congress, a political party founded in 1885 that became the principal leader of the Indian independence movement. A woman who represents an important Indian Christian voice under British rule is scholar and activist Pandita Ramabai (1858–1922).

Ramabai was born in Karnataka to a Brahmin scholar and his much younger wife (she was nine and he was over forty when they married). Despite the distinguished position her father held, the family was poor, and her father took up a nomadic life as a Puranika (or public reader of Puranic verses) when Ramabai was six months old to support the family. This lifestyle supported the family financially, and it also spread knowledge of the sacred texts. It also meant the young Ramabai would spend her childhood as a pilgrim.[21] Despite social convention, which barred it, her father taught both his wife and daughter to read Sanskrit classics. Ramabai was so accomplished that at the age of twenty, she was given the honorific title of Pandita, meaning scholar-teacher.

The life of a wanderer was difficult, and both her parents and her sister died during a famine, and Ramabai and her brother, Shrinivas, were left orphans. The two continued to travel together for years until they ended up in Calcutta in 1878. Her brother died two years later, and she married one of his friends, Bipin Behari Das, an educated man from a different

20 Bonnie G. Smith, *Women in World History: 1450 to the Present* (London: Bloomsbury Academic, 2020), 227–228.

21 Antoinette Burton, *At the Heart of the Empire: Indians and the Colonial Encounter in Late-Victorian Britain* (Berkeley: University of California Press, 1998), 76–77.

caste.[22] Her husband died shortly after, which left her a young widow with a daughter to care for alone. Through her travels and her experiences, she was acutely aware of the challenges facing women and children, and she developed a conviction to improve their lives.

She moved to Pune in 1882 where she began her career as a reformer. She established the Arya Mahila Samaj, which was a society for elite women in which she challenged the women to free themselves from the oppressive customs in society, such as child marriage, illiteracy, and the oppression of widows. In September of the same year, she testified before the Hunter Commission on Education to improve education for women.[23]

Through her relationship with St. Mary's Home in Puna, which was run by Anglicans, she went to England to receive medical training. It was there that she began serious study of the Bible and decided to be baptized. Her conversion and subsequent propagation of the faith were shocking to the Hindu community and seen as a betrayal of a faith already threatened by colonial rule. Ramabai had a complex relationship with Christianity and the Church of England in particular. Her source of authority was the Bible, so she struggled with concepts of ecclesial authority and the Trinity because she believed these were issues not explicitly present in the Bible.[24] She listed the parts of Christian doctrine she accepted and the aspects she rejected, thus creating her own creed of sorts.[25] She criticized the abundance of Christian denominations, which she argued was confusing to outsiders.

Following her time in England, she sailed to the United States, where she became a sensation. She received countless invitations to speak, and articles were written about her, particularly in women's magazines. She went on tour asking Americans to help Indian women, and she leveraged her Christian faith when appealing to Western women for financial support. She returned to India in 1889 with $25,000 in hand and another $5,000 in pledges.[26] In 1896, when another famine ravaged India, she collected abandoned or sold girls, and she began the Ramabai Mukti Mission in 1898 with donations that came in from around the world. The mission built dormitories, schools, and a meeting hall, and soon they added the Home of Mercy, the Home for the Aged and Infirm, the Home for Boys, and the Home for the Blind (where they taught Braille). Staffing for this complex came to include eighty-five women and girls.[27]

Critical for understanding Ramabai's Christian faith, especially in light of British colonialism, was her commitment to the indigenization of Christian practices. For example, she inscribed not Latin on her crucifix but Sanskrit, and she maintained her vegetarian diet, which she argued was cultural and not due to Hindu adherence. Given this commitment to indigenization and the high authority she put on scripture, it is unsurprising that she worked

---

22 Burton, *At the Heart of the Empire*, 78.

23 Robert Eric Frykenberg, "The Legacy of Pandita Ramabai: Mahatma of Mukti," *International Bulletin of Mission Research* 40, no. 1 (January 2016): 60–70.

24 Robert Ellsberg, *Blessed among all Women: Women Saints, Prophets, and Witnesses for Our Time* (New York: The Crossroads Publishing Company, 2005), 157.

25 Meera Kosambi, "Indian Response to Christianity, Church and Colonialism: Case of Pandita Ramabai," *Economic and Political Weekly* 27, nos. 43–44 (1992): 61–71.

26 Frykenberg, "The Legacy of Pandita Ramabai: Mahatma of Mukti," 64.

27 Frykenberg, 66.

on a new translation of the Bible for Indians, even learning Greek, Hebrew, Aramaic, and Latin. She completed her translation shortly before her death at the age of sixty-three.[28]

Ramabai represents a complicated picture of resistance. She undeniably held strong feminist and anti-colonial sentiments, yet many Indians were shocked by her adherence to the Christian faith and its ties to Western powers. Yet Ramabai pushed boundaries and forged her own Christian path rooted in Indian culture. She used her education and connections to promote social reform efforts to elevate women's positions in India. In the end, she was a well-respected voice both in India and around the globe.

These stories represent only a small sampling of the many women who stood up against unequitable social structures and colonial and imperialist powers. Throughout the course of the twentieth century, Western colonization began to fall apart. Imperialism was a factor in the outbreak of the world wars, and the world was left fundamentally changed in the wake of such violent conflicts. Today we continue to live in the shadow of colonialism, and women continue to campaign for equal rights and protections under the new systems that replaced the old forces, which has led to the rise of women's rights on a global scale.

THE WOMEN'S RIGHTS MOVEMENT

The importance of the global women's rights movement cannot be overestimated regarding the well-being of women and girls today. There were early harbingers of the movement such as Mary Wollstonecraft's widely distributed treaty, *A Vindication of the Rights of Woman*, published in 1792, which argued that women and men were equal but that women were at a disadvantage because of their lack of education.[29] Similarly, Sarah Grimké wrote *Letters on the Equality of the Sexes, and the Condition of Woman* in 1838, which became a classic of women's rights literature. Through this work she challenged the idea of male authority based on biblical exegesis. She argued, citing Genesis 1, that men and women were created equal: "They were both made in the image of God; dominion was given to both over every other creature, but not over each other. Created in perfect equality, they were expected to exercise the vicegerency entrusted to them by their Maker, in harmony and love."[30] However, historians often pinpoint the true beginning of the women's rights movement as the first women's rights convention, which took place in Seneca Fall, New York, in 1848. This meeting, which was organized by Elizabeth Cady Stanton and Lucretia Mott, adopted the Declaration of Sentiments, based on the Declaration of Independence, which boldly states, "We hold these truths to be self-evident: that all men *and women* are created equal."[31]

---

28 Frykenberg, 68.

29 Mary Wollstonecraft, *A Vindication of the Rights of Woman* (London: Walter Scott, 1891).

30 Sarah Moore Grimke, *Letters on the Equality of the Sexes, and the Condition of Woman: Addressed to Mary S. Parker, President of the Boston Female Anti-Slavery Society* (Boston: Isaac Knapp, 1838), 4.

31 Report of the Woman's Rights' Convention, Seneca Falls, NY, July 19 and 20, 1848. Proceedings and Declaration of Sentiments (Rochester, NY: John Dick at the North Star Office, 1848), 7. The text can be read in full at: The Library of Congress, "Image 10 of Report of the Woman's Rights Convention, held at Seneca Falls, New York, July 19th and 20th, 1848. Proceedings and Declaration of Sentiments," accessed April 24, 2022, https://www.loc.gov/resource/rbcmil.scrp4006702/?sp=10. Italics mine.

This convention began the formal organization of the women's rights movement, and it emphasized the need for women's suffrage.

Although this landmark convention was held in the United States, the fight for women's equality was truly a global movement. In Europe a number of associations were formed to fight for gender equality such as the General German Women's Association in 1865, the French Society for the Demand for Women's Rights in 1866, and the Danish Women's Society in 1871. In 1888, the International Council of Women was formed and met in Washington, DC. At the first meeting, forty-nine delegates from nine different countries attended. The general goals of the organization were to promote health, peace, equality, and education for women. The first International Women's Day was first observed in Austria, Germany, Denmark, and Switzerland in 1911 and in Russia two years later; the United Nations has observed the day since 1975.

While the fight for equal rights involved many different aspects, the fight for women's suffrage was a critical component, though also long and difficult. New Zealand was the first nation to formally allow women to vote in national elections in 1893. Liechtenstein, the last of the European countries to approve women's suffrage, did not grant women the right to vote until 1984. In Africa, 80 percent of the countries granted universal suffrage between the years 1960 and 1975. In certain areas of the globe, suffrage was granted to some women and not others. For example, Ecuador became the first country in Latin America to grant women the right to vote in 1929, but the right was only extended to literate women. India acted similarly, granting the vote to married women in 1935 and all women in 1950. Women were granted the right to vote in 1920 in the United States, but women of color were severely limited by restrictive local laws. In South Africa, white women gained the right to vote in 1930, but it was not until 1993 that Black women gained the right to vote. There are still many places around the world where women are unable to vote due to either discrimination or a lack of democratic systems.[32]

Of course, there is far more to the women's rights movement than simply gaining the right to vote, and women in different times and places have had different needs depending on their context. One prime example of conflict arising from divergent views of women's rights played out in the Inter-American Commission of Women (IACW), founded in 1928 to unite women across the Americas. Doris Stevens, an American suffragist and women's legal rights advocate who headed the IACW, came into open conflict with the Cuban feminist activist Ofelia Domíngues Navarro over tactics. Stevens heavily pushed for women's political rights, whereas Domíngues Navarro, coming from a context in which her country was suffering under American imperialism, argued that feminism was something broader than political rights—it involved economic justice and political and civil rights for all people.[33] The conflict between Stevens and Domíngues Navarro represents a larger issue within this early women's movement, which was the vastly different agendas

---

32   Katherine Schaeffer, "Key Facts about Women's Suffrage around the World, a Century after U.S. Ratified 19th Amendment," *Pew Research Center*, last modified October 5, 2020, https://www.pewresearch.org/fact-tank/2020/10/05/key-facts-about-womens-suffrage-around-the-world-a-century-after-u-s-ratified-19th-amendment/.

33   For further information on the history of Latin American feminism, see Katherine M. Marino, *Feminism for the Americas: The Making of an International Human Rights Movement* (Chapel Hill: The University of North Carolina Press, 2019).

and needs of women based on their contexts. It also underscores the elitist attitudes that women from politically powerful nations exerted over their sisters from countries suffering under oppressive imperialist regimes.

As would be expected, the relationship between women's rights and Christianity was complex. On the one hand, some of the first advocates for women's rights were committed Christians, and some of the first arguments for equality were based in scripture. On the other hand, there was a significant number of women's rights advocates who were highly critical of Christianity. Two of the most vocal critics in the nineteenth century were Elizabeth Cady Stanton and Matilda Joselyn Gage. Both women came to see the Christian church as a major obstacle to the advancement of women's rights. At the 1878 convention of the National Woman Suffrage Association (NWSA), the more liberal of the women's rights organizations, both women supported a series of controversial resolutions attacking religion that were condemned by various clergy, the American Woman Suffrage Association, and many women within the NWSA.[34] Undeterred, Cady Stanton and Gage embarked on an ambitious project, the creation of the *Woman's Bible*.[35] It is essentially a Bible commentary focused on sections of the Bible pertaining to women, but throughout the work the authors attack religious orthodoxy and the subjugation of women they identify within scripture. The first volume was released in 1895 and the second in 1898. While the work created quite a sensation and went through numerous initial printings, the reaction from many was hostile. Even some women within the NWSA were so shocked by the book that they passed a resolution distancing themselves from it. It was not until the rise of the feminist movement in the 1960s that scholars came to a new appreciation of this controversial yet quite creative take on scripture. This tension between women who adhered to the Christian faith and those who rejected it would continue throughout the women's rights movement and into the feminist movement in the second half of the twentieth century.

TEMPERANCE

Closely related to the fight for women's rights is that for temperance. The rise of this popular movement was largely American, but through international temperance organizations and foreign missions, temperance became a global issue. It was a cause that was particularly dear to many women, though its strongest supporters were typically white, middle-class Protestant women—this association stems back to the connection between religion and moral reform prominent during the Second Great Awakening. The Women's Christian Temperance Movement (WCTU) is the best known and most effective of the

---

34 Within the United States, the women's rights movement split following the American Civil War. The National Woman Suffrage Association (NWSA) was formed on May 15, 1869, and its main leaders were Susan B. Anthony and Elizabeth Cady Stanton. The American Woman Suffrage Association (AWSA) was founded the same year, with Lucy Stone as the most prominent member. The NWSA was largely considered to be more progressive, though the two organizations held different ideas on political action, with the NWSA focusing more on federal-level change and the AWSA focusing more on state-level change. The two organizations merged in 1890 to form the National American Woman Suffrage Association.

35 Elizabeth Cady Stanton, *The Woman's Bible*, 2 vols. (Boston: Northeastern University Press, 1993).

temperance societies. However, the beginnings of the temperance movement preceded the WTCU by decades. The first of the temperance societies were led by men, but soon women-led temperance societies began appearing in both the United States and Great Britain, though Britain's temperance movement was undoubtedly less passionate than its American counterpart.[36] After the American Civil War, women led a massive temperance movement that had a profound impact on society.

A little context is needed to fully understand the temperance movement. People have consumed alcohol in various forms since antiquity, but the concept of viewing alcoholism as a vice, a moral failing, or a disease is a relatively new phenomenon. It was in the late eighteenth and early nineteenth centuries that alcoholism began to be defined as a mental health issue, a physical disease, and a social problem.[37] It was not just that societal views of alcohol usage were changing—alcohol abuse was legitimately a widespread problem. In the year 1830, Americans drank an average of 7.1 gallons of pure alcohol every single year—compare that to today's still hefty 2 gallons of pure alcohol per person annually.[38] Compounding this alcohol abuse was the lack of women's rights; women had few legal recourses if their husbands drank away their fortunes or were physically abusive. Due to these circumstances, the women's temperance movement and the women's rights movement had tremendous overlap. In fact, the alcohol industry spent a fortune to keep the ballot out of women's reach.

Women's frustration with alcohol came to a breaking point in the 1870s with the militance of the Women's Crusade in the United States. It began when a group of women, inspired by a local temperance lecturer, met at a Presbyterian church in Ohio in 1873 to both pray and organize. The group went to saloons where they prayed and sang hymns with the goal of convincing the owners not to sell liquor anymore. Their actions began to spread. By the summer of 1874, over nine hundred cities in the United States had experienced this same phenomenon. Occasionally the hymn singing and praying devolved into property destruction. These crusaders were distressed, angry, and frustrated about the effects of alcohol; many had lost husbands, sons, or brothers to alcoholism, and the primary goal of this particular movement was to stop the selling of alcohol.

The crusaders were religiously inspired. Sometimes preachers and ministers supported these crusades, especially if they themselves were supporters of temperance. Other times, they criticized the crusaders' unwomanly behavior. Either way, the crusade was successful in a couple of different ways. Amazingly, the crusaders' tactics sometimes worked, at least temporarily, and saloon owners agreed to stop selling alcohol. In the long run, the crusade did not stop the liquor trade, but it did lead to the founding of the WCTU in 1874, which had profound impact on society and eventually led to the passing of Prohibition.[39]

---

36 Ian Tyrrell, *Woman's World/Woman's Empire: The Woman's Christian Temperance Union in International Perspective, 1880–1930* (Chapel Hill: University of North Carolina Press, 1991), 15.

37 William Bynum, "Chronic Alcoholism in the First Half of the 19th Century," *Bulletin of the History of Medicine* 42, no. 2 (1968): 160–185. This article provides an interesting history of alcoholism and how society viewed it in the nineteenth century.

38 Jane O'Brien, "The time when Americans drank all day long," *BBC News*, March 5, 2015, https://www.bbc.com/news/magazine-31741615.

39 Lindley, *You Have Stept Out of Your Place*, 101–103.

Even though her activities occurred after the initial Women's Crusade in the 1870s, no person represents the anger and frustration many women felt toward alcohol better than Carry A. Nation (1846–1911).[40] Nation physically destroyed saloons, often with her trusty ax—she was even able to help finance her campaigns by selling little hatchet pins to her supporters. Her determination to take down alcohol stemmed from both a deep piety and traumatic life experiences relating to alcoholism. Nation used unusually aggressive tactics in the name of reining in both the alcohol industry and alcohol abuse, but there were countless other women who held the same passion—perhaps rage is a better word—about the evils that alcohol was causing in society.[41]

The founding of the WCTU was directly related to the impassioned Women's Crusade that immediately preceded it, though not all crusaders joined the WCTU and not all members had been crusaders. The WTCU was founded in Cleveland, Ohio, in 1874. Annie Turner Wittenmyer (1827–1900), a social reformer, relief worker, and writer, was elected to be the first president. During her tenure, the WCTU grew into a network that included more than one thousand affiliate organizations and began publishing the journal *Our Union*. In 1879, Wittenmyer lost the presidency to Frances Willard (1839–1898), who would prove to be one of the most influential and effective social leaders of the nineteenth century.

Willard was born in 1839 in Churchville, New York, though as a child, her family moved first to Oberlin, Ohio, and then to Janesville in the Wisconsin Territory. In 1871, she became the president of the new Evanston College for Ladies, and when the college was absorbed into Northwestern University, Willard became the first dean of women and a professor of English and art, though she left one year later. Religiously she was a devout Methodist, a fact that can be seen both in her personal theology and in her guidance of the WCTU. When the WCTU was first formed, she was elected secretary of the state-level WCTU, and in November of the same year, she was elected the corresponding secretary of the National WCTU. Two years later she became head of its publications committee. In 1877, Willard left the WCTU due to conflict with Wittenmyer. The two women had different ideas for how the WCTU should move forward. Willard, who was younger and more radical, believed that it should be actively working for women's suffrage, rightly understanding that a women's rights and the fight against alcohol were intrinsically intertwined. Wittenmyer, who was older and more conservative, wanted the WCTU to stay focused on temperance alone. The direction of the WCTU was decided in 1878 when Willard won the presidency, a position she would hold until her death in 1898. Wittenmyer went on to establish the Nonpartisan Women's Christian Temperance Union and serve as president of the National Women's Relief Corps.

Before Willard took the reins, the WCTU's methods were focused on moral persuasion to encourage total abstinence from alcohol. Under Willard's tenure, the WCTU

---

40 Sources vary in the spelling of Nation's first name because she was not consistent in the writing of her name. She used both Carrie and Carry at different times.

41 Frances Grace Carver, "With Bible in One Hand and Battle-Axe in the Other: Carry A. Nation as Religious Performer and Self-Promoter," *Religion and American Culture: A Journal of Interpretation* 9, no. 1 (Winter 1999): 31–65.

shifted to political means of advocating both abstinence and a wide variety of other social reform efforts. The WTCU began to work toward labor laws, child welfare laws, age of consent laws, prison reform, temperance education in school, and, most notably, universal suffrage.[42] Willard and her supporters were without question more progressive than many of the WCTU's rank and file members. During this point in American history, women's suffrage was a radical concept that did not have widespread approval, especially among many of the more conservative Christian members of the WCTU. However, Willard brilliantly came up with a solution—"home protection." It is unlikely that Willard bought into Victorian ideals of womanhood or thought that women should stay within their domestic sphere—she never married, she maintained a successful career, and she spent her life with a female companion named Anna Gordon. However, through her "home protection" campaign she argued that by obtaining the vote and outlawing alcohol, women were merely holding true to their womanly nature and acting within the domestic sphere. They were not demanding suffrage because it was a universal right based on equality. They were demanding suffrage because it was the means through which women could protect the home from the evil effects of alcohol. Some of the more radical suffrage advocates, like Matilda Joslyn Gage, viewed Willard and her politics as dangerous, but Willard's tactics were wildly successful. It was Willard, not women like Gage or Anthony, who encouraged support for women's suffrage among more moderate and conservative Christian women.

The WCTU began as an American organization, but it did not stay that way. In her address to the tenth annual WCTU convention (held in Detroit), Willard called for an international campaign.[43] The WCTU then sent Mary Clement Leavitt, a former schoolteacher and divorced mother of three, to be the union's first global missionary in 1884. During her travels, she visited the Sandwich Islands, Australia, India, China, and Japan, carrying the message of temperance. Leavitt retuned to Boston in 1891 a hero and honorary president of the World Women's Christian Temperance Union (WWCTU). The WWCTU reached its peak in 1927 with more than 766,000 dues-paying members and a following of over a million.[44]

Leavitt's time in Japan was particularly successful. She landed in Yokohama in June of 1886 and spent nearly five months traveling through Japan, including visits to Kyoto, Osaka, Kobe, Wakayama, Okayama, and Nagasaki, giving her message of temperance to often mixed-gender audiences. She utilized missionary networks, though her message was distinct from theirs, actively promoting temperance and purity and encouraging Japanese women to organize.

One woman who heeded Leavitt's call to action was Yajima Kajiko (1833–1925). Yajima was born to a well-to-do peasant family. She did not receive a formal education, though her mother did teach her basic reading and writing skills. When she was twenty-five years old, she married a man named Hayashi Shichirō, who was a heavy drinker and

---

42 Francis Willard House Museum and Archives, "History of the WCTU," accessed April 24, 2022, https://franceswillardhouse .org/frances-willard/history-of-wctu/.

43 This quotation is found on the World Woman's Christian Temperance Union's website, http://www.wwctu.org/pages/history .html.

44 Tyrrell, *Woman's World/Woman's Empire*, 2–3.

physically abusive to Yajima. She endured the marriage for ten years before leaving him, which scandalized both her family and her community. Over the next few years she relied on her family, but eventually she moved to Tokyo and went to school to be a primary school teacher. In 1878, she took a job at a Presbyterian school and was baptized in 1879.[45]

In July of 1886, Yajima attended one of Leavitt's lectures, which focused on temperance and ending the practice of concubinage and public bathing. Over the next few months she participated in a series of planning meetings to establish what would become the Tokyo Fujin Kyofukai or Women's Reform Society (the literal translation is more accurately Tokyo Women's Custom-Correcting Society), sometimes called the JWCTU. This group did not act simply as an arm of the American branch of the WCTU, as is evident in both its name and its mission, which included more than just an emphasis on temperance.[46] Yajima was elected the first president, and Sasaki Toyoju (1853–1901), who was both younger and more progressive than Yajima, was elected secretary. Despite some differences in opinion between the two women over direction, over the next two years the Tokyo Fujin Kyofukai grew tremendously from 53 members at its founding to 546 members by the end of 1888. They held monthly meetings, sponsored seven different lectures, and launched their own periodical.[47]

While its successes should not be overlooked, all was not perfect with the WCTU within the United States. The WCTU has been criticized, both then and now, for pushing white Protestant values that were not shared by all. It is a valid critique. There was limited diversity regarding religious affiliation and inclusion of women of color and immigrants. Regarding race, Francis Willard told the Southern branch of the WCTU that they could exclude women of color from their membership; she found a segregated WCTU acceptable, and for too long she refused to speak out against lynching—for which she was openly criticized by Ida B. Wells.[48] There were many within the organization that expressed anti-immigrant views as well. At the 1892 WCTU convention, Willard called for Congress to "enact a stringent immigration law prohibiting the influx into our land of more of the scum of the Old World."[49] Closely related to the anti-immigrant rhetoric was a lack of religious diversity. The WCTU was overwhelmingly Protestant, and Catholic women, many of whom were immigrants, were far more likely to join separate Catholic temperance organizations, the largest being the Catholic Total Abstinence Union, which included women's societies. Catholic temperance organizations had their own history and culture, and they tended to focus more on moral persuasion over political action.

Perhaps the biggest criticism of the WCTU today is that Prohibition failed. In fact, it failed spectacularly. One may wonder, what was the lasting impact of the temperance

45 Elizabeth Dorn Lublin, "Wearing the White Ribbon of Reform and the Banner of Civic Duty: Yajima Kajiko and the Japan Woman's Christian Temperance Union in the Meiji Period." *U.S.-Japan Women's Journal*, nos. 30–31 (2006): 62–65.

46 Rumi Yasutake, *Transnational Women's Activism: The United States, Japan, and Japanese Immigrant Communities in California, 1859–1920* (New York: New York University Press, 2004), 45.

47 Elizabeth Dorn Lublin, "Wearing the White Ribbon of Reform and the Banner of Civic Duty," 66–67.

48 Dzubinski and Stasson, *Women in the Mission of the Church*, 158–159.

49 Dierdre M. Moloney, "Combatting 'Whiskey's Work': The Catholic Temperance Movement in Late Nineteenth-Century America," *U.S. Catholic Historian* 16, no. 3 (1998): 5.

movement if the main objective was temporary and ineffective? The WCTU and the WWCTU are both still in existence, and both continue to fight against alcohol and drug abuse. In fact, the WCTU was even nominated for a Nobel Prize in 2017.[50] The gains the WCTU made were not just in achieving Prohibition, however. They were instrumental in achieving women's suffrage. The members were active in schools to promote abstinence from alcohol. They worked for prison reform, and they lobbied successfully to raise the age of consent from as low as seven in some states to eighteen. So, while Prohibition was both temporary and unsuccessful, their work in a variety of other areas of women's rights was profoundly impactful in society.

CONSEQUENCES

This reform work, or social justice work, is essential to understanding the advancement of women's rights, women's place in societies, and even women's place in the church. Women have not stopped working for change; in fact, chapter 11 continues this conversation with an examination of a few other areas in which women have been influential in the twentieth century.

Just as in our overview of women in global missions, this work is not without criticism and controversy, and some of these fights are far from over. Again, like global missions, some women, especially those hailing from wealthier Western nations, operated with harmful biases against others from different cultures and races. Judging from continued racial inequalities and disparate experiences in countries often labeled the "Global South," efforts toward ending oppressive systems are still a work in progress. The improvement of women's rights on a global scale has been uneven, and women are anything but equal in far too many places around the globe. There has been conflict between women in different contexts over what is needed and why. Finally, the incredibly influential global work of the temperance movement has been largely temporary and ineffective, though some of their more tangential political fights have proved more lasting and efficacious over the years.

These three broad categories of reform—racial justice / civil rights / anti-colonialism, women's rights, and temperance—are not the only important areas of social reform in which women have been active participants, but they were three of the most influential and far-reaching mass movements of the nineteenth and early twentieth centuries. It is important to remember that countless women engaged in smaller-scale work in their neighborhoods and communities. They raised money for their churches, influenced local politics, and built kindergartens and settlements, just to name a few activities. This focus on large national and international movements should not take away from the countless smaller ways in which women, then and now, have worked to improve their lives and the lives of others.

---

50 Women's Christian Temperance Union, "Our History," accessed May 6, 2022, https://www.wctu.org/history.

CHAPTER 11

Global Christianity in a Modern World

The twentieth century was like no other. The rapid change that occurred in those one hundred years is almost unimaginable. At the turn of the twentieth century, the radio, electric lights, and the automobile were brand-new technologies, yet they were not accessible to large portions of the population. Most people, even in the United States, did not have plumbing. A mere one hundred years later—really a blink of an eye when considering the entire length of history—our lives became profoundly different. The technological gains have been astonishing, but these gains do not equate to peace or safety, and unfortunately, the twentieth century was likely also the deadliest in human history (of course, these types of things are nearly impossible to measure accurately). Humanity's technological advances resulted in mass killing on a scale never seen before. In the wake of the two world wars, borders shifted, and the imperialistic systems put into place by Western powers in the eighteenth and nineteenth centuries started to crumble and fall. Nations, most significantly the Russia and China, embraced communism, and the Cold War became a dominant theme in the second half of the century, fueling tensions and all-out warfare on numerous occasions. Human behavior, paired with technology, has resulted in a climate crisis, a topic that will certainly dominate in the twenty-first century.

Global trends in religion shifted dramatically. For centuries, Christianity had become nearly synonymous with the West, but this changed over the course of the twentieth century. In 1910, 90 percent of Europe was Christian, but as of 2018 only about 71 percent of Western Europeans identified as Christian. One must also remember that there is a difference between active participation in religious life and saying one identifies with the Christian tradition. According to polls, only about 22 percent of Western Europeans attend a religious service, of any kind, at least once a month.[1] While Europe became less and less Christian, Asia and Africa became more so. Asia was 2.4 percent Christian in 1910, and in 2010 it was 9 percent. While that may seem low, Asia has the largest population of any continent, and that mere 9 percent translates to hundreds of millions of people. The gains in Africa are even more pronounced. In 1910, Africa was 9.4 percent Christian; now it is 48 percent, an incredible growth over the course of one century. Christianity has broken from its Western corner to once again be a truly global faith as

---

1 Pew Research Forum, "Being Christian in Western Europe," Pew Research Forum, last modified May 29, 2018, https://www .pewforum.org/2018/05/29/being-christian-in-western-europe/.

it was in the time of the early church.[2] We are now in a position where missionaries from Africa and Asia are coming to the West to bring the good news.

Throughout all these changes, women's roles in both society and the Christian church have expanded. Without question, women gained rights throughout the twentieth century, likely more than in any other century on record. They made advances in political rights and positions of leadership within religious institutions and within the academy, and there are now women leading churches, parachurch organizations, religious denominations, and social justice movements. However, these advancements are not evenly distributed across traditions or geographic areas, and there are many places and spaces where women are marginalized in countless different ways.

As Christianity expands to once again be a global faith, the story of the religion grows increasingly complex. This final chapter is broken into salient themes that have emerged in women's Christian history over the past century—the first being general trends in global Christianity highlighting the shift from European/American dominance to the growth and vibrancy of African, Asian, and Latin American Christianity; the second being a focus on the persecutions and death that featured too prominently in the twentieth century's history; and the third being an examination of some important reform movements, including peace and work for the poor, and finally a look at women's advancements, particularly regarding women's ministry, leadership, ordination, and entrance into academic and theological studies.

GENERAL TRENDS IN GLOBAL RELIGION: THE GROWTH OF ASIAN AND AFRICAN CHRISTIANITY

One of the most significant religious trends in the twentieth century was the explosive growth of Christianity in Africa and Asia. Christianity's reliance on European religious culture and theology must lessen now that we have become a world in which Christianity is more active in Africa, Asia, and the Americas. While global missions play a role in the history of this story, much of this growth and development had to do with the impressive work of indigenous evangelists and church leaders within these various contexts.

Asia

While it is not the only Asian country that has experienced phenomenal Christian growth over the past century—in fact, Korea's growth was more significant—the presence and spread of Chinese Christianity were perhaps the biggest surprises to Westerners. Western missionaries flooded into China in the nineteenth and early twentieth centuries, but their time there was coming to an end by the 1930s. In 1937, Japan invaded China, thus beginning a mass exodus of Western missionaries out of the country. Some returned in 1945, but in 1950, the new communist People's Republic of China forced all missionaries out

---

2 Scott Sunquist, *The Unexpected Christian Century: The Reversal and Transformation of Global Christianity, 1900–2000* (Grand Rapids: Baker, 2015), xvii–xviii.

for good. At this time, less than I percent of China's population was Christian, and Western missionaries were certain China was lost. Despite the doom and gloom predictions from Westerners, Christianity continued to grow regardless of the restrictions against religion in China. In hindsight, one can see how it was Chinese Christians who embraced and cultivated Christianity during those years who grew the church despite the hardships these Christians endured during the Maoist regime. The seeds of this movement were already present before the expelling of Western missionaries, and one of the best-known first-generation Chinese evangelists, regardless of gender, was a woman by the name of Yu Cidu (1873–1931), better known as Dora Yu in the West.

Yu was born in an American Presbyterian Mission compound about 120 miles from Shanghai. Her father was a physician and had survived the Taiping Rebellion (1850–1864)—the deadliest civil war in global history—mainly due to his surgical skills, but he later trained to be a preacher. Yu, following in her father's footsteps, trained to be a medical doctor, finishing her education in 1896. She decided not to marry and instead went to Korea as a missionary from 1897 to 1903, which were difficult years physically and financially for her. Following her time as a missionary, she returned to China and continued her work as an evangelist.

By 1908, she was speaking throughout eastern China and cooperating with the Young Men's Christian Association, several missionary societies, and a number of other semi-autonomous Chinese evangelists. Her preaching drew large crowds, and eventually she opened her own Bible school and prayer house. Many of her early students were women who went on to be preachers and carry the faith once the country embraced communism. Yu was respected both in China and internationally, and she was even invited to be a main speaker at the International Missionary Meeting of the 1927 Keswick Convention. Four years later she died of cancer at the age of fifty-eight, leaving a long legacy of evangelism.[3]

In another context, Yu may have seemed like just another woman preacher, but she was groundbreaking in many ways. By all accounts she was one of the foremost evangelists in China in the early twentieth century. Due to her work in Korea, she was the first cross-cultural missionary of modern times. She was the first Chinese woman to establish a Bible school dedicated to training other Christian leaders. Among her many converts was Nee To-sheng, better known as Watchman Nee in the West. Nee studied for a year at Yu's Bible school in Shanghai, and Yu not only led him to faith but also discipled him.[4] But Nee was far from the only Christian Yu mentored, and many of the other less-known men and women she trained helped carry the Christian faith through the difficult years of oppression.

Another important Christian leader in early twentieth-century China was Shi Meiyu (1873–1954), who was also known as Mary Stone in the United States. Like Yu, she was trained as a physician, but unlike Yu, medicine was the primary means through which she

---

3 Mark A. Noll and Carolyn Nystrom, *Clouds of Witnesses: Christian Voices from Africa and Asia* (Downers Grove: IVP Books, 2011), 188–199.

4 Scott Sunquist, *Explorations in Asian Christianity: History, Theology, and Mission* (Downers Grove: Inter Varsity Press, 2017), 65.

evangelized. Shi was born in 1881 to Christian parents. When Shi was eight years old, her parents brought her to Dr. Katharine Bushnell and asked her to help Shi become a doctor. On Bushnell's recommendation, Shi was sent to Gertrude Howe's Rulison-Fish Memorial School where she prepared for medical school in the United States with Howe's adopted daughter, Kang Cheng (also known as Ida Kahn). In 1892, the two girls passed their entrance exams for medical school and headed to Ann Arbor, Michigan—their schooling was paid for by the Women's Foreign Missionary Society of the Methodist Episcopal Church. There had only been two other Chinese women trained at American medical schools by this point, and Shi and Kang were the first Chinese women to attend a coed medical school. It was during her time in the United States that Shi took an American name, Mary Stone, and from that point forward she used both names depending on her context.

After they finished their medical degrees Shi and Kang returned to China in 1896 and immediately established a medical dispensary in their home city of Jiujiang. Despite some concerns over whether the people would accept their Western-style medicine, they treated over 2,300 people and made hundreds of house calls within the first ten months. While they practiced Western medicine, the people were more trusting of them than Western doctors because the women were Chinese. In 1900, with donations from the United States, they were able to build a new hospital. It was not entirely smooth sailing though. The two women were forced to flee and seek refuge in Japan during the Boxer Rebellion (1898–1900), but they returned in 1901 to continue their medical practice, and they were able to serve eight thousand patients in their new hospital within their first year back. In addition to her own medical work, Shi trained Chinese women to be nurses. In fact, she refused to accept Western nurses, and over the course of her career, she trained over five hundred women in medicine.

In 1906, an American missionary named Jennie Hughs arrived at Danforth Hospital, and Hughs and Shi would become partners for life. They lived together and cared for a number of children, including four boys whom they adopted. The women lived primarily in China, though they occasionally traveled to the United States for training or medical care for themselves. In 1937, when the Japanese invaded China, the two women were forced to flee permanently. By the time the war ended, Shi was seventy-three years old, and they stayed in the United States. Regardless of where Shi ended her life, her contributions to both medicine and evangelism in China were significant.[5]

It is difficult to assess the exact number of Christians in China today, and estimates vary. Some estimate that there are thirty-eight million Protestants and ten to twelve million Catholics. This is a small percentage of the total population, but there are now more Christians in China today than in historically Christian countries like Germany or France.[6] Others have estimated the number of total Christians to be closer to one

---

5 Noll and Nystrom, *Clouds of Witnesses: Christian Voices from Africa and Asia*, 201–213.

6 "Protestant Christianity is Booming in China," *The Economist*, September 15, 2020, https://www.economist.com/graphic -detail/2020/09/15/protestant-christianity-is-booming-in-china.

hundred million.[7] However, exact numbers are impossible because Christianity is still seen as suspect by many Chinese government officials, and the situation is tenuous enough that China is now considered the seventeenth most dangerous place to be a Christian in the world.[8]

While the growth of Chinese Christianity over the past century has been significant, the growth of Christianity in South Korea has been spectacular. South Korea has no dominant religious group today, with about an estimated 46 percent of the population unaffiliated, about 23 percent Buddhist, and 29 percent Christian. As discussed in chapter 8, Catholicism has had a presence in the country since the eighteenth century, but the arrival of Protestant Christians in the late nineteenth century made a considerable impact on religious adherence.

The introduction of Bible classes and the establishment of the role of Bible Women were foundational in the spread of Protestant Christianity in Korea. Bible classes for women began with Methodist missionary Mary Scanton's Sunday school in Seoul in 1888. Through these classes, which emphasized both religion and general literacy, women were taught the Korean script, the basics of the Bible, and practical knowledge. Not all women decided to put their talents toward the church, but a good number became certified Bible Women after four years of study.[9] Bible Women played a critical role as cultural mediators between Western missionaries and Korean women in addition to their own work, which involved recruiting, organizing, and educating Korean women.[10] The role of Bible Women gave Protestant women leadership opportunities, and it also induced both the proliferation of the faith and an increase in women's overall education, eventually leading to women's schools and then colleges.

This was not the only women's outreach, however. In the 1920s, two women founded the Korean Young Woman's Christian Association (YWCA), and by 1926, there were chapters in numerous major cities. In the 1950s, in the difficult days following the Korean War, the YWCA ran widows' homes, orphanages, and training centers and provided a space for people to meet and organize.[11] Indeed, Christianity has long been credited with the significant changes in the lives of Korean women that occurred in the twentieth century, and it is estimated that Korean women make up as much as 70 percent of the Korean Christian Church; however, to this day they do not make up an equal percentage of its leadership.[12] Today there is an important field of Korean feminist theology that is helping to shape the Korean Church of the future.[13]

7   Douglas Jacobson, *Global Gospel: An Introduction to Christianity on Five Continents* (Grand Rapids: Baker Academic, 2015), 168.

8   "China," *Open Door Report*, accessed April 25, 2022, https://www.opendoorsusa.org/christian-persecution/world-watch -list/china/.

9   Lee-Ellen Strawn, "Protestant Bible Education for Women: First Steps in Professional Education for Modern Korean Women," *Journal of Korean Religions* 4, no. 1 (2013): 101–102

10 Strawn, 103, 105.

11 Donald Clark, "Christianity in Modern Korea," *Education about Asia* 11, no. 2 (Fall 2006): 35–39.

12 Hyo-jae Yi, "Christian Mission and the Liberation of Korean Women," *International Review of Mission* 74, no. 293 (1985): 93–102. (93)

13 Min-Ah Cho, "Stirring up Deep Waters: Korean Feminist Theologies Today," *Theology Today* 71, no. 2 (2014): 233–245.

Africa

Of all the Christian growth globally in the twentieth century, none was more pronounced than that in Africa. While there are ancient forms of African Christianity, most notably the Ethiopian Orthodox Church, much of its recent growth is related to the missionary activity in the nineteenth and early twentieth centuries. However, like in Asia, a great deal of the growth should be credited to indigenous evangelism and other outreaches, but the shadow of Western missionaries looms large. As Esther Mombo states in her essay on women in African Christianity, there were two overarching realities:

> In the background, the all-pervasive reality of colonialism. . . . The second influence, which was very present in the foreground, was the missionary movement. . . . Within the large scheme of things, the work among women in Africa was stumbled upon rather than thought through and executed. Moreover, it was the arrival of women missionaries from the second half of the nineteenth century which accelerated the ideology of "women's work."[14]

Despite the work of women's missionary societies to advance evangelism among women, it was often the case that outreach to women was secondary. This women's work also tended to align with Victorian views of gender, prescribing women a place within the home and caring for children, which was not necessarily the norm among the cultures missionaries were trying to convert. In the post-colonial era, particularly in churches that had connections to Western missions, women continued to hold marginalized roles in church leadership, and few denominations ordained women.[15] Despite these limitations, this work did create powerful spaces for women to connect with each other, and that legacy has continued to the present day.

While we cannot discount the work of Western missionaries in Africa, much of the success of African Christianity can be traced back to the rise of African-initiated churches (AICs), and from the beginning of the movement women have been particularly present. AICs have consistently been more open to women's leadership than African churches with ties to Western Christianity, and it is estimated that in some areas, such as Nigeria, about 70 percent of AIC membership is female as well.[16] In fact, women have been so consistently present in both AIC leadership and membership, the movement has been called a "woman's movement."[17]

One of the earliest woman-established AICs was the Seraph Society founded in Lagos, Nigeria, in 1925. As is the case in many of the following stories, the movement began

---

14 Esther Mombo, "Women in African Christianities," in *The Routledge Companion to Christianity in Africa*, ed. Elias Kifon Bongmba (New York: Routledge, 2016), 174.

15 Mombo, "Women in African Christianities," 176–177.

16 Atinuke Abdulsalami, "Distinguished church leader essay: Roles of Women in African Independent and Pentecostal Churches in Nigeria," in *African Initiated Christianity and the Decolonization of Development: Sustainable Development in Pentecostal and Independent Churches*, eds. Philip Öhlmann, Wilhelm Gräb, and Marie-Luise Frost (London: Routledge, 2020), 107.

17 Leanne M. Dzubinski and Anneke H. Strasson, *Women in the Mission of the Church: Their Opportunities and Obstacles throughout Christian History* (Grand Rapids: Baker Academic, 2021), 193.

with a dramatic religious experience. A young woman by the name of Christiana Abiodun Akinsowon began having religious visions—specifically, an angel visited her in her sleep and took her to distant places. In June of 1925, she fell into a prolonged trance that lasted seven days. Her uncle called in a local holy man by the name of Moses Orimolade who was able to wake her. After this, she said that the angel had taken her to the "Celestial City," where she had several spiritual experiences. When people heard news of this miraculous event, they flocked to her. Soon Akinsowon and Orimolade were holding regular prayer groups, and by September they had formed the interdenominational group the Seraph Society. The name was later changed to the Cherubim and Seraphim Society as the result of a vision.[18]

While initially it existed as an interdenominational entity, soon the gathering became a church. Abiodun proved to be a capable leader and a skilled preacher, and the group expanded significantly under her evangelistic efforts. According to Nigerian scholar Akinyele Omoyajowo, "Its purpose was to reinterpret Christianity to the African—to destroy the whole idea of Christianity being the white man's religion which we as Africans could ill-afford to embrace to an appreciable standard."[19] He also identified the greatest weakness of the movement as its lack of structure, which is directly related to its origin as an interdenominational society, not a church. Yet today the Cherubim and Seraphim Church is a large international denomination with churches as far away as the United States and England.

While Cherubim and Seraphim is likely the first AIC founded by a woman, there are numerous other examples of women who have emerged as leaders in various AICs. The Messianic Church of Mai Chaza was founded by Mai Chaza, a married mother with six children. In 1953, she fell ill, and her husband divorced her. Later she reportedly died and was resurrected by God with a mission. She went into the mountains, and there she received healing powers and revelations from God. From there she became a faith healer, ministering to women who were unable to have children, the blind, and the crippled. She gathered a following, mainly from Botswana, South Africa, Mozambique, Zambia, and Malawi, and they established healing centers where people plagued by spirits could be cured. Despite the fact that Mai Chaza was Methodist and had never intended to break from the Methodist Church, by 1955, her movement was independent. By the time she died in 1960, it is believed that it had over seventy thousand members.[20]

One of the most interesting examples of a woman-founded AIC is that of the Lumpa Church founded by Lenshina Mulenga (c. 1920–1978). In 1953, following an attack of cerebral malaria, Mulenga fell into a deep coma. She was so close to death that her village prepared for her burial, but after a few days she regained consciousness and claimed that she had died and met Jesus Christ, who sent her back to earth with a special mission—to begin a church for Africans only and to destroy witchcraft and sorcery. After this powerful

---

18 J Akinyele Omoyajowo, "The Cherubim and Seraphim Church," *Journal of the Interdenominational Theological Center* 16, nos. 1–2 (Fall/Spring 1988/1989): 139–140.

19 Omoyajowo, "Cherubim and Seraphim Church," 147.

20 J Akinyele Omoyajowo, "The role of women in traditional African religions and independent church movements," *Dialogue & Alliance* 2, no. 3 (Fall 1988): 77–87.

spiritual experience, she was baptized at a Presbyterian mission nearby. She began an anti-witchcraft movement in which she called on people to abandon and destroy their charms. She also preached against polygamy and adultery, which as a daughter of a second wife she may have had very personal reasons for. In 1953, she was excommunicated by the Presbyterians, and she organized her own church called the Lumpa Church. Her movement had more appeal among rural populations and women than it did urban men, though members hailed from a range of social statuses. There is also evidence that the Lumpa movement was opposed to the peasantization process that had occurred under European colonial rule, and generally it can be seen as an anti-European organization.[21]

By the late 1950s, the movement had developed a distinctive millennial bent, had become increasingly nonpolitical, and was progressively coming into conflict with the United National Independence Party (UNIP), which was the main political party contending to establish Zambian independence. By 1963, church members refused to pay taxes, and in July of 1964, violence broke out between the Lumpa Church and the UNIP. While the Lumpa religious were armed with traditional weapons, such as spears and axes, the UNIP crushed them with modern weapons. While death counts vary, it appears that at a minimum, one thousand members of the Lumpa Church died in the conflict.[22] Lenshina was imprisoned, and some of her followers sought refuge in the Democratic Republic of Congo. The movement is still in existence today under the name New Jerusalem Church. The original UNIP report established a narrative that the Lumpa–UNIP conflict was the result of a Lumpa rebellion that began in the 1950s. However, more recent scholarship has posited the conflict not as an uprising but as a massacre by the UNIP.[23]

Not all AICs have such dramatic establishment stories, and there are many AICs where women preach, lead, and support other women. In her study of modern Nigerian Pentecostal AICs, Atinuke Abdulsalami recounts how women have realized that there is a "not too hidden scripture" that puts them on the same pedestal as men. Women have come together to focus on socio-religious matters through groups such as the following:

> Married and Singles Fellowship, Praying Mothers Fellowship, Daughters of Abraham Fellowship, Women of Prayers in Nigeria Fellowship . . . Sisters Fellowship International and many more. An upsurge of fellowships began to be the approach of the modern female Pentecostal leaders to break loose from the shackles of the puppet in a box.[24]

Through these groups women have been able to impact the lives of other women via teaching the scriptures and offering support financially, politically, medically, emotionally, and even academically.

---

21 Hugo Hinfelaar, "Women's Revolt: The Lumpa Church of Lenshina Mulenga in the 1950s," *Journal of Religion in Africa* 21, no. 2 (1991): 99–129.

22 David M. Gordon, "Rebellion or Massacre? The UNIP-Lumpa Conflict Revisited," in *One Zambia, Many Histories*, eds. Jan-Bart Gewald, Marja Hinfelaar, and Giacomo Macola (Boston: Brill, 2008), 45–46.

23 Gordon, 46.

24 Abdulsalami, "Distinguished church leader essay," 108.

While there are many instances of women leading in AICs, that does not mean that women are equal leaders throughout Africa. As in most other places in the world, women are often marginalized in Christian leadership. However, there is an emerging field of African women theologians.

Through ecumenical organization women theologians and church leaders have worked for greater leadership opportunities for women. The Ecumenical Decade of Churches in Solidarity with Women (1988–1998) set up by the World Council of Churches aimed to empower women to challenge oppressive structures in the global community. It was during this period that a number of churches began having conversations about women's ordination.

In 1989, another important ecumenical group was formed. A group of approximately seventy African women met in Ghana to create a forum in which they could analyze and reflect on their experiences. They called themselves the "Circle of Concerned African Women Theologians." Notably the group did not use the word feminist, but they did highlight the fact that they were all African.[25] The founder of the group is Mercy Amba Oduyoye, who is known as the "mother of African women's theologies." In her book, *Introducing African Women's Theology*, Oduyoye explains that "though their theological heritage is made up of European and American theologies of various types, including missionary and feminist/womanist theologies, African women theologians take a critical distance from them, as their priority is to communicate African women's own understanding."[26] The Circle of Concerned African Women Theologians not only included Christian theologians but was also inclusive of women in indigenous African religions and Islam. The main aim of the circle was to encourage lay and ordained women to study and write theology that would impact churches.[27]

Considering the current shifts in Christianity, there is no doubt that as we go into the future the voices of women in Africa and Asia will become more pronounced on the global stage.

A CENTURY OF STRIFE OR A WORLD AT WAR

While the second half of the century was certainly not defined by peace, the first half of the twentieth century was in many ways dominated by the two world wars. Much of twentieth-century history is focused on military exploits and the larger-than-life personalities of the global leaders, but women were active participants in the war efforts and engaged in attempts to reign in the out-of-control violence.

During the First World War (1914–1918), women were enlisted to perform a variety of jobs previously unavailable to them. With a lack of male employees, women picked up jobs in farming, production, transportation, and trade all over the globe. They produced

---

25 Teresia Mbari Hinga, *African, Christian, Feminist: The Enduring Search of What Matters* (Maryknoll: Orbis Books, 2017), 3–4.

26 Mercy Amba Oduyoye, *Introducing African Women's Theology* (Cleveland: The Pilgrim Press, 2001), 15.

27 Mombo, "Women in African Christianities," 178.

wartime materials such as munitions, and they served as nurses on the front lines; in Russia they even fought in all-women combat units.[28] While women undeniably participated in the war effort, other women suffered terribly.

In the midst of the war years, and closely linked to their war involvement, the Ottoman government conducted a genocide of Armenian Christians living within their empire. At least 664,000 and possibly as many as 1.2 million died between spring of 1915 and fall of 1916.[29] The Armenian genocide is considered the first genocide of the twentieth century, but it was certainly not the last. In Russia, heavy war losses compounded with unhappiness with the ruling monarch led to civil war and the rise of the Soviet Union. In some ways, women gained rights under the new communist regime, but religious people were persecuted, and it is estimated that 120,000 monks and nuns were killed.[30]

The Second World War (1937–1945) similarly influenced women, though this time the loss of life was even more staggering. Once again women were called to take over production and manufacturing while men were fighting. It was largely women who kept economies and the war machines going. While women were less likely to be combatants, their lives were no less influenced by the wars. Invasions, famines, displacements, pestilence, and campaigns of rape and terror heavily affected women all over the globe. The death toll for women in World War II was enormous. It is believed that civilian deaths outnumbered combatant deaths, and women's mortality rates were even higher than those of men. In Europe, Jewish women, often the ones tasked with caring for others, were less likely to flee and thus more likely to be murdered in Germany's "final solution." In China, women were targeted in the "Rape of Nanjing" in which tens of thousands of women were raped, mutilated, and murdered by enemy soldiers. This of course was not the only instance when soldiers used rape as a tactic of terror, though it is a particularly horrific one.

The suffering and loss endured by women during the wars could fill volumes, but one story here will have to suffice, and that is of the tragic loss of Edith Stein (1891–1942), a German Jewish philosopher who converted to Christianity and became a Discalced Carmelite nun with the name Teresa Benedicta of the Cross. She was both a brilliant theologian and a tragic example of martyrdom in the twentieth century. Interest in her life and works has increased since her canonization in 1998 in which she became the first Jewish-born saint to be canonized since the days of the early church.

Edith Stein was born to Jewish parents in Breslau, Germany (now Wroclaw, Poland), in 1891. Her father died when she was two years old, and her widowed mother kept an observant home, but by her teenage years Stein had become an atheist. From a young age, she demonstrated intellectual prowess, and she earned a doctorate degree in philosophy with full honors from the University of Göttingen under the direction of Edmund Husserl. She wrote her dissertation on the theme of empathy. She served as Husserl's assistant,

---

28 Bonnie G. Smith, *Women in World History* (London: Bloomsbury Academic, 2020).

29 The United States Holocaust Museum, "The Armenian Genocide (1915–16): Overview," *Holocaust Encyclopedia*, accessed April 25, 2022, https://encyclopedia.ushmm.org/content/en/article/the-armenian-genocide-1915-16-overview.

30 Sundquist, *Unexpected Christian Century*, 78.

but due to gender discrimination at the time, she was unable to obtain a teaching post. Later her career was limited by the growing anti-Semitism in Germany.

Stein began to read the New Testament and works of Christian theology, such as the writings of Søren Kierkegaard, but Teresa of Ávila's story proved to be the most profound for the young scholar. In the summer of 1921, Stein read Teresa's autobiography and was profoundly moved. Stein was baptized into the Catholic Church in January 1922, which brought significant sadness to her mother. This sadness was only to increase when Stein became a Discalced Carmelite nun, the order that Teresa had reformed centuries before, in 1933. Her superiors recognized her intellectual talents, and they encouraged her to write articles and books, which she did. Unfortunately, the tide of Nazism was growing in Germany, and even though she was now a Catholic nun, she, too, faced persecution. For her own safety, her order moved her from Germany to a monastery in Holland, but this would only be a temporary refuge. When the Germans occupied Holland in 1940 and implemented their persecution of the Jews, all Jewish Catholics were deported to concentration camps despite the vigorous stand made by the church leadership. She and her sister Rosa were arrested in an SS raid in 1942, and she was sent to the Auschwitz death camp. She died in the gas chamber on August 9, 1942, one week after her arrival.[31]

While a convert to Christianity, Stein strongly identified with her Jewish roots, and she saw no incompatibility between these roots and her Christian faith. In fact, she even highlighted this relationship with her memoir, *Life in a Jewish Family*, which she wrote in the 1930s in an attempt to fight against the growing tide of anti-Semitism. The opening line of her foreword explains, "Recent months have catapulted the German Jews out of the peaceful existence they had come to take for granted." She goes on to say that this national attack on Judaism is what prompted her to write her reflections on her Jewish upbringing.[32]

Unfortunately, the Nazis' "final solution" was not the last genocide of the century. Countless suffered under Stalin in the Soviet Union, and genocides later occurred in Cambodia and Bosnia. The Rwandan genocide is a gut-wrenching example of Christians acting as both the aggressors and the victims. Throughout the conflict, the Hutu Christians slaughtered their Tutsi Christian neighbors. All suffered, but sexual violence was used as a terror tactic, and thousands of women were subjected to horrific acts of sexual violence and murder, and some women were held in sexual slavery.[33]

The suffering of women, whether Christian, Jewish, or of any other faith, was immense during this century. Violence and hate proved to be a powerful force, and we are still living in the shadow of many of these horrific events. Thankfully, suffering is not the only theme that was dominant in the twentieth century. It was also a time of activism and reform. On numerous occasions, it was women who fought for equality and peace.

---

31 Edith Stein, *Essential Writings* (Orbis Books, Maryknoll, 2005).

32 Edith Stein, *Life in a Jewish Family: An Autobiography 1891–1916*, eds. L. Gelber and Romaus Leuven, trans. Josephine Koeppel (Washington, DC: Institute of Carmelite Studies, ICS Publications, 1986), 23.

33 Binaifer Nowrojee and Janet Fleischman, *Shattered Lives: Sexual Violence during the Rwandan Genocide and its Aftermath* (New York: Human Rights Watch, 1996), https://www.hrw.org/reports/1996/Rwanda.htm.

GLOBAL REFORMERS

The rise of the modern peace movement is an important aspect of global women's reform movements that was particularly salient in the twentieth century. The movement has roots in the Western nineteenth-century reform movements, and women have worked both inside and outside of political movements to fight for lasting peace. As early as the Franco-Prussian war in 1870–71, American Methodist Julia Ward Howe called for a Mother's Peace Day, which was celebrated in a number of American cities and European countries. Two early but short-lived peace organizations were *L'Union international des femmes pour la paix* in 1891 and the *Alliance universelle des femmes pour la paix et pour le désarmement* in 1896. Understandably the women's peace movement gained traction with the atrocities of the two world wars. For example, Jane Addams (1860–1935), often better known for her settlement work, won the Nobel Peace Prize in 1931 for her work toward international disarmament and peace. Dorothy Day, the founder of the Catholic Worker movement, faced considerable backlash for using her paper, *Catholic Worker*, to advocate for peace, even during the Second World War. She became an important voice for nuclear disarmament and protested the Vietnam War. In 1961, the American group Women Strike for Peace formed, with over fifty thousand women across the country marching for peace and against aboveground nuclear testing.

Some of the most powerful and influential movements for peace were not national or international organizations but grassroots campaigns to stop a particular violent conflict or an oppressive regime. Both the Madres de la Plaza de Mayo movement in Argentina and the Women of Liberia Mass Action for Peace movement represent successful peace campaigns led by women in the twentieth century.

Madres de la Plaza de Mayo

In 1976 the Argentinian military, under the leadership of General Jorge Rafael Videla, overthrew the government and launched a campaign it called the "War against Subversion." The mission of this war was to wipe out all vestiges of the previous regime. Over the course of seven years, tens of thousands of civilians were killed; generally they simply disappeared—no arrests, no charges filed against them. They just vanished. Most of the victims were young—the vast majority under the age of thirty-five. They were university or high school students, young workers, and union members. Some had ties to political organizations, were activists, or were members of human rights groups, but many were simply taken because of an unlucky association or chance, though a disproportionate number of the victims were Jewish.

It was a time of terror and fear, and from 1976 to 1982, the program of repression was largely successful in silencing opposition. Out of fear, political adversaries vanished, and journalists and civic leaders fell silent. The lone voice of public opposition came from an unlikely source. It was not from students or rebels; it was from mothers. Mothers marched every Sunday, and later every Thursday, in front of the presidential palace, the Casa Rosada. First this group came together for mutual support, but then they demanded answers—they demanded to know what had happened to their children. They wore white scarves embroidered with the names of their children, symbolizing their children's diapers, and they carried photographs of their sons and daughters. It was illegal to hold any sort of public protest, and their activism was not without risk. Protestors were threatened, arrested, physically attacked, and some were murdered by the government including the founder of the movement, Azucena Villaflor (1924–1977), and two French nuns who supported the movement, Alice Damon (1937–1977) and Léonie Duquet (1916–1977).

This public display of bravery and suffering began to draw international attention to the brutal war of repression the government had been waging, and the much-too-warm relationship between the Argentinian government and the United States was exposed. The military gave up control of the country to a civilian government in 1983. Years later some former military officers came forward about their role in the disappearances. They admitted that people were taken, drugged, loaded on planes, and thrown out over the Atlantic Ocean. Mass graves of people who had washed up on the shores have also been found.[34]

Women of Liberia Mass Action for Peace Movement

In 2003 a group of Liberian women traveled to Ghana to pressure warring factions in the Second Liberian Civil War (1999–2003) to come to a peace agreement. When the talks stalled, Leymah Gbowee (b. 1972) and nearly two hundred women literally blocked the representatives of then president Charles Taylor and other rebel leaders from leaving their meeting room. This proved to be a pivotal moment in the peace process that came after years of horrific conflict during which the country suffered tremendously; the war is particularly notable for its extensive use of child soldiers on both sides of the conflict.

Gbowee was an unlikely leader. She was seventeen when the First Liberian Civil War (1987–1997) broke out, and her plans for further education were interrupted by the violence. In her autobiography she talks of seeking refuge in a church with other women only for soldiers to break in and rape and kill some of the unarmed women regardless. She and her family ended up in a refugee camp in Ghana temporarily, but she found her way back to Liberia only to endure more personal and political violence. She survived abusive relationships, poverty, and the hardships of mothering young children while her nation was at war. Yet she had the heart to help others despite, or perhaps inspired by, her own suffering.

As the first of the civil wars ended in 1996, she trained to be a trauma counselor, eventually earning a degree in 2001. Throughout her career she worked with both women and former child soldiers. When the second civil war broke out in 1999, where systematic rape and other brutalities were used as terrorism techniques in an already devastated society, she became connected with the peace organization West Africa Network for Peacebuilding. Understanding the importance of women in the fight for peace, she helped organize the Women of Liberia Mass Action for Peace, an interreligious coalition of Christian and Muslim women with the goal of bringing peace to their nation. Religion was not simply

---

34 Teresa A. Meade, *A History of Modern Latin America: 1800 to the Present* (Malden, MA: Wiley-Blackwell, 2010), 264–267; Robert Ellsberg, *Blessed among all Women: Women Saints, Prophets, and Witnesses for Our Time* (New York: The Crossroad Publishing Company, 2005), 83–84.

a means to an end for Gbowee; she was a deeply religious woman. In 2002, she fell asleep at her office and had a dream in which God told her she needed to gather the women and pray for peace. She understood this to be a divine call.

Under Gbowee's leadership, thousands of women staged pray-ins and nonviolent protests demanding reconciliation and peace talks. Their protests included threats of a curse and even a sex strike. Referring to the sex strike, Gbowee admitted it had no practical effect, but it was extremely valuable in gaining media attention. However, Gbowee was insistent that the women's greatest weapons were moral clarity, patience, and persistence.[35] They were women who were exhausted from fourteen years of violence, death, and terror and devastated from the loss of their children. In the end, their efforts were extremely successful. Within weeks of their Ghana sit-in among peace talks, Charles Taylor, who was convicted of war crimes in 2012, was pushed into exile, and a peace treaty that included a resolution for a traditional government was signed. This led the way for the election of Ellen Johnson Sirleaf, the first elected woman head of state in Africa, in 2005.[36]

Gbowee continues to be an activist. She earned a master's degree in conflict transformation from Eastern Mennonite University in 2007, and she has founded and served in a number of women's organizations focused on lasting peace. In 2011, Leymah Gbowee and Ellen Johnson Sirleaf, along with Yemini activist Tawakkol Karman, won the Nobel Peace Prize.[37]

Modern Advocates for the Poor

The world has suffered not only from armed conflict but also as a result of massive wealth inequality. There have been countless women who have served the poor in a variety of ways, but two Catholic women in the twentieth century gained international fame for their work with the poor: Dorothy Day (1897–1980) and Mother Theresa (1910–1997). They had vastly different personalities, and they approached their work in wildly different ways; therefore, they offer a fascinating comparison of how two women sharing a Catholic faith can serve others with their own unique gifts. Interestingly, both women dealt with controversy, though again for different reasons.

As *The New Yorker* once amusingly quipped, in 1941 the United States Federal Bureau of Investigation did not know what to do about Dorothy Day's onetime communism, sometime socialism, and all-the-time anarchism.[38] As a testament to their concern, her FBI file is over eight hundred pages long.[39] Day's political radicalism, paired with her devout Catholic faith, left outsiders confused, but for Day these dual commitments were at the heart of her ministry and activism. She did not wonder how to reconcile

---

35 Helen Morales, "Aristophanes' 'Lysistrata', the Liberian 'Sex Strike', and the Politics of Reception," *Greece & Rome* 60, no. 2 (October 2013): 288.

36 Leymah Gbowee and Carol Mithers, *Mighty Be Our Powers: How Sisterhood, Prayer, and Sex Changed a Nation at War* (New York: Beast Books, 2011).

37 Nobel Prize Outreach, "The Nobel Peace Prize in 2011," accessed April 25, 2022, https://www.nobelprize.org/prizes/peace/2011/summary/.

38 Casey Cep, "Dorothy Day's Radical Faith: The Life and legacy of the Catholic writer and activist, who some hope will be made a saint," *The New Yorker*, April 6, 2020, https://www.newyorker.com/magazine/2020/04/13/dorothy-days-radical-faith.

39 Federal Bureau of Investigation, "Dorothy Day," accessed April 25, 2022, https://archive.org/details/DorothyDay.

them; she wondered why more Catholics were not more concerned about the poor and the marginalized.

Day was born in Brooklyn, New York, in 1897 to a nonreligious family. When she was seven, they moved to Oakland, California. In 1906 the San Francisco earthquake hit, and while her father lost his job, Day was moved by how people came together to care for those affected by the quake. After this, the family moved to Chicago and had to live in a poor rowhouse, where she was exposed to poverty.

She won a scholarship to go to college in Illinois, where she became interested in labor history and socialism and discovered the great Russian writers Gorky, Chekhov, Dostoyevsky, and Tolstoy. When her family moved back to New York City, she dropped out of college to go with them. She took a job as a journalist for radical papers, and she was arrested in 1917 at a suffrage protest (her first stint in jail). Her young adult life was full of adventure and hardship. During the 1918 flu epidemic, she worked as a nurse. Later, she fell in love with a womanizing journalist, got pregnant, and had an abortion to save their relationship, but he left her anyway. She later called the abortion the great tragedy of her life, and she tried to die by suicide twice. Following this, she married a much older, wealthy man but left him after a year. She wrote and sold the rights to a short book, and with the money she bought herself a cottage in Staten Island. She met and fell in love with another man, named Foster Batterham, who was an atheist and anarchist. When she got pregnant again, she was thrilled, but Foster did not want the baby, and he resented Day for her growing religious affiliation. During her pregnancy she began to pray the rosary and attend Mass at a Catholic Church. She decided to have her baby baptized and prayed for faith for herself, and it was her newfound religious faith that ended her relationship with Foster and drove a wedge between her and her more radical friends.

A pivotal moment in her life occurred five years later. She was covering a hunger march organized by communists, and she could not understand why the Catholics were not there. She went to a nearby church and prayed that God would use her to help the poor. When she returned to New York, she met Frenchman Peter Maurin (1877–1949). Maurin, who had emigrated to Saskatchewan in 1909, survived for many years by taking on whatever work he could find. After years of reflection and hard labor, such as digging ditches and working in steel mills and coal mines, he came to believe that poverty was a gift from God because his transient life had allowed him plenty of time to pray and study.[40] Day viewed Maurin as the answer to her prayers, and he viewed her as a modern-day Catherine of Siena, and together they founded the *Catholic Worker* paper in 1933. The first issue covered the exploitation of Black workers in the South, child labor, and local strikes over wages. It sold for a penny a copy. Day was both a journalist and the editor.

Along with this came the Catholic Worker Houses, first in New York, then elsewhere. Central to these houses was the concept of radical hospitality whereby people would bring the poor into their own homes. The three core Catholic Worker principles are voluntary

---

40 Jim Forest, "Biography of Peter Maurin," *The Catholic Worker Movement*, accessed April 25, 2022, https://www .catholicworker.org/petermaurin/pm-biography.html.

poverty, personalism, and pacifism. It was Day's pacifism, especially during the Second World War, that proved to be the most controversial of all her stances.[41]

Likely her most famous quote is "Don't call me a saint, I don't want to be dismissed so easily." However, in 1997, Cardinal John O'Connor, archbishop of New York, launched her canonization process, and in 2012 the Catholic bishops of the United States unanimously recommended her for canonization.[42] Whether the world sees a St. Dorothy Day in the upcoming years is still up in the air, but she continues to be a tremendous inspiration for many today.

In many ways Agnes Gonxha Bojaxhiu, better known as Mother Teresa (1910–1997), is Day's opposite, yet they both had a concern for the poor that defined their ministries. Mother Teresa was born to Albanian parents in Skopje, Macedonia, in 1910. From a very young age she felt called to the ministry, and at the age of eighteen she joined the Sisters of Loreto. After training in Ireland, she was sent to India as a missionary. From 1931 to 1948 Teresa taught at a high school in Calcutta, but she was so moved by the poverty and suffering outside of the convent walls that she received permission from her superiors to start an open-air school for poor children in the city. Soon she was joined by volunteers who helped her extend the scope of her work.

She was adamant that this was not work that she chose but work to which she was called, and in 1950, she received permission to establish the Missionaries of Charity in Calcutta, a religious order dedicated to ministering to the neediest and the dying. She began with only thirteen sisters, but the movement has grown to more than four thousand religious in over one hundred countries. The order comprises both active and contemplative branches of both sisters and brothers. The Missionaries of Charity has undertaken relief work in the wake of natural disasters and other humanitarian crises. The members manage homes for people who are dying of HIV/AIDS, leprosy, and tuberculosis. They also run soup kitchens, mobile medical clinics, counseling programs, orphanages, and schools. In addition to the usual three vows, nuns of this particular order make a fourth vow to give wholehearted free service to the poorest of the poor.[43]

Through her activities Mother Teresa gained international recognition, which included receiving the Nobel Peace Prize in 1979.[44] Despite the incredible reach her ministry had, she struggled personally with feelings of darkness and separation from God. In fact, she said she felt nothing of God's presence for forty-nine years, yet she continued in obedience for decades. Her actions were also not completely without controversy. Some have criticized her for her vocal opposition to both contraceptives and abortion, and there have been accusations of cruelty as well.[45]

41 Dorothy Day, *The Long Loneliness* (New York: Harper & Row Publishers, Inc., 1952).

42 Jim Forest, "Servant of God Dorothy Day," *The Catholic Worker Movement*, accessed April 25, 2022, https://www.catholicworker.org/dorothyday/servant-of-god.html.

43 Sunquist, *The Unexpected Christian Century*, 48–49.

44 Nobel Prize Outreach, "The Nobel Peace Prize 1979," accessed April 25, 2022, https://www.nobelprize.org/prizes/peace/1979/summary/.

45 Matt Bradley, "Mother Teresa's Canonization: Controversy Mars Nun's Work," *CBS News*, September 16, 2021, https://www.nbcnews.com/news/world/mother-teresa-s-canonization-controversy-clouds-nun-s-work-n641181.

She will be remembered not only for her good works but also as an example of one who has wrestled with their faith. In September 2016, Mother Teresa, now known as St. Teresa of Calcutta, was canonized by Pope Francis, and one year later she was named the co-patron saint, along with St. Francis Xavier, of the archdiocese of Calcutta.

A CENTURY OF ADVANCEMENTS

While women made advancements in a plethora of areas during the twentieth century, few are more relevant for us than those in women's ordination. The story of women's ordination is not the triumphal tale of steady progress toward equality that many wish it to be, though significant gains have been made. It is a winding and complicated tale filled with steps forward and steps backward among a diverse collection of traditions. The motivations for women's ordination are varied, though common themes of call, need, and equality do emerge.

It is critical to understand that the majority of the world's Christians attend churches that do not ordain women. The members of the Catholic Church and the various Orthodox churches, none of which ordain women, make up the largest group of Christians by far. When we discuss women's ordination, we are talking about Protestant churches, and within that broad category, only some church bodies ordain women. It is also important to understand that women's ordination does not necessarily mean equality within a denomination. Conversely, it should not be assumed that women do not have any power or influence in traditions that do not ordain them. As we have seen in previous chapters, women in a variety of traditions that do not ordain women have been highly influential members of their church bodies, and this continues to be the case. However, the path toward ordination is an important story and one that has highly influenced Christianity, especially in the past fifty to one hundred years. Women in greater numbers than ever are joining the pastorate and serving in a variety of capacities, including parish pastors, bishops, and other important ministry positions.

Chapter 9 explored a limited number of early nineteenth-century ordinations, but these appointments were few and far between. They did not open the floodgates to a world of equality within the church. It was not until the second half of the twentieth century that women made significant progress toward both ordination and other leadership roles within their denominations. The following stories of ordination are a combination of significant "firsts" and influential women and events that have helped shape the current landscape. This topic within Christian history is not over though. This is an active conversation today and will continue to be so in the foreseeable future. In our current context, added into this story of women's ordination are questions of race, sexual orientation, and gender identity, and these topics have rightfully expanded the conversation.

The first sixty years of the century, while filled with immense progress for women regarding access to education, political influence, and entrance into the workforce, saw little movement regarding women's ordination. In fact, according to the National Council of Churches' 1978 survey on women clergy, there was actually a slight *decrease* in women clergy between the years 1930 and 1970 within the United States, though the number of women with theological degrees increased.[46] Undoubtedly the Great Depression was a setback for women clergy. With jobs scarce on a global scale, there was a general feeling that women should not take men's jobs, and the pastorate was an area in which this sentiment was particularly prevalent. Churches were hiring more women, but into lower-level positions, and popular arguments against women clergy, such as the wildly misogynistic book by John Rice titled *Bobbed Hair, Bossy Wives, and Women Preachers*, were becoming disconcertingly popular.[47]

There were exceptions to this, of course. The Methodist Episcopal Church, North affirmed the right to ordain women in 1924, and this was extended to Southern Methodists when the Methodist Episcopal Churches, North and South merged in 1939, though women were not granted full membership in the General Council until 1956. Also in 1956, Margaret Towner became the first woman ordained in the Presbyterian Church (USA). Most mainline denominations still only ordained men, though movements to allow women clergy were actively working to change this.

When comparing the different streams of Christianity, we find there was significantly more flexibility for women clergy in the Holiness and Pentecostal traditions in the first sixty years of the twentieth century than in mainline denominations. As demonstrated in chapter 9, women in these traditions had long been leaders in evangelism and preaching. It must be noted that there was disagreement in Holiness and Pentecostal denominations on the issue of women clergy, and there were even denominational splits over the issue, but regardless of conflicts, women did more commonly have ministry opportunities in these traditions. At the turn of the twentieth century, the Free Church Conference was sending ordained women as missionaries. The Church of the Nazarene included a provision for women preachers in its 1894 constitution, and Santos Elizondo (1867–1941), who was likely the first ordained Mexican American woman, served as a pastor in El Paso, Texas. In 1902, 25 percent of the leaders in the Church of God were women. Notable leaders include Emma Alberta Nelson Crosswhite (b. 1882), who helped build an interracial Church of God fellowship that she pastored for forty-seven years, and Ozie Garrett, who pastored an all-white church in Columbus, Nebraska, where she was the only person of color in the town and the only woman minister in the state.[48] Ironically, as mainline churches began to ordain more women, women clergy within Holiness and Pentecostal churches began to decline. This trend has continued into the present day.

One of the most fascinating stories of women's ordination during the first half of the twentieth century is that of the first woman priest in the Anglican Communion. Florence Li Tim-Oi (1907–1992) was born in Hong Kong and ordained fifty years before the Church of England officially began ordaining women. She joined the Anglican Church while she was in college; she began her studies at Union Theological College in Canton in 1934, and three years later the Japanese invaded China, beginning the Second

---

46 Carl J. and Dorothy Schneider, *In Their Own Right: The History of American Clergywomen* (New York: A Crossroad Book), 127.

47 John Rice, *Bobbed Hair, Bossy Wives, and Women Preachers* (Murfreesboro, TN: Sword of the Lord Publishers, 1941).

48 Schneider and Schneider, *In Their Own Right*, 150–151.

World War. As the chairman of the college student union, she took on fundraising and first aid training, and she finished her theological training among sirens and bombings. After her graduation in 1938, she was sent to Hong Kong, and in 1940 she was moved to the Portuguese colony of Macao to serve the growing Chinese refugee population on the island. The next year she was ordained as a deaconess. The island did not have a permanent priest, but in her role as a deaconess, she could baptize, officiate marriages, preach, teach, and preside over funerals. Visiting priests would preside over the Eucharist. In addition to her work in administering the sacraments, she actively ministered to the people, meeting both their spiritual and physical needs, such as by providing food and clothing to refugees.

As the war progressed, the Japanese blockade of the island made it impossible for priests to visit, and Li was authorized to perform the Eucharist due to exceptional wartime circumstance. On Easter Sunday in 1942, she celebrated the Eucharist for the first time. Then in 1944 she traveled through Japanese-occupied territory to be ordained a priest by Bishop Raymond Hall. Li's ordination was not a progressive statement—it was a matter of practicality. The people of Macao needed a priest, and she was capable, willing, and already engaged in ministry. To deny the people of Macao the sacraments based on Li's gender was simply not acceptable to Bishop Hall.[49]

After the war ended, her ordination began to cause controversy. She was asked to relinquish her priest's license, to which she agreed. Under communist rule in China, her history as a priest caused her hardships. She was forced to destroy her vestments and was sent to be "re-educated" during China's Cultural Revolution. After thirty years, she was granted permission to leave the country. She moved to Canada in 1983, and in 1984 she was reinstated as a priest in the Anglican Church of Canada. She served in that role until her death in 1992.[50]

The feminist movement of the 1960s and 1970s radically changed opportunities for women seeking ordination, even if those changes took longer than women might have hoped. In 1963 Betty Friedan published *The Feminine Mystique*, and in 1968 Mary Daly published *The Church and the Second Sex*. Both of these books were revolutionary regarding feminist thought and feminist theology. And thus began a shift in larger society often referred to as second-wave feminism. Women engaged in both social and political movements that fought for a number of issues regarding equality, including but not limited to women's liberation, reproductive rights, equal pay, and an end to domestic and sexual violence. It is important to understand that the feminist movement was not limited to the United States and Western Europe. There were similar movements that arose in many places across the globe in the second half of the twentieth century.

The feminist movement led to an enormous increase in women's enrollment in seminaries. From 1972 to 1980, their enrollment in American seminaries increased 223 percent as

49 Florence Li Tim-Oi, *Raindrops of my Life, Memoirs of the Reverend Florence Li Tim-Oi* (Toronto: Anglican Book Centre, 1996), 1–24.

50 Edmund B. Der, "Florence Tim Oi Li: Pioneer & Mentor of the Women Priests' Movement," The Anglican Church of Canada, accessed April 25, 2022, https://www.anglican.ca/faith/worship/resources/li-tim-oi/li-tim-oi-der/.

opposed to 31 percent for men. Increased enrollment was not even between traditions. For example, between 1970 and 1980, American Baptist seminaries saw a 9 percent increase in men enrolled and a 597 percent increase in women enrolled. For predominantly Black seminaries in the United States, there was a 317 percent increase in women's enrollment. In turn, seminary faculties were changing, with an increase in women professors.[51] The transition was difficult; women faced discrimination, and change did not happen easily or quickly, but nonetheless there was progress.

Globally, the status of women's ordination varies wildly, and it is often a point of contention in ecumenical dialogue. An interesting example of the global difference in ordination opportunities is the Anglican Communion. In many churches around the world, especially churches situated in countries in the Global North, women are ordained as priests, and some have even become bishops. However, not all Anglican member churches ordain women, and one may describe the opportunities for women in other churches as an uphill battle. Women consistently have more difficulty seeking a pastorate, and other issues include lower pay, fewer advancements, less support from within parishes and from supervisors, and resistance to leadership.[52]

While some denominations now ordain women, the largest denomination in the world, the Catholic Church, does not. In his apostolic letter *Ordinatio Sacerdotalis*, from May of 1994, Pope John Paul II states that the church has no authority to ordain women to the priesthood despite active campaigning by those wishing for women's ordination. While the Catholic Church maintains that the priesthood is closed to women, there was a sharp increase in the number of women actively participating in Catholic ministry in other ways in the second half of the twentieth century. Since 1983, women have served as lectors, and since 1994, women and girls have been allowed to be altar servers. In places in the world where priest shortages are particularly acute, women often catechize their communities and distribute Communion when a priest cannot be present. In January of 2021, Pope Francis changed church law to allow women to be permanently installed as lectors or acolytes, though it is important to note that women have been performing those roles for decades in various capacities.[53]

There has been interest in reinstating the diaconate for women within the Catholic Church in modern times as well (the diaconate for men was reinstated in the 1970s). In 2002, the Internal Theological Commission put out a document that was submitted to Cardinal Joseph Ratzinger (later Pope Benedict XVI) called "From the Diakonia of Christ to the Diakonia of the Apostle," which explores the role of the historic diaconate. Section IV: The Ministry of Deaconesses recognizes the role of the deaconess: "In the

---

51 Schneider and Schneider, *In Their Own Right*, 185–186.

52 World Council of Church, "Faith and Order on women's Ordination," last modified June 1, 1998, https://www.oikoumene.org/resources/documents/faith-and-order-on-womens-ordination.

53 Colleen Dulle, "Explainer: The history of women lectors and altar servers—and what Pope Francis has changed," *America: The Jesuit Review*, January 11, 2021, https://www.americamagazine.org/faith/2021/01/11/explainer-women-lectors-acolytes-catholic-church-239694.

apostolic era different forms of diaconal assistance offered to the Apostles and communities by women seem to have been institutional."[54]

In 2016, Pope Francis established a commission to further study the topic of women deaconesses. Then in 2020, after the Synod of Bishops in the Amazon, where the majority of bishops were in favor of ordaining women to the diaconate, Francis established a renewed commission. At this point in time, it is unknown what future the diaconate has for women in the Catholic Church.[55]

The ancient deaconess movement was more prevalent in the East than in the West, and within the Orthodox tradition there have been modest attempts to reinstate deaconesses, beginning in the nineteenth century. Fr. Makarii Glukharev, a Russia archimandrite and missionary, proposed the idea of missionary deaconesses. His proposal was rejected by the hierarchy, though he accepted a number of women to serve on his mission anyway. While not ordained into the diaconate, these women acted in that capacity. Throughout the twentieth century, there were various other attempts to reinstate the diaconate. In 1952, the Church of Greece established a graduate college that served as a school for "lay" deaconesses. In 1953, the archbishop of the Greek Orthodox Archdiocese of North and South America encouraged women to join the ministry. Eight women responded to his call. Despite the interest of both certain members of the hierarchy and some women, neither attempt led to a reinstatement of the diaconate. The movement did again gain traction in the 1980s and 1990s, with even the ecumenical patriarch in Constantinople expressing support.[56] In 1988, a Pan-Orthodox group produced a statement calling for the reinstatement of the apostolic order of the deaconess. Interestingly, little happened until 2017, when Theodoros II, patriarch of Alexandria and all Africa, consecrated five women to the diaconate in the Democratic Republic of Congo. Their mission is primarily to assist the missionary churches there. Reports indicate that the women were consecrated and not ordained, however.[57] The ramifications of this action are yet to be seen.

Closely tied to the issue of women's ordination is that of the appointment of women bishops. The case of America's first bishop is a lesson in the complexities of early women's ordination, especially regarding race, power, and privilege. Alma White (1862–1946) was married to a Methodist pastor, though she had a gift for preaching. The two led revivals in the American West and founded Pillar of Fire, a small separate Methodist denomination that is still in existence. White headquartered the church in a community she began in New Jersey called Zarephath. White and her husband separated, and she continued to lead the denomination until her death in 1946. In 1918, she was consecrated as a bishop, making her the first woman to achieve that in the Americas.

---

54 International Theological Commission, "From the Diakonia of Christ to the Diakonia of the Apostle," accessed April 25, 2022, https://www.vatican.va/roman_curia/congregations/cfaith/cti_documents/rc_con_cfaith_pro_05072004_diaconate_en .html.

55 Discerning Deacons, "Background," accessed April 25, 2022, https://discerningdeacons.org/about/.

56 Kyriaki Karidoyanes FitzGerald, *Women Deacons in the Orthodox Church: Called to Holiness and Ministry* (Brookline: MA, Holy Cross Orthodox Press, 1999), 149–178.

57 James Dearie, "Orthodox move for women deacons is 'revitalization' not 'innovation,'" *National Catholic Reporter*, November 30, 2017, https://www.ncronline.org/news/theology/orthodox-move-women-deacons-called-revitalization-not -innovation.

White's legacy is more than a little complicated. While she does have the honor of being the first American woman bishop, she also closely aligned herself with the Ku Klux Klan. Though she could not be an official member because she was a woman, she allowed and sometimes participated in Klan events at her church, and she even wrote books, such as *The Ku Klux Klan in Prophecy* (1925) and *Klansmen: Guardians of Liberty* (1926), in support of the hate organization. She enthusiastically supported their anti-immigrant and anti-Catholic agenda, though she certainly was not opposed to their racist and anti-Semitic ideologies either. While some scholars of women's history have highlighted her strong commitment to feminism and her accomplishments, her active support of a hate organization and promotion of discrimination cannot be overlooked. Some may believe it would be convenient to forget about her, but the truth is, this is part of the history of women's Christianity too. We cannot hold up only the successes. White demonstrates the dangers of Christians holding hateful and harmful beliefs and then using their religious authority to push these types of beliefs.[58]

White's elevation to bishop was not entirely surprising considering she founded the very denomination in which she became a bishop. It took much longer for other women to rise to the rank of bishop in established churches. The following is not an extensive list of all first women bishops, though it does highlight some firsts in a variety of large Protestant denominations: Marjorie Matthews (1916–1986), ordained in 1965, was the first woman to serve as a Methodist bishop. She was appointed in 1980 and served for four years before retiring. Barbara Clementine Harris, an Episcopalian, was elected bishop in 1989. Interestingly, and perhaps prophetically, she participated in the irregular ordination of the "Philadelphia Eleven" about fifteen years earlier. Katharine Jefferts Schori was elected the first presiding bishop in the American Episcopal Church in 2006 and was the first woman elected primate in the Anglican Communion. April Ulring Larson (b. 1950) was the first woman bishop in the Evangelical Lutheran Church in America (ELCA) in 1992, and Elizabeth Eaton (b. 1955), the first woman to serve as presiding bishop in the ELCA, was elected in 2013. Libby Lane (b. 1966) was the first woman to serve as a bishop in the Anglican Church, appointed right after the General Synod voted in 2014 to allow women to serve as bishops. Christina Odenberg (b. 1940) became the first bishop in the Church of Sweden, serving in the diocese of Lund until 2007.

Women in the Academy: Theology Takes a Turn

There are three movements, all of which are related, that led to the development of feminist theologies in the second half of the twentieth century. First was the feminist movement that emerged in the 1960s. Second was the increase in ordained women, particularly in mainline Protestant churches. Third was the increase in women, even those from traditions that did not ordain women, being able to access a theological education at seminaries. More Christian women were earning doctorates in theological fields and entering seminary faculties as well. The first woman theologian to teach in a Protestant seminary in the United States was Methodist Georgia Harkness (1891–1974). She served as a

---

58 Lindley, *You Have Stept Out of Your Place*, 329–331.

professor of applied theology at Garret Biblical Institute from 1939 to 1950 and at Pacific School of Religion from 1950 until her retirement in 1961. She authored nearly forty books, and she was an important early figure in women's theological contributions to the academy.[59]

Interestingly, however, a number of pioneering feminist theologians, such as Mary Daly, Rosemary Radford Ruether, Elisabeth Schüssler Fiorenza, and Elizabeth Johnson, emerged from the Catholic tradition, which points to an increase in ecumenical activity following the Second Vatican Council. It might seem paradoxical, but Ruether has suggested that the dominance of early Catholic feminist theologians could be in part because they are barred from the priesthood. While Protestant women can go into ordained ministry, academia is one way in which Catholic women can and do make significant theological contributions within their own traditions.[60]

While the emergence of feminist theology in the 1960s and 1970s represents an important step, the field has been rightly criticized for its emphasis on white women's experiences and its lack of attention to race. In the 1980s, womanist theology emerged, adding a needed voice of African American women into the theological conversation. Theologians such as Delores Williams, Jacquelyn Grant, Katie Cannon, and Emilie Townes were pioneers in the emerging field. Jacquelyn Grant provides a critical explanation of her own work in response to feminist and Black theologies:

> In other words, Black theologians and feminist theologians have argued that the universalism which classical theologians attempt to uphold represents merely the particular experiences of the dominant culture. Blacks identify that experience as White experience; and women identify it as male experience. The question then is, if universalism is the criterion for valid theology, how is such a universalism achieved? What I will be exploring here is how Black women's experiences can provide some insights into this question. In doing so, Black women not only join Blacks and feminists in their challenge of theology but they also provide an internal critique for Black men as well as for White women.[61]

In more recent years there has been an emergence of feminist theologies coming from all over the globe, including Latin America, Asia, and Africa. Just as white feminist theology cannot speak to the lived experiences of African American women, distinct feminist theologies are needed for different contexts and experiences.

---

59 Rosemary Skinner Keller, "Georgia Harkness—Theologian of the People: Evangelical Liberal and Social Prophet," in *Spirituality & Social Responsibility: Vocational Vision of Women in The United Methodist Tradition*, ed. Rosemary Skinner Keller (Nashville: Abingdon Press, 1993), 205–206.

60 Rosemary Radford Ruether, "The Emergency of Christian Feminist Theology," in *The Cambridge Companion to Feminist Theology* (Cambridge: Cambridge University Press, 2002): 8.

61 Jacquelyn Grant, "Womanist Theology: Black Women's Experience as a Source for Doing Theology, with Special Reference to Christology," *Journal of the Interdenominational Theological Center* 13, no. 2 (Spring 1986): 197.

GOING FORWARD

Undoubtedly, the dominant story of the twentieth and early twenty-first centuries has been one of growth in the Global South and of stagnation and decline in the Global North. These shifts in global Christianity indicate an evolving faith, but they do not indicate any sort of death of the religion. If the history of the past two thousand years has shown us anything, it is that women will continue to be active participants in the Christian faith. There are now more opportunities for women to lead, preach, teach, engage in missions and evangelism, and minister to others than ever before. Even if we cannot claim total equality today, we have come a long way.

Conclusion

In 1577, toward the end of her life, Teresa of Ávila was commanded to write a book on prayer for her fellow nuns. She makes it clear in her preface, and sporadically throughout the book, that she did not want to write it. Her opening line is "Few tasks that I have been commanded by obedience to undertake have been as difficult as this one."[1] She is self-deprecating at points, which is almost universal for women writers of the time. She also states that if anything she writes is unorthodox, it is a result of ignorance, not malice—a necessary disclaimer in a time and place in which the Inquisition was so zealous. However, throughout the book, there are moments when she is funny and biting. She famously quips that half-learned men have cost her dearly and that even though she is being obedient in writing the book, she is not going to pretend to be happy about it.[2] The result of her labors, unwelcome as they were, is her seminal work, *The Interior Castle*. Eleven years later it was published in Salamanca, and since then the book has become a classic of Spanish literature and has been an inspiration and comfort to countless Christians over the centuries.

This story of Teresa and the book she did not want to write is in some ways symbolic of women's place in the history of Christianity. Teresa was a pioneer in monastic reform and a renowned mystic, and to this day, she is considered one of the great figures of the faith, but she was never a completely free agent either. She consistently had her detractors, who accused her of both insanity and acting outside her appropriate gender role. She had to work within the limited options open to women in her context, and she was always subject to a hierarchy that only sometimes understood her. Yet during her life, she had friends and allies (both within the Catholic hierarchy and outside of it) who recognized her brilliance and promoted her causes, and in the years since, the church and many individual Christians have embraced her as a scholar and saint. She is far from the only woman to be in this position—this volume is filled with brilliant and influential women who pushed boundaries and expectations, sometimes meeting support, other times meeting opposition, and oftentimes meeting both.

In the introduction to this volume, I state that this book is a story about Christian women and that it is also about martyrs, mystics, missionaries, leaders, preachers, theologians, saints, and prophets. Women have performed all these different roles throughout the long history of the Christian church, and they will continue to do so, but their experiences have been anything but equal.

---

1 Teresa of Ávila, *The Interior Castle*, trans. Mirabai Star (New York: Riverhead Books, 2003), 29.

2 Teresa of Ávila, 122.

Throughout most of Christian history (and one could argue that this is still the case today), women were limited in what they could do, where they could go, and in what ways they could participate in the faith. Women also largely operated outside of official power structures. This is a broad statement, and there *are* exceptions, especially as we move closer to the present day; however, throughout most of history women could not be priests, bishops, or pastors or even vote on church boards. Despite these limitations, women did gain power and authority through alternative methods. During the early church, women founded and participated in monastic communities; in the Middle Ages, women acted as mystics, gaining their authority directly from God, not the church; in the Victorian era, women used reform efforts to shape the world around them when they lacked voting rights in either the church or society. These are just a few of the countless ways in which women operated outside of official power structures to influence their world and faith.

Even today, as women gain more rights on a global scale, there are still limitations, biases, and closed doors. When I teach women's history, students are shocked at how much they did not know—how common it is to assume women were always followers or listeners but never leaders. There are still many who would deny women a place both at the table and in the history books—those who fail to see that women have contributed in countless ways over the past two millennia and that they continue to do so. Yet women have always been integral to the Christian faith. Their contributions have never been supplemental or tangential to the "real story" of Christianity. Women, too, are the story.

As we reach the end of a volume such as this, we may ask, Why does knowing the history of women in the Christian tradition matter in our world today?

History is profoundly important to our identity as human beings. To see ourselves in history, or people that look like us or act like us, is a powerful thing. That is why it is so critical that the historical record better reflect our diverse world. As for our subject at hand, there are numerous reasons these stories need to be told, though I will highlight only a few. First, there is so much to gain and nothing to lose by learning more about the women who contributed to our rich Christian history. These stories can empower women to preach, lead, write, and act as agents of change. Second, to deny the contributions of women in the past is to justify exclusion in the present. Finally, Christians are a diverse group with a history spanning two thousand years on six different continents; it is important to recognize the contributions of all people to better understand the history of the Christian faith.

In many places in the world today, women are more visible and have larger roles in churches than ever before, though this advancement has been uneven. Women will continue to preach, pastor, teach, and participate in evangelism and missions in the years to come. However, the church, particularly in the West, is becoming less relevant. There are declining memberships and an overall feeling of apathy toward the faith. The articles and books written on the "nones" and the "dones" seem endless. There are too many leaders and scholars who have argued that it is only a matter of time before the religion declines into nothingness. I am not so pessimistic about the future.

Once you understand the history, you see that Christianity has had its times of decay and renewal over the centuries—times of corruption, stagnation, and decline followed by times of vibrancy and growth. Christianity is growing in many places in the world—these places just happen to be outside of the historic European and North American strongholds. I am both comforted and excited about the future when I look back at our past. Women's Christian history is critical for understanding that the Christian faith is not going to slowly die. Women have often led the charge in evangelism and revival; women have often made up the majority of church memberships; and women have frequently kept the faith alive in its darkest hours.

.

Bibliography

Abdulsalami, Atinuke. "Roles of Women in African Independent and Pentecostal Churches in Nigeria." In *African Initiated Christianity and the Decolonization of Development: Sustainable Development in Pentecostal and Independent Churches*, edited by Philip Öhlmann, Wilhelm Gräb, and Marie-Luise Frost, 105–114. London: Routledge, 2020.

"The Acts of John." In *The Apocryphal Acts of the New Testament*. Translated by M. R. James. Oxford: Clarendon Press, 1924.

"Acts of Paul and Thecla." In *Women in the Early Church*, edited by Elizabeth Clark, 79–88. Wilmington, DE: Michael Glazier, 1983.

"Acts of the Martyrs." In *In Her Words*, edited by Amy Oden, 38–46. Nashville: Abingdon Press, 1994.

Alexander, Estrelda. *The Women of Azusa Street*. Cleveland: Pilgrim Press, 2005.

Allen, Catherine B. "The Legacy of Lottie Moon." *International Bulletin of Mission Research* 17, no. 4 (October 1993): 146–152.

"Another General Booth Enters Heaven." *Christian Century* 67, no. 31 (August 1950): 909.

Augustine of Hippo. *Confessions*. Oxford: Oxford University Press, 2009.

Battis, Emery. *Saints and Sectaries: Anne Hutchinson and the Antinomian Controversy in the Massachusetts Bay Colony*. Chapel Hill: University of North Carolina Press, 1962.

Bede. *The Ecclesiastical History of England*. Translated by A. M. Sellar. London: George Bell and Sons, 1907.

———. *Ecclesiastical History of the English Nation*. Translated by Lewis Gidley. Oxford: Oxford University Press, 1870.

Bolívar, Simón. *Obras completes*. Volume 3. Havana: Editorial Lex, 1950.

Bradley, Matt. "Mother Teresa's Canonization: Controversy Mars Nun's Work." *CBS News*, September 16, 2021. https://www.nbcnews.com/news/world/mother-teresa-s-canonization-controversy-clouds-nun-s-work-n641181.

Bradstreet, Anne. "Upon a Fit of Sickness, Anno 1632." Accessed May 6, 2022. https://www.findinganne.org/blog-1/2019/2/6/on-deaths-door.

Brock, Sebastian P., and Susan Ashbrook Harvey, eds. and trans. *Holy Women of the Syrian Orient*. Berkeley: University of California Press, 2008.

Bryant, Gwendolyn. "Caritas Pirckheimer." In *Women Writers of the Renaissance and Reformation*, edited by Katharina M. Wilson, 287–303. Athens: University of Georgia Press, 1987.

Buchberger, Erica. *Shifting Ethnic Identities in Spain and Gaul, 500–700: From Romans to Goths and Franks*. Amsterdam: Amsterdam University Press, 2017.

Burton, Antoinette. *At the Heart of the Empire: Indians and the Colonial Encounter in Late-Victorian Britain*. Berkeley: University of California Press, 1998.

Butcher, Carmen Acevedo. *St. Hildegard of Bingen: Doctor of the Church, A Spiritual Reader*. Brewster, MA: Paraclete Press, 2007.

Bynum, Caroline Walker. *Holy Feast and Holy Fast: The Religious Significance of Food to Medieval Women*. Berkeley: University of California Press, 1987.

Bynum, William F. "Chronic Alcoholism in the First Half of the 19th Century." *Bulletin of the History of Medicine* 42, no. 2 (1968): 160–185.

Carver, Frances Grace. "With Bible in One Hand and Battle-Axe in the Other: Carry A. Nation as Religious Performer and Self-Promoter." *Religion and American Culture: A Journal of Interpretation* 9, no. 1 (1999): 31–65.

Catherine of Sienna. *Dialogue of Saint Catherine of Siena*. Translated by Algar Labouchere Thorold. London: Kegan Paul, Trench, Trubner & Co., Ltd., 1907.

Cep, Casey. "Dorothy Day's Radical Faith: The Life and Legacy of the Catholic Writer and Activist, Who Some Hope Will Be Made a Saint." *The New Yorker*, April 6, 2020. https://www.newyorker.com/magazine/2020/04/13/dorothy-days-radical-faith.

Chadwick, Nora. *The Beginnings of Russian History: An Enquiry into Sources*. Cambridge: Cambridge University Press, 1946.

Cho, Min-Ah. "Stirring up Deep Waters: Korean Feminist Theologies Today." *Theology Today* 71, no. 2 (June 2014): 233–45.

Clark, Donald. "Christianity in Modern Korea." *Education about Asia* 11, no. 2 (Fall 2006): 35–39.

Clark, Elizabeth A. *Women in the Early Church*. Collegeville: The Liturgical Press, 1983.

Clements, Barbara Evans. *A History of Women in Russia: From Earliest Times to the Present*. Bloomington: Indiana University Press, 2012.

Cloke, Gillian. "Mater or Martyr: Christianity and the Alienation of Women within the Family in the Later Roman Empire." *Theology & Sexuality* 5 (September 1996): 37–57.

———. *This Female Man of God: Women and Spiritual Power in the Patristic Age, AD 350–450*. London: Routledge, 1995.

Connor, Carolyn L. *Women of Byzantium*. New Haven: Yale, 2004.

Connor, Phillip. "6 Facts about South Korea's growing Christian population." *Pew Research Center*. Last modified August 12, 2014. https://www.pewresearch.org/fact-tank/2014/08/12/6-facts-about-christianity-in-south-korea/.

"Correspondence of Pliny and Trajan." In *Readings in World Christian History, Volume 1: Earliest Christianity to 1453*, edited by John W. Coakley and Andrea Sterk. Maryknoll: Orbis Books, 2018.

Corrigan, John, and Winthrop S. Hudson. *Religions in America: An Historical Account of the Development of American Religious Life*. 7th ed. Upper Saddle River, NJ: Pearson, 2004.

Dailey, Patricia. *Promised Bodies: Time, Language, and Corporeality in Medieval Women's Mystical Texts*. New York: Columbia University Press, 2013.

Dearie, James. "Orthodox move for women deacons is 'revitalization' not 'innovation.'" *National Catholic Reporter*, November 30, 2017. https://www.ncronline.org/news/theology/orthodox-move-women-deacons-called-revitalization-not-innovation.

Deen, Edith. *All of the Women of the Bible*. New York: Harper & Brothers Publishers, 1955.

Dentière, Marie. "A Most Beneficial Letter, Prepared and Written Down by a Christian Woman of Tournai, and Sent to the Queen of Navarre, Sister of the King of France, Against the Turks, the Jews, the Infidels, the False Christians, the Anabaptists and the Lutherans." In *Women Writers of the Renaissance and Reformation*, edited by Katharina M. Wilson, 275–280. Athens: University of Georgia Press, 1987.

Der, Edmund B. "Florence Tim Oi Li: Pioneer & Mentor of the Women Priests' Movement." The Anglican Church of Canada. Accessed April 22, 2022. https://www.anglican.ca/faith/worship/resources/li-tim-oi/li-tim-oi-der/

Diakonia World Federation. http://dwfmembers.org/.

"The Didache, or Teaching of the Twelve Apostles." In *The Apostolic Fathers*. Vol. 1. Translated by Kirsopp Lake. London: William Heinemann, 1919.

Didascalia Apostolorum. Translated by Margaret Dunlop Gibson. London: C. J. Clay and Sons, 1903.

Didion, Joan. *The White Album*. New York: Simon & Schuster, 1979.

Discerning Deacons. "Background." Accessed April 22, 2022. https://discerningdeacons.org/about/.

Dobson, Jualynne E. *Engendering Church: Women, Power, and the AME Church*. Lanham: Rowman & Littlefield Publishers, Inc., 2002.

Duffy, Eamon. *Fires of Faith: Catholic England under Mary Tudor*. New Haven: Yale University Press, 2009.

Dulle, Colleen. "Explainer: The history of women lectors and altar servers—and what Pope Francis has changed." *America: The Jesuit Review*, January 11, 2021. https://www.americamagazine.org/faith/2021/01/11/explainer-women-lectors-acolytes-catholic-church-239694.

Du Mez, Kristin Kobes. "Reorienting American Religious History in the Age of Global Christianity: The Case of Katharine Bushnell." In *American Evangelicalism: George Marsden and the State of American Religious History*, edited by Darren Dochuk, Thomas S. Kidd, and Kurt W. Peterson, 180–98. Notre Dame: University of Notre Dame Press, 2014.

Dzubinski, Leanne M., and Anneke H. Strasson. *Women in the Mission of the Church: Their Opportunities and Obstacles throughout Christian History*. Grand Rapids: Baker Academic, 2021.

Earle, Mary C. *The Desert Mothers: Spiritual Practices from the Women of the Wilderness*. Harrisburg, PA: Morehouse Publishing, 2007.

Eire, Carlos. *The Life of Saint Teresa of Avila*. Princeton: Princeton University Press, 2019.

Ellsberg, Robert. *Blessed among all Women: Women Saints, Prophets, and Witnesses for Our Time*. New York: The Crossroads Publishing Company, 2005.

Épiney-Burgard, Georgette. "Hadewijch of Antwerp." In *Encyclopedia of the Middle Ages*. Cambridge: James Clarke & Co, 2002.

Epp, Eldon Jay. *Junia: The First Woman Apostle*. Minneapolis: Augsburg Fortress, 2005.

Espin, Oliva M. "The Enduring Popularity of Rosa de Lima, First Saint of the Americas: Women, Bodies, Sainthood, and National Identity." *Cross Currents* 61, no. 1 (March 2011): 6–26.

Eusebius. "Acts of the Martyrs." In *In Her Words*, edited by Amy Oden. Nashville: Abingdon Press, 1994.

Evans, Christopher. *The Social Gospel in American Religion: A History.* New York: New York University Press, 2017.

Evans, James Allan. *The Empress Theodora: Partner of Justinian.* Austin: University of Texas Press, 2002.

Federal Bureau of Investigation. "Dorothy Day." Accessed April 26, 2022. https://archive .org/details/DorothyDay.

Fell, Margaret. *Women's Speaking Justified, Proved, and Allowed of by the Scriptures, All Such as Speak by the Spirit and Power of the Lord Jesus.* London: 1666.

Field, Sean L. *The Beguine, the Angel, and the Inquisitor: The Trials of Marguerite Porete and Guiard of Cressonessart.* Notre Dame: University of Notre Dame Press, 2012.

Fisher, James T. *Catholics in America.* Oxford: Oxford University Press, 2000.

FitzGerald, Kyriaki Karidoyanes. *Women Deacons in the Orthodox Church: Called to Holiness and Ministry.* Brookline, MA: Holy Cross Orthodox Press, 1999.

Flowers, Elizabeth H. "The Contested Legacy of Lottie Moon: Southern Baptists, Women, and Partisan Protestantism." *Fides et Historia* 43, no. 1 (2011): 15–40.

Forest, Jim. "Biography of Peter Maurin." *The Catholic Worker Movement.* Accessed April 22, 2022. https://www.catholicworker.org/petermaurin/pm-biography.html.

———. "Servant of God Dorothy Day." *The Catholic Worker Movement.* Accessed May 6, 2022. https://www.catholicworker.org/dorothyday/servant-of-god.html.

The Foursquare Church. *A Simplified Guide to Foursquare Belief.* Los Angeles: International Church of the Foursquare Gospel. Accessed April 22, 2022. https://s3.amazonaws .com/foursquare.org/wp-content/uploads/sites/2/2019/11/08165309/ SimplifiedGuideBrochure_WEB_FINAL.pdf.

Foxe, John. *Foxe's Book of Martyrs Or A History of the Lives, Sufferings, and Triumphant Deaths of the Primitive Protestant Martyrs.* Chicago: The John C. Winston Co, 2007. https://www .gutenberg.org/files/22400/22400-h/22400-h.htm.

Francis Willard House Museum and Archives. "History of the WCTU." Accessed April 22, 2022. https://franceswillardhouse.org/frances-willard/history-of-wctu/.

Franklin, Simon, and Jonathan Shepard. *The Emergence of Russia 750–1200.* New York: Routledge, 1998.

Frykenberg, Robert Eric. "The Legacy of Pandita Ramabai: Mahatma of Mukti." *International Bulletin of Mission Research* 40, no. 1 (January 2016): 60–70.

Gabriele, Matthew and David M. Perry. *The Bright Ages: A New History of Medieval History* New York: HarperOne, 2021.

Galawdewos. *The Life and Struggles of Our Mother Walatta Petros: A Seventeenth-Century African Biography of an Ethiopian Woman.* Translated and edited by Wendy Laura Belcher and Michael Kleiner. Princeton: Princeton University Press, 2015.

———. *The Life and Struggles of Our Mother Walatta Petros: A Seventeenth-Century African Biography of an Ethiopian Woman.* Concise ed. Translated and edited by Wendy Laura Belcher and Michael Kleiner. Princeton: Princeton University Press, 2015.

Garland, Lynda. *Byzantine Empresses: Women and Power in Byzantium, AD 527–1204.* London: Routledge, 1999.

Garver, Valerie L. *Women and Aristocratic Culture in the Carolingian World*. Ithaca: Cornell University Press, 2009.

Gbowee, Leymah, and Carol Mithers, *Mighty Be Our Powers: How Sisterhood, Prayer, and Sex Changed a Nation at War*. New York: Beast Books, 2011.

Geary, Patrick J. *Before France and Germany: The Creation and Transformation of the Merovingian World*. New York: Oxford University Press, 1988.

Georgiadou, Aristoula. "Marguerite Porete." In *Women in the Middle Ages: An Encyclopedia*, vol. 2., edited by Katharina M. Wilson and Nadia Margolis. Westport, CT: Greenwood, 2004.

Gonzalés, Justo L. *The Story of Christianity, Volume 1: The Earliest Church to the Dawn of the Reformation*. Revised ed. New York: HarperOne, 2010.

Gonzalés, Ondina E., and Justo Gonzalés. *Christianity in Latin America: A History*. Cambridge: Cambridge University Press, 2008.

Gordon, David M. "Rebellion or Massacre? The UNIP-Lumpa Conflict Revisited." In *One Zambia, Many Histories*, edited by Jan-Bart Gewald, Marja Hinfelaar, and Giacomo Macola. Boston: Brill, 2008.

Gorski, Philip. American Covenant: A History of Civil Religion from the Puritans to the Present. Princeton: Princeton University Press, 2017.

Grant, Jacquelyn. "Womanist Theology: Black Women's Experience as a Source for Doing Theology, with Special Reference to Christology." *Journal of the Interdenominational Theological Center* 13, no. 2 (1986): 195–212.

Green, Monica H. "The Four Black Deaths." *The American Historical Review* 125, no. 5 (December 2020): 1601–1631.

Gregory of Nyssa. "Life of Macrina." In *Readings in World Christian History, Volume 1: Earliest Christianity to 1453*, edited by John W. Coakly and Andrea Sterk. Maryknoll, NY: Orbis Books, 2018.

Grimke, Sarah Moore. *Letters on the Equality of the Sexes, and the Condition of Woman: Addressed to Mary S. Parker, President of the Boston Female Anti-Slavery Society*. Boston: Isaac Knapp, 1838.

Grumbach, Argula von. "To the University of Ingolstadt." In *Argula von Grumbach: A Woman's Voice in the Reformation*, edited by Peter Matheson. Edinburgh: T & T Clark, 1995.

Grundmann, Herbert. *Religious Movements in the Middle Ages*. Translated by Steven Rowan. Notre Dame: University of Notre Dame Press, 1995.

Grundmann, Herbert, Steven Rowan, and Robert E. Lerner. "The Incorporation of the Women's Religious Movement into the Mendicant Orders." In *Religious Movements in the Middle Ages*. Notre Dame: University of Notre Dame Press, 1995.

Haigh, Christopher. *Elizabeth I*. London: Longman, 1988.

Hamm, Thomas D. *Quakers in America*. New York: Columbia, 2003.

Hanawalt, Barbara A. "Medieval English Women in Rural and Urban Domestic Space." *Dumbarton Oaks Papers* 52 (1998): 19–26.

Hardwick, Dana. "Man's Prattle, Woman's Words: The Biblical Mission of Katharine Bushnell." In *Spirituality & Social Responsibility: Vocational Vision of Women in The United Methodist*

Tradition, edited by Rosemary Skinner Keller, 165–182. Nashville: Abingdon Press, 1993.

Harvey, Susan Ashbrook. *Asceticism and Society in Crisis: John of Ephesus and the Lives of the Eastern Saints*. Berkeley: University of California Press, 1990.

Hatcher, John. "Women's Work Reconsidered: Gender and Wage Differentiation in Late Medieval England." *Past & Present*, no. 173 (2001): 191–198.

Head, Thomas. "Clare of Assisi." In *Women in the Middle Ages: An Encyclopedia*, vol. 2, edited by Katharina M. Wilson and Nadia Margolis. Westport, CT: Greenwood, 2004.

Heath, Elaine A. *Naked Faith: The Mystical Theology of Phoebe Palmer*. Cambridge, UK: James Clark & Co., 2010.

Herlihy, David. "Land, Family, and Women in Continental Europe, 701–1200." In *Women in Medieval Society*, edited by Stuard Susan Mosher, 13–46. Philadelphia: University of Pennsylvania Press, 1976.

Herrin, Judith. *Women In Purple: Rulers of Medieval Byzantium*. Princeton.: Princeton University Press, 2001.

Hildegard of Bingen. *Scivias*. Translated by Mother Columba Hart and Jane Bishop. New York: Paulist Press, 1900.

Hillerbrand, Hans J. *The Division of Christendom: Christianity in the Sixteenth Century*. Louisville: Westminster John Knox Press, 2007.

Hinfelaar, Hugo. "Women's Revolt: The Lumpa Church of Lenshina Mulenga in the 1950s." *Journal of Religion in Africa* 21, no. 2 (1991): 99–129.

Hinga, Teresia Mbari. *African, Christian, Feminist: The Enduring Search of What Matters*. Maryknoll: Orbis Books, 2017.

Hippolytus of Rome. *The Apostolic Tradition of Hippolytus*. Translated by Burton Scott Easton. Cambridge: Cambridge University Press, 1934.

Hollis, Stephanie. *Anglo-Saxon Women and the Church*. Woodbridge, Suffolk: Boydell Press, 1992.

Holum, Kenneth G. *Theodosian Empresses: Women and Imperial Dominion in Late Antiquity*. Berkeley: University of California Press, 1989.

Imb. "Lottie Moon Christmas Offering: Your 2020 Gifts at Work." Accessed April 22, 2022. https://www.imb.org/generosity/lottie-moon-christmas-offering/.

Ingham, Mary Beth. "The Logic of the Gift: Clare of Assisi and Franciscan Evangelical Life" *The Greek Orthodox Theological Review* 60, nos. 1–2 (2015): 129–142.

Inman, Anne E. *Hild of Whitby and the Ministry of Women in the Anglo-Saxon World*. Lanham: Lexington Books/Fortress Academic, 2019.

International Theological Commission. "From the Diakonia of Christ to the Diakonia of the Apostle." Accessed April 26, 2022. https://www.vatican.va/roman_curia/congregations/cfaith/cti_documents/rc_con_cfaith_pro_05072004_diaconate_en.html.

Irving, Dale T., and Scott W. Sunquist. *History of the World Christian Movement, Volume 1: Earliest Christianity to 1453*. Maryknoll: Orbis, 2001.

———. *History of the World Christian Movement, Volume 2: Modern Christianity from 1454–1800*. Maryknoll: Orbis, 2001.

Israel, Adrienne. *Amanda Berry Smith, From Washerwoman to Evangelist*. Lanham, MD: The Scarecrow Press, Inc., 1998.

Jacobs, Sylvia M. "The Historical Roles of Afro-Americans in American Missionary Efforts in Africa." In *Black Americans and the Missionary Movement in Africa*, edited by Sylvia M. Jacobs. Westport, CT: Greenwood Press, 1982.

Jacobson, Douglas. *Global Gospel: An Introduction to Christianity on Five Continents*. Grand Rapids: Baker Academic, 2015.

Jerome. "To Eustochium Letter 108." In *From Nicene and Post-Nicene Fathers*, 2nd ser., vol. 6, edited by Philip Schaff and Henry Wace. Translated by W. H. Fremantle, G. Lewis, and W. G. Martley. Buffalo, NY: Christian Literature Publishing Co., 1893. Revised edition for New Advent by Kevin Knight. http://www.newadvent.org/fathers/3001108.htm.

———. "To Principia, Letter 127." In *From Nicene and Post-Nicene Fathers*, 2nd ser., vol. 6, edited by Philip Schaff and Henry Wace. Translated by W. H. Fremantle, G. Lewis, and W. G. Martley. Buffalo, NY: Christian Literature Publishing Co., 1893. Revised edition for New Advent by Kevin Knight, https://www.newadvent.org/fathers/3001127.htm.

Johnson, Elizabeth. *Truly Our Sister: A Theology of Mary in the Community of Saints*. New York: Continuum International Publishing Group, 2003.

Johnson, Scott F. *The Life and Miracles of Thekla: A Literary Study*. Hellenic Studies Series 13. Washington, DC: Center for Hellenic Studies, 2006.

Julian of Norwich. "A Revelation of Love." In *The Writings of Julian of Norwich: A Vision Showed to a Devout Woman and a Revelation of Love*, edited by Nicholas Watson and Jacqueline Jenkins. University Park: University of Pennsylvania, 2006.

Karant-Nunn, Susan C., and Merry E. Wiesner-Hanks. *Luther on Women: A Sourcebook*. Cambridge: Cambridge University Press, 2003.

Keller, Rosemary Skinner. "Georgia Harkness—Theologian of the People: Evangelical Liberal and Social Prophet." In *Spirituality & Social Responsibility: Vocational Vision of Women in The United Methodist Tradition*, edited by Rosemary Skinner Keller, 205–229. Nashville: Abingdon Press, 1993.

Kelly, Joan. *Women, History, and Theory*. Chicago: University of Chicago Press, 1984.

Kim, Sebastian C. H., and Kirsteen Kim. *A History of Korean Christianity*. New York: Cambridge University Press, 2015.

Kissane, Noel. *Saint Brigid of Kildare: Life, Legend, and Cult*. Dublin: Open Air, 2017.

Kittelson, James M., and Hans Wiersma. *Luther the Reformer: The Story of the Man and this Career*. 2nd ed. Minneapolis: Fortress Press, 2016.

Kosambi, Meera. "Indian Response to Christianity, Church and Colonialism: Case of Pandita Ramabai." *Economic and Political Weekly* 27, nos. 43–44 (1992): WS61–71.

Kulzer, Linda, and Miriam Schmitt. *Medieval Women Monastics: Wisdom's Wellsprings*. Collegeville: Liturgical Press, 1996.

Lagerquist, DeAne. *From My Mother's Arms*. Minneapolis: Augsburg Fortress, 1991.

Ledyard, Gari. "Kollumba Kang Wansuk, an Early Catholic Activist and Martyr." In *Christianity in Korea*, edited by Robert E. Buswell and Timothy S. Lee, 38–71. Honolulu: University of Hawai'i Press, 2006.

Lee, Jarena. *Religious Experience and Journal of Mrs. Jarena Lee, Giving an Account of her Call to Preach the Gospel.* Philadelphia: 1849.

Legath, Jenny Wiley. *Sanctified Sisters: A History of Protestant Deaconesses.* New York: New York University Press, 2019.

Leonard, Bill J., and Jill Y. Crainshaw. *Encyclopedia of Religious Controversies in the United States.* Vol. 1. Santa Barbara: ABC-CLIO, 2013.

Library of Congress. "Books that Shaped America: Harriet Beecher Stowe, Uncle Tom's Cabin (1852)." Accessed April 22, 2022. https://www.loc.gov/exhibits/books-that -shaped-america/1850-to-1900.html.

Life of Olympias, Deaconess. In *Messages of the Fathers of the Church: Women in the Early Church*, edited by Elizabeth Clark, 224–231. Wilmington: Michael Glazier, Inc., 1983.

Lindley, Susan. *You Have Stept Out of Your Place: A History of Women and Religion in America.* Louisville: Westminster John Knox Press, 1996.

Lublin, Elizabeth Dorn. "Wearing the White Ribbon of Reform and the Banner of Civic Duty: Yajima Kajiko and the Japan Woman's Christian Temperance Union in the Meiji Period." *U.S.-Japan Women's Journal*, nos. 30–31 (2006): 60–79.

Luongo, Thomas F. *The Saintly Politics of Catherine of Siena.* Ithaca: Cornell University Press, 2006.

Ma, Li. *Christian Women and Modern China: Recovering a Women's History of Chinese Protestantism.* Lanham, MD: Lexington Books, 2021.

MacHaffie, Barbara J. *Her Story: Women the Christian Tradition.* 2nd ed. Minneapolis: Fortress Press, 2006.

MacLachland, Bonnie. *Women in Ancient Rome: A Sourcebook.* London, Bloomsbury, 2013.

Makowski, Elizabeth. *A Pernicious Sort of Woman: Quasi-religious Women and Canon Lawyers in the Later Middle Ages.* Washington, DC: Catholic University of America Press, 2005.

Malone, Mary T. *Women & Christianity: The First Thousand Years.* Vol. 1. Maryknoll: Orbis, 2001.

Marino, Katherine M. *Feminism for the Americas: The Making of an International Human Rights Movement.* Chapel Hill: The University of North Carolina Press, 2019.

"The Martyrdom of Martha, Daughter of Posi who was a Daughter of the Covenant." In *Holy Women of the Syrian Orient.* Translated and edited by Sebastian P. Brock and Susan Ashbrook Harvey. Berkeley: University of California Press, 2008.

"The Martyrdom of Perpetua and Felicity." In *Readings in World Christian History, Volume 1: Earliest Christianity to 1453*, edited by John Coakley and Andrea Sterk. Maryknoll: Orbis, 2004.

"The Martyrdom of Tarbo, her Sister, and her Servant." In *Holy Women of the Syrian Orient.* Translated and edited by Sebastian P. Brock and Susan Ashbrook Harvey. Berkeley: University of California Press, 2008.

Matheson, Peter. *Argula von Grumbach: A Woman's Voice in the Reformation.* Edinburgh: T & T Clark, 1995.

Matthews, Shelly. *First Converts: Rich Pagan Women and the Rhetoric of Mission in Early Judaism and Christianity.* Stanford: Stanford University Press, 2001.

Mayhew, Experience. *Indian Converts: Or, Some Account of the Lives and Dying Speeches of a Considerable Number of the Christianized Indians of Martha's Vineyard, in New England, by Experience*

Mayhew. London: printed for Samuel Gerrish, bookseller in Boston, 1727, excerpted in *Women and Religion in America, Volume 2: The Colonial Period and Revolutionary Periods*, edited by Rosemary Radford Ruether and Rosemary Skinner Keller, 34–36. Cambridge: Harper and Row, 1983.

McAvoy, Liz Herbert, ed. *A Companion to Julian of Norwich*. Woodbridge, Suffolk: Boydell & Brewer, 2008.

McFadden, Margaret. "The Ironies of Pentecost: Phoebe Palmer, World Evangelism, and Female Networks." *Methodist History* 31, no. 2 (January 1993): 63–75.

McGowan, Anne, and Paul F. Bradshaw. *The Pilgrimage of Egeria*. Collegeville, MN: Liturgical Press, 2018.

McIntosh, J. L. *From Heads of Household to Heads of State: the Preaccession Households of Mary and Elizabeth Tudor, 1516–1558*. New York: Columbia University Press, 2013,

McNamara, Jo Ann. *Sainted Women of the Dark Ages*. Durham: Duke University Press, 1992.

Meade, Teresa A. *A History of Modern Latin America: 1800 to the Present*. Malden, MA: Wiley-Blackwell, 2010.

Meconi, Honey. *Hildegard of Bingen*. Urbana: University of Illinois Press. 2018.

Medwick, Cathleen. *Teresa of Avila: The Progress of a Soul*. London: Duckworth, 2000.

Meier, Matt S., Conchita Franco Serri, and Richard A. Garcia. *Notable Latino Americans*. Westport, CT: ABC-CLIO, 1997.

Melton, J. Gordon. *A Will to Choose: The Origins of African American Methodism*. Lanham: Rowman & Littlefield Publishers, Inc., 2007.

Menthuen, Charlotte. "Preaching the Gospel through Love of Neighbour: The Ministry of Katharina Schütz Zell." *Journal of Ecclesiastical History* 61, no. 4 (October 2010): 707–728.

Michaud-Fréjaville, Francois. "St. Joan of Arc." In *Women in the Middle Ages: An Encyclopedia*, vol. 2, edited by Katharina M. Wilson and Nadia Margolis. Westport, CT: Greenwood, 2004.

Moloney, Dierdre M. "Combatting 'Whiskey's Work': The Catholic Temperance Movement in Late Nineteenth-Century America." *U.S. Catholic Historian* 16, no. 3 (1998): 1–23.

Mombo, Esther. "Women in African Christianities." In *The Routledge Companion to Christianity in Africa*, edited by Elias Kifon Bongmba, 173–186. New York: Routledge, 2016.

Mooney, Catherine M. *Clare of Assisi and the Thirteenth-Century Church: Religious Women, Rules, and Resistance*. Philadelphia: University of Pennsylvania Press, 2016.

Moore, Rebecca. *Women in Christian Traditions*. New York: New York University Press, 2015.

Morales, Helen, "Aristophanes' 'Lysistrata', the Liberian 'Sex Strike', and the Politics of Reception," *Greece & Rome* 60, no. 2 (October 2013): 281–295.

Moretti, Paola Francesca. "The Two Ephesian Matrons: Drusiana's Story in the Acts of John as a Possible Christian Response to Milesian Narrative." In *The Ancient Novel and Early Christian and Jewish Narrative: Fictional Intersections*, edited by Marília P. Futre Pinheiro, Judith Perkins, and Richard Pervo, 35–48. Groningen: Barkhuis, 2012.

Mott, Lucretia. "Why Shouldn't a Woman be a Reformer?" In *In our own Voices: Four Centuries of American Women's Religious Writings*, edited by Rosemary Skinner Keller and Rosemary Radford Ruether. Louisville: Westminster John Knox Press, 1995.

Mueller, Joan. *The Privilege of Poverty: Clare of Assisi, Agnes of Prague, and the Struggle for a Franciscan Rule for Women.* University Park: The Pennsylvania State University Press, 2006.

Myers, Kathleen Ann. *Neither Saints Nor Sinners: Writing the Lives of Women in Spanish America.* Oxford: Oxford University Press, 2003.

Nightingale, Florence. *The Institution of Kaiserswerth on the Rhine for the Practical Training of Deaconesses, etc.* London: London Training Ragged Colonial Training School, 1851.

Nobel Prize Outreach. "The Nobel Peace Prize 2011." Accessed April 25, 2022. https://www.nobelprize.org/prizes/peace/1979/summary/.

Nobel Prize Outreach. "The Nobel Peace Prize 1979." Accessed April 25, 2022. https://www.nobelprize.org/prizes/peace/1979/summary/.

Noll, Mark A., and Carolyn Nystrom, *Clouds of Witnesses: Christian Voices from Africa and Asia.* Downers Grove: IVP Books, 2011.

Nowrojee, Binaifer, and Janet Fleischman. "Shattered Lives: Sexual Violence during the Rwandan Genocide and its Aftermath." New York: Human Rights Watch, 1996. https://www.hrw.org/reports/1996/Rwanda.htm.

NPR. "Mixed Reactions to First Native American Saint." Last updated February 10, 2012. https://www.npr.org/2012/02/10/146695395/mixed-reactions-to-first-native-american-saint.

O'Brien, Jane. "The time when Americans drank all day long." *BBC News,* March 5, 2015. https://www.bbc.com/news/magazine-31741615.

Octavio. "The Sons of La Malinche." In *Labyrinth of Solitude.* Translated by Lysander Kemp. New York: Grove Atlantic Press, 1994.

Oduyoye, Mercy Amba. *Introducing African Women's Theology.* Cleveland: The Pilgrim Press, 2001.

Oen, Maria H., and Unn Falkeid. "Introduction." In *Sanctity and Female Authorship: Brigitta of Sweden & Catherine of Siena,* edited by Maria H. Oen and Unn Falkeid. New York: Routledge, 2020.

Omoyajowo, J. Akinyele. "The Cherubim and Seraphim Church." *Journal of the Interdenominational Theological Center* 16, nos. 1–2 (Fall/Spring 1988/1989): 137–151.

———. "The role of women in traditional African religions and independent church movements." *Dialogue & Alliance* 2, no. 3 (Fall 1988): 77–87.

O'Neale, Sondra. "A Slave's Subtle War: Phillis Wheatley's Use of Biblical Myth and Symbol." *Early American Literature* 21, no. 2 (Fall 1986): 144–165.

Open Door Report. "China." Accessed April 26, 2022. https://www.opendoorsusa.org/christian-persecution/world-watch-list/china/.

Osiek, Carolyn, and Margaret Y. MacDonald. *A Women's Place: House Churches in the Earliest Christianity.* Minneapolis: Augsburg Fortress Press, 2006.

Painter, Christine Valters. *Desert Fathers and Mothers: Early Christian Wisdom Sayings.* Woodstock, VT: Skylight Path, 2012.

Pak, Sujin G. "Three early female Protestant reforms' appropriation of prophecy as interpretation of Scripture." *Church History* 84, no. 1 (March 2015): 90–123.

Palladius of Aspuna. *The Lausiac History.* Translated by John Wortley. Collegeville: Liturgical Press, 2015.

Palmer, Phoebe. *The Way of Holiness.* New York: Piercy and Reed Printers, 1843.

PBS Online. "Sara Allen." *Africans in America, Part 3: Brotherly Love.* Accessed February 3, 2022. https://www.pbs.org/wgbh/aia/part3/3p246.html.

Peterson, Jaqueline, and Mary Druke. "American Indian Women and Religion." In *Women and Religion in America, Volume 2: The Colonial Period and Revolutionary Periods,* edited by Rosemary Radford Ruether and Rosemary Skinner Keller, 1–14. Cambridge: Harper and Row, 1983.

Pettegree, Andrew. *Brand Luther: 1517, Printing, and the Making of the Reformation.* New York: Penguin Press, 2015.

Pew Research Forum. "Being Christian in Western Europe." Last modified May 29, 2018. https://www.pewforum.org/2018/05/29/being-christian-in-western-europe/.

Pirckheimer, Caritas. "Denkwürdigkeiten." In *Women Writers of the Renaissance and Reformation,* edited by Katharina M. Wilson, 296–301. Athens: University of Georgia Press, 1987.

Plummer, Marjorie Elizabeth. *From Priest's Whore to Pastor's Wife: Clerical Marriage and the Process of Reform in the Early German Reformation.* Burlington: VA: Ashgate, 2012.

Poor, Sara S. *Mechthild of Magdeburg and Her Book: Gender and the Making of Textual Authority.* Philadelphia: University of Pennsylvania Press, 2004.

"Protestant Christianity is Booming in China." *The Economist,* September 15, 2020. https://www.economist.com/graphic-detail/2020/09/15/protestant-christianity-is-booming-in-china.

Protoevangelium of James. In *From Ante-Nicene Fathers,* vol. 8, edited by Alexander Roberts, James Donaldson, and A. Cleveland Coxe. Translated by Alexander Walker. Buffalo, NY: Christian Literature Publishing Co., 1886. Revised and edited for New Advent by Kevin Knight, http://www.newadvent.org/fathers/0847.htm.

Pruitt, Lisa Joy. *A Looking Glass for Ladies: American Protestant Women and the Orient in the Nineteenth Century.* Macon, GA: Mercer University Press, 2005.

Quinn, Frederick. *African Saints: Saints Martyrs, and Holy People from the Continent of Africa.* New York: A Crossroads Book, 2002.

Raymond of Capua. *The Life of St. Catherine of Siena.* Dublin: James Duffy and Co.

Read, John. *Catherine Booth: Laying the Theological Foundations of a Radical Movement,* 1–27. Cambridge, UK: Lutterworth Press, 2013.

Reyerson, Kathryn. "Urban Economies." In *The Oxford Handbook of Women & Gender in Medieval Europe,* edited by Judith M. Bennet and Ruth Mazo Karras. Oxford: Oxford University Press, 2013.

Rice, John. *Bobbed Hair, Bossy Wives, and Women Preachers.* Murfreesboro, TN: Sword of the Lord Publishers, 1941.

Rix, Robert William. "Joanna Southcott and the Strange Effects of Printing: Publishing Prophesies in the Early Nineteenth Century." *History of Religions* 55, no. 1 (August 2015): 65–88.

Robert, Dana L. *American Women in Mission: A Social History of their Thought and Practice Mission.* Macon, GA: Mercer University Press, 1996.

Robins, Roger. "Anglican Prophetess Joanna Southcott and the Gospel Story." *Anglican and Episcopal History* 61, no. 3 (September 1992): 277–302.

Ronda, James P. "Generation of Faith: The Christian Indians of Martha's Vineyard." *William and Mary Quarterly* 38, no. 3 (July 1981): 369–394.

Rudolf of Fulda. *Life of Leoba*. Fordham University. Accessed April 26, 2022. https://sourcebooks.fordham.edu/basis/leoba.asp.

Ruether, Rosemary Radford. "The Emergency of Christian Feminist Theology." In *The Cambridge Companion to Feminist Theology*, edited by Susan Franks Parsons, 3–22. Cambridge: Cambridge University Press, 2002.

The Russian Primary Chronicle: Laurentian Text. Translated and edited by Samuel Hazzard Cross and Olgerd P. Sherbowitz-Wetzor. The Mediaeval Academy of America. Cambridge: Crimson Printing Co., 1953.

Sahlin, Claire L. *Birgitta of Sweden and the Voice of Prophecy*. Rochester, NY: Boydell Press, 2001.

Sanford, Arthur Benton. *Methodist Yearbook, 1897*. New York: Eaton and Mains, 1897.

Savery, William. *A Journal of the Life, Travels and Religious Labors of William Savery*. London: C. Gilpin, 1844.

Schaeffer, Katherine. "Key Facts about Women's Suffrage around the World, a Century after U.S. Ratified 19th Amendment." *Pew Research Center*. Last modified October 5, 2020. https://www.pewresearch.org/fact-tank/2020/10/05/key-facts-about-womens-suffrage-around-the-world-a-century-after-u-s-ratified-19th-amendment/.

Schenk, Christine. *Crispina and Her Sisters: Women and Authority in Early Christianity*. Minneapolis: Fortress, 2017.

Schneider, Carl J., and Dorothy Schneider. *In Their Own Right: The History of American Clergywomen*. New York: A Crossroad Book, 1997.

Semple, Rhonda Anne. *Missionary Women: Gender, Professionalism and the Victorian Idea of Christian Mission*. Woodbridge, NY: Boydell & Brewer, 2003.

Sidwell, Mark. "Did Women Have a Reformation?: The Case of Katherine Zell." *Puritan Reformed Journal* 10, no. 1 (January 2018): 140–153.

Sivan, Hagith. "Who was Egeria: Piety and pilgrimage in the age of Gratian." *Harvard Theological Review* 81, no. 1 (1988): 59–72.

Smith, Amanda Berry. *An Autobiography. The Story of the Lord's Dealings with Mrs. Amanda Smith: The Colored Evangelist; Containing an Account of her Life Work of Faith, and her Travels in America, England, Ireland, Scotland, India, and Africa, as an Independent Missionary*. Chicago: Meyer & Brother, Publishers, 1893.

Smith, Bonnie G. *Women in World History: 1450 to the Present*. London: Bloomsbury Academic, 2020.

Smith, Eleanor. "Phillis Wheatley: A Black Perspective." *Journal of Negro Education* 43, no. 3 (Summer 1974): 401–407.

Socolow, Susan Migden. *The Women of Colonial Latin America*. 2nd ed. Cambridge: Cambridge University Press, 2015.

Soranus of Ephesus. *Gynecology*. Translated by Oswei Temkin. Baltimore: Johns Hopkin's University Press, 1991.

Southern, R. W. *Western Society and the Church in the Middle Ages*. Baltimore: Penguin Books Inc., 1979.

Stanton, Elizabeth Cady. *Declaration of Sentiments*. Rochester, NY: John Dick at the North Star Office, 1848.

———. *The Woman's Bible*, 2 vols. Boston: Northeastern University Press, 1993.

Steffan, Melissa. "The Surprising Countries Most Missionaries are Sent From and Go To." *Christianity Today*, July 25, 2013. https://www.christianitytoday.com/news/2013/july/missionaries-countries-sent-received-csgc-gordon-conwell.html.

Stein, Edith. *Essential Writings*. Maryknoll: Orbis Books, 2005.

———. *Life in a Jewish Family: An Autobiography 1891–1916*. Edited by L. Gelber and Romaus Leuven. Translated by Josephine Koeppel. Washington, DC: Institute of Carmelite Studies Publications, 1986.

Sticca, Sandro. "St. Birgitta of Sweden." In *Women in the Middle Ages: An Encyclopedia*, vol. 2, edited by Katharina M. Wilson and Nadia Margolis. Westport, CT: Greenwood, 2004.

Stjerna, Kirsi. *Women and the Reformation*. Malden, MA: Blackwell, 2009.

Strawn, Lee-Ellen. "Protestant Bible Education for Women: First Steps in Professional Education for Modern Korean Women." *Journal of Korean Religions* 4, no. 1 (2013): 99–121.

Stuard, Susan Mosher, ed. *Women in Medieval Society*. Philadelphia: University of Pennsylvania Press, 1976.

Sunquist, Scott. *Explorations in Asian Christianity: History, Theology, and Mission*. Downers Grove: Inter Varsity Press, 2017.

———. *The Unexpected Christian Century: The Reversal and Transformation of Global Christianity, 1900–2000*. Grand Rapids: Baker, 2015.

Swan, Laura. *The Forgotten Desert Mothers: Sayings, Lives, and Stories of Early Christian Women*. New York: Paulist Press, 2001.

Talbot, Alice-Mary. "The Devotional life of Laywomen." In *A People's History of Christianity, Vol. 3: Byzantine Christianity*. Minneapolis: Fortress Press, 2006.

Teresa of Ávila. *Autobiography of St. Teresa of Ávila*. Translated and edited by E. Allison Peers. Mineola, NY: Dover Publications, Inc., 2010.

———. *The Interior Castle*. Translated by Mirabai Star. New York: Riverhead Books, 2003.

Thelmadatter, Leigh. "An unlikely modern icon, Sor Juana's celebrity cuts across age and class." *Mexico News Daily*, February 13, 2021. https://mexiconewsdaily.com/mexicolife/sor-juanas-celebrity-cuts-across-age-and-class/.

Theodossiou, E., V. N. Manimanis, and E. Danezis. "The Russian Calendars after the Christianization of the Country." *Astronomical & Astrophysical Transactions* 21, nos. 1–3 (2002): 149–153.

Theriot, Nancy M. *Mothers and Daughters in Nineteenth-Century America: The Biosocial Construction of Femininity*. Lexington, KY: University Press of Kentucky, 1996.

Throughline. "Public Universal Friend." Produced by Rund Abdelfatah. NPR, March 5, 2020. Podcast, 48:00. https://www.npr.org/2020/03/04/812092399/public-universal-friend.

Townes, Emilie M. "Because God Gave Her Vision: The Religious Impulse of Ida B. Wells-Barnett." In *Spirituality & Social Responsibility: Vocational Vision of Women in The United*

Methodist Tradition, edited by Rosemary Radford Ruether, 139–163. Nashville: Abingdon Press, 1993.

Truth, Sojourner. *The Narrative of Sojourner Truth*. Edited by Olive Gilbert. Boston: printed by the author, 1850.

Tucker, Ruth. *Katie Luther, First Lady of the Reformation: The Unconventional Life of Katharina von Bora*. Grand Rapids: Zondervan, 2017.

Tyrrell, Ian. *Woman's World/Woman's Empire: The Woman's Christian Temperance Union in International Perspective, 1880–1930*. Chapel Hill: University of North Carolina Press, 1991.

The United States Holocaust Museum, "The Armenian Genocide (1915–16): Overview," in *Holocaust Encyclopedia*. Accessed April 25, 2022. https://encyclopedia.ushmm.org/content/en/article/the-armenian-genocide-1915-16-overview.

Vivian, Tim. *Witness to Holiness: Abba Daniel of Scetis: Translations of the Greek, Coptic, Ethiopic, Syriac, Armenian, Latin, Old Church Slavonic, and Arabic Accounts*. Kalamazoo: Cistercian Publications, 2008.

Walker, Pamela J. "A Chaste and Fervid Eloquence Catherine Booth and the Ministry of Women in the Salvation Army." In *Women Preachers and Prophets through Two Millennia of Christianity*, edited by Beverly Kienzle and Pamela J. Walker, 288–302. Berkeley: University of California Press, 1998.

Walsh, Walter. *The Jesuits in Great Britain: An Historical Inquiry into their Political Influence*. New York: George Routledge and Sons, 1903.

Watson, Nicholas, and Jacqueline Jenkins, eds. *The Writings of Julian of Norwich: A Vision Showed to a Devout Woman and a Revelation of Love*. University Park: The University of Pennsylvania, 2006.

Weber, Alison. *Teresa of Avila and the Rhetoric of Femininity*. Princeton: Princeton University Press, 1990.

Wemple, Suzanne Fonay. *Women in Frankish Society: Marriage and the Cloisters 500 to 900*. Philadelphia: University of Pennsylvania Press, 1981.

Wengert, Timothy J., Mark Granquist, Mary Jane Haemig, Robert Kolb, Mark C. Mattes, and Jonathan Strom. *Dictionary of Luther and the Lutheran Traditions*. Grand Rapids: Baker Academic, 2017.

Wesley, Susanna. "To Samuel Wesley Sr., 25 February 1711/12." In *Susanna Wesley: The Complete Writings*, edited by Charles Wallace, 13. New York: Oxford University Press, 1997.

Wheatley, Phillis. "Letter to Reverent Samson Occum (1774)." *The Connecticut Gazette*, March 77, 1774. https://www.learningforjustice.org/classroom-resources/texts/hard-history/letter-to-reverend-samson-occum.

White, Charles Edward. *The Beauty of Holiness: Phoebe Palmer as Theologian, Revivalist, Feminist, and Humanitarian*. Eugene, OR: Wipf & Stock, 1986.

White, Ellen G. "Ellen Harmon White, Seventh Day Adventist Prophetess." In *Women and Religion in America, Volume 1: The Nineteenth Century*, edited by Rosemary Radford Ruether and Rosemary Skinner Keller, 80–81. Cambridge: Harper and Row, 1981.

Whittle, Jane. "Rural Economies." In *The Oxford Handbook of Women & Gender in Medieval Europe*, edited by Judith M. Bennet and Ruth Mazo Karras, 311–326. Oxford: Oxford University Press, 2013.

Willard, Frances. *Woman in the Pulpit*. Chicago: Woman's Temperance Publication Association, 1889.

Winthrop, John. *The History of New England from 1630 to 1649*. Edited by James Savage. Boston: Phelps & Farnham, 1825.

WMF Minutes, 1 September 1919, WMF Papers (ELC), ALC Archives, St. Paul, quoted in DeAne Lagerquist, *From My Mother's Arms*. Minneapolis, Augsburg Fortress, 1991.

Wojciechowski, Jennifer Hornyak. "Bringing the Kingdom: Religious Women's Engagement in Social Reform in Minnesota from 1880 to 1920." PhD diss., Luther Seminary, 2019.

———. "William J. Seymore." In *The World's Greatest Religious Leaders: How Religious Leaders Helped Shape World History*, edited by Scott Hendrix and Uchenna Okeja. Santa Barbara: ABC-CIO, 2018.

Wollstonecraft, Mary. *A Vindication of the Rights of Woman*. London: Walter Scott, 1891.

Women's Christian Temperance Union. "Our History." Accessed April 26, 2022. https://www.wctu.org/history.

Wong, R. Bin. "Early Modern Economic History in the Long Run." *Science & Society* 68, no. 1 (2004): 80–90.

World Council of Church. "Faith and Order on women's Ordination." Last modified June 1, 1998. https://www.oikoumene.org/resources/documents/faith-and-order-on-womens-ordination.

Wright, N. T. *The Resurrection of the Son of God*. Minneapolis: Fortress, 2003.

Yasutake, Rumi. *Transnational Women's Activism: The United States, Japan, and Japanese Immigrant Communities in California, 1859–1920*. New York: New York University Press, 2004.

Yi, Hyo-jae. "Christian Mission and the Liberation of Korean Women." *International Review of Mission* 74, no. 293 (January 1985): 93–102.

Yoido Full Gospel Church, "About us," *Yoido Full Gospel Church*. Accessed April 23, 2022. https://english.fgtv.com/a01/01.asp.

Zell, Katharina Schütz. *Defending Clerical Marriage*. 1524, *German History in Documents and Images*. Accessed April 26, 2022. https://ghdi.ghi-dc.org/docpage.cfm?docpage_id=5313.

Zhang, Sarah. "Why a Medieval Woman had Lapis Lazuli Hidden in her Teeth." *Atlantic*, January 9, 2019.

Zurlo, Gina A., Todd M. Johnson, and Peter F. Crossing. "World Christianity and Mission 2021: Questions about the Future." *International Bulletin of Mission Research* 45, no. 1 (December 2020): 15–25.

Index